P9-APT-089

Youth Unemployment and Society

Youth Unemployment and Society is a timely and important volume that examines the phenomenon of prolonged adolescence. Historians, psychologists, economists, and sociologists join forces to provide a cross-national examination of trends in youth unemployment and intervention strategies in the United States and Europe. Assessing the causes of aggregate societal unemployment rates, the authors address factors that make individuals more vulnerable to unemployment and consider the developmental consequences of this experience. The volume also examines how persistently high rates of youth unemployment feed back on society, affecting its values, beliefs, and institutions.

Youth Unemployment and Society

Edited by
Anne C. Petersen
and
Jeylan T. Mortimer

CAMBRIDGE
UNIVERSITY PRESS

HD
6270
Y678
1994

Published by the Press Syndicate of the University of Cambridge
The Pitt Building, Trumpington Street, Cambridge CB2 1RP
40 West 20th Street, New York, NY 10011-4211, USA
10 Stamford Road, Oakleigh, Melbourne 3166, Australia

First published 1994

Printed in the United States of America

Library of Congress *Cataloging-in-Publication Data*

Youth unemployment and society / edited by Anne C. Peterssen, Jeylan T.
  Mortimer.
    p. cm.
    Includes index.
    ISBN 0-521-44473-X
    1. Youth – Employment – Congresses. 2. Unemployment – Social
aspects – Congresses. 3. Unemployment – Pscyhological aspects –
Congresses. 4. Unemployment – Social conditions – Congresses.
5. Unemployed – Psychology – Congresses. 8. Social problems –
Congresses. I. Petersen, Anne C. II. Mortimer, Jeylan T., 1943–   .

  HD6270.Y678   1994
  331.13'73'0835–dc20   93-14237

A catalog record for this book is available from the British Library

ISBN 0-521-44473-X hardback

Contents

Contributors

Hans Bertram, Humboldt-Universität zu Berlin, Fachbereich Sozial-wissen-Schäften Institut für Soziologie, Berlin, Germany

James Coleman, Department of Sociology, University of Chicago, Chicago, IL, U.S.A.

Helmut Fend, Padagogisches Institut der Universität Zürich, Switzerland

Adrian Furnham, Department of Psychology, Business Psychology Unit, University College, London, England

Hannie te Grotenhuis, B&A Group Policy Research and Consultancy, Rotterdam, The Netherlands

Stephen Hamilton, Department of Human Development and Family Studies, Cornell University, Ithaca, NY, U.S.A.

Walter R. Heinz, Statuspassagen und Risikolagen im Lebensverlauf, Universität Bremen, Bremen, Germany

Laura E. Hess, Max Planck Institute for Human Development and Education, Berlin, Germany

Frans Meijers, University of Leiden, The Netherlands

John Modell, Department of History, Carnegie Mellon University, Pittsburgh, PA

Jeylan T. Mortimer, Department of Sociology, University of Minnesota, Minneapolis, MN, U.S.A.

Anne C. Petersen, Dean, Graduate School, University of Minnesota, Minneapolis, MN, U.S.A.

Michael Rutter, Institute of Psychiatry, Department of Child and Adolescent Psychiatry, London, England

David J. Smith, Policy Studies Institute, London, England

Michael White, Policy Studies Institute, London, England

Foreword

KLAUS J. JACOBS
Chairman of the Board
Johann Jacobs Foundation

This volume is the first title, it is hoped, of a long series devoted to the better understanding of human development, particularly that of adolescents and young people. The chapters published in this book were presented from November 7–9, 1991, at the Johann Jacobs Communication Center, Marbach Castle, Germany, during a conference sponsored by the foundation of the same name. The event was organized by Anne C. Petersen, then dean of the College of Health and Human Development at the Pennsylvania State University and now, since March 1992, vice-president for research and dean of the Graduate School, University of Minnesota.

The goal of the conference was to examine the causes and consequences of youth unemployment, for both society and the individual. In addition, part of the conference was devoted to the analysis of policies and programs to prevent the causes and treat the consequences.

Forty-five scientists and young scholars from Europe and the United States also studied some of the misconceptions about youth unemployment, which may lead to both wasteful government programs and missed opportunities. In addition, they analyzed some of the existing successful programs and considered how these might be exported to other countries and other cultures. Finally, they looked at the need for ongoing research to help render interventions by government, industry, or families as effective as possible.

Most people will agree that the theme of this first Johann Jacobs conference is an important one, and I am afraid its importance will continue to increase. Although the Johann Jacobs Foundation is aware of the limited impact of such a conference, we are pleased to have had the opportunity to improve the knowledge on such a critical problem as youth unemployment and its consequences for society.

x   K. J. Jacobs

It only remains for me to thank Anne C. Petersen for her enthusiasm and competence in organizing this first Johann Jacobs conference.

Finally, I would like to convey my gratitude to the speakers, discussants, and other participants, who all contributed to the success of the event to which this volume is devoted.

Johann Jacobs Foundation
Zürich, Switzerland

Introduction

JEYLAN T. MORTIMER
Life Course Center
University of Minnesota

Youth unemployment and marginality are multifaceted problems, having complex multiple causes and requiring diverse strategies of remedial action. This major premise was used both in developing this volume and in generating the conference that preceded it. The causes, consequences, and remedial actions are construed as having their locus at both the individual and societal levels. Thus, this collection is interdisciplinary, bringing together the thinking of social scientists representing the fields of psychology, sociology, history, and economics. A further assumption is that cross-national comparisons greatly enhance our understanding of the causes of the problem of youth unemployment, as well as providing us with insight into its solution.

In the first chapter, Hess, Petersen, and Mortimer provide a general orientation to what follows, discussing the meaning and sources of youth marginality, trends in unemployment in industrialized countries, and the causes thereof. The particular consequences of unemployment for adolescents are featured, with emphasis on identity formation, career development, and mental health. The authors examine the programs and policies that have been developed to cope with high youth unemployment rates in the industrialized countries of Japan, Western Europe, and the United States, identifying the features of programs that have proven to be most successful. Finally, they alert us to the possibilities of other social roles that may function as viable alternatives to paid employment, such as volunteer work, which offer youth meaningful connection to society and socialization experiences that will help to prepare them for their adult social roles.

In the following section on societal investment in youth, Coleman and Modell debate whether adults' interest in directing their resources of time, energy, and money toward the preparation of youth for adulthood has diminished during the course of societal modernization, that is, during the movement from agrarian, to industrial, to postindustrial society. Turning to macrosocial perspectives on youth employment, Fend examines changes in the patterns of transition to adulthood and, consequently, the meaning of unemployment through historical time, from premodern Europe, through the period of industrialization, and into the twentieth century. White and Smith then offer an economic analysis of the causes of persistently high unemployment in modern societies, with special attention to the implications for youth.

Whereas the macrosocial perspectives of historical and economic analysis draw attention to the effects of broad societal forces on unemployment, and illuminate factors that influence aggregate levels of unemployment, a microsocial, or social psychological, perspective is necessary to understand the implications of unemployment for individuals. In the initial chapter of the section titled "Individual Perspectives," Rutter alerts us to the complexities of causal analysis, pointing to diverse conceptualizations of causation, means of testing causal hypotheses, and the implications of the insights generated by these considerations for intervention programs. Because the probability of unemployment is not the same for all persons, factors that distinguish unemployed and employed youth may be either the result of prior differences or consequences of the unemployment experience itself. Hence, cross-sectional studies, in which data are collected at a single point, have limited value. Instead, there is a great need for longitudinal studies that follow the same individuals through time. Mortimer reviews longitudinal studies that address the problem of selection into employment, identifying those prior characteristics that may predispose an individual to become unemployed. Furnham summarizes the evidence, also mainly drawn from longitudinal studies, with respect to the psychosocial consequences of unemployment. After examining the distinctive features and outcomes of youth unemployment (as opposed to unemployment in older age groups), he cogently argues that the experience of unemployment is not the same for all youth and that key individual attributes importantly moderate the experience and the consequences of being without work.

The next section of the volume recognizes that unemployment and society are reciprocally related. Whereas societal, and especially economic, forces determine the aggregate level, distribution, and social meaning of unemployment, the phenomenon of unemployment feeds back on society, affecting its values, belief systems, and institutions. Te Grotenhuis and Meijers raise the issue as to whether large numbers of unemployed youth in modern, postindustrial societies are fostering alternative value systems that deemphasize the importance of work and threaten the ideological premises of the welfare state. They also assess whether high rates of youth unemployment foster deviance and the emergence of a permanent, marginalized underclass. Hamilton addresses the intervention strategies societies have undertaken to ease the transition of youth to adult work roles, focusing on the institution of apprenticeship in the Federal Republic of Germany. He identifies several criteria that can be used to evaluate the measures societies take to reduce youth unemployment.

In the last section of the volume, Bertram outlines several productive strategies for international comparative research, in response to recent changes surrounding German reunification and developments in Central Europe. He proposes that the extension of general schooling, intended as a means of preparing youth for increasingly complex occupational tasks, may actually be dysfunctional given that it neither imparts specific occupational training nor links youth to particular employers. Lengthy academic training in secondary schools may be particularly disadvantageous to youth who are not oriented toward university entrance. He urges that investigators from several countries undertake collaborative studies of the linkages between educational policy and youth unemployment.

In his critical overview of the contents of the volume, Heinz addresses the macrolevel and microsocial processes that channel the movement of young people into the labor force and determine individual and societal reactions when such movement does not successfully occur. Heinz places special emphasis on a convergent theme: that free-market processes must be supplemented by structural mechanisms to facilitate the transition of young people from school to work. Coordinated action on the part of the state, employers, and the educational system is needed both to enhance investment in the human capital of young people who do not enter universities and to prevent the development of a permanent underclass of marginalized and discouraged workers.

I. Investment in youth

1. Youth, unemployment and marginality: The problem and the solution

LAURA E. HESS
Max Planck Institute for
Human Development and Education

ANNE C. PETERSEN
University of Minnesota

JEYLAN T. MORTIMER
University of Minnesota

All societies invest in the socialization of their young to roles valued for adults. Whereas traditionally the locus of this socialization was the family, with industrialization, adult work roles increasingly moved outside of family control. Many societies began compulsory education for all young people, and extended it to older ages. These social changes subsequently postponed the age at which young people began to work and extended the responsibility for socialization of youth from families to schools. Extended schooling with same-age peers especially influenced the nature of adolescence, the transition period between childhood and adulthood.

These social changes have made responsibility for socialization of youth more diffuse, thereby increasing the likelihood that young people are not well integrated into society (e.g., Rutter, 1980). Indeed, several scholars (e.g., Lewin, 1939; Muuss, 1975) consider the period of adolescence to be an inherently marginal one, a time when individuals may possess the requisite competence for adult work and family roles but are denied access to these roles. Such adolescent problems as alienation, delinquency, and substance use are frequently attributed to the lack of a challenging social role (e.g., Conger & Petersen, 1984; Erikson, 1968). This is not meant to imply that adolescents are without roles. By definition adolescents occupy social roles in several contexts (e.g., family, school, peer group). The premise is that adolescents are alienated or marginalized

3

in such a way that they cannot assume active, meaningful, and productive roles in adult society (Nightingale & Wolverton, 1988).

A major adult role that is outside the purview of many adolescents is the work role. A shortage of work opportunities or difficulty in attaining those jobs that do exist can pose major problems for adolescents. Over the past few decades, the labor markets in postindustrial societies have experienced profound changes due to rapid technological advances. Youth have come to experience increasingly heavy demands for the proper education and socialization to prepare them to meet the requirements for jobs or careers.

Coupled with these technological advances have been changes in the structures and functioning of the family, the primary institution responsible for the socialization of children. Most industrialized societies are experiencing increasing rates of divorce, remarriage, and single-parent households, along with sharply rising maternal employment rates. As a result, many modern households are becoming less capable of performing the educational and supportive functions of "traditional" families. Due in part to the changing nature of family relations, the responsibility for providing the necessary education and support to prepare youth for successful adult life has increasingly shifted to formal educational institutions and community-based organizations (Hamburg, 1990).

Employment is generally recognized as a significant step in the socialization of adolescents, allowing them to take on responsible, productive adult roles in society. Working not only provides vocational experience but also affords youth a valuable opportunity to interact with people other than family and peers. In addition, work environments force adolescents to make decisions under a variety of circumstances, thereby giving youth feelings of responsibility and independence. Furthermore, the money earned on the job reduces financial dependence upon adults, helping adults to recognize adolescents as contributing to family well-being, as well as to society in general (Peters, 1987; Phillips & Sandstrom, 1990).

Current Trends in Unemployment

Youth unemployment has become an issue of widespread concern throughout the world, especially in western industrialized economies (Glover, 1986; Levin, 1983; Melvyn & Freedman, 1979). The U.S. government has expressed concern over youth joblessness since the 1960s, but over the past decade, western European countries began to confront massive youth unemployment for the first time in more than 30 years (Lerman, 1986). Table 1.1 summarizes youth unemployment trends from 1981

Table 1.1 *Youth unemployment percentage rates in 12 OECD countries[1]*

	1981	1983	1985	1987	1989
Australia	10.8	17.9	14.3	14.6	10.4
Canada	13.3	19.8	16.3	13.7	11.3
Finland	9.2	10.5	9.1	9.0	6.1
France	17.0	19.7	25.6	23.0	19.0
Germany	6.5	10.7	9.5	8.1	n/a
Italy	25.8	30.5	33.9	35.5	35.6
Japan	4.0	4.5	4.8	5.2	4.5
Norway	5.7	8.9	6.5	5.3	11.5
Spain	31.1	37.6	43.8	40.2	32.0
Sweden	6.3	8.0	5.8	4.2	3.0
United Kingdom	17.9	23.4	21.8	17.4	8.6
United States	14.3	16.4	13.0	11.7	10.5
Average of countries	13.5	17.3	17.0	15.7	13.9

[1]The term *youth* refers to the 15–24 age group in all countries except the United States (14–24) and the United Kingdom, Italy, Norway, Spain, and Sweden (16–24). Dates and methods of statistical collection vary slightly from country to country. Compiled from Tables in *Labour Force Statistics 1968–1988* (OECD, 1990).

to 1989 in the 12 member countries of the Organization for Economic Cooperation and Development (OECD) (Organization for Economic Cooperation and Development, 1990).[1]

Although the most recent trends seem promising for these OECD member countries, it is important to remember that the percentage of unemployed youth throughout the 1980s represents the highest incidence of unemployment in the industrialized nations since World War II, and the highest absolute number of unemployed workers since the Great Depression of the 1930s (Borowski, 1984).

In most of these countries, certain groups are more prone to joblessness than others. For instance, the proportion of adolescents who are unemployed is typically two to three times greater than that of adults (Banducci, 1984; Markey, 1988). In the United States, minority groups such as blacks and Hispanics have far higher unemployment rates than whites (Borowski, 1984; Levin, 1983). In addition, the United States and other industrialized nations share the problem of a higher concentration of unemployment among youth from lower socioeconomic backgrounds (Lerman, 1986).

Causes of Youth Unemployment

Adolescent joblessness has been attributed to four factors: (1) a demographic increase in youth entering the labor force, (2) social policies such as mandatory minimum wages that exceed youthful workers' productivity value to employers, (3) insufficient education and training, and (4) generally poor economic conditions under which youth suffer more than older adults (Levin, 1983).

Changing demographics of youth

One of the most popular explanations for the deterioration of youth employment opportunity is that the number of youth entering the labor force has risen at a rate far higher than the rate at which jobs for youth are created (Levin, 1983). In the decades following the U.S. "baby boom" after World War II, there have been large increases in the number of 16- to 24-year-olds; the population of baby-boomers reached its peak around 1978 (Markey, 1988). The number of high school graduates entering the U.S. labor market steadily declined throughout the 1980s (Herr & Long, 1983). However, though demographic factors may account for some change in youth unemployment, they are not a major or singular cause. First, not all youth experience the same employment opportunities. In the United States, black, Hispanic, and low-income youth have endured much greater unemployment than have whites or other youth from families of high socioeconomic status (Lerman, 1986; Levin, 1983). In fact, in the United States, the proportion of employed white youths actually improved between 1969 and 1977, whereas that of nonwhites deteriorated (Bowers, 1979; Freeman & Wise, 1982; Ginzberg, 1980; Newman, 1979). Second, although the population of youth peaked in the late 1970s and began declining in the 1980s, job opportunities still have not been sufficient to meet the demand (Levin, 1983). Third, some countries have experienced increased youth unemployment with no corresponding rise in the population of youth.

Minimum wages

A second explanation for high youth unemployment is that minimum wage requirements for youth have "priced them out" of jobs, because youths' productive contributions to the employer are not worth the mandatory wages (Levin, 1983). In other words, it is assumed that employers either will hire "more productive" adults or will invest capital in more cost-effective production methods, instead of giving jobs to youth. But despite increases in minimum wages in countries such as the United States and Australia in the 1970s, the relative earnings of youth as compared to adults still declined, suggesting that minimum wages—at least in these two countries—are not primary causes of youth unemployment in recent years.

Inadequate education and training

A third rationale for the youth unemployment crisis focuses on the decrease in the quality of education and training. According to this view, adolescents are becoming less and less equipped with the skills required for productive employment (Levin, 1983). Proponents of this view claim that if the educational system were functioning adequately, creating a more qualified and skilled youth population, such youth would not face unemployment (Hoare, 1980).

In general, more highly educated youth are in fact less likely to face unemployment than are less educated ones (Levin, 1983). However, rather widespread evidence indicates that educational standards in the United States have fallen since the late 1960s, based on the results of standardized tests of basic reading and math skills administered to secondary school students (Levin, 1983). Although there is considerable debate as to whether such achievement tests adequately reflect student job skills, some have argued that these declines mean that increasing numbers of post–high school students lack the requisite skills to obtain productive jobs. Falling test scores may reflect young people's decreasing effort in school as the benefits from secondary education (such as access to decent jobs) decline.

Although some claim that technological advances create more complex jobs that require higher skill levels, the bulk of research evidence suggests that technology and automation have actually "deskilled" entry-level jobs, particularly when computers have replaced human decision making (see Berg, Freedman, & Freedman, 1978; Braverman, 1974; Rumberger, 1981). The deteriorating job performances (Williams, 1979) and the high quit rates (Lerman, 1986) of youth may be responses to the routinization and boredom of many jobs, as well as the discontinuity between youth employment opportunities and long-term career development (Brown, 1990).

In sum, for the most part, youth with higher levels of education do appear to have greater access to available employment. However, it may be that declines in educational attainment among youth are in fact responses to the depressed job market and the lessening of challenges on the job, rather than causes of youth unemployment (Levin, 1983).

Poor economic conditions

Although youth population increases, minimum wage standards, and declining education and training all may have some impact, the factor that has proven to be most consistently related to youth unemployment throughout the world has been the general state of the economy (Levin, 1983). Poor economic conditions, reflected in societal unemployment rates, appear to be the most important single factor in youth unemployment (Borowski, 1984; Levin, 1983). As the overall employment rate for industrialized nations deteriorates, the rates of youth unemployment rise commensurately. In industrialized countries, youth seem to be the prime targets when there is economic decline. The U.S. Department of Labor (1979) concluded:

> Perhaps the most significant fact about the youth labor market from a policy viewpoint is the severe disruption brought about by declining aggregate economic conditions. The initial job is more difficult to procure, young workers are more likely to be pushed out of their jobs, the duration of unemployment is extended, and wage growth is depressed. (pp. 163–164)

Although the state of the economy may be the major cause of unemployment for the youth population in general, the factors determining the employment situation of economically disadvantaged and minority youths—who are at highest risk of marginalization—are multidimensional (Herr & Long, 1983). Quarles and Hannenberg (1982) describe the causes of unemployment for these youth as follows:

> A substantial proportion of youths are disadvantaged, facing barriers in finding employment. These barriers include inadequate training and marginal basic skills. Moreover, many are lacking the attitudinal and job-seeking skills necessary to gain and maintain jobs. For the most part, the jobs available to teenagers are at the bottom of the scale. Predictably, many of these jobs have few incentives for the employer and the employee to develop long-term relationships. Dead-end jobs tend to produce high turnover and high unemployment even when overall unemployment is low. Fundamentally, the problem of youth unemployment is the same as that of the adult population—*not enough jobs to go around*. The rate of youth unemployment mirrors and magnifies the larger problem of the

economy. However, unemployment hits young people from poverty-level and working-class families hardest. (p. 63)

Adolescent Development

Adolescence is a period in which youth make a transition from the security of their family in childhood to the autonomy and responsibility of adulthood. To achieve a comprehensive sense of physical, mental, and social well-being, essential for healthy adulthood (Hurrelmann, 1990), it is necessary for adolescents to develop in ways that permit them to identify their needs and hopes, and to feel effective in their achievements (Hurrelmann & Engel, 1989).

Identity formation

An adolescent's functioning in various social domains influences, and is influenced by, identity formation. During adolescence, cognitive gains in abstract reasoning ability are used to reevaluate and reintegrate one's self-definition or self-concept, and to begin the process of committing oneself to meaningful adult roles (Erikson, 1968). Erikson (1955) claims that societies universally grant terms of *moratorium* to adolescents, defining it as an "institutionalized period of delay granted to someone who is not ready to meet an obligation or forced on somebody who should give himself time to do so" (p. 5). During this period, adolescents have the opportunity to experiment freely with different roles and psychological states and are exempt from taking on full adult responsibilities and commitments (Rapoport, 1988). Osterman (1978) characterizes this "moratorium stage" as a period in which "weak labor force attachments" permit many youth to change jobs and move in and out of the workforce often (Herr & Long, 1983).

However, many societies now prolong this period of moratorium, due in part to failing economic conditions that have decreased job opportunities for youth. Thus, the period of adolescent uncertainty is moving further and further into ages that once were considered to be adult.

Career development

One of the primary roles adolescents begin to prepare for is the work role. Given this, there is a growing interest among social scientists, the business community, and policy makers in the processes by which youth form their occupational identities and later perform in their careers. Recently, several

U.S. social scientists have pointed out shortcomings in the theory, research, and practice (vocational guidance) of career development, especially with respect to marginal youth.

Led by Super (1953, 1957, 1963), the major theoretical contributions to career development during adolescence have focused on (1) comparing the characteristics of the individual (e.g., gender, race, personality characteristics) to characteristics of occupations and (2) the crystallization of vocational *choice* via the development and testing of occupational preferences (Hamilton, 1987b; Vondracek, Lerner, & Schulenberg, 1986). Thinking of the occupational development of socioeconomically disadvantaged youth in terms of career choice is misleading, because as Hamilton (1987b) points out, for these youth, "the process of finding employment is not terribly rational, is seriously constrained by labor market conditions, and represents an accommodation to economic reality rather than an optimal matching" (p. 286). Further, research has been for the most part non-developmental and descriptive, and has not enhanced understanding of the conditions that influence the quality of the fit between the individual and the demands of the job (cf. Vondracek, Lerner, & Schulenberg, 1986).

Super's (1957) theoretical framework has had a substantial impact on vocational guidance in the United States, where vocational guidance counselors help individuals to assess their occupational interests, strengths, and weaknesses and to find relevant occupations. This approach to intervention bypasses the needs of marginal youth, most of whom do not have the luxury of choosing among several plausible careers. For many disadvantaged youth, "careers" may be limited to employment in low-paying, low-status jobs in the secondary labor market. These youth need help in developing traits that will enhance their employability, such as punctuality, grooming, respect for authority, and problem-solving and social skills (Hamilton, 1987b).

Developmental Transitions

Periods of life in which there is significant change in social roles, biological status, or both have been termed *developmental transitions* (e.g., Petersen, Kennedy, & Sullivan, in press; Petersen, Susman, & Beard, 1989). Because adolescence now is prolonged in many societies, it has become a period of life itself, and not simply a transition from childhood to adulthood.

The transition out of adolescence is most typically defined by the entry into adult roles (e.g., Petersen et al., 1989). In most developed societies, however, there is no clearly defined, single time of entry into adult roles. This current status of the transition to adulthood contrasts sharply with that of traditional times, in which entry into adult society was marked by a *rite de passage*. In many societies currently, there is one age at which one can vote and another at which one may be considered legally responsible. Initiation of the two major adult social roles—work and family—may occur at entirely different times from each other and from legally defined adulthood.

Gradual acquisition of adult status may be an advantage for some youth, easing the transition to adulthood and the accommodation to new roles. However, when the work role is delayed significantly several negative consequences may result.

Marginality of Youth: The Lack of a Social Role

A major stress for an increasing number of youth stems from their lack of a meaningful place or role in industrialized societies. The quotations that follow point to the detrimental consequences of societal changes for the adolescent transition from childhood into adulthood.

> Being a teenager is not easy. The opportunities are few and far between for taking on meaningful roles that are valued by others. Unable to demonstrate their own capabilities and lacking the classic rites of passage, youth become strangers. The avenues one must travel to achieve adult status are unmarked. The process must be perplexing no less than lonely. . . . While education, employment, and military sectors do absorb large numbers of youth and slot them into roles that, at least, "keep them busy," there are large numbers of other youth who fall through the cracks. . . . This (marginal) group is of particular concern, not only because of the individual tragedies but because of the cumulative impact on the social fabric. These youth are highly prone to have sustained periods of unemployment, to be in conflict with the law, and to be caught in a spiral of defeat. (Rist, 1981, pp. 3–4)

The advance of technological society has drastically altered the status of young people: where once there were useful outlets for youthful energies in forms that included work on family farms and small businesses and unskilled labor in developing industries, changing economic realities have foreclosed many or most of these outlets. As a result, many young people have been forced to postpone their entry into, or often even their exposure to, adult activities. Today's jobs require greater skills, and the economy and the labor market can now barely support the adult population. The consequent economic marginality of youth (except as consumers) is reflected in an unemployment rate several times higher than that for adults. (Kohler & Dollar, 1976, p. 20)

The marginality of youth has reached near-crisis proportions in many countries. In the United States and Great Britain, youth who are most at risk for economic marginality (notably, minorities of color) are at an extreme disadvantage due to poor familial economic resources, parental divorce and the lack of significant adult role models, dropping out of high school, drug and alcohol abuse, pregnancy, and crime (Farrington, Gallagher, Morley, St. Ledger, & West, 1986; Hamburg, 1990; Sherraden & Adamek, 1984). Such youth are alienated from society in multiple ways. Their multilevel conditions of disadvantage place marginal youth at risk for continuous labor-market problems through adulthood. In 1980, for instance, unemployment among white U.S. teenagers was roughly 15 percent, among Hispanics it was 22 percent, and among blacks it was 39 percent. U.S. adults within these groups maintained such differentials, despite their much lower unemployment rates: 5 percent for white males, 8 percent for Hispanic males, and 12 percent for Black males (Saks & Smith, 1981).

Although the U.S. government has been preoccupied with the impact of unemployment and marginality on the futures of disadvantaged minority youth, a variety of social indicators document deteriorating conditions among youth in general, white as well as nonwhite, rural as well as urban. Although nonwhite youth maintain the most marginal and deteriorated position in the labor market, white youth have been rapidly narrowing the gap during the past few decades. Between 1961 and 1982, the nonwhite unemployment rate increased 35.2 percent, whereas the white rate increased 60.3 percent (Sherraden & Adamek, 1984).

Sherraden and Adamek (1984) examined several indicators of the increasing alienation of young people in the United States in recent years. This pattern of expansion of marginality is seen in other countries as well. For instance, as the figures in Table 1.1 indicate, many European countries are narrowing the gap between their own rates and the U.S. youth unemployment rates, sometimes even surpassing the U.S. rates. It is, of course, impossible to generalize from the situation of youth in the United States to youth in other industrialized nations, due to the wide variation in sociocultural, sociopolitical, and socioeconomic conditions, all of which are inextricably linked to the socialization patterns within which youth must develop into productive and contributing adult members of society. However, by gaining insight into the societal conditions leading to alienation of youth within the United States, other countries may be able to work toward avoiding similar situations. As Hamilton (1987a) warned the Federal Republic of Germany (FRG):

> Continued deterioration in the labor market will have disastrous consequences for the youth who are left out. When they begin to believe that their apprenticeships or their vocational schooling are not pathways to careers, when they conclude that their failure to enter a career is not a consequence of their lack of effort but of an institutional breakdown that is beyond their control, then they will become alienated from society and lose their motivation to behave responsibly. . . . If the FRG responds to these challenges with nothing better than an "Americanization" of their system—prolonged secondary schooling followed by delayed career entry—then their rates of youth problem behavior may take an American direction as well. (pp. 201–202)

With this in mind, it is useful to look at the U.S. evidence that suggests youth are becoming increasingly isolated from the social and economic mainstream of society:

> Young people under the age of 21 now account for more than half of all arrests for serious crimes. . . . Also increasing among young people are vandalism and physical violence . . . the use of drugs, previously associated with urban minorities, became common among the White middle class during the 1960s and 1970s. . . . American young people use more drugs than the young people of any other industrialized nation. . . . Alcohol abuse is a still greater problem. Alcohol is used far more frequently than other drugs, and first use of alcohol is occurring at younger ages. (Sherraden & Adamek, 1984, p. 545)

> Young people seem to be demonstrating, as a group, more limited commitment to the activities and responsibilities they assume. According to the Committee for the Study of National Service (1979), over a third of young people who enlisted in the armed forces are discharged before the first term of enlistment is completed. Dropout rates in the Job Corps are over 50 percent. Dropout rates in the Peace Corps have gone from the lowest of any overseas assistance program in the early 1960s to almost a third of enrollees. . . . Low rates of participation in the electoral process by young people are another indicator of alienation . . . (as is) the high number of young people, largely middle class, who have joined charismatic communal religious organizations, or "cults." (Sherraden & Adamek, 1984, p. 546)

"Runaways" are another growing problem. . . . Another indicator of alienation and cultural disengagement is the rate of out-of-wedlock pregnancies and childbirths. . . . While the rate of out-of-wedlock births among non-Whites has been much higher than that of Whites, it is noteworthy that the White rate grew 109.1 percent between 1960 and 1978, while the non-White rate grew only 9.7 percent during this period. Whites are beginning to "close the gap" in out-of-wedlock childbirths. (Sherraden & Adamek, 1984, p. 547)

Finally, the most disturbing indicators of a troubled youth are increased death rates by homicide and suicide . . . the homicide rate for non-White young people has been much higher than that of Whites; however, between 1950 and 1978 the White rate increased 232.0 percent, while the non-White rate increased only 15.7 percent. Again, Whites are beginning to close the gap. . . . Sharply increasing suicide rates among both Whites and non-Whites are perhaps more disturbing. . . . According to Hendin (1982), "The U.S. now ranks among the highest countries in the world in the suicide rate of its young men, surpassing Japan and Sweden, countries long identified with the problem of suicide." (Sherraden & Adamek, 1984, p. 548)

In sum, the alienation and expanding marginality of youth in many industrialized societies today is not the result of belonging to a particular "social address" (i.e., a particular ethnic or racial background), but rather it is due to youth's daily experience of "restricted opportunity, frustration, anger, resignation, and self-destruction" (Sherraden & Adamek, 1984, p. 549).

Psychosocial consequences of post-school unemployment

The experience of being unemployed differs substantially for adolescents who are still in school full-time versus adolescents who are out of school and looking for work. Research suggests that out-of-school youth who are dropouts are at a much higher risk for unemployment than those who completed high school (Herr & Long, 1983).

The degree to which a given youngster may successfully (or unsuccessfully) cope with being unemployed may depend on a number of psychosocial factors. A brief review of the literature (Hendry & Raymond, 1986; Kieselbach, 1988) will help to illustrate the diversity of young people's reactions to unemployment, as well as the potential for many psychosocial factors to foster either positive or negative psychological consequences of unemployment.

Some researchers have examined the "hypothesis of skill utilization" to study the influence of unemployment on adolescents' identity formation (Kieselbach, 1988). According to this approach, a positive self-concept or identity results from "perceiving the efficacy of one's own actions and by successfully coping with role requirements" (p. 87), based on experiences at home, at school, and on the job. Kieselbach concludes that the negative impact of unemployment on identity development is not due to joblessness per se, but rather to the denial of opportunities for personality and identity formation. Gurney (1980) found that youth employment leads to a stabilization of identity, whereas unemployment results in identity diffusion and lack of a meaningful social role. Conversely, some researchers have found that youth do not necessarily view unemployment as a trauma, but rather as a *psychosocial moratorium* (Erikson, 1968), or a *floundering period* (Hamilton, 1990) of relief from the job-related demands of adulthood (Gurney, 1980).

Youth who are denied access to meaningful societal roles by virtue of their unemployment may be at risk for more serious psychiatric disorders. In one of the more comprehensive Australian studies investigating 16- to 24-year-old unemployed youngsters, roughly 56 percent of the youth questioned were classified as in need of psychiatric treatment, and the majority of these were clinically depressed (Finlay-Jones & Eckhardt, 1982). Similarly, McPherson and Hall (1983) found increased vulnerability to psychiatric disorders for unemployed youth; Tiggemann and Winefield (1980) also report that youth who remained unemployed seven months after leaving school felt more depressed, unhappy, and lonely, and were less satisfied with themselves. In addition to these Australian studies, a study conducted in Great Britain (Warr, Banks, & Ullah, 1985) found that unemployed youth attributed 82 percent of their negative psychological symptoms to being unemployed. Additional support for the notion that youth may be especially vulnerable to the negative psychological effects of unemployment has been provided by Viney (1983), who found significantly higher rates of anxiety, anger, helplessness, guilt and shame for jobless youth under age 20 than for unemployed people over age 20. Several investigators have concluded that young people are especially vulnerable to psychosocial stress during unemployment (Kieselbach, 1988; Roberts, 1984; Schwefel, 1986; Spruit & Svennson, 1987; Warr, 1984).

A psychosocial factor that may moderate the way in which youngsters cope with unemployment (and other stressful life events) is the amount of "social support" available to them (Gore, 1978). Kieselbach (1988) explains the effect of social support as follows:

In the hypothesis of social support, effects of unemployment are explained by the assumption that an unemployed person, by enjoying emotional support from the closer or wider social network, conceives of himself as a part of this frame of reference which he himself values positively. The feeling of being respected as a friend, child, or member of a social group and not to be stigmatized as one of the unemployed enables him to recentrate his self-perception and, thus, to counteract tendencies of social disorientation, induced by unemployment. (p. 88)

Because the family is the social institution of primary influence, the psychosocial adjustment of adolescents is greatly influenced by relationships within the family (Hendry & Raymond, 1986). Empirical evidence for the significance of social support has been provided by Clark and Clissold (1982), who found that unemployed youngsters who felt they were receiving support from family, friends, and community social services were likely to have a more positive and optimistic orientation toward the future. However, several studies have found that unemployed youth are likely to experience decreased familial social support and increased family conflict and tensions (Burger & Seidenspinner, 1977; Clark & Clissold, 1982; Fagin & Little, 1984; Fineman, 1983; Hendry & Raymond, 1986; Schober, 1978).

Relations with peers represent another potential buffer from the stresses of unemployment. Roberts (1983) has suggested that groups of unemployed young people are able to develop their own positive identity. Donovan and Oddy (1982) found poor psychological adjustment among unemployed adolescents who had little social contact with other unemployed youth, and speculated that jobless youngsters in areas of high unemployment enjoy a more supportive peer environment than those in areas of relatively low unemployment.

The way in which unemployed adolescents make use of their free time appears to be another important indicator of psychological coping (Hendry & Raymond, 1986). Hepworth (1980) and Warr and Payne (1983) have emphasized the negative psychological consequences of unstructured and directionless free time. However, lack of financial resources often excludes unemployed youth from leisure activities assumed by their working peers, which alienates them even more from the world of work (Coffield, Burrill, & Marshall, 1983; Hendry & Raymond, 1986; Hendry, Raymond, & Stewart, 1984; Roberts, 1983). Informal, community-based youth organizations have taken up the challenge of providing support for the young unemployed (James, Livingston, & Walker, 1983). However, empirical evidence regarding the effectiveness of youth organizations as a whole in meeting the needs of the young unemployed is lacking (Hendry & Raymond, 1983).

The nature of their belief systems (encompassing values, beliefs, and expectations) influences how adolescents experience the transition from childhood into adult roles. Ogbu (1989) recently has examined the role that cultural knowledge and belief systems may play in the marginalization (in terms of school failure and limited career development) of minority black youths in the United States. According to his analysis, a reciprocal relationship exists between (1) societal opportunities and rewards for educational attainment (e.g., employment and career development) and (2) the efforts expended by youth to achieve in school and participate in the workforce. A key factor in this relationship is the belief system (folk theory or status mobility system, cf. LeVine, 1967) that youth have of how to "get ahead" in society. Youth are more likely to develop adaptive belief systems when many of the people they know have found jobs and earned money commensurate with their educational qualifications. Similarly, parents and other key socializers (e.g., neighbors, older peers, teachers, youth leaders) who have experienced similar societal recognition of their effort (by achieving jobs commensurate with their abilities) are more likely to socialize youth to be achievement oriented in school, and thereby increase their chances of employability. Conversely, when youth and socializing adults become aware that they are limited—via job ceilings imposed on them by the majority population—in terms of the opportunities for obtaining desirable occupations (see Mickelson, 1984; Ogbu, 1978, 1989), they learn that jobs and career advancement are not always based upon academic achievement or individual ability and effort. As a consequence, many black minority youth develop a fatalistic attitude or belief system, which can be summed up in the phrase, "What's the use of trying?" These beliefs influence behaviors— black youth in general are likely to develop an oppositional identity, and are less likely to behave in school and on the job market in ways that the majority reference group (which in most cases are the people holding the jobs and running the schools) view as conducive to being successful. Thus, an important step in reducing marginalization of minority youth may be to expose them to significant adult role models or "success stories," so they can adopt the belief that effort in school and at work can lead to success.

In sum, adolescents' ability to successfully manage the transition from childhood to adulthood, including their ability to cope with unemployment during adolescence, depends on the cumulative effect of a number of psychosocial factors. Youth who are most at risk for becoming alienated or marginal as a consequence of unemployment are those who experience a number of negative factors concurrently and cumulatively (Hendry & Raymond, 1986).

Traditionally, lower-income youth have been most vulnerable to multiple negative life events (such as parental divorce, loss of parental income, school failure and dropout, unemployment, and crime), and these concurrent disadvantages placed them at high risk for marginality and alienation from society. However, today many middle-class youth in industrialized societies are facing increasing exposure to psychosocial stressors (e.g., rising divorce rates, economic decline, and unemployment). Thus, restricted employment opportunities are problematic for an increasing number of teenagers and young adults, regardless of geographical location or income level.

Many governments have recognized the growing problem of marginal youth and have developed numerous national policies and programs in an attempt to remediate the situation. The section that follows reviews some of these attempts at improving employment prospects for youth.

A Review of Existing Programs and Policies to Enhance Youth Employment Opportunities in Industrialized Regions

George (1987) presents an overview of the policies and programs of 11 industrialized countries—Australia, Britain, Canada, Finland, France, West Germany, Hungary, Ireland, Japan, Norway, and Sweden—designed to smooth the transition of non-college-bound youth into the workplace. Although she presents a succinct (and optimistic) overview of national policies and programs, her analysis is for the most part descriptive, rather than evaluative. Given that our goal in reviewing national programs and policies is to understand what aspects of government programs and policies seem to be most effective in encouraging the employability of youth, we refer the reader to George (1987) for a broad overview in these countries, and concentrate our efforts on more in-depth reviews of programs and policies among a narrower range of industrialized nations.

Japan

Economic conditions have had less serious impacts on the employment of youth in Japan relative to other nations. In fact, young people have been less affected by economic recessions than older adults (Kato, 1978).

Demand has often exceeded supply in the youth labor market, and employers often have difficulty finding 15- to 19-year-olds who are willing to work either part- or full-time. Although junior or senior high school graduates experience quite a bit of job security, college and university graduates experience more insecurity with regard to employment opportunities because their education narrows the range of potential jobs (Kato, 1978).

Many Japanese youths are careless about choosing an occupation because of the high demand for them from prospective employers. Thus, rather than develop programs for reducing youth unemployment, the Japanese government has focused its efforts on *stabilizing* employment, by reducing the number of youth who leave their jobs or change jobs numerous times (Kato, 1978). The national Employment Security Office (ESO), in cooperation with high schools, offers vocational counseling and lectures for students entering the job market. At the local level, government schools provide training in such fields as automotive repair, plastics, and textiles (Kato, 1978). Such schools provide training at no cost to the adolescent, and trainees may receive a modest amount of monthly interest-free financial aid, which they pay back after they get jobs.

Private industries also have invested heavily in youth employment training, by establishing their own specialized vocational high schools (Kato, 1978). Graduates of these high schools earn a diploma equal to that earned in the traditional senior high schools and are given full-time positions with the corporation. These training schools have been extremely successful because they are beneficial to both management and youth. From management's perspective, the schools provide a highly reliable source of labor, because graduates are trained to meet the specific demands of each firm. Students also are attracted to such schools, because they do not need to pay for education expenses (such as tuition, fees, books, and dormitories), which frees up their energies to concentrate on their academic and technical training. Furthermore, admission to such schools offers them instant job security with large corporations as early as age 15, and also affords them a very smooth and successful transition from school to the world of work.

Western Europe

As illustrated in Table 1.1, European countries vary greatly with respect to their youth unemployment problems. A brief look at some of the youth employment programs may clarify why some countries have been more successful in helping youth to find occupations.

During the past decade, the youth unemployment rate soared to unprecedented levels in the *United Kingdom* (Hart, 1988). The Manpower Service Commission (MSC) has developed numerous training programs to reduce youth unemployment, including the Work Experience Programme, the Youth Opportunities Programme, and the Youth Training Schemes (for critiques of these and other training schemes in the United Kingdom, see Breen, 1985; Hart, 1988; Main, 1985; McDermott, 1985; Solomos, 1985).

The MSC has sought to build a more effective "bridge from school to work," by providing programs of work experience, basic training, and social skills (McDermott, 1985). However, the evidence thus far suggests that this has proven to be more of an ideological objective than an actual achievement (Solomos, 1985). For instance, Youth Training Schemes (YST) may contribute to the long-term employability of participants, but they do not appear to contribute significantly to the financial independence of youth, either from their parents or from the Social Security system (Harris, 1988). Furthermore, although the training allowance given to YTS employees is 50 to 75 percent higher than the equivalent rate of government income support, it is far below the typical pay scale for young people in the labor market. Moreover, the YTS allowance does not vary according to financial need of the applicants, and most trainees feel the pay level is inadequate for their efforts on the job (Harris, 1988). Thus, some critics have suggested that the ultimate impact of the YTS has been to reduce independence and enforce dependence of youth on their family and/or on the social welfare system, which in turn impedes the transition of adolescents into adulthood (Harris, 1988; Hedges & Hyatt, 1985; Schostak, 1983).

The tremendous increase in youth unemployment in the *United Kingdom* since the mid-1970s has been mirrored (or even surpassed) in *France*. This dramatic increase in the mid-1970s led the French government to launch several policies and programs to address the youth unemployment problem. Most notable is the employment-cum-training contract program, called *contrat emploi-formation*, or CEF (Caspar, 1988). Its three objectives are (1) to promote new job creation by stimulating labor demand, (2) to improve the labor supply by enhancing youths' learning of a trade, and (3) to offer incentives for employers to take on youth (i.e., when there is state subsidy of CEF employees' salaries). Caspar (1988) evaluated the effectiveness of CEF in reaching these objectives and concluded that the program has "fallen somewhat short of its aim of offering a second chance to the most disadvantaged" (p. 453). Youth with the most educational training benefitted most from the program, whereas disadvantaged youth were underrepresented. Moreover, the program was more effective in improving youth entry into employment than in teaching real skills on the job, especially to disadvantaged youth.

In comparison to neighboring European countries, apprenticeship training has played a minor role in France. However, in 1987 the government passed legislation to update and broaden its apprenticeship system, in order to cover a wide range of economic activities, including those involving the most advanced technologies (Oechslin, 1987). This legislation extended apprenticeships beyond the traditional (modestly paid) occupations, by making apprenticeship contracts renewable through secondary schooling or advanced-level schooling, and even beyond.

Of all the Western European countries, the *Federal Republic of Germany* (FGR) has been most successful at restricting youth unemployment. Approximately two-thirds of young people on the job market in the Federal Republic of Germany (740,000 in 1986) receive apprenticeship training, called two-track or "dual" training (Oechslin, 1987). Under these contracts, training occurs both at the factory or workshop and at sessions in vocational schools. The cost to businesses that finance the on-the-job training sessions is much higher than the gain added by the apprentice, and there is no guarantee that the apprentice will stay with the particular business in which he or she trained. Nevertheless, employers continue to provide strong support for this system, because it provides them with skilled staff who are familiar with the enterprise's work requirements (Oechslin, 1987).

Hamilton (1987b, 1990) offers an in-depth analysis of the impact of the apprenticeship system on the occupational socialization of West German youth. Although the system hinders occupational flexibility and has been criticized for perpetuation of social-class stratification, Hamilton views the benefits as far outweighing these costs. First, apprenticeship helps to greatly reduce the "floundering period" for noncollege youth, by providing them with training in a specific occupation at an early age. Perhaps more important, West German youth who participate in apprenticeships are not alienated from work roles, nor do they feel marginal to society. Apprenticeship training is seen as a central part of their identity and a source of status and potential career advancement.

Scandinavia

Scandinavian countries have made systematic efforts to introduce young people to the realities of the work world, in order for them to experience personally the need for training and the completion of school coursework.

The Practical Vocational Guidance Programme (PRYO) has enabled students in their last two years of compulsory education to attend courses in businesses for six to eight weeks as part of their standard curriculum (Oechslin, 1987). This program is coordinated locally by the schools, the employment offices, and business organizations. A parallel program exists in which teachers also go to business enterprises, to become familiar with the settings in which their students will be working and to help them adapt their teaching methods and motivation tactics to the demands of the workplace.

The United States

A myriad of federal government–sponsored programs has been developed in the United States since the mid-1960s to remedy the youth unemployment crisis, including the Comprehensive Employment and Training Act, Job Corps, the Job Training Partnership Act, the Summer Youth Employment Program, and the Youth Employment Demonstration Project Act. Evaluations of such programs (e.g., Adams & Magnum, 1978; Barton & Fraser, 1978) are not optimistic. Hamilton and Claus (1981) succinctly summarize such evaluations:

> Many programs have no measurable effects; those that do move some participants a bit higher on the scale of employment and earnings. . . . Three explanations tend to recur for the modesty of measured program effects: design problems, implementation problems, and the magnitude of the resocialization task . . . (such as) conflicts between attitudes and behavior prevalent among disadvantaged youth and those required for successful participation in the primary labor market. (p. 114)

The *Job Corps* is the most expensive, but yet the longest lived and most effective of the U.S. government's employment training programs for disadvantaged youth (Hamilton, 1990). Initiated in 1964, the program enrolls 14- to 21-year-old low-income youths (Hamilton, 1990). Ramsey and Ramsey (1983) discuss six integrated factors that are responsible for the success of the Job Corps program:

1. *Voluntary participation*: Job Corps is available only to out-of-school, unemployed youngsters who are lacking in job skills and do not have active criminal records, substance abuse problems, or mental disorders.

2. *Open entry—open exit*: The program is based on highly individualized and self-paced progression through well-developed stages.

3. *Individualization*: Participants are taught as individuals rather than as a group or by classroom-based instruction.
4. *Accountability*: Every component of the Job Corps is audited by the U.S. Department of Labor, ranging from individual client performance statistics (termination, graduation, job placement rate), to statistics on safety of staff and trainees, to statistics on the efficiency and accuracy of staff reporting.
5. *Comprehensiveness*: The program not only works on improving disadvantaged youths' job skills, but also includes a thorough orientation, academic training, health care, and instruction in other life-skill areas such as nutrition, hygiene, problem solving, and personal counseling.
6. *Contractor competition*: Service companies (some of which are not-for-profit social service agencies) apply to the U.S. Department of Labor for funding of their programs. Centers are typically funded for two-year contracts with third-year extension options. The companies and agencies that operate Job Corps centers are responsible for staff training, inspection, and program development, but also must make sure their centers meet the standards set by the U.S. Department of Labor to remain in the Job Corps system.

Apprenticeship has always played a much more limited role in the transition of youth from school to work in the United States than in European countries (Glover, 1986; Hamilton, 1990; Mangum, 1987). The U.S. apprenticeship system is privately sponsored and funded primarily through private enterprises (Glover, 1986). A primary reason U.S. employers have invested less in apprenticeship is the high mobility of U.S. workers, especially youth (Mangum, 1987). Employers have been resistant to invest the time and money necessary to train an apprentice, who may in turn take these skills to another (possibly competing) employer. To date, apprenticeship training in the United States is available almost exclusively to white males, and is usually made available to young adults rather than youth (Hamilton, 1990). The median age for U.S. apprentices is 25, and less than 5 percent of youth receive apprenticeship training after leaving school (Hamilton, 1990).

Modifying the youth work experience

In most industrialized countries, employment during adolescence can be characterized by the following: low-skill, low-paid, short-term, part-time, and sporadic work (Hamilton & Claus, 1981). Although many youth outgrow this pattern as they obtain further education and move into the "primary" labor market in adulthood, a disproportionate number of economically disadvantaged minority youth are forced into this "secondary" labor market for the long term or are denied access to employment altogether (Hamilton & Claus, 1981).

Most employment and training programs have been directed at alleviating the problems faced by these marginalized or alienated youth. Unfortunately, most programs have invested primarily in enhancing skills for job placement, rather than in providing disadvantaged youth with *meaningful* employment opportunities. Although such efforts have offered some disadvantaged youth the opportunity to gain employment, the frustrations and lack of incentive characteristic of these unchallenging and uninteresting jobs have contributed to the marginalization of disadvantaged youth. According to Hamilton and Claus (1981), "subsidized employment in low-paid, low-status, low-responsibility jobs may unintentionally confirm the subordinate status of disadvantaged youth because it is continuous with their experience at home and in school and with the experiences of their friends, neighbors, and relatives" (p. 119). Thus, by denying disadvantaged minority youth opportunities to gain the skills and experience necessary to move them out of the secondary job market and into careers that allow for increases in status, responsibility, and income, work programs are perpetuating racial and social-class distinctions (Hamilton & Claus, 1981). The transition into adult occupational roles might be made much smoother for disadvantaged or marginal adolescents if governments would focus more on enhancing the quality of the employment experience for high-risk youth.

It is difficult to make recommendations for youth employment training programs that are relevant and practical for all countries, as there obviously is great political, economic, and cultural variation. However, most countries today share the experience of the increasing marginalization of their youth, especially those who come from disadvantaged or impoverished economic backgrounds. Thus, most nations recognize the importance of improving the access of school-leavers to job opportunities that provide solid training in job skills (*The Forgotten Half*, 1988b). Moreover, because youth are harbingers of the future, it may be beneficial for other countries to pattern their own youth training programs after the training schemes of prosperous nations.

As was illustrated earlier, the two strongest economies in the world today—Germany and Japan—invest heavily in the future via well-developed youth training programs. These programs emphasize on-the-job training (OJT) and apprenticeship experiences.

The central goal of OJT is learning useful job skills by working on the job. However, most researchers agree now that work-only OJT programs do not have positive long-lasting effects, because they overlook other areas of the personal development of disadvantaged youth, such as developing basic academic skills (*The Forgotten Half*, 1988b).

Apprenticeship—which is most well developed in West Germany and the German-speaking regions of Switzerland and Austria—has several appealing features: (1) it is recognized as a transitional social status between adolescence and adulthood, it confers prestige on the trainee and the employer; (2) on-the-job training is combined with academic training; (3) certification of apprenticeship graduates leads to advantages on the job market; and (4) training is specific enough to train youth for highly qualified, highly skilled occupations, but also broad enough to provide a basic foundation that can lead to upward mobility in the same job or to further development in a related occupation (*The Forgotten Half*, 1988b).

Apprenticeship training is not necessarily regarded by these societies as lower status than postsecondary education, but rather is viewed as a respected alternative from which students can benefit in terms of gaining good employment and continuing their education. Thus, the time has come for industrialized nations to build upon the successes of strong economic nations (such as Japan and Germany) by upgrading and improving their apprenticeship education and training (*The Forgotten Half*, 1988b; Glover, 1986; Hamilton, 1990).

In addition to urging countries to expand their apprenticeship training, Hamilton and his colleagues have called repeatedly for modification of the youth work experience via movement toward more participatory-democratic and entrepreneurial work programs for disadvantaged youth (Hamilton, Basseches, & Richards, 1985; Hamilton & Claus, 1981). Participatory-democratic work organizations provide all workers with the power and responsibility to make informed decisions regarding organizational policy, such as production, communication with outside organizations, and coordination of employees (Hamilton et al., 1985). Thus, in participatory-democratic entrepreneurships, all workers are involved in group decision making, work tasks are shared and rotated to provide flexibility and diversity on the job, and any profits generated are controlled by the entire group (Hamilton & Claus, 1981).

As Hamilton and his colleagues recognize, entrepreneurial ventures place heavy demands on youth employment programs, in terms of both financial burden (generating capital to establish a youth business and assist failing businesses), and human resources (adult guidance and supervision). However, the benefits to disadvantaged youth would far outweigh the costs. Disadvantaged youth would have a rare opportunity to assume technical and managerial positions that otherwise would be inaccessible to them. This experience also would enhance the self-image of disadvantaged youth and give them the motivation to work hard and develop skills that will move them up in the occupational hierarchy. The Boys Club of America's Youth Entrepreneurs Program illustrates one successful attempt at such a venture.

Creating meaningful alternatives to youth employment

Young people are vital resources, and society needs their active participation, not only as employees contributing to economic growth, but also as responsible citizens who uphold the values and rules of their communities. Inevitably, a portion of the youth population in every country will be denied access to meaningful employment. Most countries have much work to be done, but not enough paying jobs to do it. Thus, a meaningful alternative to employment for marginal youth is community service and volunteerism. The William T. Grant Foundation Commission on Work, Family, and Citizenship provides the following rationale for service:

> young people need experience not only as workers but especially as citizens. Undue emphasis on paid employment impoverishes education and may hamper personal and intellectual development. Just as we should not expect young people to take a single long step from being full-time students to being full-time workers, we should not expect them to be transformed overnight . . . from passive recipients of society's beneficence to active and concerned citizens. (*The Forgotten Half*, 1988a, p. 48)

Although government support of youth service is important at the national level, community-based design and implementation of youth service experiences are critical. Thus, at the local level, neighborhoods, communities, and cities should tailor their programs to the specific needs of their environments. The commission points out two key objectives of such a volunteer community effort: "(1) citizenship education, bringing together both poor and privileged youth to develop a service-oriented, lifelong commitment to others; and (2) exposure to fundamental social needs that are the common civic obligation of all of us" (*The Forgotten Half*, 1988a, p. 49).

Typically, youth volunteers work in service agencies operated by adults (e.g., hospitals, day-care centers, nursing homes). However, youth also could be organized to develop their own services to the community (e.g., neighborhood cleanup efforts, preservation of the environment). Regardless of the specific services rendered, voluntary service helps to socialize youth to become more responsible and productive adults, and also promotes skills that are useful on the job market in the future (e.g., promptness, teamwork, responsibility, cooperation, motivation, decision making, goal setting, etc.). Moreover, because the community values the services provided by youth volunteers, service programs enhance the self-respect of disadvantaged youth.

Teaching life skills to youth in and out of work

Hamburg (1990) defines life-skills training as "the formal teaching of requisite skills for surviving, living with others, and succeeding in a complex society" (p. 3). As societies become more technologically advanced, the responsibility for socializing youth to become valued and productive citizens is shifting away from the institution of the family and being placed more and more on the formal and informal institutions of communities (e.g., schools and youth organizations). Therefore, programs designed to help marginal youth make a smoother transition from adolescence into adulthood need to pay more attention to preparing youth in critical life skills, which extend beyond the boundaries of knowledge acquisition in schools or skill training on the job. Two general features that seem critical to the success of programs are (1) clear indications that youth contributions and responsibility are valued and facilitated and (2) provision of specific skills to help youth. Youth-serving organizations that enhance the status of youth tend to be particularly successful. Among the specific features identified in successful programs are voluntary participation, decision-making activities or tasks that are rewarding both for their own sake and as a means of achieving future goals, shared values among participants and leaders, and multiple activities to provide opportunities for role experimentation.

Particularly in adolescence, the importance of experimentation cannot be overemphasized. Youngsters should be given the opportunity to experiment, in as realistic a way as possible, so they can begin to get a sense of their own strengths and preferences. The acquisition of skills is important but should not be the sole focus of these programs. Small groups appear to be more successful than larger groups, and activities that afford individualization appear to be highly successful. Programs that combine workshops, discussion groups, and experience-gaining activities appear to be most effective. Youth accomplishments in these programs should be recognized and rewarded.

Youth are our most important resource for the future. It is extremely important that we find ways to integrate young people into meaningful and valued roles for adulthood, both for the sake of developing youth and for the betterment of society. Any efforts to increase youth integration and decrease marginality have tremendous potential.

Acknowledgements

The authors gratefully acknowledge Rachel Seidensticker and Phame Camarena for their research assistance and Amy Schultz and Linda Stahl for their technical support.

Note

1. The way in which unemployment is defined can greatly influence national statistics. For example, some countries may include all jobless non-school youth in their figures, whereas others may exclude non-employed youth (who are not actively in search of employment).

References

Adams, V., & Magnum, G. L. (1978). *The lingering crisis of youth unemployment.* Kalamazoo, MI: W. E. Upjohn Institute for Employment Research.

Banducci, R. (1984). Youth employment: International perspectives on transition. *School Counselor, 31,* 414–421.

Barton, P. E., & Fraser, B. S. (1978). *Between two worlds: Youth transition from school to work* (Vol. 2). Washington, DC: Center for Education and Work, National Manpower Institute.

Berg, I., Freedman, M., & Freedman, M. (1978). *Managers and work reform.* New York: Free Press.

Borowski, A. (1984). A comparison of youth unemployment in Australia and the United States. *Monthly Labor Review, 107,* 30–36.

Bowers, N. (1979). Young and marginal: An overview of youth unemployment. In U.S. Department of Labor, Bureau of Labor Statistics, *Young workers and families: A special section* (Special Labor Force Report 233) (pp. 4–18). Washington, DC: U.S. Department of Labor,Bureau of Labor Statistics.

Braverman, H. (1974). *Labor and monopoly capital.* New York: Monthly Review Press.

Breen, R. (1985). The work experience programme in Ireland. *International Labour Review, 127*(4), 429–443.

Brown, B. B. (1990). Peer groups and peer cultures. In S. S. Feldman & G. R. Elliott (Eds.), *At the threshold: The developing adolescent.* Cambridge, MA: Harvard University Press.

Burger, A., & Seidenspinner, G. (1977). *Jugend unter dem druck der arbeitslosigkeit.* Munich: Juventa.

Caspar, M. L. (1988). Employment-cum-training contracts in France: The 1975–85 record. *International Labour Review, 127*(4), 445–461.

Clark, A. W., & Clissold, M. P. (1982). Correlates of adaptation among unemployed and employed young men. *Psychological Reports, 50*(3), 887–893.

Coffield, F., Burrill, C., & Marshall, S. (1983). How young people try to survive being unemployed. *New Society, 2*, 332–334.

Conger, J. J., & Petersen, A. C. (1984). *Adolescence and youth* (3rd ed.). New York: Harper & Row.

Donovan, A., & Oddy, M. (1982). Psychological aspects of unemployment: An investigation into the emotional and social adjustment of school leavers. *Journal of Adolescence, 5*, 15–30.

Erikson, E. H. (1955). Ego identify and the psychosocial moratorium. In H. L. Winter & R. Kotinsky (Eds.), *New perspectives in juvenile delinquency.* Washington, DC: U.S. Department of Health, Education, and Welfare.

Erikson, E. H. (1968). *Identity: Youth and crisis.* New York: Norton.

Fagin, L. H., & Little, M. (1984). *The forsaken families.* Harmondsworth, UK: Penguin.

Farrington, D. P., Gallagher, B., Morley, L., St. Ledger, R. J., & West, D. J. (1986, October). Unemployment, school leaving, and crime. *British Journal of Criminology, 26*(4), 335–356.

Fineman, S. (1983). Counseling the unemployed: Help and helplessness. *British Journal of Guidance and Counseling, 11*, 1–9.

Finlay-Jones, R., & Eckhardt, B. (1982). *A survey of psychiatric disorder among the young unemployed of Canberra* (final report). A report submitted to the Research and Development Grants Advisory Committee. Australian Department of Health.

Freeman, R. B., & Wise, P. A. (Eds.). (1982). *The youth labor market problem: Its nature, causes, and consequences.* Chicago: University of Chicago Press.

George, R. (1987). *Youth policies and programs in selected countries.* Washington, DC: Youth and America's Future: The William T. Grant Foundation Commission on Work, Family and Citizenship.

Ginzberg, E. (1980). Youth unemployment. *Scientific American, 242*(5), 43–49.

Glover, R. W. (1986). *Apprenticeship lessons from abroad.* Columbus, OH: National Center for Research in Vocational Education.

Gore, S. (1978). The effect of social support in moderating the health consequences of unemployment. *Journal of Health and Social Behavior, 19*, 157–165.

Gurney, R. M. (1980). The effects of unemployment on the psycho-social development of school leavers. *Journal of Occupational Psychology, 53*, 205–213.

Hamburg, B. A. (1990). *Life skills training: Preventive interventions for young adolescents.* Report of the Life Skills Training Working Group, Carnegie Council on Adolescent Development. Washington, DC.

Hamilton, S. F. (1987a). *Adolescent problem behavior in the United States and the Federal Republic of Germany: Implications for prevention.* In K. Hurrelmann, F. Kaufmann, and F. Lösel (Eds.), *Social intervention: potential and constraints.* New York: de Gruyter.

Hamilton, S. F. (1987b). Work and maturity: Occupational socialization of noncollege youth in the United States and West Germany. *Research in the Sociology of Education and Socialization, 7*, 283–312.

Hamilton, S. F. (1990). *Apprenticeship for adulthood: Preparing youth for the future.* New York: Free Press.

Hamilton, S. F., Basseches, M., & Richards, F. A. (1985). *Participatory democratic work and adolescents' mental health* (pp. 467–487). New York: Plenum.

Hamilton, S. F., & Claus, J. F. (1981). Inequality and youth employment: Can work programs work? *Education and Urban Society, 14,* 103–126.

Harris, N. (1988). Social security and the transition to adulthood (survey article). *Journal of Social Politics, 17*(4), 501–523.

Hart, P. E. (1988). *Youth unemployment in Great Britain.* Cambridge: Cambridge University Press.

Hedges, A., & Hyatt, J. (1985). *Attitudes of beneficiaries to child benefit and benefits for young people.* London: Social and Community Planning Research.

Hendry, L. B., & Raymond, M. J. (1983). Youth unemployment, leisure and lifestyles: Some educational considerations. *Scottish Educational Review, 15,* 28–40.

Hendry, L. B., & Raymond, M. J. (1986). Psycho-social aspects of youth unemployment: An interpretive theoretical model. *Journal of Adolescence, 9,* 355–366.

Hendry, L. B., Raymond, M. J., & Stewart, C. (1984). Unemployment, school and leisure: An adolescent study. *Leisure Studies, 3,* 175–187.

Hepworth, J. T. (1980). Moderating factors of the psychological impact of unemployment. *Journal of Occupational Psychology, 53,* 139–145.

Herr, E. L., & Long, T. E. (1983). Counseling youth for employability: Unlearning the potential. Ann Arbor, MI: ERIC/CAPS Invited Monograph Series.

Hoare, J. (1980). Fraser gives the schools a serve. *Financial Review, 26,* 7.

Hurrelmann, K. (1990). Health promotion for adolescents: Preventive and corrective strategies against problem behavior. *Journal of Adolescence, 13,* 231–250.

Hurrelmann, K., & Engel, U. (Eds.). (1989). *The social world of adolescents: International perspectives.* Berlin/New York: De Gruyter.

James, P., Livingston, R., & Walker, C. (1983). *Sense of direction: Explaining new prospects with unemployed young people.* London: Community Projects Foundation.

Kato, H. (1978). *Education and youth employment in Japan.* Berkeley, CA: Carnegie Council on Policy Studies in Higher Education.

Kieselbach, J. (1988). Youth unemployment and health effects. *The International Journal of Social Psychiatry, 34*(2), 83–96.

Kohler, M. C., & Dollar, B. (1976, May/June). Youth service work: An antidote to alienation. *The Center Magazine, 9* (3) 20–27.

Lerman, R. I. (1986). Unemployment among low-income and black youth: A review of causes, programs, and policies. *Youth and Society, 17,* 237–266.

Levin, H. M. (1983). Youth unemployment and its educational consequences. *Educational Evaluation and Policy Analysis, 5*(2), 231–247.

LeVine, R. A. (1967). *Dreams and deeds: Achievement motivation in Nigeria.* Chicago: University of Chicago Press.

Lewin, K. (1939). Field theory and experiment in social psychology: Concepts and methods. *American Journal of Sociology, 44*(6), 868–896.

Main, B. G. M. (1985). School-leaver unemployment and the youth opportunities programme in Scotland. *Oxford Economic Papers, 37,* 426–447.

Mangum, G. L. (1987). Youth transition from adolescence to the world of work. In M. W. Young (Ed.), *Youth and America's Future:.* Washington, DC: William T. Grant Foundation.

Markey, J. P. (1988). The labor market problems of today's high school dropouts. *Monthly Labor Review, 111,* 36–43.

McDermott, K. (1985). All dressed up and nowhere to go: Youth unemployment and state policy in Britain. *Urban Anthropology, 14*(1–3), 91–108.

McPherson, A., & Hall, W. (1983). Psychiatric impairment, physical health and work values among unemployed and apprenticed young men. *Australian and New Zealand Journal of Psychiatry, 17*(4), 335–340.

Melvyn, P., & Freedman, D. H. (1979). Youth unemployment: A worsening situation. In D. H. Freedman (Ed.), *Employment outlook and insights* (pp. 81–92). Geneva: International Labor Office.

Mickelson, R. A. (1984). *Race, class, and gender differences in adolescent academic achievement attitudes and behaviors.* Unpublished doctoral dissertation, Graduate School of Education, University of California, Los Angeles.

Muuss, R. E. (1975). *Theories of adolescence.* New York: Random House.

Newman, M. J. (1979). The labor market experience of black youth, 1954–78. In U.S. Department of Labor, Bureau of Labor Statistics, *Young workers and families: A special section* (Special Labor Force Report 233) (pp.19–27). Washington, DC: U.S. Department of Labor, Bureau of Labor Statistics.

Nightingale, E. O., & Wolverton, L. (1988). *Adolescent rolelessness in modern society.* Invited address for the American Medical Association, National Congress on Adolescent Health: Charting a course through turbulent times, Chicago, May 12–14.

Oechslin, J. (1987). Training and the business world: The French experience. *International Labour Review, 126*(6), 653–667.

Ogbu, J. (1978). *Minority education and caste: The American system in cross-cultural perspective.* New York: Academic Press.

Ogbu, J. (1989). Cultural boundaries and minority youth orientation toward work preparation. In D. Stern & D. Eichorn (Eds.), *Adolescence and work: Influences of social structure, labor markets, and culture.* Hillsdale, NJ: Lawrence Erlbaum.

Osterman, P. (1978). Youth, work, and unemployment. *Challenge, 21*(2), 65–72.

Organization for Economic Cooperation and Development. (1990). *Labour Force Statistics, 1968–1988.* Paris: Author.

Peters, J. F. (1987). Youth, family, and employment. *Adolescence, 22*(86), 456–473.

Petersen, A. C., Kennedy, R. E., & Sullivan, P. (1991). Coping with adolescence. In M. E. Colten & S. Gore (Eds.), *Adolescent stress: Causes and consequences.* Hawthorne, NY: Aldine.

Petersen, A. C., Susman, E. J., & Beard, J. L. (1989). The development of coping responses during adolescence: Endocrine and behavioral aspects. In D. S. Palermo (Ed.), *Coping with uncertainty: Behavioral and developmental perspectives* (pp. 151–172). Hillsdale, NJ: Lawrence Erlbaum.

Phillips, S., & Sandstrom, K. (1990). Parental attitudes toward "youthwork." *Youth and Society, 22,* 160–183.

Quarles, G. R., & Hannenberg, V. L. (1982). Meeting the challenge of unemployed youth. In N. Christian (Ed.), *Education in the 80's: Vocational education.* Washington, DC: National Education Association.

Ramsey, R. S., & Ramsey, R. W. (1983). So why does Job Corps work? *College Student Journal, 17,* 2–9.

Rapoport, T. (1988). Socialization patterns in the family, the school, and the youth movement. *Youth and Society, 20,* 159–179.

Rist, R. C. (1981). Walking through a house of mirrors: Youth education and employment training. *Education and Urban Society, 14*(1), 3–14.

Roberts, K. (1983). *Youth and leisure.* London: Allen & Unwin.

Roberts, K. (1984). Problems and initiatives in youth unemployment. *Journal of Community Health Care*, *62*(8), 320–326.

Rumberger, R. (1981). *Overeducation in the U.S. labor market*. New York: Praeger.

Rutter, M. (1980). *Changing youth in a changing society: Patterns of adolescent development and disorder*. Cambridge, MA: Harvard University Press.

Saks, D. H., & Smith, R. E. (1981). Youth with poor job prospects. *Education and Urban Society*, *14*(1), 15–32.

Schober, K. (1978). Arbeitslose jugendliche: Belastungen und reaktionen du betroffenen. *Mitteilungen fur Arbeitsmaskt-und Berufsforschung*, *11*(2), 198–215.

Schostak, J. F. (1983). Race, riots and unemployment. In R. Fiddy (Ed.), *In place of work: Policy and provision for the young unemployed*. Lewes, UK: Falmer Press, Ltd.

Schwefel, D. (1986). Unemployment, health, and health services in German-speaking countries. *Social Science and Medicine*, *22*(4), 409–430.

Sherraden, M. W., & Adamek, M. E. (1984, December). Explosive imagery and misguided policy. *Social Service Review*, *58*(4), 539–555.

Solomos, J. (1985). Problems, but whose problems: The social construction of black youth unemployment and state policies. *Journal of Social Policy*, *14*, 527–554.

Spruit, I. P., & Svensson, P. G. (1987). Young and unemployed: Special problems. In Schwefel, D., & Svensson, P. G. (Eds.), *Unemployment, social vulnerability, and health in Europe* (pp. 196–210). Berlin, New York: Springer-Verlag.

Super, D. E. (1953). A theory of vocational development. *American Psychologist, 8*, 185–190.

Super, D. E. (1957). *The psychology of careers*. New York: Harper & Row.

Super, D. E. (1963). Self-concepts in vocational development. In D. E. Super, R. Stavishevsky, N. Matlin, & J. P. Jordaan (Eds.), *Career development: Self-concept theory* (Research Monograph No. 4). New York: College Entrance Examination Board.

Tiggeman, M., & Winefield, A. H. (1980). Some psychological effects of unemployment in school-leavers. *Australian Journal of Social Issues*, *15*(4), 269–276.

U.S. Department of Labor. (1979). *Toward the ideal journeyman*. Employment and Training Administration Apprenticeship and CETA Technical Assistance Guide. Washington, DC: Government Printing Office.

Viney, L. (1983). Psychological reactions of young people to unemployment. *Youth and Society*, *14*(4), 457–474.

Vondracek, F. W., Lerner, R. M., & Schulenberg, J. E. (1986). *Career development: A life-span developmental approach*. Hillsdale, NJ: Lawrence Erlbaum.

Warr, P. B. (1984). Job loss, unemployment, and psychological well-being. In V. Allen & E. Van de Vliert (Eds.), *Role transitions* (pp. 263–286). New York: Plenum.

Warr, P. B., Banks, M. H., & Ullah, P. (1985). The experience of unemployment among black and white urban teenagers. *British Journal of Psychology, 76*, 75–87.

Warr, P. B., & Payne, R. (1983). Social class and reported changes in behavior after job loss. *Journal of Applied Social Psychology, 13*, 206–222.

The William T. Grant Commission on Work, Family and Citizenship. (1988a). *The forgotten half: Non-college youth in America*. Washington, DC: William T. Grant Foundation.

The William T. Grant Commission on Work, Family and Citizenship. (1988b). *The forgotten half: Pathways to success for America's youth and young families.* Washington, DC: William T. Grant Foundation.

Williams, B. R. Chair, Committee of Inquiry into Education and Training. (1979) *Education, training, and employment* (Vol. 1). Canberra: Australian Goverment Publishing Service.

2. Social capital, human capital, and investment in youth

JAMES S. COLEMAN
Department of Sociology
The University of Chicago

I start with an observation that I attempt later to account for: Youth are coming to be increasingly marginalized in modern society. In attempting to account for this, I will ask just why this should be; what is it about modern society that leads to the marginalization of youth? We take this fact as if it were natural, but there is nothing natural about it. Why increasingly marginalized? Why not increasingly central?

Figure 2.1 is an indicator of the marginalization. Shown in the figure are ratios of male youth (young men ages 15 to 19) unemployment to the male adult (25 and over) unemployment rate, in 1965 and in 1979, 14 years later. In all countries but one, the ratio is greater than 1.0, and in nearly every country for which data are shown these ratios have increased during that period. In Canada and the United States, the ratios were already high; in some other countries, they became high during this period.

What makes this result especially striking is that during this same period, a great increase occurred in the proportion of youth not in the labor market, but in full-time education. Taking the two results together, the picture is one of a radical change for youth, from being part of the productive economy to being outside it in "holding tanks," so to speak, with difficulty in moving from the holding tanks to the productive economy.

Youth are not marginal in consumption. Since the 1960s there has emerged in industrialized societies an extensive youth market for certain consumption goods—in particular, clothes, music, and entertainment services. The discretionary income of youth is high despite the fact that youth are increasingly marginal to the production side of the economy and find it increasingly difficult to enter into employment.

This is the starting point. In attempting to answer why this is so, and how it might change, I sketch what I see as three separate phases in the

34

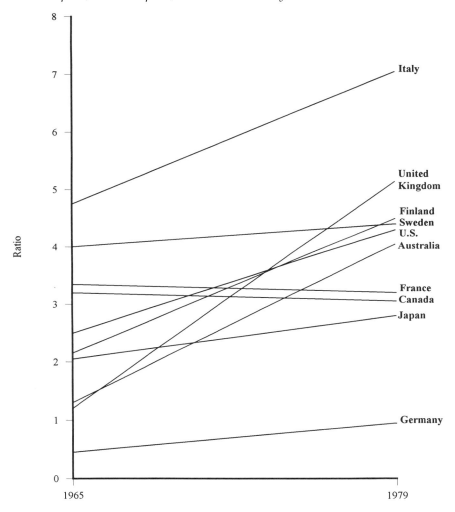

SOURCE: Youth Unemployment: The Causes and Consequences. Paris, OECD, 1980.

Figure 2.1. Ratio of teenage male unemployment to adult unemployment rates, 1965 and 1979 in ten OECD countries

relationship of children and youth to society. These phases can be distinguished by their potential for investment in the human capital of the next generation. This investment in human capital occurs by applying the social and financial resources of adults toward the development of productive skills in children. It can be quite simply described as the investment of the social and financial capital of one generation toward the creation of human capital in the next generation. The social capital consists of the social relationships within the family and the community that generate the attention and time spent by parents and community members in the development of children and youth. The financial capital consists of the monetary expenditures of formal institutions designed toward that same goal. The principal such institution is, of course, the school.

Phase 1: The exploitation of children's labor

A household in phase 1 is a household living near a subsistence level. A phase 1 economy is one in which most households are near a subsistence level. An economy based largely on subsistence farming is the most widespread example, though extractive economies in general—in which most occupations are in the primary economic sector—fit this phase, as do village-based societies in which most households are engaged in herding. In such social structures, households directly produce most of what they consume; economic exchange and division of labor are minimal.

In such societies, the household is the principal productive institution. The household has both responsibility for its children and authority over them. In economists' terms, property rights over children are vested in the family.[1] The labor of children is useful to the household, both because in the diversified activities of the household there are always tasks that children can carry out and because the economic level of the household is sufficiently low that the effort of all is needed. The cost of children to the family is low, because food is ordinarily produced at home. Families exercise their property rights in children through having many of them and then exploiting their capacity for labor, with little regard for the impact of this upon the children's opportunities. Such societies are ordinarily stable over generations, and there is little of what is, in modern societies, described as "opportunity." Families have narrow horizons, are inwardly focused, and have little interest in or resources for extending their children's horizons broadly.

In this stage, the family makes little financial investment in its children beyond that implicit in the "on-the-job training" the child gets through labor in the household or apprenticeship in a nearby household. The family's investments of social capital consist primarily of the informal social resources of family and proximate community members, and these investments are directed to short-term payoffs in productivity of the young. Long-term investments are limited, because the family requires productive activity from its young as soon as they are able. Investments with longer-term payoffs are limited to those skills that will help perpetuate the family and support parents in old age. In a stable society, this means learning the relevant skills of father or mother (or of other adults in the vicinity), and these may be acquired as a by-product of the father's or mother's daily occupations. Formal schooling is hardly necessary, and for societies at this stage schools are scarce.

This can be seen even in relatively recent times, by examining trends in the number of boys not in school as the society shifts out of stage 1. Figure 2.2 shows the proportion of boys ages 5 to 19 not in school in the United States from 1840 (the earliest date for which data exist) to 1970; alongside it runs the graph indicating the proportion of men in agriculture (which traditionally has largely been family farming and continued to remain so until at least the 1940s). The fact that the proportion of boys not in school closely tracks the proportion of men in agriculture is suggestive evidence of the irrelevance of formal schooling for raising children in stable subsistence-farming societies.

Phase 2: Children as investments for the family

A postagricultural, urban, industrial society engaged largely in manufacturing and some commerce defines phase 2. Here the economy is an exchange economy, most labor is performed in full-time jobs, and the family's economic needs are provided mainly through the exchange of wages for goods. Children's labor is no longer needed for the household's economy, fewer possibilities exist for productive work of children within the household. In such a society, and even in the movement from phase 1 to phase 2, "opportunity" for the young begins to take on meaning.

In such a society the family continues to have a strong interest in children, for a more long-range goal. The family retains its implicit property rights in its children, in part as a residue from phase 1. Families are still the central institutions of society, again in part as a residue from phase 1. Although the household is no longer the principal locus of production in the society, the full implications of this have not been realized, because the family retains many related functions. "The family's interests" are still closely linked to each of its members' interests.

Children are the carriers of the family across generations from the past into future, and parents' investment in children is an investment in human capital for their own old age as well as for the family's future. A large number of children is no longer valuable for this latter purpose, but

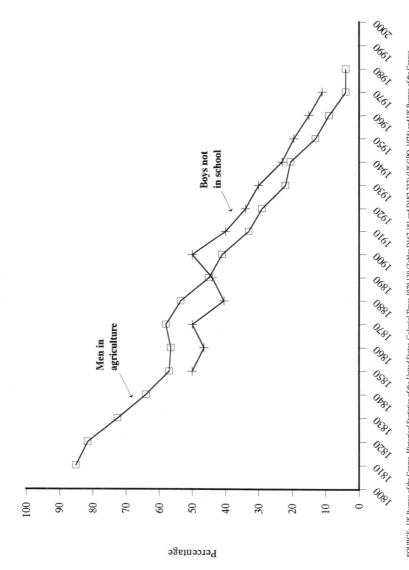

SOURCE: US Bureau of the Census, *Historical Statistics of the United States, Colonial Times 1970* 139 (Tables D167-181 and D182-232) (US GPO, 1975) and US Bureau of the Census, *Statistical Abstracts of the United States* 417 (Table 693) (US GPO, 1984). For the data on boys' school attendance, US Bureau of the Census, *Historical Statistics* at 370 (Table H433-441).

Figure 2.2.   Percentage of male labor force working in agriculture, 1810–1980, and percentage of boys aged 5–10 not attending school, 1850–1970

38

the high investments made in each child—to increase the status, economic position, and social respectability of the family in the next generation—are of value.

It is especially important to recognize two points about this phase, points that are relevant to the problems youth face today. The first is that the productive capacity of a family's children is important for the family's future, both for the parents' own well-being in the dependency of old age and for the well-being of the family as a corporate body extending over generations. Second, the value of the child to the family is not in terms of current production, but in terms of future productive capacity.

The first point implies that the family has a direct material interest in developing its children's productive capacity. Investments in the child's education and skill development are not merely investments for the child's future welfare; they are investments for the parents' future welfare as well, and for the family's standing in the community.[2] The second point implies that the family's interest is in future productivity over the whole course of adulthood, rather than in immediate benefits, as is true in phase 1. The two points taken together imply that the family will have a strong material interest in the child's welfare that coincides largely with the child's own long-range interest. Exploitation of the child is no longer in the family's interest if it will reduce the child's future productive potential. (There are a few forms of exploitation of the child that will still be in the parents' interest, cases in which the child's current earning power is high relative to that of the parents. The best-known example is exploitation of children as potential movie stars. But such circumstances are few.)

Phase 2 is associated with social change, especially beginning with the Industrial Revolution. This implies not only that the family can afford investments in the future, but also that the social resources of the family and its immediate environment are insufficient and even inappropriate for the skills the young will need.[3] Financial investments in training the young are necessary, and these investments are primarily in a specialized institution: the school. Schooling of the child comes to be important to the family.

This can be seen especially well in Europe, where many families left the first phase only after World War II. Before that time, secondary education was not universal; a large portion of the population gained employment immediately after elementary school. After 1945, a strong demand for equal educational opportunity was created, secondary education became universal, and, in the 1960s, there arose a demand to replace the two-tiered secondary educational system with comprehensive schools enrolling all youth in the cohort.

Phase 2 is a transitional phase, as suggested by the earlier point. The centrality of the family exists in part as a residue of its functional strength in phase 1. Over time this residue comes to be washed away, and the connection of individual interests to family interests is weakened. In developed societies this second phase in the relationship of youth to society has begun to be replaced by a third phase.

Phase 3: Children as irrelevant

Phase 3 is an advanced industrial society (what Daniel Bell has called a postindustrial society) or a welfare state with a high degree of affluence. In this phase the family's central role in the economy has vanished, and the family itself has become a kind of appendage to the economic structure. It is an institution relevant to consumption but no longer important to production. Its functional role has been reduced to that of child rearing.

The family's central place in the economy and in society has been taken over by large and small corporate bodies, and industrial and commercial corporations. When the economic functions of the household are siphoned off to other institutions, the family can retain its *raison d'être* only for a period of time. It is no longer an institution spanning lifetimes, but one that forms anew with each successive generation. Its interest in children to carry the family into the future declines. The stability of marriages (and thus of households) has declined; the extended family is no longer able to restrain its members from choosing individualistic solutions at the expense of the family.

Other changes in advanced societies are also consistent with the irrelevance of children in phase 3. More couples choose not to have children. Those who do have children spend less time with their pre-adolescent and adolescent children, and children spend less time with parents in whole-family settings. Leisure activities take place increasingly in age-segregated settings, exemplified by cocktail parties for the adults and rock concerts for the youth. The gulf between adults, in their work institutions, and youth, in their educational institutions, has increased. Increasing numbers of children are abandoned, run away from home, become addicted to drugs, or commit suicide. In the United States there is evidence that immigrant parents make greater investments in their children's futures than do nonimmigrant parents.

As the above discussion indicates, the potential for investment in the next generation changes as society itself changes. If we think of investments in youth as investments in the next generation's human capital, it is useful to distinguish investments of two kinds: first, investment of time, effort, and attention of adults in the family and in the informal community surrounding the family—what I have earlier described as investments of social capital—and second, investments through employment of professionals in formal organizations, in particular, schools. I have described these as investments of financial capital.

The relations as I have described them, between the investments of social capital and the investments of financial capital in the human capital of the next generation, can be described schematically (see Figure 2.3).

This figure shows the continually increasing investment of financial capital in the creation of human capital and the equally continually *decreasing* investment of social capital. The increasing investment of financial capital is a direct consequence of economic development. Such growth leads to an increase in the affluence of the society, and of the families within it. The decreasing investment in social capital reflects an indirect consequence of that same economic development. The family—a specialized institution in an exchange economy—is less likely to be a place where the everyday activities lead toward a focus on developing productive skills.

The investments of financial capital and social capital might combine in various ways to produce human capital in the young. Three of these (see Figure 2.4a–c) show outputs of human capital corresponding to the investments shown in Figure 2.3. Figure 2.4a, with a horizontal line, shows the level of human capital produced if the human capital product was merely the sum of the two types of investment, which means one was perfectly substitutable for the other. The curve in Figure 2.4b shows the human capital produced if the two types of investment combined multiplicatively. Figure 2.4c, labeled "Minimum input," shows the human capital produced if the product depended on the minimum of the two investments. As we can see by referring back to Figure 2.3, this output is limited by the lower of the two investment lines—constricted by financial investment on the left and confined by social investment on the right.

Evidence comparing less-developed countries with more-developed countries, discussed below, indicates that the production function for human capital is not additive, but is rather something like that of the multiplicative or the minimum-input function. Both functions imply that financial and social capital are not substitutes for one another.[4] Substantively, this suggests that two different kinds of resources are necessary for the growth of human capital: (1) the existence of educational opportuni-

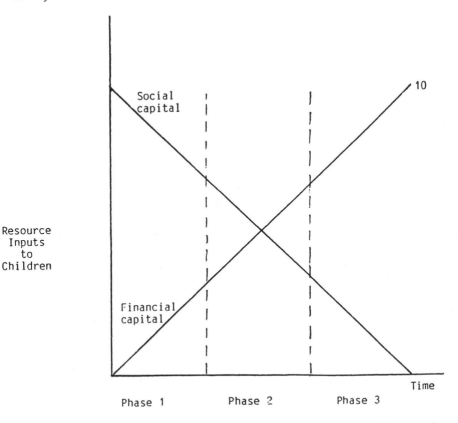

Figure 2.3.   Financial capital and social capital resource inputs into development of human capital in children and youth

ties and (2) the presence of motivation and interest that will lead to taking advantage of these opportunities. If either is missing, human capital development is blocked. In Figure 2.3, human capital development is blocked or impeded in phase 1, to the left, by a deficiency of opportunity brought about by a deficiency of financial capital. It is blocked or impeded in phase 3 by a deficiency of motivation, resulting from a deficiency in social capital. In phase 1, financial capital is in short supply and constitutes what may be called the "limiting factor." In phase 3 the limiting factor is declining social capital. This implies that in phase 1 an increase in finances for education will make great differences in human capital development; in phase 3 an increase in the social capital (provided by family and community) would have a comparable effect. In modern society, vari-

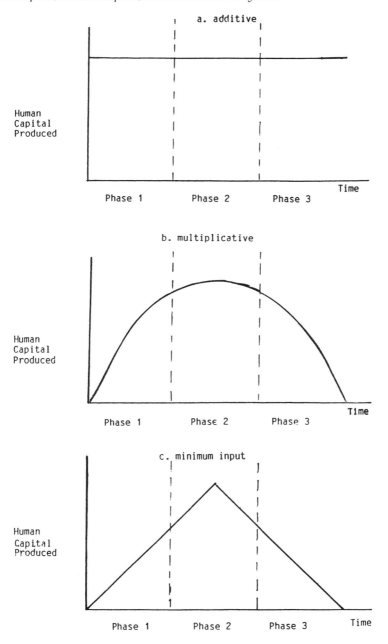

Figure 2.4. Production of human capital in three phases of society, according to three different production functions

ations in family background matter much more than variations in school achievement outcomes.

Heyneman (1990), an educational researcher whose research has been focused in less-developed countries (principally Africa and Southeast Asia) supports this view of human capital development:

> Since the beginning of systematic cognitive testing at the turn of the century, students from middle-class backgrounds have often outperformed students from lower income families. In the early 1970s, however, large-scale testing began in developing countries, and it was discovered that this "iron rule" was far from universal. In fact, there are circumstances in which the typical student from a low social status home environment performs every bit as well as those from a middle class background. . . .
>
> Why is this relevant to the U.S.? Lack of money is not the principal cause of ineffective schools or low quality education [in the United States]. The lack of pupil motivation and therefore, discipline is the principal cause. When ministers of education from developing countries are asked about the most important problems in education, pupil motivation or discipline isn't even on this list. (29–30)

In the United States, the achievement attributable to the school itself is almost independent of the level of tangible school resources provided by the community or the nation. The achievement is not independent of the way the school is organized, the disciplinary constraints it imposes on students, and the academic demands it makes on them. But a school with excellent physical resources, laboratories, books, and teacher qualifications, a school with high per pupil expenditures, does not produce high achievement if these less tangible organizational elements are missing. Even more important are the social resources provided by parents. The presence (or absence) of such resources accounts for much more variation in school outcomes than does the amount of financial resources put into the school. In contrast, these differences in background matter little in less-developed countries.

If this picture is correct, highly developed countries are currently moving into phase 3, a place in which tangible school resources—the financial investments in education—are in oversupply, not only in the school itself, but also in the home, and quite generally throughout society. Tangible resources are not in short supply in the affluent phase 3. Social capital, however, the motivations that strong families—interested in investing time, effort, and attention in their children—provided in phase 2, are lacking in phase 3. The schools that are most effective in this third phase are those able to supply this social capital, to furnish the intangible qualities that impel students to take full advantage of the opportunities provided by the tangible resources. The school, in phase 3, is one of the many elements competing for the attention and interests of children and youth, and what cannot be taken for granted are the motivational forces that direct attention and interest toward school learning, rather than toward the other attractive competitors for this attention and interest.

Investment in human capital

The preceding sections have given a partial diagnosis of the problems of bringing children and youth into adulthood in modern society—or, as an economist might put it, the problems of developing human capital in the next generation. In those sections, I argued that the growth of human capital requires investments not only of financial capital, but also of social capital. I argued also that parents, who in phase 2 of society's develop- ment made those investments, now in phase 3 have far fewer incentives for doing so. Those incentives always depended on the parents being able to count on support from children when the parents were old. Stated differently, the parents had partial property rights in the production of their children when those children were adults and the parents were dependent.

The arguments of the preceding section also imply that these incen- tives have been destroyed by the weakening of the family, and the loss of those property rights. In this section I suggest that appropriate invest- ments in the human capital of the next generation will occur only when there comes once again to be some actor with property rights in the production of the next generation. Furthermore, if the property rights are appropriately allocated, the incentives thus created will be far more effec- tive than those of the past, because the property rights in the past were not well specified and enforced, even at best.

By *property rights* in the present context, I mean the obligation on the part of children to do honor to the family name, and their obligation to care for dependent parents (or others in the family who become depen- dent). This can be seen as part of a set of norms that once gave the family as an institution informal property rights over some unspecified part of each of its members' production. The norms included also the bearing of children to carry on the family name and the raising of these children in such a way that they will bring honor to the family name. These property rights were not enforceable by law, but only by informal norms, norms that were enforced first of all by family members on one another, and second by members of the community of which the family was a part. These norms, however, were effective only so long as the social structure facilitated their enforcement through sanctions (as described in Coleman, 1990, Chapter 11). Once that structure breaks down, there are numerous consequences. Of interest here is only a subset of these consequences: It releases adult family members from the obligation to have children and raise them well, and it releases children, once adult, from the obligations to care for parents and to carry on the family name with honor. The negative impact on investments in the human capital of the children lies in the elimination of both the carrot and the stick. The carrot is the potential return to the parents on the investment, in the care and responsibility they can expect from their children as they become dependent and the psychic benefits they can expect when the children as adults bring honor to the family. The stick is the obligation they have toward the family, as an abstract entity, to spend the necessary resources, financial and social, to bring children well prepared into adulthood.

What, then, can be done?

It seems clear from this diagnosis that what is necessary is some means of restructuring property rights to make it to some actor's best interest to invest social capital in the next generation's human capital. It is inappropriate on several counts to aim for a reconstitution of the family's property rights. First, the social structure necessary for enforcement has gone and is unlikely to return. Both the community surrounding the family and the older generations within the family have largely lost the capacity for imposing effective sanctions on parents in bearing and properly raising children, and on children (as adults) in accepting obligations for dependent parents. Second, that social structure had inherent biases leading to differential effectiveness of the property rights allocation, and thus to great inequalities among children from different social strata. Third, the property rights allocation that brought about investments of social capital in the young depended as much on the stick as on the carrot, as much on negative sanctions for nonperformance of duty as on positive rewards for performance. In the voluntaristic social structure that increasingly characterizes society, negative sanctions for nonperformance are hardly effective, because relationships can easily be broken with little cost.

A second direction that is inappropriate is suggested by a recent announcement of new books by the Committee for Economic Development (CED), a business-financed and business-oriented group concerned with educational issues. Two titles announced are *Investing in Our Children: Business and the Public Schools* and *Children in Need: Investment Strategies for the Educationally Disadvantaged*. Both titles suggest what the books discuss in full: investment strategies for business firms, benefitting either all children (the first book) or solely "educationally disadvantaged" children (the second book). There is only one difficulty with the investment strategies discussed in these books: No business firm can expect a return on its investments. The authors indeed do not expect the investments to give a positive return to the business firm that makes the investment. The reason, of course, is that the firm has no property rights in the value created by its investment. If the investment is a good one—if it does create value by increasing the future productive potential of the children affected—the value will accrue to all firms in the relevant labor market area, an area that is continuing to expand and for some occupations constitutes the whole of the United States, or even the world. The value created is a public good, not a private one. Thus the general prescription to business firms or to any other actor to invest in children has a fatal flaw, a "tragedy of the commons" flaw that will deter any reasonable firm from making the investment, unless it expects to use the fact of the investment itself to exhibit its philanthropic character.

A third direction is suggested by a common response to public-goods problems such as this one: to move the investment up to a level such that the benefits of the investment can be captured by the investing actor. In this scenario, a consortium of actors (such as business firms) would cover a whole market area, taxing themselves in order to create the resources necessary to develop the human capital that would otherwise remain undeveloped in the young. The result would be, as it turns out, something like what already exists: a government, complete with the power to tax. This is precisely the way in which financial resources for public schooling are already provided. Even the division between levels of government, and changes in that division over time, correspond to the changes in labor-market areas that have occurred. In the early days of public education in the United States, nearly all the funding was at the local school district level, through real estate taxes, and nearly all labor markets were confined to that level. Over time, state income tax funding has increased; it currently constitutes about half of public education costs (averaged over all states). Federal income tax funding, which once was minuscule, now constitutes 7 to 8 percent of that total.

This approach to solving the public-goods problem for children, however, has defects. It does overcome the public-goods problem of educating children and youth. But as indicated earlier, financial capital is not a substitute for social capital in the production of human capital. As Heyneman's comparison of education in more-developed and less-developed countries indicates—and as Hanushek's review of research shows—additional financial resources make little difference for education in developed countries. The social capital, however, provided by parents' involvement with the child's education, does. A second defect is that social action, via taxation and the distribution of resources to many actors (schools, teachers, and, ultimately, children), is subject to conflicts over what constitutes fair distribution of the burden or the benefit. These conflicts are a major source of the misallocation of funds found in countries possessing a command rather than a market economy.

An illustration of this defect is given by a simple example. As I was writing this chapter, my eye chanced upon a reprint of a short article from the *Los Angeles Times* by Charles Wolf, Jr. (1991). Part of the headline was covered, and I could read only, "Change, Not Tons of Money." I read also the subhead: "With appropriate reform, aid will not be needed. Without it, aid will be wasted." I, writing about education, assumed that the article was about schools. But when I uncovered the full headline, it read, "Soviets Need Change, Not Tons of Money." The mistake was not coincidental. The distribution of tax-generated educational resources by federal, state, and local education districts is distribution through a command economy—and the current complaints about that system are almost indistinguishable from those made about state socialist economic systems: Money is used for unproductive purposes, incentive systems are inappropriate, and so on.

What, then, is the correct direction? The answer is to get the property rights right. Once this is done, it will automatically overcome the public-goods problem, and it will do so by introducing the proper incentives into the system.

How can "getting the property rights right" be accomplished in this case? The following costs of nondevelopment of human capital accrue to governments: costs of schooling; costs of crime, including costs of apprehension and incarceration of criminals; costs of welfare payments; medical costs induced by lifestyle; costs associated with alcohol and drug use; and, finally, the loss of benefits from income taxes. Governments would gain by vesting rights to a portion of both the realized benefits and the unrealized costs to any actor that, with parents' approval, would undertake to reduce the costs and increase the benefits for particular children. This would necessitate use of social science methods to make a statistical prediction, on the basis of background characteristics, of the expected costs and benefits to government of a given child. Such predictions certainly are possible. For example, one study of out-of-wedlock births concludes from its analysis that, considering only one type of cost, AFDC (Aid to Families with Dependent Children) payments, "Each family that began with a birth to a teen-ager will cost the public an average of $14,000 over the next twenty years" (An, Haveman, & Wolfe, 1991).

What is proposed is, in effect, a "bounty" on the head of each child in the system, a bounty collectible by whatever actor undertook to develop the child in a way that would reduce the costs and increase the benefits. Because the costs and benefits occur over the lifetime of the child in question, the return on the investment made by the responsible actor would accrue to that actor as the young person passed the age at which the costs and benefits would be expected to occur.

This vesting of property rights in actors that would take responsibility for specific children may seem unrealistic. I contend that it is the only viable direction for the future task of bringing the young into adulthood. The task of "getting the property rights right" without introducing new perverse incentives (such as incentives on the part of low-income adults to produce children who would command a bounty) is not a simple one. Nevertheless, the welfare of future generations depends on our capacity to do so.

Notes

1. Vivid descriptions of such households in seventeenth-century America can be found in Demos (1970). For characterization of English households at about the same time, see Laslett (1971). Laslett (1972) gives some information about households and the treatment of children throughout Europe, although the focus is primarily demographic.
2. There still may be underinvestment in the child's educational development because the parent captures only a part of the benefits of that education. The situation is like that of a firm investing in the creation of human capital in its employees, largely specific human capital (benefits captured by the firm) but with some general human capital (benefits not captured by the firm) as well. To the extent that the general human capital is inextricably bound with the specific human capital, the firm, not able to capture all the benefits, will underinvest (see Becker, 1964)
3. Immigration can show especially well the different roles of schooling in phases 1 and 2. For example, a high proportion of immigrants from rural Mexico to the United States drop out of school as soon as permitted by law, because schooling was not regarded as important in their pre-immigration setting (see Kett, 1977).
4. This does not imply that no possibility of convertibility exists between social capital and financial capital. It implies only that given the existing educational practices,

more money invested in education will not bring about greater achievement. This is certainly what has been found in education. See Hanushek (1986) for a review of studies in U.S. education.

References

An, C. B., Haveman, R., & Wolfe, B. (1991). Reducing teen out-of-wedlock births: The role of parental education and family stability. *The La Follette Policy Report*, 4(1), 8.

Becker, G. (1964). *Human capital*. New York: National Bureau of Economic Research, Columbia University Press.

Coleman, J. S. (1990). *Foundations of social theory*. Cambridge, MA: Harvard University Press.

Demos, J. (1970). *A little commonwealth family life in Plymouth colony*. Oxford: Oxford University Press.

Hanushek, E. A. (1986). The economics of schooling production and efficiency in public schools. *Journal of Economic Literature, 24*, 1141–1177.

Heyneman, S. (1990, March). Education on the world market. *American School Board Journal, 177*(3) 28–30.

Kett, J. (1977). *Rites of passage: Adolescents in America, 1790 to the present*. New York: Basic Books.

Laslett, P. (1971). *The world we have lost*. London: Methuen.

Wolf, C., Jr. (1991, September 12). Soviets need change, not tons of money. *Los Angeles Times*, p. 87.

3. When may social capital influence children's school performance?

JOHN MODELL
Department of History
Carnegie Mellon University

For several years, James Coleman has been working out the notion of "social capital," employing it provisionally in various settings as a possible key link in his theoretical effort to "import the economists' principle of rational action for use in the analysis of social systems proper...without discarding social organization in the process" (Coleman, 1988, p. S97; Coleman, 1990). Coleman asks us to think of structured sentiment and behavior as *resources*, the availability of which facilitates and, by facilitating, guides the choices of individuals conceived of as rational actors.

In his chapter in this volume, Coleman brings this theoretical perspective to bear on the emergence of many poorly schooled youth into a too-demanding labor market. In keeping with Coleman's focus, I pass over structural aspects of the school-work tie, directing my attention instead to students in school, in order to "unpack" the schematic notion of "social capital" (Coleman, 1988, p. S101) as it applies to school learning. In this chapter I nibble around the edges of "social capital," leaving the concept possibly better trimmed to its particular application, although (a conclusion I leave to the reader) also possibly drained of some of its analytic crispness.

Overall, my argument suggests that little evidence exists of a straightforward trend in the reduction of social capital employed by U.S. parents on behalf of their children's school learning. More broadly, the account I offer argues that any meaningful notion of social capital must be situated in a larger set of social and cultural relations that surround the way children grow up in any given society.

Evidence of Decline

If the combination of cognitive achievement and gumption required to complete high school is a relevant measure of human capital formation in U.S. children, then we may ask whether things are actually getting worse. For the past generation and more, the proportion of those completing high school has remained within the 70 to 75 percent range, reaching something of a peak when Vietnam draft calls provided incentive for remaining in school and declining to a low point around 1980. It has been trending upward since. During that same period, the number receiving equivalency degrees (which may or may not mark the same human capital investment, but which are nominally recognized by next-stage gatekeepers as an equivalent achievement) has been roughly complementary (U.S. National Center for Educational Statistics, 1991, pp. 105, 107). If we measure U.S. children's achievement at school by scores on standardized tests, the balance of evidence suggests that the once alarming test-score decline in the 1970s was brief and since has been more than overcome (Stedman & Kaestle, 1991). Seen in long-term perspective, U.S. schoolchildren are as knowledgeable—even about U.S. history—as at earlier dates (Whittington, 1991) and are, in IQ terms, smarter than they used to be (Flynn, 1984).

We ought not infer that important downward trends in the provision of social capital to children result directly from structural changes in society (even though, at first glance, these changes do suggest a trend toward adult selfishness, such as the increased prevalence of divorce and hence children being raised by one rather than both parents). If sharply reduced marital fertility is an indicator of a lessened regard for the obligatory nature of bearing and raising children, no less is it the case that couples who choose to have small families devote on average more time and cultural resources to each child (Alwin & Thornton, 1984; Blake, 1989, chapters 6–7). A recent longitudinal study (Astone & McLanahan, 1991) asked how differently do one- and two-parent families rear their adolescent children, and what are the implications of this for school achievement? There were substantial deficits, as predicted, in the amount of monitoring and supervision that single parents versus couples provided (net of the influence of various correlates), but no differences were revealed in single parents' aspirations for their children's education. Indeed, they spent more rather than less time in conversation with their children. As anticipated, the lesser monitoring and supervision did have a deleterious effect upon their children's school performance, but these were strong only with regard to children's engagement in school (attendance, attitude) and not with regard to grades or dropping out. Measured differences in parenting practices—social capital expended—explained only one-tenth of the observed difference in high school graduation rates between children from two-parent and one-parent families.

School as Arena

Whatever else it is, the school is a setting in which generations meet on special terms, an institution within which children—under evident compulsion, and massed according to their age—are asked to perform according to specifications laid down by adults. Children experience home and school as distinct spheres (Goodnow & Burns, 1985). Home is where goals are diffuse, instruction is mixed with encouragement, and one can remain confident of one's good standing. School is where the rhythm of the day is out of the child's control and where humiliation may occur at any moment, along with quick anger and the possibility of banishment. When U.S. children locate the goal of learning outside themselves, they learn more reluctantly and less effectively; indeed, many U.S. children seem to hold an uncertain enough view of the value of learning for learning's sake that when external rewards for learning are offered, existing intrinsic motivations are weakened (Lepper & Hodell, 1989). As U.S. children grow up, their schools are increasingly structured in ways that invite, even demand, competitive comparisons with peers. Children closely monitor teachers' explicit and implicit judgments both of them and of them in comparison with their classmates, and they become increasingly acute at reading the cues, which become increasingly explicit and objectively based (Weinstein, 1989). Rosenholtz and Simpson (1984) stated:

> The between-student comparison process becomes less a way of asking how smart each [child] is *becoming*, than of measuring minute differences in how smart each *is*. Attributions explaining performance turn to ability as a stable aspect of the individual, and performance comparisons take on added importance to the student['s] world. (p. 57)

In the United States, it has been observed that children approach the learning tasks they are confronted with in school with one of two characteristic emphases. One embraces working for the sake of satisfying others and making a good show of oneself; the other, for the sake of accomplishing the task as a goal in itself (Dweck, 1986; Dweck & Elliott, 1983). Correspondingly, and empirically related, children from an early age begin to learn from parents, and from the way learning is staged in classrooms, one of two differing accounts of intelligence. To some children, intelligence is by and large fixed in quantity, essentially unified across realms, and visible in performances of all sorts. For others, it "consists of an ever-expanding repertoire of skills and knowledge, one that is increased through one's own instrumental behavior" (Dweck & Bempechat, 1983, p. 244; Nicholls, Patashnick, & Nolen, 1985). These kinds of differences in perspective about the appropriate strategy for school learning vary markedly among parents, too, and presumably are often transmitted from parent to child from an early stage in the latter's formal education (Ames & Archer, 1987).

These "theories" about the nature of intelligence and the nature of school performance matter because students' motivation to take intellectual risks in learning derive in part from how their theories lead them to interpret the classroom arena. Children whose views of competence depend on competitive comparison, however, will eventually compare; if their early showings are not favorable, they are likely to learn to stop caring about the activity in the arena in question so as to avoid generalizing their negative self-evaluation to ever more inclusive realms. They will learn early to avoid trying to learn anything genuinely difficult, seeking instead a face-saving way out or, alternatively, choosing a task so mountainously difficult that any student would fail, so that failure in this particular instance does not prove stupidity. If they are deep believers in the notion of intelligence as fixed, the conclusion to be drawn from repeated trials and failures may be devastating, and may understandably lead them to seek other spheres of publicly legitimated competence in which they can shine. Such patterns of behavior increase in prevalence with children's ages, along with a shift in children's view of school subjects from inherently interesting to instrumentally worthwhile (Harter, 1981; Licht, Stader, & Swenson, 1989; Nicholls, 1989).

In the U.S. setting, many parents seek to play a considerable role in helping their children succeed at school by helping them overcome momentary discouragement and by enabling them to maintain the manner and engagement of a learner. U.S. parents on the whole tend to rate their children's capacity relatively favorably, and, when a child finds reason to doubt his or her own ability, this can keep the child in the fight. At the level of children's motivation to learn, however, there are critical limits to what even the most committed parent can do. For one, parents derive some of their sense of their children's school ability from the usual school cues, and this, too, feeds back into their children's self-evaluation (Parsons, Adler, & Kaczala, 1982). In any case, parents' engagement in their children's schooling seems more to influence behavior in the short run than to induce long-term confidence or successful learning strategies in their children (Ensminger & Slusarick, 1992; Hess & Holloway, 1984). In no small part, this is because of the increasingly fixed interaction patterns, built around the child's particular pattern of "working the system" at school (Entwisle & Hayduk, 1988). Teachers understand, respond to, and reinforce these patterns, which become children's public *and* private school identities.

What parents can give directly to their children that will aid their school success depends upon its fit with the school as arena. Thus, children in predominantly middle-class grade schools achieved more when their parents—valuing autonomy in their children—encouraged in them "independent problem solving, choice, and participations in decisions" (Grolnick & Ryan, 1989; Grolnick, Ryan, & Deci, 1991; cf. Skinner, Wellborn, & Connell, 1990). These children, in general, acted "right": Teachers appreciated the orientation to school that the children had learned at home, and responded warmly; children reciprocated by demonstrating the kind of effort required to learn in a setting of this kind. Child rearing values matched school values. But they do not and cannot always do so.

Children's commitment to working and learning in school, certainly by the time they are adolescents, is considerably influenced by their own anticipations of whether or not they will be continuing in school after completing high school. Adolescent educational plans do, to a considerable extent, reflect their own evaluation of whether they are well suited to school, but their parents' aspirations are also highly influential (Hossler & Stage, 1992). Even when scholastic aptitude and the characteristics of both student and school are controlled statistically, students' plans to continue their education exercise a significant influence on how much time they will spend in study and on the grades that they achieve. It is partly through aspirations for subsequent education that parents from early on continue to influence their children's academic performance through the maintenance of goals for further education (Reynolds & Walberg, 1991; Shanahan & Walberg, 1985). Postsecondary education is seen by U.S. children as an objective reality to which they legitimately might be asked (or not be asked) by parents to orient themselves, and this reality in turn may operate to legitimize (or delegitimize) the subject matter and perhaps even more so the procedures of their current school.

Such motivation appeals to a remote future, of course, a future sometimes subject to considerable discount owing to the state of the labor market or to the absence of sufficiently vivid, plausible local exemplars of the educational and occupational future that parents urge. In a period and among a population where mobility through education seems rather unproblematic, parental ambitions might not be undercut by parents' own relatively poor educational background (Cohen, 1987). But in times and places in which the world beyond the family seems less benign, children may well believe less readily in the future that their parents want for them (Ogbu, 1974).

Learning now, however, may in some settings be its own current reward. In contemporary France, for instance, there is widespread concurrence with the idea that what is taught at schools is the essence of "civilization."

> French schools have a reputation for starting children with difficult subjects at an early age and forcing them through memorization and repetition to struggle toward learning them. . . . The cultural capital of one generation is transmitted via the schools to the next. This principle has been an important one for the French government, which [from the early nineteenth century] used the primary school to build loyalty for the nation-state and to spread the French language. (Lees, 1992)

South Korean children, from the time of Korea's liberation from Japan at the end of World War II to the present, have been catechized at school in the Charter of National Education. This document, the explicit ideological basis for education throughout the nation, underlines for children that they share with others at their age in years past and years to come the duty to study and learn, because it will be through the learned abilities of its people that the Korean nation will be able to overcome its legacy of colonial abasement. This is a living belief among Koreans, including schoolchildren (Sorensen, 1992). Such beliefs provide considerable ideological underpinning for an authority structure within the school that focuses closely upon cognitive tasks.

Auspices of the Life Course of Youth

As Coleman discusses, a century and more ago, social-structural change—urbanization, the decline of family-run businesses, the increased availability of reliable, remunerative work for adults—came to render children's work rarely needed to sustain the family economy. Schooling opportunities were increased, regulations passed designed to drive children from common employments, and means devised to enforce children's enrollment in and attendance at school. The life-stage construct "adolescence" emerged as a vehicle for finding an acceptable psychological handle for understanding their parents' sometimes tense relation to young people for whom society provided little current purpose (Katz & Davey, 1978; Kett, 1977; Modell & Goodman, 1990).

Zelizer's account (1985) aptly emphasizes the cultural elaboration with which Americans interpreted the structural change within the family economy:

> In an increasingly commercialized world, children were reserved a separate noncommercial place, extra-commercium. The economic and sentimental value of children were thereby declared to be radically incompatible. . . . Properly loved children, regardless of social class, belonged in a domesticated, nonproductive world of lessons, games, and token money. (p. 11)

Under such a regime, even such seemingly useful activities as household chores were to be reinterpreted as inherently useless but developmentally valuable. "House chores were therefore not to be 'real' work, but lessons in helpfulness, order, and unselfishness." (p. 99) Likewise, "the expanding school system attempted to incorporate 'good' work into their curricula." (p. 100) As [the Progressive reformer] Edward T. Devine explained [in 1908], " 'work which we deny . . . in the factory, for profit, may be demanded in school . . . for education and training'." (p. 100)

Those aspects of childhood under parental control that once shared the educational structure of *apprenticeship* have been exorcised, in favor of explicitly schooled learning, mainly in school but also in the home (e.g., allowances). Apprenticeship is learning within context, learning by guided doing rather than learning of abstracted material; it rests on a relationship of the exchange of useful work for skills training that visibly produces increasing value for both parties (Lave, 1990). Formal education tacks in the opposite direction, extracting an explicit curriculum from the stream of knowledge and practice so essentials can be transmitted concisely and uniformly, at the cost of adding third and fourth parties—the parents and the state—to the learning relationship, and typically postponing the enjoyment of the skills themselves until a remote future. Schooled learning increases the need for children to draw emotional support for their efforts to learn from beyond the classroom. In the United States, society at large never could provide this kind of support (as in France or Korea): Parents (or a very close circle focusing upon them) must do it.

The sentimentalization of childhood has provided the ideological basis for a closely attentive, developmentally oriented definition of good parenting. The congruence of this underlying concept with increasingly nonauthoritarian parenting practices is obvious—and this congruence has been made all the stronger in recent decades by the increasing convergence (in belief, surely, if not so fully in practice) of the fathering role upon the mothering (Stearns & Parke, 1992). Increasingly, parents have sought to raise their children in such fashion as to encourage them in the ability and inclination to think for themselves, rather than simply to obey authoritative cues (Alwin, 1984; Kohn & Schoenbach, 1983). Home discipline has correspondingly moved away from corporal punishment—enforcing explicitly enunciated parental rules—to a search for a negotiated consensus in which persuasion and the implied threat of the withdrawal of approval are key to the parents' advantage. Since the publication of Dr. Benjamin Spock's famous child-care book, little now remains of the notion that children's naturally disorderly inclinations must be suppressed. When children confute parents' proffered judgments, their reasons are to be taken seriously for the openings they offer for personal development.

Over the past several generations, U.S. schoolchildren have gained an increasing measure of control of their life course. No adolescent institution better exemplifies that proposition than *dating*, that now ubiquitous but once uniquely American form of heterosexual sociability (ambiguously connected with the course to marriage that gradually and subtly came to admit initially chaste then normatively hedonistic sexuality). Dating took place within definite, peer-administered limits—and was tied loosely and ambiguously to courtship (Modell, 1983). One can read contemporaneous documentation of dating to observe the elaboration within its compass of a vocabulary and rules for promoting and controlling enhanced, voluntary, nonmarital emotional intimacy; and one can read in contemporaneous adult publications the path they followed to accept and finally embrace their children's institutional innovation for the broadening and deepening of experience it was said to promote.

In the 1920s and 1930s, the characteristic social institution *dating* was elaborated and spread within high schools. The mesh between dating and the high school was strong, in part because educators themselves sought to enliven school for adolescents (competitively with such aspects of commercial culture as dance halls and roadhouses) by highlighting dating in school-sponsored venues such as dances and by interweaving dating and school sports. The classic documentation of the educational outcome of this coevolution is James Coleman's own *The Adolescent Society* (1961; and see Marini, 1978), which shows, among other things, that in admitting and even encouraging the development of dating, schools had allowed children to erect within the halls of the institution a pupil-governed reward structure (and path to adulthood) that conflicted with the school's academic goals, especially for girls.[1]

In his sociological overview of the past fifty years, Janowitz (1978, pp. 297–300) describes the breakdown of an older, relatively unitary, hierarchical, and legitimated authority structure in U.S. schools, driven by the near-universalization of high school, by the administratively rational enlargement of individual schools, and by the tendency toward age-homogenization of classes. In schools, young people's world is now to a fair degree their own, and this world is one in which regularly reevaluated merit (on their own terms) rather than adult-promulgated authority organizes students' choices. The schools' former role as institutions highly relevant to young people's transitions to the adult occupational world has been considerably vitiated, owing in no small part to the widespread presumption of postsecondary education as the appropriate terminal point for the majority of children (Rosenbaum & Kariya, 1989, 1991). Daily social relations in the high school, Janowitz (1978) argues, "is more disarticulated and more removed from the reality and symbolic presence of work and employment" (pp. 297–300).

Comparisons of the relation of family background, school performance, and subsequent occupational choice of the 1960 high school senior cohort and its successor 20 years later led Buchmann (1989, also, see Lueptow, 1984, pp. 261–266) to discern a general decline in "obligation to social collectivities" on the part of young people, including family and local community, rendering "social identifications and identity constructions based on membership in these collectivities increasingly obsolete" (Buchmann, 1989, pp. 184–185). Instead, the life course itself, as a cultural construct, directs young people's choices. "Life is less constrained by traditions and customs and thus more susceptible to individualized action orientations; these potential individual choices, however, must be made within the context of standardized and bureaucratized life patterns" (p. 185). Children, then, are actors on their own behalf, and, when in school, they choose to work hard and learn (or not to do so) in the face of other organized activities sanctioned not only by the adolescent society, but in many ways by the adult society as well.

Gainful employment in the private sector has become one of these. This pattern grew irregularly during the first three decades of the postwar era, but especially in the 1960s and early 1970s; by 1980, three-quarters of high school seniors worked (an average of 12–13 hours a week) or sought work, a figure that was hardly lower for college-bound students than for those in vocational tracks (Lewin-Epstein, 1981; U.S. Department of Labor, 1978, 1983). Since that date, the employment of high school students has fluctuated with the business cycle, but has not changed markedly (U.S.

Department of Labor, 1989, p. 257 Table 62). Only modest competitive relationships with homework are revealed by the 1980 data: What mattered about jobs was not so much the time they demanded that might better have been spent on homework, but rather the wages they brought. Where students' work was directed toward spending-money, their earning bought them entree into the liberal republic of consumption, whose egalitarianism bore flattering comparison to their subordinated roles at school. Students who had worked in order to save money toward future college expenses, on the other hand, expressed and achieved higher educational aspirations than did those of like background and school characteristics who had not worked (Marsh, 1991).

Homework no longer takes up much time in U.S. children's lives—something like four hours a week for high school seniors. An extensive literature (Fehrmann, Keith, & Reimers, 1987; Lueptow, 1984, pp. 196–198; Walberg, Fraser, & Welch, 1986) has pointed to the considerable (although possibly—and intriguingly—declining) relationship of the amount of homework U.S. students carry out to their success within the formal curriculum. What is particularly striking is that despite the fit of the empirical findings with what seems intuitive to most people, the amount of homework that schools can successfully ask of their students seems to have declined sharply. A comparison of representative 1960 and 1976 high school student surveys, for instance, suggests that median weekly hours of homework dropped by more than half (Modell, 1989, pp. 296–297). If anything, there has been a slight additional decline since then, perhaps responding to sharp student distaste for homework (Bezilla, 1988, pp. 49, 51; Mullis, Dossey, Foertsch, Jones, & Gentile, 1991, p. 136).[2]

Close examination of a large but not national sample of U.S. high school students in 1964–65, who on average did about seven and a half hours of homework a week, indicates the wide range of (possibly intersecting) supports that undergirded some students' willingness to do relatively more homework. Parents' rules about doing homework—one in four parents had such rules—were among the more effective of these, being associated statistically with an added two-thirds of an hour more homework per week, net of a wide range of background and context variables. (Interestingly, the mother's college aspirations for her child were statistically significant—the father's were not—but, net of correlates, added only ten minutes of homework a week.) Where teachers insisted that work not mastered in class be completed at home, more than a half-hour increment in homework was found. Even more effective (over an hour more homework a week) was placement in the college track, so much more influential than the (nevertheless significant) measure of the student's own educational aspirations that one imagines the added hour a week was seen as a legitimate price exacted for being in the favored track (Natriello & McDill, 1986).

National high school samples both from 1960 and from the late 1970s point to the importance in explaining young people's school behaviors of a characteristic usually treated as outside the relevant theoretical framework for such discussions: the student's religious beliefs and practices. The essential finding seems to be that young people in whose lives organized religion plays a large role, net of other relevant background characteristics, work harder and perhaps more comfortably within the formal demands that school places upon them, tend to remain outside of those student-organized activities that place them in conflict with adults, tend to achieve higher grades, and tend to have higher educational aspirations (Herzog & Bachman, 1982; Modell, 1989). These are evidently "good" children, children who embrace rather than subvert the margins of the adult-sponsored authority structure in the school. My point here is not identical with that of Coleman and his colleagues (Coleman, Hoffer, & Kilgore, 1982) when they note the superior ability of religious schools to enforce discipline within the classroom. Their level of analysis is the school, and mine here is the student. They point to the possibility of broader resources for social capital investment in a school based upon common belief. I suggest that the underlying structure of our formal education system may presuppose a generalized authority that is less and less prevalent, but that nevertheless is relatively present in the belief (and perhaps psychological makeup) of many students, the religious prominent among these.

Rowing Hard Against the Current?

Contrary to what many imagine, U.S. parents' involvement in their children's school life is high, both absolutely and by international standards. Parents themselves report an extent of involvement in their high school–age children's school lives that might offer some comfort to those concerned about the simple *availability* of social capital in the family. Overall, almost half of parents say they or their spouse talk with their child "regularly" about high school plans, and slightly fewer talk about post–high school plans. Seven in ten report that at least sometimes they help their child with homework. Half have contacted the school about their child's academic performance. Three in four have family rules about

Table 3.1 *Family involvement in 13-year-old children's mathematics schoolwork, 20 societies arranged by GDP/capita, 1991*

Less Economically Developed		Intermediate Development		Highly Developed	
Mozambique	1.60	Jordan	1.22	Italy	1.18
China	1.22	Hungary	1.65	Spain	1.39
		Brazil	1.25	Israel	1.33
		Slovenia	1.47	Scotland	1.34
		Russia	1.03	England	1.39
		Portugal	1.04	France	1.19
		Korea	1.05	Canada	1.33
		Ireland	1.31	United States	1.42
		Taiwan	1.25	Switzerland	1.09

attaining a given grade point average; nine in ten have rules about homework. Virtually all of these social capital investments, to be sure, are made more uniformly by parents in educationally and socioeconomically advantaged families, but single-headed families show no sharp deficits (U.S. National Center for Educational Statistics, 1991, p. 29).

Coleman and colleagues, very plausibly, hypothesize a curvilinear historical development of parental direct investment of their own time and emotion in their children's formal educations, with the peak of social investment at middle levels of economic development. But among the set of 20 societies whose 13-year-old children participated in the International Assessment of Educational Progress in mathematics (IAEP, 1991; Lapointe, Mead, & Askew, 1992), this kind of provision of social capital was not found to be related at all straightforwardly to economic development. Table 3.1 indicates this. (The level is the average number of "yes" answers to the pair of questions asked the children: "Does anyone at home ever talk to you about what you are learning in mathematics class?" and "Does anyone at home ever help you with your mathematics homework?")[3]

Although cross-sectional observations of this sort cannot discern historical trends within any single society, the table certainly suggests that the extent of parental involvement in children's schooling in any given society is set in some considerable part by the kinds of relations of school to society that evolved when institutions of formal education first took control of the cognitive aspects of young people's learning. U.S. parents, by this measure, are highly involved in their children's school learning, as are their counterparts in Canada, among nations at the high end of economic development. But France and Switzerland, likewise wealthy nations, have rather uninvolved parents.

Is it that U.S. parents' involvement with their children's school learning is inefficacious because U.S. families have become so incoherent that they have little social capital to expend, even where parents try to call it forth? Table 3.2, again based on the IAEP data, suggests otherwise. Here we see a rough cross-tabulation of the unique contribution among each society's 13-year-olds of parental involvement to how much homework the students do, and to how readily the children concur in the statement that "it is important to know some mathematics in order to get a good job." Virtually all of these relationships are positive: Everywhere parents' involvement (as perceived) counts at least something with their children. Even when a long list of related background items is in the equation, three-quarters of the correlations with homework performed are statistically significant, and half of those with the ascription to mathematics of vocational usefulness. Although there are differing emphases from society to society in which sort of impact family involvement most affects, there also is a clear tendency for strength along one dimension to correspond to strength along the other dimension.

And on both dimensions, family involvement matters in the United States, as it does in Israel (Jewish children) and Scotland, among the economically most-developed societies, and in Hungary. In all of these societies, we should note, families were relatively seriously engaged in their children's mathematics learning. Among societies in which family engagement most affected either children's carrying out of homework or the usefulness they perceive for mathematics, in fact, only Russian parents were not at least considerably engaged. Putatively, "social capital" is a bundle that includes both parental willingness to involve themselves in their children's school learning and the resources inhering in this connection that leads children to respond favorably to such involvement. By this line of reasoning, the United States is rather high, not low, in social capital relevant to school learning.

At the low end of Table 3.2 we find the two nations that we discussed earlier in terms of a living *national* ideology supporting children's efforts at school: Korea and France. In both of these countries, as Table 3.1 shows, parents are relatively unengaged in their children's schoolwork, at least on the level of individual efforts as distinct from a background-level shared belief in the importance to children of being engaged in learning.

The picture that emerges from all of this is a world in which, for a set of historical reasons unique in any given society, the academic component

Table 3.2 *Net impact of family involvement on children's homework and belief in need for mathematics in jobs*

	Jobs		
	Low	Medium	High
Homework			
Low	Korea France		China Mozambique
Medium	Brazil Italy Portugal Spain	Ireland Jordan Switzerland	Russia Taiwan England
High		Canada Slovenia	Israel Hungary Scotland United States

Note: "Low," "medium," and "high" represent arbitrary subdivisions of nations based on the metric regression coefficient of (1) a 5-category self-report by child of daily homework in all subjects and (2) a 5-category response to the assertion that "it is important to know some mathematics in order to get a good job" on parental involvement in children's mathematics (see Table 3.1 and text for discussion). In all cases, the coefficient is calculated with grade and sex of child, number of siblings, and number of books in the home already in the regression equation. N's varied from society to society, but on the whole, no "low," most "medium," and almost all "high" coefficients were statistically significant at the 0.05 level or better.

of schooling enjoys a legitimacy that varies a good deal from society to society. Where this dimension is relatively favorable to children's continuing brave and hard work at the cognitive side of school—whether by enlarging the immediate public evaluation of simply being engaged at the work or by lowering by comparison the local prestige available to a child who shifts his or her effort to another sphere of activity—more local forms of social capital perhaps need not be called upon. Where, on the other hand, the rewards for schoolwork are remote or not outstanding among other possibilities—especially in those societies in which schools are so structured as to create public tests of prior school learning in which there are repeated losers—and where children recognize that they are forever sorted into the smart and the less smart, where smartness is understood as generalized capacity and virtually inborn, there even the deepest parental commitment may not be able to meet the demands made upon it.

The social capital that U.S. parents invest, of course, may be the wrong capital: tougher love, laced more with authority, might better help U.S. children persist at schoolwork. But how we love our children is historically grounded. Can we so finely tune our requirements for "social capital" in a given situation, and yet derive from the concept much guidance for policy?

Notes

1. To be sure, the institution of dating did not forever command the unquestioned allegiance of young people: Beginning in the late 1960s, it was gradually supplemented by a more amorphous, more group-based form of heterosexual sociability. This less fully institutionalized form of behavior, however, may be even more competitive in its relationship to the formal academic goals of high schools than dating (Modell, 1989, pp. 291–305).
2. The Gallup Youth Survey found that in 1984, 49 percent of 13- to 17-year-olds said they felt that they "should receive" less homework, and only 40 percent said they should receive more. By contrast, in 1986, 48 percent of the young people said they thought "the requirements of graduation from the public high schools" should "be made more strict." The latter opinion was related to grade point average; distaste for homework, however, was about ubiquitous. The youth surveys were representative national samples with N's of slightly more than 500.
3. Of course, the indicator of family involvement is not optimal, but its components are things the children are capable of reporting accurately, and we can be reassured by the roughly equal degrees of correlation between the two items from society to society. Samples were at least 1,500 except in England, and represented national samples (with 100 or more schools as sampling points) except in China (many exclusions), Mozambique (only two cities), Brazil (only two cities), Portugal (school progress cut off), Israel (Jewish population only), Switzerland (a few omitted cantons), and Italy (one province only). The data have been provided to me by the Educational Testing Service, Center for Assessment of Educational Progress.

References

Alwin, D. F. (1984). Trends in parental socialization values: Detroit, 1958–1983. *American Journal of Sociology, 90,* 359–382.

Alwin, D. F., & Thornton, A. (1984). Family origins and the schooling process: Early versus late influence of parental characteristics. *American Sociological Review, 49,* 784–802.

Ames, C., & Archer, A. (1987). Mothers' beliefs about the role of ability and effort in school learning. *Journal of Educational Psychology, 79,* 409–414.

Astone, N. M., & McLanahan, S. S. (1991). Family structure, parental practices and high school completion. *American Sociological Review, 56,* 309–320.

Bezilla, R. (Ed.). (1988). *America's youth 1977–1988.* Princeton, NJ: Gallup Organization.

Blake, J. (1989). *Family size and achievement.* Berkeley: University of California Press.

Buchmann, M. (1989). *The script of life in modern society.* Chicago: University of Chicago Press.

Cohen, J. (1987). Parents as educational models and definers. *Journal of Marriage and the Family, 49,* 339–351.

Coleman, J. S. (1961). *The adolescent society.* New York: Free Press.

Coleman, J. S. (1988). Social capital in the creation of human capital. In C. Winship & S. Rosen (Eds.), *Organizations and institutions: Sociological and economic approaches to the analysis of social structure.* Supplement to *American Journal of Sociology, 94,* S95-S120.

Coleman, J. S. (1990). *Foundations of social theory.* Cambridge, MA: Harvard University Press.

Coleman, J. S., Hoffer, T., & Kilgore, S. (1982). *High school achievement.* New York: Basic Books.

Dweck, C. S. (1986). Motivational processes affecting learning. *American Psychologist, 41,* 1040–1048.

Dweck, C. S., & Bempechat, J. (1983). Children's theories of intelligence: Consequences for learning. In S. G. Paris, G. M. Olson, & H. W. Stevenson (Eds.), *Learning and motivation in the classroom* (pp. 239–256). Hillsdale, NJ: Lawrence Erlbaum.

Dweck, C. S., & Elliott, E. S. (1983). Achievement motivation. In E. M. Hetherington (Ed.), *Handbook of child psychology IV* (4th ed.) (pp. 643–691). New York: John Wiley.

Ensminger, M. E., & Slusarick, A. L. (1992). Paths to high school graduation or dropout: A longitudinal study of a first-grade cohort. *Sociology of Education, 65,* 95–113.

Entwisle, D. R., & Hayduk, L. A. (1988). Lasting effects of elementary school. *Sociology of Education, 61,* 147–159.

Fehrmann, P. G., Keith, T. Z., & Reimers, T. M. (1987). Home influence on school learning: Direct and indirect effects of parental involvement on high school grades. *Journal of Educational Research, 80,* 330–337.

Flynn, J. R. (1984). The mean I.Q. of Americans: Massive gains, 1923 to 1978. *Psychological Bulletin, 95,* 29–51.

Goodnow, J., & Burns, A. (1985). *Home and school: A child's-eye view.* Sydney: Allen & Unwin.

Grolnick, W. S., & Ryan, R. M. (1989). Parent styles associated with children's self-regulation and competence at school. *Journal of Educational Psychology, 81,* 143–154.

Grolnick, W. S., Ryan, R. M., & Deci, E. L. (1991). Inner resources for school achievement: Motivational mediators of children's perceptions of their parents. *Journal of Educational Psychology, 83,* 508–517.

Harter, S. (1981). A new self-report scale of intrinsic versus extrinsic orientation in the classroom: Motivational and informational components. *Developmental Psychology, 17,* 300–312.

Herzog, A. R., & Bachman, J. G. (1982). *Sex role attitudes among high school seniors.* Ann Arbor: University of Michigan, Survey Research Center, .

Hess, R. D., & Holloway, S. D. (1984). Family and school as educational institutions. In R. D. Parke (Ed.), *Review of child development research: Vol. 7. The Family.* (pp. 179–222). Chicago: University of Chicago Press.

Hossler, D., & Stage, F. K. (1992). Family and high school experience influences on the postsecondary educational plans of ninth-grade students. *American Educational Research Journal, 29*, 425–451.

International Assessment of Educational Progress. (1991). *The 1991 IAEP assessment objectives for mathematics, science, and geography.* Princeton, NJ: Educational Testing Service, Center for the Assessment of Educational Progress.

Janowitz, M. (1978). *The last half-century.* Chicago: University of Chicago Press.

Katz, M. B., & Davey, I. E. (1978). Youth and early industrialization in a Canadian city. In J. Demos & S.S. Boocock (Eds.), *Turning points: Historical and sociological essays on the family.* Supplement to *American Journal of Sociology, 84*, S81-S119.

Kett, J. F. (1977). *Rites of passage: Adolescence in America 1790 to the present.* New York: Basic Books.

Kohn, M. L. & Schoenbach, C. (1983). Class, stratification, and psychological functioning. In M. L. Kohn & C. Schooler (Eds.), *Work and personality: An inquiry into the impact of social stratification* (pp. 154–189). Norwood, NJ: Ablex.

Lapointe, A. E., Mead, N. A., & Askew, J. M. (1992). *Learning mathematics.* Princeton, NJ: Educational Testing Service, Center for the Assessment of Educational Progress.

Lave, J. (1990). The culture of acquisition and the practice of understanding. In J. W. Stigler, R. A. Schweder, & G. Herdt (Eds.), *Cultural psychology: Essays on comparative human development* (pp. 309–327). Chicago: University of Chicago Press

Lees, L. H. (1992). *Two styles of educational inequality: England and France in the 1980s.* Unpublished paper, University of Pennsylvania, Philadelphia, PA.

Lepper, M. R., & Hodell, L. (1989). Intrinsic motivation in the classroom. In C. Ames & R. Ames (Eds.), *Research on motivation in education: Vol. 3. Goals and cognitions* (pp. 73–105). New York: Academic Press.

Lewin-Epstein, N. (1981). *Youth employment during high school* (NCES 81–249). Washington, DC: National Center for Educational Statistics.

Licht, B. G., Stader, S. R., & Swenson, C. C. (1989). Children's achievement-related beliefs: Effects of academic area, sex, and achievement level. *Journal of Educational Research, 82*, 253–260.

Lueptow, L. B. (1984). *Adolescent sex roles and social change.* New York: Columbia University Press.

Marini, M. M. (1978). The transition to adulthood: Sex differences in educational attainment and age at marriage. *American Sociological Review, 43*, 483–507.

Marsh, H. W. (1991). Employment during high school: Character building or a subversion of academic goals. *Sociology of Education, 64*, 172–189.

Modell, J. (1983). Dating becomes the way of American youth. In L. P. Moch & G. D. Stark, (Eds.), *Essays on the family and historical change* (pp. 91–126). College Station: Texas A & M University Press.

Modell, J. (1989). *Into one's own: From youth to adulthood in the United States, 1920–1975.* Berkeley: University of California Press.

Modell, J., & Goodman, M. (1990). Historical perspectives. In S. S. Feldman & G. R. Elliott (Eds.), *At the threshold: The developing adolescent* (pp. 93–122). Cambridge, MA Harvard University Press.

Mullis, I. V. S., Dossey, J. A., Foertsch, M., Jones, L., & Gentile, C. (1991). *Trends in academic progress.* Educational Testing Service Report No. 21-T-01. Washington, DC: Government Printing Office.

Natriello, G., & McDill, E. L. (1986). Performance standards, student effort on homework, and academic achievement. *Sociology of Education, 59*, 18–31.

Nicholls, J. G. (1989). *The competitive ethos and democratic education.* Cambridge, MA: Harvard University Press.

Nicholls, J. G., Patashnick, M., & Nolen, S. B. (1985). Adolescents' theories of education. *Journal of Educational Psychology, 77*(6), 683–692.

Ogbu, J. U. (1974). *The next generation: An ethnography of education in an urban neighborhood.* New York: Academic Press.

Parke, R.D., & Sterns, P.N. (1992). Fathers and childrearing. In G. H. Elder, Jr., J. Modell, & R. D. Parke (Eds.), *Children in time and place.* (pp.147–170), New-York: Cambridge University Press.

Parsons, J. E., Adler, T. F., & Kaczala, C. M. (1982). Socialization of achievement attitudes and beliefs: Parental influences. *Child Development, 53*, 310–321.

Reynolds, A. J., & Walberg, H. J. (1991). A structural model of science achievement. *Journal of Educational Psychology, 83*, 97–107.

Rosenbaum, J. E., & Kariya, T. (1989). From high school to work: Market and institutional mechanisms in Japan. *American Journal of Sociology, 94*, 1334–1365.

Rosenbaum, J. E., & Kariya, T. (1991). Do school achievements affect the early jobs of high school graduates in the United States and Japan? *Sociology of Education, 64*, 78–95.

Rosenholtz, S. J., & Simpson. C. (1984). The formation of ability conceptions: Developmental trend or social construction. *Review of Educational Research, 54*, 31–63.

Shanahan, T., & Walberg, H. J. (1985). Productive influences on high school student achievement. *Journal of Educational Research, 78*, 357–363.

Skinner, E. A., Wellborn, J. G., & Connell, J. P. (1990). What it takes to do well in school and whether I've got it: A process model of perceived control and children's engagement and achievement in school. *Journal of Educational Psychology, 82*, 22–32.

Sorensen, C. (1992). *Success and education in contemporary South Korea.* Unpublished paper, University of Washington, Seattle.

Stedman, L. C., & Kaestle, C. F. (1991). The great test-score decline: A closer look. In C. Kaestle, H. Damon-Moore, K. Tinsley, & W. V. Trollinger, Jr. (Eds.), *Literacy in the United States* (pp. 129–145). New Haven, CT: Yale University Press.

U.S. Department of Labor. (1978, 1983). *President's report on manpower and training.* Washington, DC: Government Printing Office.

U.S Department of Labor (1989). Bureau of Labor Statistics. *Handbook of Labor Statistics.*Bulletin 2340. Washington, DC: Government Printing Office.

U.S. National Center for Educational Statistics (1991). *Digest of educational statistics.* Washington, DC: Government Printing Office.

Walberg, H. J., Fraser, B. J., & Welch, W. W. (1986). A test of a model of educational productivity among senior high school students. *Journal of Educational Research, 79*, 133–139.

Weinstein, R. S. (1989). Perceptions of classroom processes and student motivation: Children's views of self-fulfilling prophecies. In C. Ames & R. Ames (Eds.), *Research on motivation in education: Vol. 3. Goals and cognitions* (pp. 187–221) New York: Academic Press.

Whittington, D. (1991). What have 17-year-olds known in the past? *American Educational Research Journal, 28*, 759–789.

Zelizer, V. (1985). *Pricing the priceless child.* New York: Basic Books.

Reply to John Modell

JAMES S. COLEMAN

John Modell's chapter in this volume argues that there has not been a decline in social capital provided by the family for schoolchildren in the United States, and that the social capital U.S. parents provide for their children is higher than that in many other countries. This, of course, goes directly against the arguments of my chapter, so it is useful to add a word about the divergence. First a correction to Modell's contention that the decline in test scores has been "more than overcome." The decline in SAT test scores has stabilized in mathematics, but remains 20 points below its pre-decline (1952–1963) level, whereas the verbal score has continued to decline—in 1991, it was 50 points below the pre-decline level (Murray & Herrnstein, 1992). Furthermore, the decline has been particularly great at the upper end of the distribution, implying that the decline is not merely compositional, or due to an influx at the lower end of the distribution.

Another point about the relative decline in mathematics and verbal skills suggests the loss of social capital in the family, rather than merely decreased effectiveness of the school. Extensive evidence indicates that a greater portion of mathematics than of verbal skills learned is learned in school (Coleman, 1993). Crudely put, mathematics is learned in school, verbal skills at home. The greater decline in verbal skills versus mathematics indicates a greater decline in the family's educational strength rather than in that of the school.

Social capital within the family and within the community directed toward children's education is not measured by the amount of talk about school between parents and children. In the U.S. Department of Education's nationwide study of eighth-grade students in 1988, Asian-American parents were lowest (compared to African Americans, Hispanics, and whites) in helping with homework and in talking with their children about school. Do Asian-American parents exhibit less social capital directed to their children's education? The same research shows that they have the highest rate of enrollment of children in classes outside school, the highest use (controlling on income) of private schools, and the highest frequency of involving their children in the public library, concerts, art museums, science museums, and history museums (Muller, 1993). These indicators of the employment of social capital are paralleled by indicators of the structural supports for family social capital: Asian-American parents exhibit by far the lowest divorce rate of these four racial-ethnic groups and have by far the largest proportion of their eighth-grade children in intact families.

A major transformation that has occurred in the U.S. family is the change in the adolescent's role. As Modell himself describes, teenagers in school at all social levels work at jobs more than in the early postwar years. They have greater control over their school activities than ever before and are less under parental authority in both school and nonschool activities. As Powell and his colleagues (1985) describe an emergent pattern of course selection in modern U.S. high schools, it is a "shopping mall" in which students pick and choose among a widening array of courses. This is in contrast to the classical pattern, in which the college-bound child not only knew which courses were college preparatory, but also took courses in compliance with parents' demands.

In 1924, the Lynds carried out a survey of parents' preferences concerning traits in their children (Lynd & Lynd, 1929), and in 1978 a second survey was carried out of parents in the same city (Muncie, Indiana). Alwin (1988) reports the following comparisons, showing a sharp decline in authority-related preferences and an even sharper increase in the desire for their children to be "independent":

	1924 (%)	1978 (%)	Difference (%)
Strict obedience	45	17	−28
Loyalty to church	58	22	−30
Independence	25	76	+51

All this fits together, giving a picture of the modern high school student as one who selects undemanding courses (without effective protest from parents), does little homework (according to Modell, a decline from 7.5 hours a week as recently as 1965 to 4 hours currently), and has a job to provide income for increasingly extensive consumption connected with a vigorous social life.

Modell would not disagree greatly with this picture, and its contrast with that of U.S. high school students before about 1965, for he describes many aspects of it in his chapter. Where we part company is not only in describing the consequences of that change, but also more fundamentally in describing the parents' changes that have brought it about. What is the source of parents' desire not to exercise authority, but to engender independence in their children? I suggest that this aim of independence in children is a desire of the parents for early freedom from the responsibilities of parenthood, responsibilities of the sort that always accompany authority. What would generate such a change in orientation? Exactly the things I describe in the body of my chapter as characteristic of a society in phase 3: The future performance of the children as adults has come to be irrelevant to the parents' futures. The parents' standing in the community and their material welfare are largely independent of the child's performance as an adult, and the family as an institution to be preserved over generations is largely a thing of the past. In such a circumstance, a parent's orientation can well be that the child should be set free as soon as possible, so the child can "do his or her own thing" and the parent can be free from the responsibility that goes with authority.

The modern family thus moves in the direction of becoming a set of independent parties, each going his or her own way, residing together for the material or psychic benefits common residence provides. It is not a family in which social capital exists and is directed toward educational development of the child, once that child has reached high school age.

References

Alwin, D.F. (1988). From obedience to autonomy. *Public Opinion Quarterly*, 52:33–52

Coleman, J.S. (1993, forthcoming). What is learned in schools and what is learned outside. In festschrift for Julian Stanley.

Lynd, R., & Lynd, H. (1929). *Middletown*. New York: Harcourt, Brace & World.

Muller, C. (1993). Parent involvement in the home, schools and community. In B. Schneider & J. S Coleman (Eds.), *Parents, their children and schools* (pp. 77–113). Boulder: Westview Press.

Murray, C., & Herrnstein, R.J. (1992). What's really behind the SAT-score decline? *The Public Interest*, 106, 32–56.

Reply to James S. Coleman

JOHN MODELL

The strategy of my chapter in this volume is announced by its title, which asks, "When May Social Capital Influence Children's School Performance?" The implication of my question is that the chapter by James S. Coleman (to which mine is a response) employs the intriguing notion of "social capital" in such a sketchily developed historical context that it neither "works" nor "doesn't work." In my account, family social capital does not operate directly upon children's school-based cognitive achievements, but rather through children's motivations to learn school subjects that are themselves culturally organized and subject to socially sanctioned competing concerns. I argue that Coleman overlooks historical changes that as well explain U.S. children's mediocre (and arguably declining) success in school as does the decline in family social capital that he has imputed.

Coleman's rejoinder suggests another problem that deserves some thought if social capital theory is to be developed—this time essentially a measurement problem. In his chapter, Coleman describes social capital as consisting of "social relationships within the family and community that generate the attention and time spent by parents and community members in the development of children and youth." In his rejoinder, however, Coleman maintains that social capital "is not measured by the amount of talk about school between parents and children . . . [or] the frequency of helping their child with homework," indicators to which I have referred. Shortly thereafter, however, Coleman indicates Asian-American parents' considerable "social capital directed to their children's education" by the rate of enrollment of their children in extraschool classes and at private schools, and their "frequency of involving their children" in a variety of mainline extraschool cultural activities.

Coleman does not explain why these latter parental behaviors are better suited to the analytic purpose of indicating the employment of parental social capital than are the ones I cited. Perhaps they represent qualitatively greater investments of social capital, but if so we need to think about the characteristics of the "market" in which social capital is deployed that might make large investments "count," but not small investments. If Coleman instead intends to suggest that visits to museums differ from help with homework not in degree but in kind, then the difficulty with "my" parents would not be that they did not employ *enough* social capital but that they did not expend it *wisely*. But if so, our analytic concern shifts from insufficiency of social resources to a morally tinged failure of discernment.

A key theoretical virtue that Coleman means to claim by developing the notion of "social capital" as an analogue to financial capital is its generality. In a modern economy, financial capital is an extremely fungible resource. Social capital, in Coleman's account, must likewise be a resource capable of taking a variety of forms, of being spent on (or withheld from) a variety of projects. To be a meaningful concept, capital of whatever sort must be measurable in the aggregate apart from its effects. The thought-provoking argument of Coleman's chapter holds that changes in the family's institutional role and organization have reduced the aggregate of social capital generated by family relationships and hence available to families. But for Coleman to declare that helping one's children with their homework is not an expenditure of social capital while taking them to a museum is, is to vacate his own theoretical point.

An example of how this plays out may be seen by contrasting the way my chapter and Coleman's response interpret the historical trend (the existence of which we both assert) from the inculcation of obedience as a goal of U.S. child rearing to training for independence. In my presentation, this trend is treated as an aspect of "the sentimentalization of childhood"; in Coleman's, it reflects "the desire of the parents for early freedom from the responsibilities of parenthood, responsibilities of the sort that always accompany authority." Coleman's interpretation must contend with a variety of commonly accepted factual observations: that the sentimentalization of childhood considerably predated the schooling consequences that distress him; that the value of independence-training spread from the education-conscious middle class to others in the society; that the kind of watchful self-restraint involved in the independence-training mode of child rearing was understood by its proponents to involve especially heavy investments of time and attention by parents and has as one of its presumed virtues closer emotional ties of parent and child.

Of course, these conventional understandings may be incorrect. But to ignore them as Coleman does in inferring U.S. parents' motives is to risk building a theoretical structure on a shaky basis. The danger is that the "social capital" construct may come to be seen as a screen for social prescription rather than a tool for social analysis. To overcome this danger, in my reading, test and refinement are demanded.

II. Macrosocial perspectives

4. The historical context of transition to work and youth unemployment

HELMUT FEND
University of Zürich
Institute of Education

The Conceptual Framework: Historical Context and Human Development

The transition to adulthood implies two processes of initiation into adult roles. One is connected with family roles, the second with work roles. The survival of humankind is dependent upon both. Biological reproduction is tied to some kind of family role; physical survival is tied to economic subsistence in some kind of work role.

These transition processes not only are preconditions of inter-generational continuity, but also they are, more importantly, *highly variable and context specific*. This became obvious for the first time in the research of cultural anthropologists that demonstrated the great variation in these transition processes from culture to culture. The context specificity has been shown even more impressively in sociohistorical research, which also helped to illuminate the social conditions generating the phenomenon of youth unemployment. It is a very late product of industrialization and marks only in this context a temporary or permanent failure of a regular transition to the adult work role. Today, it constitutes a problem for society, as well as a problem for a productive individual human development.

This way of analyzing youth unemployment is characteristic of the even more general approach of considering the whole human life span as embedded in a changing historical context. To take *sociohistorical context factors* seriously when analyzing determinants of human development is by now a well-established perspective (Elder, 1980; Elder, Pavalko, & Hastings, 1991; Lerner, 1991; Modell & Goodman, 1990; Ryder, 1965; Stewart &

Healy, 1989). In this paradigm, change at the macro level of society is related to change at the microlevel of the immediate context of growing up, which in turn has consequences for developmental pathways of individuals.

Therefore, it is the first aim of a sociohistorical introduction to document on *the level of society* the specific *social changes that create the phenomenon of unemployment* and, specifically, of youth unemployment. Furthermore, the historical and societal context determines the pattern of individual properties that lead to individual risks of youth unemployment; they determine *who is at risk of becoming unemployed* in the transition from school to work. In technical terms, societal context functions as a *moderating factor* in determining *causes* of youth unemployment.

A sociohistorical description is also necessary to demonstrate, on the *individual level*, why the experience of unemployment constitutes potentially one of the main *risk factors in human development* today, and therefore determines the *consequences* of youth unemployment. It is connected with cultural expectations of an optimal human life course.

Social Change and the Life Course: The General Pattern

To understand the "script for life in modern society" (Buchmann, 1989), it is necessary to consider the "long wave" (Braudel, 1985) of historical development related to fundamental changes in living conditions. Several formats in sequencing this long wave to describe the historical development of the adolescent life span have been applied. Some prefer the description of *distinct periods* (e.g., the time from the Renaissance to the end of the eighteenth century, the time of industrialization in the nineteenth century, and the modern period in the twentieth century; Modell & Goodman, 1990, p. 94); others assume a *continuous process* of modernization. For illustrative purposes, a *typology* of traditional and modern societies is useful. All of them refer to Europe and North America.

The context for growing up in traditional and modern societies

Childhood and adolescence in the mainly agrarian European societies were structured by close-knit social relationships in extended families and local communities. The conditions for mere survival created a high demand for labor. Even children had a highly visible economic value for coping with daily work and for the subsistence of parents in old age.

The central core of traditional society consists of small close-knit communities of which the human being, with many needs and potentials, was an integral part, and on which the person was completely dependent for existence. The individual necessities of survival, such as provision for old age, sickness, and invalidity, and the provision of nourishment and shelter were organized on a small scale in local communities. There were scarcely any alternative means of survival, nor were alternative systems of belief available other than the beliefs held by the community and its culture. Such communities have dissolved in the modern era.

This pattern of change is usually labeled as the transition from "Gemeinschaft" to "Gesellschaft," summarized by Hoffmann-Nowotny (1989) in a concise form:

> "Gesellschaft" in contrast to "Gemeinschaft" is marked by a highly differentiated, functionally interdependent structure whose most pronounced features are bureaucratic institutions. Their necessary cultural counterpart is the rise of universalistic values and norms, as expressed by specific social sub-systems orientated towards the achievement of special purposes. . . . "Gesellschaft", in contrast to "Gemeinschaft", is characterized by relatively open structures implying higher chances of social mobility. In principle, social positions and life chances are achievable and not ascribed. Inevitably, the cultural equivalent of such an open structure is an ideology of achievement and a climate of competition. (pp. 28–30)

Of course, a typology simplifies a complex and continuous process of social change, involving dramatic change in production (i.e., industrialization, rise of capitalism, development of technology, development of science) and social relations (i.e., rise of the bourgeois family, rise of democracies) during the nineteenth century.

The most important indicators of this process are the changes in the occupational structure and the production sector, indicating the transition from an agrarian to an industrialized society (Germany in 1849: 56.7% agrarian sector, 24.5% industry, mining, traffic, and manufacturing; in 1882: 44.2% in the primary sector [e.g., farming], 32.9% in the secondary sector [e.g. manufacturing], 22.9% in the tertiary sector [e.g., services]; in 1970: 7.7% in the primary sector, 49.4% in the secondary sector; 42.9% in the tertiary sector; Conce, 1976, p. 437; Kleber, 1983, p. 70). This process was accompanied by several similarly dramatic changes contributing to the urbanization of society: population growth, mass migration from Europe to America, expansion of the educational system, and a rise in life expectancy.

In the twentieth century we have witnessed a continuation of this process of social change but with important modifications from the 1960's onward. During this period there have been a massive decline in fertility, an increase in divorce, increasingly diverse family structures, and an increase in female employment (Hess, 1992). The increasing number of students attending universities is the most visible indicator of change in the educational system (Germany in 1964–65: 7.3% university entrance examination; in 1970–71: 18.1%; in 1986–87: 22.5%; Kühler, 1991, p. 54). Finally, the growth in women's participation in higher education and employment is the most outstanding indicator of change in life styles.

The social definition of adolescence as a phase in life

The sociohistorical changes described above have led to a restructuring of the course of life (Kohli, 1985). It is now possible to plan phases of preparation for a profession, one's work life, and retirement. As a result, adolescence has emerged as a phase of preparation for working that is embedded in the educational system. The magnitude of change is illustrated by the fact that, approximately 150 years ago, the onset of menstruation of young girls in Nordic countries occurred at about 17 years of age (cf. Steinberg, 1989, p. 40), whereas integration into the work process took place at an early stage. In rural areas, young boys and girls were completely integrated members of the workforce. Today, the situation is reversed. Sexual maturity is attained at less than 13 years of age, whereas for large numbers of adolescents, working does not begin until they are 17. In short, sexual maturity is achieved earlier in life, and economic and social independence is achieved later. There is frequently a gap of more than ten years between sexual maturity and entry into marriage, as well as for the achievement of economic independence. But we find historical as well as national (England and Wales as compared to the United States) variations in the gaps between leaving school, entering an occupation, and getting married (Modell & Goodman, 1990, p. 110).

Adolescence as a phase in life in its own right has emerged within the past century as a consequence of both changes in the economic sector and attendant changes in the educational system. The prolongation of this period, due to an increase in the time required for professional training, is the most important aspect of the institutionalization of adolescence as a unique phase of life. Therefore, more adolescents experience this phase as a period in which their principal task is to determine what they want to become and what they want to achieve.

In the course of social development from traditional to modern society, the transition from childhood to adulthood has changed dramatically.

Besides transitions to marriage in the framework of the European marriage pattern (Mitterauer, 1986), the transitions to work have marked the overall process of growing into adulthood (Modell & Goodman, 1990). In the transition to work, three periods can be distinguished: premodern Europe, the period of industrialization, and the twentieth century.

Transition to work in premodern Europe

In the period before the rapid growth of industrialization *children had to contribute to the struggle for survival as early as their physical abilities permitted*. Their economic value was unquestioned. Unemployment was no problem, but the means of subsistence were scarce. Therefore, the transition to adulthood was, for large parts of the age cohort, very difficult. This problem was often solved by migration, including the migration of children.

In the area of Lake Constance at the German-Swiss border, for example, it was an established, centuries-old custom for children to migrate from poor farming areas in Tyrol and Vorarlberg for seasonal work in South Germany. There they were hired out to farmers in the child markets of Friedrichshafen and Ravensburg for summer work from March to October (see Uhlig, 1978). In this way, many children contributed to family survival by *taking care of themselves*.

These remarks may suggest a homogenous picture of transition processes, which in fact did not exist. A great variety of transitions and local diversity can be found for limited numbers of children and adolescents in the feudal sectors, the monasteries, the church and schools, the military sector, the manufacturing sector, and so on (cf. Mitterauer, 1986).

Transition to work and youth unemployment in the process of industrialization

With growing industrialization, the overall picture begins to change. Growing numbers of workers find employment in the expanding industries. Production is increasingly based on scientifically developed technologies, goods are produced for expanding markets, and capital becomes an important means of developing the industrial complex. Labor has to be cheap and the supply of children and young men willing to work must be abundant.

Children's and adolescents' transition to adulthood now takes the form of at least temporarily *contributing to family income*. The main social policies are directed toward the "breadwinner" and *adolescent work is regarded as a supplement*. Girls also are occupied in industry, but large numbers are absorbed in household work.

This situation is illustrated by Modell, Furstenberg, and Hershberg (1976). They compared the transition to the status of adulthood in Philadelphia around the year 1880 with transition in 1970. Toward the end of the nineteenth century, the family still played a central role in ensuring survival. *Unemployment was dealt with within the family*. Whoever was employed, whether it was the children or the parents, had to contribute to the family's survival. At this time children still contributed to the family income for an average period of 7.5 years. In 1970, this period had been shortened to 2.5 years. Moreover, children typically spent their money on investment in their own future or on individual consumption, rather than contributing to the family directly. This is a clear indicator of reduced family responsibility on the part of adolescents in modern times and the loosening of social bonds. In earlier times, however, it was more common for the lives of young people to be interrupted by phases of unemployment than is the case today. Children and adolescents were important as an *emergency backup system*.

Transition into adulthood and youth unemployment in the twentieth century

The modern script of transition to adulthood emerged slowly during the past hundred years, but varied for different groups (e.g., females, youth in the countryside, etc.) as part of a sociohistorical process known as individualization (Kohli, 1985, 1989). An institutionalized structure of the life course was the result.

The main feature of the modern transition from adolescence into adulthood is the task of *preparing for an individually chosen occupational career*. Life is thought of as an ordered sequence of developmental tasks; the failure to fulfill age-specific tasks is the main obstacle for making a transition to the next stage of life. Life now has a structure, determined by the individual's need to work to support himself or herself, to be independent, and eventually to retire. These stages are designed to lead to the optimal point at which the human being, on the basis of his or her economic situation, can make decisions about the important things in life (i.e., the purchase of goods, choice of services, political and philosophical orientations, and private life with a family and children). His or her life takes the form of a planful sequence of events, embedded in a system of societal support and aid. This state of affairs describes the *expectations* that maturing people encounter, expectations that they internalize in their earliest years at school.

Children are not expected to work for the family, to support their parents, or to contribute to the family income, but rather to prepare themselves for an independent life, for which earning an income is essential. In this context *personal* achievement and responsibilities become the focus of goals. Such achievements engender pride as well as anxiety about potential failures.

Social Policies Against Youth Unemployment in Historical Perspective

The different nature of transition to work roles in traditional, industrial, and modern societies is mirrored in the changing concerns for the young generation.

Because of the high mortality rate of women in agrarian society many children grew up without parents. They either were placed in the kinship systems and had to work very early or they relied on the charity of the church as the only "social policy institution" of those times. Begging children, and homeless children without any prospect of a foreseeable future, were common features of daily life.

Two problems begin to occupy public attention in the period of early industrialization: the inhumane conditions of child and adolescent labor (see, for example, the official inquiries under the aegis of the Children's Employment Act in England) and the neglect of working-class street youth (see Rühle, 1922). In this historical context, social policies do not depend on charity but emerge as a representation of the legitimate interests of unions and parliamentary commissions.

On the way to the modern welfare state, the agencies of social policy dealing with unemployment again change. Neither charitable organizations nor interest groups (such as unions) are responsible for protecting youth. Rather, the state as a public agency assumes responsibility. Different agencies also address different social support systems. Neither the extended family and the local community nor the nuclear family are any longer considered the primary agencies of assistance—public institutions and the adolescents themselves are now responsible. In this respect we find noticeable national variations, sometimes mirrored in the authorship of documents containing statistics of employment and youth unemployment. Germany is an example of such a pattern, where statistics about unemployment were first collected at the end of the nineteenth century by the unions and later by public agencies. In some regions of the United States, from about 1870 on, statistics were already a public responsibility.

Keyssar (1986) evaluated the best statistics available in Massachusetts from 1885. Because this information was categorized by age, it is here that we first learn in detail about unemployment among young people running at about 10 percent in the age groups 10–13, 14–19, and 20–29. These statistics also are arranged according to sex, type of work, and the period of unemployment. It is here, too, that we find a situation that we will come across again and again. The age group under 20 always has a higher percentage of unemployment than that between 20 and 40. Moreover, the duration of unemployment for adults is always shorter (approximately 4 to 5 months) and female adolescents are disproportionately affected, although they are less likely than their male peers to be represented in the statistics in this period.

England is another example of national variation in the locus of social policy responsibilities for unemployment. Around the turn of the nineteenth century greater efforts were made (based on private philanthropic initiative) to document the exact rate of unemployment. One such study was made for the City of York, located in northeastern England (82,000 inhabitants, of whom 5.5% were unemployed), by Rowntree and Lasker (1911). "The inquiry . . . described was made in York on the 7th of June 1910. The weather was fine, and had been so for a week" (p. vii). Thus the authors anticipated the target date method that became so important later in the analysis of the numbers of those unemployed who were actively in search of employment but unable to find a job.

It is here that we also find the first attempts to reconstruct the biographies of the unemployed youngsters. Eighty percent of the unemployed young people had had a bad start in life both within the family and in school. The fact that their parents were unemployed was significant as well. This bad start also led to reduced "employability." This was not the case to the same degree with the adult unemployed (i.e., 50% of them were described as reproachless with regard to their abilities and character). Thus it has already become clear that neither the general picture of the unemployed nor the reasons for their unemployment were homogeneous.

Rowntree and Lasker concentrated on male adolescents. The social history of female unemployment seems to be a quite different story to which no attention was paid.

The next great advance in the investigation of unemployment takes place within the framework of the Great Depression, the worldwide economic crisis in 1929.

Overall we observe changes of *targets*, *agents*, *aims*, and *means* in social policy for those who were at the transition from childhood to adulthood. Responsible agents changed from charity to private initiative and from group interests to the welfare state. The aims of social policy changed from "saving the soul," preventing starvation and death, survival of the family, and protection from being overworked to providing optimal conditions for personal development and for individual mastery of life. The targets were originally the poor; orphans; and victims of war, famine, and illness. Later children in the workforce and the children of laborers were the prime targets of help. During the late nineteenth century, the family—especially the breadwinner—was the target of social policy in order to secure at least the survival of the family. Today the whole age group growing into adulthood is under scrutiny and a target in need of help. The means of social policy has changed, too, from voluntary donations to support by semiprivate agencies and public subsidies by the welfare state.

Today public responsibility for taking action to combat youth unemployment has reached a high level of sophistication, at least in terms of documenting the *sociography of youth unemployment*. The period of unemployment, the social composition of those youth who are officially employed, the percentages of the unemployed population whom they represent, and the duration of unemployment are all recorded at a national and international level (see the reports compiled under the aegis of the OECD: 1978, 1980, 1984, 1988, 1991). The complex interplay between supply and demand with respect to labor is thus analyzed in great detail at the aggregate level. In OECD publications we can also find excellent documentation of national measures taken to prevent youth unemployment.

There now is an extensive literature on the structure of the youth labor market (Franz, 1982; Freeman & Wise, 1982; Organization for Economic Cooperation and Development, 1978, 1984, 1991; Reubens, Harrison & Rupp, 1981), the causes of youth unemployment (cf. *Australian Journal of Statistics*, 1989; Trewin, Bade, Bual,& Newton, 1989; White & Smith, this volume), and the effects of unemployment (cf. Furnham, this volume).

Societal Context Factors as Causes of Youth Unemployment

Returning to the first question in this introductory chapter, we can now summarize the specific social context conditions that generate differential rates of youth unemployment in modern societies. We analyze this on the *aggregate level* and focus therefore on the societal level. Thereby we consider determinants of rates of youth unemployment.

According to a common line of thinking, the main economic factor determining the rise and degree of unemployment is the rise of a market economy and of capitalist production. As part of this process *work becomes a cost factor* that has to be minimized or at least optimized.

Changes in the production of goods determine the costs of labor and therefore render children's or adolescents' employment more or less profitable. In a low-capitalized production system, children's work is cheap and therefore in high demand. This is documented in early phases of the process of industrialization and in third-world countries. When workplaces are cost-intensive and working conditions demand a high level of skill and responsibility, the industry depends on a highly reliable workforce. Under these conditions of production, the likelihood of unemployment in younger cohorts is higher than in middle-aged cohorts. The employment of adolescents can additionally be rendered more or less economically attractive by social policy measures aimed at protecting children and adolescents. Adolescents are highly demanded in part-time jobs of the service sector where labor is cheap and regulations are missing.

Demographic developments, on the other hand, determine the supply of labor and may lead to scarcity or to surplus conditions. But demographic factors (Rindfuss & Sweet, 1977) regulate youth labor supply only in conjunction with the *educational system*. Adolescents can be absorbed by the educational system for a shorter or longer period. In addition, that system can provide more or fewer adolescents seeking work in different sectors of the economy. In the simplest case, the supply of a young workforce becomes compartmentalized into a well-educated group, where private and public agencies have assumed the burden of investment, and into a poorly educated group, where to a large extent employability depends upon the short-term costs of their employment.

Four factors interact in determining the amount of youth unemployment in the course of history: the *quantitative supply-demand relationship*, the *cost of youthful labor*, the *regulations for the employability* of adolescents, and the *qualitative* employability of different segments of the supply side. They determine the historical and societal employment *opportunity structure* (see White & Smith, this volume).

The Influence of the Societal Context on Individual Development

The predominant mode of thinking about the *individual significance of youth unemployment* focuses on the aforementioned concept of individualization. This concept refers to a development in the history of civilization that has reached a climax in the past few decades, which has resulted in the individual becoming the central, responsible agent in shaping his or her own life. What one ultimately wants to achieve in life becomes the central point of reference in one's own planning and in the exercise of responsibility. Success or failure depends, in large measure, on assuming a normative allocation of individual responsibility. Neither conformity and the patient acceptance of given circumstances nor personal sacrifice for a great collective cause form the central reference point for the organization of life. Rather, life is focused around personal development, not in the restricted hedonistic sense of a good life, but more in the sense of extending one's potential to lead a fulfilling life.

Several social developments that have objectively created ever greater individual scope and increased the need to make decisions are responsible for the emergence of this normative code:

- Developments in the science of medicine have made life and reproduction predictable, have made health largely dependent on personal lifestyle, and have made family planning dependent on individual decisions.
- The invention and spread of democratic political systems have made political power dependent on individual decisions to agree or disagree with governmental policies.
- The development of market-oriented economies has, in addition, led to what is today called the "sovereignty of the consumer." The individual may decide in favor of certain products on the basis of consideration of personal costs and benefits.
- The availability of paid employment for both men and women has made it possible for both to lead an independent economic existence and has also made it possible for women to shape their own destinies on a sound economic basis.

At the level of individual life history, the process of *individuation* corresponds to the sociohistorical process of the *individualization* of opportunities and prospects in life. A personal program for life today no longer consists of conforming to predetermined, stereotyped patterns for shaping one's life, but rather of developing a personal perspective on life. The "cultural newcomers" have to adopt their own personal position on all important questions of life concerning work or choice of partner, politics, or worldview. The culture provides relevant constructs and models but these are today very heterogeneous and open to personal selection.

It is particularly during adolescence that the corresponding decision and search processes enter a critical phase. They are focused on the tasks of constructing an individual identity via identification with one's work, and of accommodating one's own psychosocial structure to the goal-oriented and highly structured world of the occupational sector in society. Within such a framework for an individual life course, prolonged unemployment among youth may be the first great catastrophe in life. Although it may only be caused by a historically unfavorable relationship between supply and demand with regard to the workforce, prolonged unemployment could initiate a negative developmental pathway in the life history of a person.

In sum, the conceptual framework of individualization is useful to specify the *differential biographical importance of youth employment under different social and historical conditions*. Youth unemployment becomes an indicator of risk for personal life only under the modern conditions outlined above and under the social conditions of transition into the workforce.

Historical and Societal Moderator Variables of the Individual Consequences of Youth Unemployment

Attempts to illustrate the differential individual significance of youth unemployment in the historical process of industrialization should caution us against assuming uniform effects of youth unemployment on the development of adolescents. *Today's* youth unemployment is connected with a fairly uniform picture of precursors as well as consequences of unemployment in several aspects of personality of those affected (e.g., in the area of work habits, work values, and future expectations; in the area of the self-concept; and in indicators of stress and pathology; see Mortimer, this volume). Youth unemployment is further associated with drug abuse, delinquency, and premature pregnancies in adolescent girls. Future career patterns become erratic and a sizable group suffers from long-term impairment in their occupational trajectory. Furthermore, the groups most endangered are the same in all cultures and nations: those with a deficient school career, school dropouts, youth from the working class, minorities, immigrants, and, under certain conditions, girls.

These risk groups *are more evident under adverse economic conditions, where general unemployment constitutes up to 15 percent of the labor force*. Modern conditions of life in Western societies create those problem groups that experience difficulties in the transition to work. Under premodern living conditions and in the transition to industrialization, the sectors of a youth cohort at risk have been quite different.

Furthermore, the direct effect of youth unemployment on personality is moderated by the societal configurations emerging in the social history of Western societies. This is the second main thesis of this chapter, which relates individual development to societal context. It was difficult to substantiate this for premodern societies as we have only scattered sources that adequately demonstrate the problem of transition into work. Because in premodern Europe only a small segment of the young cohorts could achieve an adult position of economic self-subsistence, this adult status did not function as the universal formula for the life course. Poverty did not create unemployment, but it did create a higher demand for the work of children and youth. Where scarcity of food supply was intensifying, migration was often the only solution. In many areas of the third world (and even in rural areas of the Western world), we can observe similar effects of social conditions on the transition to adulthood.

As Elder (1991) demonstrated in his Iowa study, economic crisis in rural areas can lead even today to more mature responsibilities of adolescents. Girls have to take greater responsibility for the household and the care of younger siblings and boys have to assume more work in the fields as substitutes for unaffordable external help. This situation does not lead necessarily to depressed personalities or character deficits. On the contrary, it can serve as training for strength and survival.

Moreover, the effect of youth unemployment on personality is moderated by the *level of unemployment in general*. The effects are different if about half of the younger population is afflicted, versus only 5 to 10 percent unemployment among a cohort. In the first situation (which we can find according to statistics of the OECD in countries such as Italy or Spain), different subgroups are differentially affected. The stigma of being unemployed in this situation is not as pronounced, and the problem may be defined in a completely different way. Research comparing these situations systematically is almost nonexistent.

Up till now we have applied a model of *direct effects* of societal variables on personality. A *multilevel model*, in which the intermediate levels of family, peers, and neighborhood are taken into consideration, may be more appropriate. These intermediate levels moderate the relationship between distal unemployment rates and proximal experiences of unemployment. For instance, the effect of one's own unemployment could be tempered by the number of acquaintances or even relatives who are out of work. This should apply even more when somebody else in the family— especially the father— is unemployed.

The effects of youth unemployment are additionally moderated by the *context-relative* position of individuals and by *properties of the individuals* themselves. An illustration for such a pattern of effects is again provided by Elder and his pioneering work on the influence of the Great Depression. He demonstrated that the effects of this historic event cannot be understood adequately without taking family structures into account. But not only this intermediate level of the social context proved to be important. The same holds true for individual-level properties such as the age and gender of the children in a family.

Economic decline affected the family intensely. Those who were highly dependent on the family (i.e., the younger children) were even more drastically influenced. Adolescents were not as strongly affected by the mediating family structure because they had more resources to take initiative on their own. Moreover, the effects differed for boys and for girls. Adolescent boys in cohesive families did well even under the adverse conditions of the Great Depression. By providing additional income for the survival of the family they gained in self-respect and responsibility. On the other hand, girls experienced greater deprivation for solving their sex-specific tasks of forming relationships and marrying. By missing any means to make themselves look attractive to the opposite sex, they suffered a loss of recognition and success and consequently felt depressed and worthless (Elder, Caspi, & Burton, 1988).

As impressive as these findings are, we would not expect to see them in the young generation of today, when about 10 percent of the school-leaving cohorts cannot find training and work opportunities. Here we find a more uniform pattern of negative effects of economic crisis on adolescents—especially on boys—mediated by a higher rate of conflicts within a family (Flanagan, 1990).

Nevertheless, it seems important when analyzing the effects of youth unemployment to take into account at least the following moderator variables:

- The regional context (for instance, rural or urban) and the degree of concentration of unemployment in an area. The *percentage of unemployed persons in a local context* seems to be an important moderator of the effects of unemployment on psychosocial adaptation.
- The *gender* of those affected by unemployment. The situation of unemployed girls seems very often to be very different from that of boys. More often girls are absorbed in the household, lack any future prospects, and are in a difficult situation in cross-sex relationships.

- The *educational level* of the adolescents. Certain context variables extend the risk of unemployment to persons with higher levels of education, as we find at present in Germany with those graduating from the university.

An important moderator for the effects of unemployment is, of course, the *age* at which someone becomes unemployed. Because this theme is the focus of this whole volume, a few illustrations will suffice to underline the main point.

Several theories of adolescence stress that this age span is—under modern conditions of growing up—a crucial period in personality development. In particular, Erikson (1968) has stressed that this is the time when human beings develop their identities by formulating a goal structure. *Adolescence is a phase in life in which establishing one's goal orientation enters a critical period* (see also Fend, 1990, 1991). Activities must now become more purposeful, the time perspective longer and directed toward the future. Energies must be oriented toward activities in the external world. Self-reflections and motives now must be tested in reality. Without a clearly sequenced opportunity structure (training, first job, advancements, career), the development of an independent person, capable of taking care of himself or herself, is impaired.

We have impressive early pioneering research on this question. According to Jahoda (1983), unemployed people miss all the experiences linked to contemporary wage earning. These are:

> the imposition of a strict temporal structure, the extension of social experience into spheres that are less emotionally charged than family life, participation in collective goals and efforts, the allocation of status and identity through the wage earning process and the regular activity that this necessitates. (p. 99)

In their research, Jahoda, Lazarsfeld, and Zeisel (1933/1975) investigated the effects of unemployment that affected almost the entire village of Marienthal near Vienna after the main factory shut down in 1929. Their comprehensive investigation involved more than six weeks of active observation and the collection of diverse materials. Their central conclusions were recorded in formulas such as "shrinkage of psychological living space" and the "collapse of temporal structure." Thus their study documented the reversal of "the production of employability."

Being employed leads to a goal-oriented structure of daily life and to a positive psychological outlook. This goal structure breaks down in times of unemployment. The unemployed of Marienthal lost all sense of purpose, which a productive working life both demands and generates. Such loss finds its expression in the most diverse phenomena: in boredom, in the loss of interest in long-term future prospects, in a withdrawal from externally directed activities (social contacts, the borrowing of books, reading the newspaper), in the inability to recall events, indeed, even in a reduction in walking speed.

The question raised here with regard to youth unemployment is an obvious one: What happens when such positive work experiences are lacking in adolescence during the transition from the educational system to the employment system? The answer today is often formulated in terms of Erikson's theoretical framework. Under conditions of unemployment, youth are deprived of essential experiences for optimal development. Because they are on the way to adulthood, they are affected more severely than grownups, who already have developed an identity.

Although we find a great bulk of research on the psychosocial effects of unemployment, we miss systematic comparisons of different age groups, groups that experience unemployment in different phases of the life course. Although many longitudinal studies investigate the future life course and occupational careers as a function of unemployment, the question of the long-term consequences of youth unemployment for the adult psychological structure is not often addressed. Elder's approach represents an important milestone and demonstrates the unexpected consequences of historic experiences during the formative years. He stressed the importance of taking historical events seriously, which, for instance, were not even mentioned in the famous study of Elmtown's youth (Hollingshead, 1949) or in The Adolescent Society (Coleman, 1961).

Roughly 10 percent of youth are unemployed in the modern context of a market economy and a welfare state. The subgroups most in danger under these context conditions are well known (see Mortimer, this volume). In a worldwide perspective, we confront a greater variety of contextual conditions that sometimes resemble situations we can only find in our social history. Youth in Asia or Africa, in the Eastern countries, in distant rural areas, or in the megacities of our time confront a wider variety of unemployment-related tasks and problems than do those we usually analyze in a rather standardized situation of modernity in Western countries. We have to take into account these conditions in order to understand the context-specific patterns of effects.

Although we know the general causes of youth unemployment, we do not know precisely how to combat them. Different pathways may lead to the same goal. A productive approach could be to compare in detail those countries that managed to keep unemployment low in the face of economic crises (Hamilton, 1990; Schmidt, 1987).

References

Australian Journal of Statistics. (1989, 31A). *Youth unemployment.* Canberra: Science Text.

Braudel, F. (1985). *Der Alltag.* Munich, FRG: Kindler.

Buchmann, M. (1989). *The script of life in modern society: Entry into adulthood in a changing world.* Chicago: Chicago University Press.

Coleman, J. S. (1961). *The adolescent society: The social life of the teenager and its impact on education.* New York: Free Press.

Elder, G. H. (1980). Adolescence in Historical Perspective. In J. Adelson, ed. *Handbook of Adolescent Psychology.* New York: John Wiley, (pp. 3–46).

Elder, G. H. (1991). *Children in the household economy.* Unpublished Manuscript.

Elder, G. H., Caspi, A., & Burton, L. M. (1988). Adolescent transitions in developmental perspective: Sociological and historical insights. In M. R. Gunnar & W. A. Collins (Eds.), *Development during the transition to adolescence (Minnesota Symposia on Child Psychology)* (pp. 151–180). Hillsdale, NJ: Lawrence Erlbaum.

Elder, G. H., Pavalko, E. K., & Hastings, T. J. (1991). Talent, history, and the fulfillment of promise. *Psychiatry, 54,* 251–267.

Fend, H. (1990). *Vom Kind zum Jugendlichen: Der übergang und seine Risiken* (Entwicklungspsychologie der Adoleszenz in der Moderne, Bd. 1). Bern: Huber.

Fend, H. (1991). *Identitätsentwicklung in der Adoleszenz.* Lebensentwürfe, Selbstfindung und Weltaneignung in berufliche, familiären und politisch-weltanschaulichen Bereichen (Entwicklungspsychologie der Adoleszenz in der Moderne, Bd. 2). Bern: Huber.

Flanagan, C. A. (1990). Change in Family Work Status: Effects on Parent-Adolescent Decision Making. *Child Development,* 61 (Feb) 163–177.

Franz, W. (1982). *Youth unemployment in the Federal Republic of Germany.* Tübingen, FRG: J.C.B. Mohr (Paul Siebeck).

Freeman, R.B., & Wise, D. A. (Hrsg.). (1982). *The youth labor market problem: Its nature, causes and consequences.* Chicago: University of Chicago Press.

Hamilton, S. F. (1990). *Apprenticeship for adulthood.* New York: Free Press.

Hess, L. E. (1992). *Changing family patterns in Western Europe: Opportunity and risk factors for adolescent development.* Unpublished Manuscript.

Hoffmann-Nowotny, H. J. (1989). The situation of young people in the context of socio-cultural change: Changing patterns of collective living and family structures. In H. Bertram et al. (Hrsg.), *Blickpunkt Jugend und Familie: Internationale Beiträge zum Wandel der Generationen* (pp. 27–40). Munich, FRG: Deutsches Jugendinstitut Materialien.

Hollingshead, A. B. (1949). *Elmtown's youth.* New York: Science Edition.

Jahoda, M. (1983). *Wieviel arbeit braucht der mensch?* (Engl. Orgi. Aufl.). Weinheim, FRG: Beltz Verlag.

Jahoda, M., Lazarsfeld, P. F., & Zeisel, H. (1975). *Die arbeitslosen von marienthal .* Leipzig, GDR: Verlag S. Hirzel. (Original work puglished 1933)

Kühler, H. (1991). Hat sich ein neues übergangssystem entwickelt? Anmerkungen zu ausgewählten Trends der Entwicklung im Bildungswesen. In D.

Brock et al. (Hrsg.), *Übergänge in den beruf* (pp. 39–55). Munich, FRG: DJI-Verlag.

Kohli, M. (1985). Die Institutionalisierung des Lebenslaufs: Historische Befunde und theoretische Argumente. *Kölner Zeitschrift für Soziologie und Sozialpsychologie, 37*, 1–29.

Kohli, M. (1989). Institutionalisierung und Individualisierung der Erwerbsbiographie. In D. Brock et al. (Hrsg.), *Subjektivät im gesellschaftlichen Wandel* (pp. 249–278). München: DJI-Verlag.

Lerner, R. M. (1991). Continuities and changes in the scientific study of adolescence. *Journal of Research on Adolescence, 1* (1), 1–5.

Mitterauer, M. (1986). *Sozialgeschichte der Jugend.* Frankfurt am Main, FRG: Suhrkamp.

Modell, J., Furstenberg, J. F. F., & Hershberg, T. (1976). Social change and transitions to adulthood in historical perspective. *Family History, 1* (1), 7–32.

Modell, J., & Goodman, M. (1990). Historical perspectives. In S. S. Feldman & G. R. Elliott (Eds.), *At the threshold* (pp. 93–122). Cambridge, MA: Harvard University Press.

OECD. (1978). *Youth unemployment.* Paris: Author.

OECD. (1980). *Youth unemployment: The causes and consequences.* Paris: Author.

OECD. (1984). *The nature of youth unemployment.* Paris: Author.

OECD. (1988). *Employment outlook: September 1988.* Paris: Author.

OECD. (1991). *OECD: Employment outlook:* Paris: Author.

Reubens, B. G., Harrison, J. A. C., & Rupp, K. (1981). *The youth labor force 1945–1995.* Totowa, NJ: Allenheld, Osmun.

Rindfuss, R R. & Sweet, J. A. (1977). *Postwar fertility trends and differentials in the United States.* New York: Academic Press.

Rowntree, S. B., & Lasker, B. (1911). *Unemployment: A social study.* London: Macmillan.

Rühle, O. (1922.) *Das proletarische Kind.* Munich, FRG: Albert Langen.

Ryder, N. B. (1965). The cohort as a concept in the study of social change. *American Sociological Review, 30*, 843–861.

Schmidt, M. (1987). The politics of full employment in Western democracies. In R. D. Lambert & A. W. Heston (Eds.), *The annals of the American Academy of Political and Social Science* (pp. 171–181). Newbury Park, CA: Sage.

Steinberg, L. (1989). *Adolescence.* New York: Knopf.

Stewart, A. J., & Healy, J. J. M. (1989). Linking individual development and social change. *American Psychologist, 44*, 30–42.

Trewin, D., Bode, G., Boal, P., & Newton, D. (1989). An automatic interaction detection analysis on unemployed youth. *Australian Journal of Statistics, 31A*, 24–45.

Uhlig, O. (1978.). *Die Schwabenkinder aus Tirol und Vorarlberg.* (Tiroler Wirtschaftsstudien, 34. Folge). Innsbruck/Stuttgart: Allen.

5. The causes of persistently high unemployment

MICHAEL WHITE

DAVID J. SMITH
Policy Studies Institute
London

Introduction

Since about 1980, most industrial nations have experienced persistently high unemployment, which has affected young people along with the rest of the population. Although the young account for a varying proportion of the unemployed from one country to another, a strong correlation exists within any country between changes over time in the overall level of unemployment and the level of youth unemployment. It follows that high youth unemployment is, to a large extent, a reflection of high unemployment overall.

This chapter therefore considers why unemployment overall has risen and remained high in most (but not all) industrial nations since about 1980, although it also gives attention to the special position of young people in the labor market. It explores the general structural causes of high unemployment rather than individual factors.

Explanations of the rise in unemployment and its persistently high level in most countries must be found within broad features of the social and economic structure. Individual factors, which are considered in another chapter, help to determine who is selected for unemployment, but these cannot explain the high level of unemployment overall.

A great wealth of information is now available about unemployment and the structures of employment from which it arises. During the past decade rich comparative data covering the developed countries have become available, primarily through the work of the Organization for Economic Cooperation and Development (OECD). Over the same period, great advances also have been made in detailed studies of unemployment within individual countries and in the study of institutions that shape employment relations. In spite of this wealth of information—or perhaps because of it—it is not easy to give a credible or worthwhile account of the determinants of unemployment. The social and economic processes involved are of great complexity; the data themselves are intricate; they relate in indirect ways to the dynamics that produce them; and the explanations put forward from the perspective of different disciplines, such as economics, political science, and sociology, often may be expressions of equivalent (though not identical) ideas in contrasting language.

This chapter is in two sections. The first briefly sets out some of the central facts about unemployment in advanced industrial economies since 1973. It summarizes some of the main points about the dynamics of unemployment and about the way it is distributed among social groups.

The second section reviews explanations of rising and persistently high unemployment, and assesses their value, by referring to a wide range of evidence. Although the chapter presents more detailed evidence for the United Kingdom than for other countries, it adopts a transnational perspective wherever possible.

Unemployment Since 1973

Historical development

From about 1948 until the beginning of the 1970s there was a period of very low unemployment in most developed countries. Economic historians agree (Maddison, 1982; van der Wee, 1986) that nervousness set in at the end of the 1960s, when it became clear that the U.S. dollar could no longer function as the bedrock of the world financial system. Confirmation of this came in 1971, when the United States unilaterally cancelled the gold-dollar convertibility standard. The world's finances were still in turmoil when, in November 1973, the leading oil-producing countries succeeded in imposing a huge rise in crude-oil prices (a quadrupling) upon the rest of the world. This first "oil shock" of 1973 was repeated in 1979 as a result of the Iranian political crisis.

Equally important, as background to the high unemployment of the 1980s, was the upsurge of wage demands throughout many Western countries in the late 1960s and early 1970s, which resulted in a growth of wage-induced inflationary pressures. Trade-union bargaining power had been growing steadily in the postwar period, in Britain as in many other countries. Now unions were learning to anticipate inflation and build a provision for it into their wage claims, so real wages would continue to increase.

To avoid the dangers of instability, many governments imposed public budget cuts and huge increases in interest rates for borrowers. With economies already stagnating through low profitability and productivity (partly brought about by wage pressures and partly by the slowdown in international trade), such actions were bound to precipitate recession and unemployment. The period of mass unemployment of the 1980s and its aftermath had begun.

Table 5.1 *Unemployment rate by country, 1973–1988*

	1973	1983	1988
United States	4.9	9.6	5.5
Canada	5.5	11.9	7.8
Japan	1.3	2.7	2.5
France	2.7	8.4	10.3
Germany	1.0	8.2	7.9
Italy	5.9	9.2	11.1
United Kingdom	2.1	11.2	8.5
Austria	0.9	3.7	3.7
Belgium	2.3	12.9	10.5
Denmark	1.0	10.4	8.5
Finland	2.5	5.4	4.7
Ireland	5.7	14.0	16.6
Netherlands	3.1	15.0	12.5
Norway	1.6	3.4	3.1
Portugal	2.2	7.9	6.5
Spain	2.2	18.2	1.7
Sweden	2.0	2.9	1.7
Switzerland	0	0.8	0.7
Australia	2.3	9.9	7.4
New Zealand	0.2	5.4	5.3
Total OECD	3.5	8.9	7.4
OECD Europe[a]	3.5	10.4	10.3
Of which:			
Low-unemployment countries[b]	1.3	3.1	2.6
High-unemployment countries[c]	2.7	10.6	10.6
Low-unemployment countries[d]	3.4	7.2	4.6

[a]Excluding Greece, Turkey, Yugoslavia.
[b]Austria, Finland, Norway, Sweden, Switzerland.
[c]Germany, France, United Kingdom, Italy, Belgium, Denmark, Netherlands, Portugal, Spain.
[d]Countries listed in (b) above plus United States, Japan, Canada.

Source: OECD, *Economies in Transition*, (Paris: OECD, 1989).

During the decade from 1973 to 1983, the unemployment rate in the OECD area rose from 3.5 percent to 9 percent; it then fell slowly each year to reach 7.5 percent by 1988 before the onset of the present recession (Table 5.1). However, this OECD average conceals remarkable differences among countries in their experiences during recession. In bringing together its recent research on these issues, the OECD (1989a) distinguishes among three groups of countries:

1. In the first group unemployment rates have been brought down almost to their 1973 levels. Within this group, two more specific categories can be distinguished:
The first includes *Japan* (where the unemployment rate was 2.5% in 1988 compared with 1.3% in 1973) and those European countries where unemployment has for many years been low and stable, namely *Austria, Finland, Norway, Sweden,* and *Switzerland*. In these European low-unemployment countries, the rate was 2.6 percent in 1988 compared with 1.3 percent in 1973.
The second category includes the *United States* and *Canada*, where the unemployment rate was about twice as high as in the European low-unemployment countries or Japan but had almost returned to its 1973 level.

2. In a second group of countries, unemployment was, by 1988, still close to its peak rate. This includes most European countries (*France, Germany, Italy, the United Kingdom, Belgium, Denmark, Ireland, the Netherlands, Portugal,* and *Spain*). In these high-unemployment countries, the rate rose steeply from 2.7 percent in 1973 to 10.6 percent in 1983, and then remained at the same level. In some countries the increase was far more extreme: In Spain, for example, the rate was 2.2 percent in 1973 compared with 19.5 percent in 1988.

3. In *Australia* and *New Zealand* unemployment has remained much higher than at the beginning of the 1970s, but not as high as in the second group of countries. Also, the rate began to fall substantially in Australia after 1983.

Significant measurement difficulties are involved in making cross-country comparisons of unemployment rates (see the following section). These can be reduced (though never eliminated) by focusing on relative changes in the aggregate level of unemployment. Table 5.2 shows the annual percentage increase in unemployment between 1973 and 1987 for the main industrial nations. It broadly confirms the pattern of striking differences summarized above.

Table 5.2 *Change in unemployment by country, 1973–1987*
(The measure is the change in the rate of unemployment [%] between 1973 and 1987:
The larger the figure, the greater the increase in unemployment.)

Countries with large increases	
Australia	5.7
Belgium	8.9
Denmark	7.0
France	8.0
Germany	7.0
Italy	5.1
Netherlands	8.3
United Kingdom	9.2
Countries with small increases	
Austria	2.6
Canada	3.4
Finland	2.6
Japan	1.5
Sweden	−0.1
Switzerland	0.6
United States	2.4

Source: OECD, *Economies in Transition* (Paris: OECD, 1989).

Uneven rates of unemployment across countries reflect, in part, different growth of output. In the low-unemployment countries, average growth of gross domestic product (GDP) accelerated from a little more than 2 percent over the period 1973–1983 to about 4 percent after 1983. In the high-unemployment group, growth picked up to only around 2 percent.

The labor intensity of growth also differed considerably among countries. Expansion was most labour intensive in North America. Not only did output grow rather more slowly in low-unemployment European countries than in North America, but also employment expanded more slowly still (at about .5 percent a year). For most of the countries in the high-unemployment European group, employment in 1988 was still below the 1973 level: The notable exceptions were *Italy* and *Portugal*.

A number of the OECD's surveys of individual countries have examined the role of international mobility in changes in the supply of labor. In *Switzerland*, the supply of immigrant labour has been controlled as a method of adjusting to changes in the labor market (OECD, 1985a): As a result, *Switzerland* is the only country where the labor force actually fell (by almost 3 percent) in the period 1973–1983, following the same trend as employment.

Migration has also been an important countercyclical adjustment mechanism in *New Zealand*. A resumption of large-scale emigration from *Ireland* prevented its unemployment from rising still higher. In the case of *Portugal*, however, immigration aggravated the unemployment problem, as the massive return of Portuguese from former colonies after 1974 coincided with the international recession.

The growth of unemployment in the United Kingdom

Table 5.2 shows that the *United Kingdom* had one of the greatest increases in unemployment during the period from 1973 to 1987. It is worth describing this development in more detail.

Changes in the official definition of unemployment mean that aggregate unemployment cannot be compared over time in a strict or precise sense, but there is ample evidence to support the following account of the broad pattern of change. By the late 1960s the first substantial rise in unemployment was taking place. This rise could not be interpreted as wholly cyclical, because in the following period of recovery, unemployment did not fall to its previous level. A pattern had thus commenced, which was to continue until the end of the 1980s (and perhaps beyond). Successive economic crises resulted in sharp increases in unemployment, and because on each occasion the subsequent fall was incomplete, the overall result was one of a cumulatively rising level of aggregate unemployment. Figure 5.1 shows this development.

Although the rise in aggregate unemployment of the 1980s could be seen as a continuation of the earlier pattern, this pattern was also aggravated in an important way. Not only was recovery incomplete, but also it was greatly delayed. An economic recession of about two years was associated with a high level of unemployment that persisted for seven years (see Figure 5.1). Furthermore, in 1988 and 1989, unemployment eventually fell only in response to a massive fiscal stimulus to consumer spending—now widely regarded as imprudent (Godley, 1991; OECD, 1990a, pp. 11–13). This suggests that, if more prudent fiscal policies had been maintained, aggregate unemployment would have continued at a high level throughout the 1980s, despite the fact that, after 1982, there was a continuous economic "boom."

This brief résumé of developments in the United Kindom has identified three important observations that stand in need of explanation:

1. The change from a long period of consistently low unemployment to an equally long period of rising and high unemployment

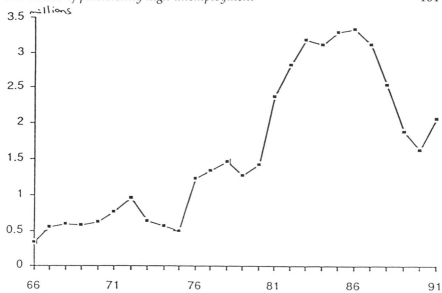

Source: Department of Employment Gazette and Employment Gazette, statistical series:
April of each year.
Note: Changes in the definition of unemployment mean that aggregate unemploy-
ment cannot be compared over the long-term in a strict or precise sense.
Figure 5.1. Aggregate unemployment in Great Britain, 1966–1991

2. The incomplete recoveries in the economic cycles of the latter period
3. The full emergence of persistent high unemployment in the 1980s during a period of economic growth

An important part of the context of changes in unemployment is
changes in the numbers in employment. The general picture in the United
Kingdom during the postwar period as a whole has been one of slow
growth in this respect. The phases of postwar employment can be aligned
with those of postwar unemployment in the following way:

1. Period of low unemployment: steady employment growth
2. Initial period of rising unemployment: moderately fluctuating employment with little overall growth
3. Period of persistent high unemployment: turbulent change in employment with some overall growth

Evidently, if aggregate employment has increased even in the period
of high and rising unemployment, then the supply of labor must have

been growing more rapidly than employment. In fact, in the sluggish 1970s the labor supply increased by 1.2 million, and this growth of supply has been repeated in the 1980s. In other words, employment growth has been weak relative to the growth in the number of people offering their labor.

The dynamics of unemployment

The aggregate rate of unemployment is the number of unemployed people expressed as a percentage of the number of people in the labor force, where those in the labor force are those in employment (who worked for pay or profit during a reference week) plus the unemployed. The International Labor Office (ILO) guidelines define the unemployed as those who meet three criteria: They are without work, currently available for work, and seeking work. There is considerable room for different interpretations of all three criteria, so considerable measurement issues can arise when comparing unemployment rates among countries (or even within the same country over time, where definitions and administrative procedures have changed). Even where different definitions give similar totals, they may identify different individuals as unemployed.

It is increasingly recognized that aggregate unemployment is a measure giving a static, cross-sectional view that in some respects is unhelpful. One of the developments over the period of rising and persistent high unemployment has been a rise in long-term unemployment, which may be defined as a continuous period of unemployment of at least one year (although any such definition is to some degree arbitrary). This is a rise not only in the *number* of the long-term unemployed, but also in the *proportion* of those unemployed at any one time who have been unemployed for at least one year.

In the *United Kingdom*, for example, during the period of low unemployment, the long-term unemployed rarely accounted for as much as 20 percent of all of those unemployed at any one time. By 1980, this proportion had risen to about 25 percent, and by 1985, to about 40 percent; with the eventual recovery, it fell back, by the end of 1990, to 30 percent. The decade of high and persistent unemployment was also a decade of persistent long-term unemployment.

The OECD has collated similar data for 15 countries for the period 1979–1986 (OECD, 1987, pp. 171–184). A positive correlation exists between the aggregate level of unemployment and the proportion of unemployed who are long term: As the unemployment rate rises, the proportion of the unemployed who have been unemployed for more than a year also rises. However, when the unemployment rate ceases to rise, the long-term proportion does not, at least initially. There appears to be a new pattern of persistent long-term unemployment that reduces only after a considerable time lag.

When aggregate unemployment is plotted against the share of long-term unemployment, most countries lie within a "band" extending up from the origin: Within this band, the countries with low rates of unemployment have low long-term proportions, and those with high unemployment rates have high proportions. There are, however, two groups of countries outside this band. The countries of *North America* have a lower incidence of long-term unemployment than countries with similar rates of aggregate unemployment, such as *Sweden, Norway, Austria,* and *Japan.* Conversely, *Belgium,* the *United Kingdom,* and *France* have a higher incidence of long-term unemployment than would be expected from their rates of aggregate unemployment.

Of course, the long-term unemployed cannot be regarded as a separate group, but the trends in long-term unemployment are significant and show the importance of analyzing the dynamics that underlie the aggregate unemployment rate. Aggregate unemployment (the number of people unemployed at a particular time) represents the cumulative balance between rates of inflow and outflow; it changes continuously as a result of these flows. There is a popular tendency to equate unemployment with job loss, but it is possible that an increased rate of job loss, if balanced by an increased rate of outflow, should result in no net increase in unemployment.

Similarly, the average duration of unemployment is a function of the stock of unemployment and the outflow rate per unit of time. In general, an increasing average duration of unemployment arises because the inflow rate is increasing more quickly than the outflow rate. An increasing aggregate level of unemployment can result either from increasing inflow to unemployment, from increasing average duration of unemployment, or from both.

In the *United Kingdom,* adequate data on unemployment flows only became available in the early 1980s (Hughes, 1982). These data show that the great rise in unemployment in the early 1980s arose from both an increased inflow to unemployment and an increased duration (or reduced outflow relative to the unemployment level). Specifically, the duration of male unemployment increased (on average) by more than one-half during the period 1978–1982, and the inflow of men to unemployment increased by about one-third. In the case of women, too, both components increased considerably, although the inflow to unemployment increased at a higher rate than the average duration. Thus, the great rise in unemployment reflected both an acceleration of the inflow and an obstruction of the outflow.

The increasing inflow to unemployment of the early 1980s was partly the result of an increased loss of jobs because of business closures and redundancies. In 1980 there was, in addition, a substantial increase in the number of school-leavers registering as unemployed because of difficulty in finding an initial job; in later years, however, this inflow was checked by the provision of the Youth Training Scheme as an alternative to unemployment.

The outflows from unemployment during the recession of the early 1980s were at a lower level than the inflows, but it is worth emphasizing that they grew in absolute terms: They simply did not grow fast enough. The average difference between inflows and outflows was 18 percent during the peak period of recession in 1980–1981, sufficient to add 1.6 million to aggregate unemployment in two years. Even these figures, however, somewhat understate the depression of the labor market during this period. Vacancies notified by employers to the state employment offices fell by one-half in 18 months. This tends to confirm that the problem was more one of obstruction to recruitment than of job loss.

Some confirmation of this is provided by the Workplace Industrial Relations Surveys of 1980 and 1984 (a national sample of more than 2,000 workplaces with 25 or more workers), which showed that it was more common for employers to adjust their workforce by restraining recruitment than to use redundancies (Millward & Stevens, 1986, Table 8.8). Unemployment would have been considerably higher during this period if it were not for increased outflows to destinations other than employment, including early retirement (encouraged by government policy) and state-provided work programs and training schemes for the unemployed.

Distribution of unemployment

Unemployment is distributed very unevenly among population groups according to age, sex, region, and occupational level. Any adequate explanation of unemployment needs to account for such differences.

Age. When age is plotted against the unemployment rate, in the great majority of countries the resulting curve is in the shape of a "reverse J": Unemployment rates are highest for youths, then decline with age, and then remain fairly flat for the prime age groups. At the other end of the age spectrum, at least in some countries, the unemployment rate increases for people ages 55–59 (OECD, 1988, pp. 26–29). A number of factors have been suggested to account for the relatively high level of youth unemployment. As recent entrants to the labor market, young people are highly mobile between jobs and, therefore, more likely to experience a number of spells of unemployment before settling into a more permanent career.

Demographic developments also may be important: Members of the baby boom generation faced increased competition with their contemporaries. On the demand side, the competitive position of young compared with older workers varies widely among countries, depending on the system of youth training and the associated wage structures.

Unemployment rates for the 16–19 age group are strongly affected by government schemes and associated counting rules in Labour Force Surveys: For example, in the *United Kingdom*, the rate of unemployment for males ages 16–19 apparently declined from 32.3 percent in 1983 to 6.8 percent in 1990, largely as a result of government programs that took youths out of the group counted as unemployed (see Table 5.3a). It must also be remembered that the proportion of the 16–19 age group who are counted as part of the labor force ranges from 8 percent in *Belgium* to 57 percent in *Denmark* (see Table 5.4). At the peak of unemployment, in 1983, the rate for males ages 16–19 reached 45 percent in *Spain* and around 33 percent in *Italy* and in the *United Kingdom*. The rate for this age group did not exceed 10 percent in *Germany, Japan,* or *Sweden.* In 1983, the rate of unemployment for the 16–19 age group was well over twice the total rate in the case of all OECD countries except *Germany;* the ratio between the 16–19 rate and the total rate was particularly high in *Italy.* By 1990, when there had been a substantial decline in the total rate of unemployment from its peak in 1983, the rate for the 16–19 group remained much higher than the total rate in most countries.

Among young adults ages 20–24, the rate of participation in the labour force is around two-thirds to three-quarters in most countries (see Table 5.4). Rates of unemployment for the 20–24 age group tend to be somewhat lower than for youths ages 16–19, but in many countries they are around twice as high as for all age groups. *Germany* is again the major exception: There, youth unemployment rates are only slightly higher than the overall rate.

In the 12 EC countries, people up to the age of 24 account for more than one-third of the unemployed. In some southern European countries (*Italy, Greece,* and *Portugal*), they account for around one-half of the unem-

Table 5.3a *Youth unemployment for selected OECD countries: Males*

	Youth unemployment rates			Ratio of youth to total unemployment rates		
	1973	1983	1990	1973	1983	1990
France						
15–19	4.1	20.3	13.3	2.7	3.3	1.8
20–24	2.5	13.5	15.9	1.7	2.2	2.2
Germany						
15–19	0.6	7.9	6.0[a]	1.0	1.2	1.0[a]
20–24	0.6	10.4	7.8[a]	0.8	1.6	1.3[a]
Italy						
14–19	15.8	32.9	32.5	5.3	5.5	4.5
20–24	10.3	21.3	23.1	7.7	3.6	3.2
Japan						
15–19	3.8	7.1	7.4	2.9	2.6	3.7
20–24	2.2	3.8	3.7	1.7	1.4	1.9
Spain						
16–19	7.1	44.5	30.8	3.4	2.9	2.6
20–24	3.5	27.9	24.4	1.7	1.8	2.0
Sweden						
16–19	5.8	10.0	4.1	2.6	2.9	2.7
20–24	4.2	6.7	3.3	1.9	2.0	2.2
United Kingdom						
16–19	4.2	32.3	6.8	1.4	2.2	0.9
20–24	3.6	22.1	12.2	1.2	1.5	1.7
United States						
16–19	12.9	22.1	15.6	3.2	2.3	2.9
20–24	6.5	14.6	8.4	1.6	1.5	1.6

[a] 1987

Source: OECD, *Labour Force Statistics 1967–1989* (Paris: OECD, 1991).

ployed, whereas in *Germany* they account for less than one-fifth (see Table 5.4). Any adequate explanation of unemployment must be able to account for these wide differences in the relative importance of youth unemployment in different countries.

Some of the complexities underlying these aggregate unemployment rates can be illustrated by referring to the evidence on the dynamics of youth unemployment in the *United Kingdom*. It long has been recognized that young people are in a specially dangerous position at times of eco-

Table 5.3b *Youth unemployment for selected OECD countries: Females*

	Youth unemployment rates			Ratio of youth to total unemployment rates		
	1973	1983	1990	1973	1983	1990
France						
15–19	8.0	42.0	29.9	2.6	4.0	2.5
20–24	4.5	21.9	23.2	1.5	2.1	1.9
Germany						
15–19	1.2	11.3	8.4[a]	1.1	1.2	1.0[a]
20–24	1.4	12.8	9.3[a]	1.3	1.4	1.1[a]
Italy						
15–19	15.7	47.3	46.6	3.3	3.1	2.7
20–24	10.7	30.1	34.3	2.3	2.0	2.0
Japan						
15–19	1.8	5.1	5.7	1.5	2.0	2.6
20–24	2.3	4.3	3.7	1.9	1.7	1.7
Spain						
16–19	6.0	52.5	43.0	2.7	2.6	1.8
20–24	3.1	38.4	38.3	1.4	1.9	1.6
Sweden						
16–19	8.0	10.8	4.9	2.9	3.0	3.3
20–24	4.7	6.9	2.7	1.7	1.9	1.8
United Kingdom						
16–19	2.6	25.5	4.7	2.9	2.9	1.3
20–24	1.8	15.2	6.5	2.0	1.7	1.9
United States						
16–19	15.2	21.2	14.6	2.5	2.3	2.7
20–24	8.4	12.7	8.4	1.4	1.4	1.6

[a]1987

Source: OECD, *Labour Force Statistics 1967–1989* (Paris: OECD, 1991).

nomic recession. This is because of their higher job mobility, which is two to three times greater than the national average (source: General Household Survey, 1992, Table 9.3 p. 207). Because young people's jobs are more frequently terminated, they naturally flow into unemployment at a higher rate. Although their outflow is also particularly high (Daniel, 1990), this may well be checked when (as in the first half of the 1980s) employers restrict their recruitment.

Table 5.4 *Youth participation and unemployment in EC countries, 1989: Males and females*

	14–19		20–24		14–24		
	Part. rate	% of unemp.	Part. rate	% of unemp.	Part. rate	% of unemp.	Unemp. rate
Belgium	7.7	4.2	60.6	20.2	33.1	24.4	15.5
Denmark	57.0	8.8	84.3	19.6	70.4	28.4	11.5
Germany	33.8	4.5	74.8	12.4	55.6	16.9	5.5
Greece	17.7	12.9	62.2	32.5	36.4	45.4	24.8
Spain	22.6	13.4	68.6	27.6	42.8	41.0	34.3
France	15.3	6.5	71.8	22.4	41.3	28.9	19.6
Ireland	23.9	13.3	78.8	18.0	45.7	31.3	21.9
Italy	23.6	17.3	69.6	33.1	44.4	50.4	31.9
Luxembourg	22.5	—	73.4	—	48.6	—	(3.3)
Netherlands	34.4	14.1	75.0	17.2	54.1	31.3	13.4
Portugal	41.2	20.8	75.5	25.8	54.8	46.6	11.7
United Kingdom	50.9	12.0	84.0	18.1	67.2	30.1	10.3
Total EC	29.4	11.5	73.8	23.5	50.4	35.0	17.6

Source: Eurostat, *Labour Force Survey: Results 1989* (Luxembourg, Eurostat 1991).

To leave school at 16 is more common in the United Kingdom than in most other European countries: About one-half of young people currently do so. Assessing the position of school-leavers has been complicated by the extensive programs of temporary employment and subsidized training introduced by the government. The worsening position of school-leavers was cause for concern early in the period of rising unemployment; as early as 1978 there was a national guarantee to all school-leavers of a place on a six-month work experience scheme if no normal job was available. This guarantee has progressively been extended, and since 1986 every 16-year-old school-leaver has had the entitlement of entering the two-year Youth Training Scheme (recently adapted into a more flexible program, called simply Youth Training). Those school-leavers not entering the various youth programs have had high rates of unemployment—typically in excess of 20 percent, and much higher in the more depressed areas (Roberts & Parsell, 1988)—but these tend to be young people with particularly low educational qualifications, from urban areas, and with other disadvantages. Initial unemployment rates among those leaving Youth Training and its predecessors have varied from more than 40 percent—in the depths of the early 1980s recession—to around 15 percent under more favorable conditions in the late 1980s.

Although it is hard to summarize unemployment among 16– to 19-year-olds in a single figure, there is little doubt that their labor market position has worsened in the long term (see Wells, 1983, for a review of the evidence). A separate indication of this has been the collapse of the British apprenticeship system since the late 1970s. But for the subsidy provided through Youth Training, there would have been little training on offer to school-leavers by the early 1980s.

Young adults (usually defined in the United Kingdom as 18– to 24-year-olds) also experienced a deteriorating position during the recession of the early 1980s. This deterioration, however, was expressed only in terms of long-term unemployment: Young adults accounted for a more or less constant proportion of aggregate unemployment, and also of unemployment of 6 to 12 months' duration, but constituted a rapidly increasing proportion of those unemployed for one year or more (White & McRae, 1989).

During the recession, not only did recent school-leavers find it difficult to enter employment, but also many young adults with previously stable jobs were displaced and suffered prolonged unemployment. In the subsequent upturn of the economy, the highest risk of remaining unemployed applied to the older part (21 years plus) rather than the young (18–20 years), despite the greater job experience of the former group (White & McRae, 1989).

The position of older workers is, once more, only properly understood by observing the distinction between flows and stocks. Workers of 55 and over constitute about one in eight of the U.K. male labor force. Their rate of inflow to unemployment has been roughly in line with this, but their rate of outflow has been less than two-thirds the average for all ages (Daniel, 1990). Accordingly, among long-term unemployed males, those aged 55 or older are overrepresented by a factor of about two relative to their labor-force participation. Older workers are often subject to ill health or the victims of large-scale redundancies at the time when they enter long-term unemployment (White, 1983).

Sex The distribution of unemployment between men and women has to be seen in the context of changes in the rate of participation by the two sexes in the labor force. Table 5.5 summarizes the relevant statistics for eight OECD countries, taking the year before the first oil shock (1973), the peak year for unemployment (1983), and the most recent year (1990). Wide differences exist among countries in the female participation rate. *Sweden* and *Japan* show the highest rates, and the southern European

Table 5.5 *Rate of unemployment and rate of participation in the labor force for selected OECD countries*

	Participation rates			Unemployment rates			
	1973	1983	1990	1973	1983	1990	1983/1973
France							
Males	86.1	79.7	72.9	1.5	6.1	7.3	4.1
Females	51.2	55.8	57.7	3.1	10.6	12.1	3.4
Germany							
Males	89.1	80.6	83.0[a]	0.6	6.7	6.1[a]	11.2
Females	49.6	49.7	54.5[a]	1.1	9.3	8.8[a]	8.5
Italy							
Males	80.0	79.1	76.6	3.0	6.2	7.3	2.1
Females	29.0	39.8	44.1	4.7	15.4	17.1	3.3
Japan							
Males	90.3	89.0	88.1	1.3	2.7	2.0	2.1
Females	54.1	73.0	74.3	1.2	2.6	2.2	2.2
Spain							
Males	92.7	85.0	79.3	2.1	15.6	12.0	7.4
Females	34.8	34.7	42.2	2.2	20.5	24.2	9.3
Sweden							
Males	90.0	87.7	88.5	2.2	3.4	1.5	1.5
Females	63.9	78.3	83.5	2.8	3.6	1.5	1.3
United Kingdom							
Males	90.0	87.7	88.5	2.2	3.4	1.5	1.5
Females	57.2	60.2	68.4	0.9	8.9	3.5	9.9
United States							
Males	89.1	87.0	87.6	4.0	9.6	5.4	2.4
Females	52.7	63.4	69.6	6.0	9.2	5.4	1.5

[a]1987

Source: OECD, *Labour Force Statistics 1967–1989* (Paris: OECD, 1991).

countries, *Italy* and *Spain*, show the lowest ones. In all eight countries the female participation rate has increased; these increases have been most marked in *Sweden* and *Japan*, but there have also been sharp increases from a low base in *Italy* and *Spain*. Male participation rates have tended to decline in all eight countries, but these declines have been substantial only in *France* and *Spain*, as a result of state policies encouraging early retirement during the recession.

In four of the eight countries (*France, Germany, Italy,* and *Spain*) the rate of unemployment in 1990 is higher among women than among men, and for three of these countries, the exception being *Germany,* the difference is substantial. In the *United Kingdom,* the rate of unemployment is substantially higher among men than among women. In the remaining three countries (*Japan, Sweden,* and the *United States*) the male and female unemployment rates are closely similar. These differences among countries are probably connected with differences in the social security systems, which may or may not encourage married women who cannot find a job to withdraw from the labor market.

The increase in the rate of unemployment between 1973 and 1983 (rightmost column of Table 5.5) was substantially higher among women than among men in the *United Kingdom,* and somewhat higher in *Spain* and *Italy.* In the case of the *United Kingdom,* however, this result is probably spurious, being caused by a radical understatement of female unemployment in the 1970s due to nonregistration. The increase in the rate of unemployment was substantially higher among men than among women only in *Germany.*

More research is needed before the distribution of unemployment between men and women, and its pattern of variation among countries, can be adequately described. What makes description particularly difficult is that both the numerator (the number of the unemployed) and the denominator (the number participating in the labor force) may be influenced by the way the social security system regards women who are part of family units where a man is working or drawing social security benefits. In the *United Kingdom,* for example, the inflow of women to unemployment rose faster than that of men during the economic recession of the early 1980s, but their outflow has also been greater. In part, however, this has been outflow into economic inactivity, conditioned by the system of income support.

Region. Table 5.6 summarizes disparities in unemployment rates among regions within each OECD country. The two right-hand columns are derived from a ranking of the regions within each country according to the unemployment rate. They show the unemployment rate for the regions containing the top and bottom quarter of the labor force on this criterion. In smaller countries, the ratio between the unemployment rates for regions in the top and bottom quarters is usually below 2; for the five largest European countries, *Japan,* and the *United States,* the ratio is about 2. Both in Europe and in Japan, unemployment rates tend to be higher in peripheral than in central regions.

Table 5.6 *Regional unemployment disparities: Annual averages, 1987*

	Number of regions	Unemployment top quarter[a]	Rate bottom quarter[a]
Nordic countries	17	6.4	1.5
Denmark	3	6.8	4.8
Finland	4	7.5	2.3
Norway	5	2.8	1.7
Sweden	5	2.6	1.1
Central and Western Europe	48	12.9	4.9
Austria	3	4.1	3.1
Belgium	3	14.2	9.3
France	11	12.9	8.6
Germany	11	8.5	3.8
Ireland	4	18.8	17.0
Netherlands	4	10.4	9.2
United Kingdom	11	13.6	7.6
Southern Europe	36	21.2	6.6
Greece	3	8.3	5.8
Italy	12	19.4	6.6
Portugal	5	10.3	4.7
Spain	11	27.7	14.7
Turkey	5	13.1	7.6
Japan	10	3.8	2.0
	10	9.3	4.7
Oceania			
Australia	8	9.4	6.2
New Zealand	2	4.9	3.7
North America	61	9.1	4.2
Canada	10	12.2	6.1
United States	51	8.4	4.1

[a]Unemployment rates for the bottom quarter of the labor force by region were calculated by ordering regions in terms of ascending unemployment rate, taking regions until the cumulative labor force passed one-quarter of the total, and including the last region in the calculation with an appropriate fractional weight, and similarly for the top quarter.
Source: OECD, *Employment Outlook 1991* (Paris; OECD 1991).

This center-versus-periphery effect is evident among the regions within a particular country, not among the regions of a number of countries considered together. This suggests that within each country there is a pull toward the capital or other large city that is stronger than any pull toward centers outside the national boundaries. No center-periphery pattern of this kind is evident in the *United States*.

Regional differentials increased during the 1980s in a majority of the OECD countries. In *Finland, France, Italy,* the *United Kingdom,* and the *United States,* the rise followed a certain fall in differentials during the

1970s. In some European countries, these changes in the *size* of regional differentials have done little or nothing to upset the *pattern*: The regional pattern has remained particularly stable in *Finland*, *Italy*, and the *United Kingdom*. In some other European countries, such as *France* and *Germany*, and also in *Australia* and *Canada*, significant changes in the regional pattern have occurred. In the *United States*, regional patterns have reversed since 1975. The much greater change in the relative position of regions within the United States than within other countries may reflect the larger scale of the country and the greater power and independence of state and local compared with central government (OECD, 1991, pp. 95–131).

Occupation

Statistics collected for eight major industrial nations by the OECD show that in all except *Germany* the rate of unemployment is considerably higher among manual than among nonmanual workers (OECD, 1987, pp. 84–90). Whether occupation is defined by reference to the last job or the normal job, concentration of unemployment among manual workers is particularly strong in the *United Kingdom*. It is worth briefly considering the dynamics underlying these differences in the aggregate unemployment rate.

A study of the inflow into unemployment (Daniel, 1990) shows that two-thirds of male and one-half of female entrants have come from manual jobs. Furthermore, the majority of the remaining female entrants have come from routine service and clerical jobs. It is now customary (in the United Kingdom) to classify these as "working class" positions (see, e.g., Goldthorpe, 1983). A study of the long-term unemployed (White, 1983) shows that 80 percent of males have come from manual occupations, wheras virtually all the females have come from manual, lower service, or clerical occupations. Further, the minority of white-collar workers in long-term unemployment have been shown to be untypical in having exceptionally low levels of educational qualification (White, 1983; see also White & McRae, 1989). Accordingly, those in long-term unemployment during the recessionary period of the 1980s could be generally characterized as "from lower occupations and/or lower qualified."

Explanations of Persistent High Unemployment

A satisfactory explanation of unemployment will address the remarkable divergence between the high- and low-unemployment countries in the postwar period, and the emergence of persistent high unemployment in many (but not all) countries since 1980. A successful explanation is likely to rely on a dynamic model that takes account of inflows and outflows within the wider framework of individual mobility and employer workforce adjustment. An explanation of this kind will, intrinsically, incorporate long-term unemployment. It should also take account of differential rates of unemployment between family units. On most of these detailed matters, it is not practicable to review transnational research. The approach adopted here is more selective. Reference to international comparative research is made at strategic points, but much of the analysis uses more detailed evidence about the *United Kingdom* to explain the development of persistent high unemployment in that country.

Macroeconomic policy

A simple and bold explanation is that unemployment has increased because governments changed their macroeconomic policies. For example, the account given by Maddison (1982) is that, faced with an increasingly chaotic international financial system, governments overreacted in shifting policies in the direction of caution, conservatism, and hence contraction. In this view, if governments had shown more determination and finesse in dealing with international pressures, rising and persistently high unemployment might have been avoided or at least mitigated.

But though governments must be seen as actors making choices, and not as passive transmitters of economic forces, these choices are subject to important constraints. Despite common international trading and financial conditions, several European countries (*Austria, Norway, Sweden, Switzerland*) followed quite distinctive macroeconomic policies and were successful in avoiding high unemployment. This might be taken to indicate that nations could "choose" low or high unemployment, but more probably it shows instead that the internal constraints on macroeconomic policy differed between the low-unemployment and high-unemployment countries.

In the United Kingdom at least, there are particular reasons for thinking that macroeconomic policy has been severely constrained. One is that broadly similar monetarist economic policies were followed by both Labour and Conservative governments during the 1975–1986 period, despite their very different priorities and rhetoric: Both governments presided over a doubling of aggregate unemployment. Another is that, beginning in 1987, the United Kingdom did in fact experiment with a return to expansionary fiscal policy. This did have a rapid and massive impact in reducing unemployment, but expansion was followed by rapidly rising pressures of inflation. To deal with inflation, the government was soon led to abandon expansion, thus introducing a further period of deep economic recession.

Wage rigidity

The development of high unemployment in certain countries and not in others cannot be explained by differences in labor costs. The low-unemployment countries in fact tend strongly to be high-wage economies; also, they did not have a higher than average increase in labor costs between 1970 and 1983 (Therborn, 1986, Table 14, p. 60).

Furthermore, *before* the onset of high unemployment, the countries of future mass unemployment had *lower* manufacturing unit labor costs than the others (Therborn, 1986, p. 61). However, wage rigidity—the failure of wages to respond quickly to changes in the economic climate—can be shown to have explanatory power.

The classical economic theory of the labor market assumes that the supply of labor creates sufficient demand by offering itself at a sufficiently low wage. Hence, the labor market should "clear." British economists were among the first to develop theories of why the labor market, in practice, often does not clear. For example, Pigou (1927, 1933) stressed the role of constraints to mobility on the supply side (such as workers' attachment to an area or lack of skill to change occupation), which reduced effective wage competition. Keynes (1936/1964), while primarily developing a new view of the demand side, also believed that "wage stickiness" was caused by the reluctance of workers to see existing wage differentials upset and by employers' desire to avoid conflict.

Steady growth and low unemployment after the war led to rising levels of wages and to expectations of continuing increases in personal consumption and collective prosperity. By the 1970s economists of the neoclassical school were incorporating expectations within their econometric models. The implication of such models was that policies of fiscal and monetary expansion would be self-defeating under conditions where workers and trade unions raised their wage demands to anticipate the expected rise in inflation, hence generating further inflation. This would prevent rising unemployment from being corrected by downward adjustment in wages.

Brittan (1975) influentially argued that for the U.K. restrictive monetary policies were essential to counteract trade-union power in wage bargaining, and that the labor could only be made to respond to market forces through long-term structural changes on the supply side, such as

reform of the trade unions, and increased spatial mobility through housing policy. The Canadian economist Cornwall (1983), writing from a neo-
Keynesian rather than monetarist viewpoint, nevertheless came to
remarkably similar analytical (though not policy) conclusions concerning
trade unions and the movement of wages. Cornwall argued, indeed, that
unionized industrial economies were inherently inflation-prone and that
for the Anglo-Saxon countries, deep-rooted social conflict between labor
and capital rendered any short-term solution impossible. There is much to
be said for the view that inflexibility on the supply side of the labor
market arising from the bargaining strategies of strong trade unions
largely explains the failure to adjust to the oil shocks of the 1970s.

Specifically, evidence that the functioning of wages has been a crucial
element in the growth of unemployment is strong. An analysis by the
OECD (1989a) related the change in national aggregate unemployment
between 1973 and 1987, for 16 industrialized economies, to a measure of
wage rigidity in those countries.

Wage rigidity consists of a lack of correlation between movements in
wages and movements in unemployment; wage flexibility is its opposite.
The outcome of this analysis, reproduced in Figure 5.2, indicates a strong
cross-national relationship between wage rigidity and change in aggregate unemployment. The United Kingdom is in the top right corner of the
chart, indicating its exceptionally high level of wage rigidity over the
period, coupled with an exceptionally large rise in unemployment.

A more detailed analysis of the cross-national OECD database
(Layard, Nickell, & Jackman, 1991) confirms the conclusion that wage
rigidity is the most important factor so far identified in explaining
national aggregate unemployment. (The second explanatory factor identified by this study—the nature of the benefit system—is discussed in the
next section.)

The notion of wage rigidity suggests that there is a lack of responsiveness or adaptability to changing pressures or to shocks from outside
the economy. In the period of low unemployment, this lack of responsiveness was unimportant because a highly secure environment was created,
with a sellers' market for goods and services, a substantial degree of trade
protection, and steady growth under conditions of relatively low wage
expectations. As external conditions became less favorable (because of the
post-1971 international financial crisis, the post-1973 oil shock, etc.), wage
flexibility became more important as a means of adaptation; simultaneously, however, rising wage expectations were adding to pressures
rather than helping with adaptation. The persistence of high unemploy-

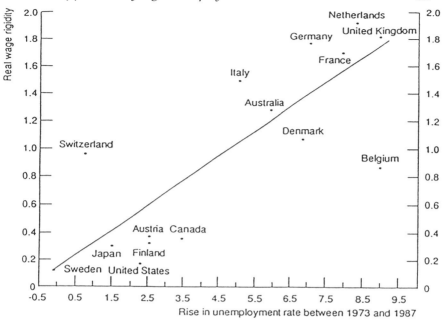

The figure is reproduced from: OECD, Economies in Transition , 1989, Diagram 2.6 (q.v. for further details and definitions).
Note that the unemployment measure is change in the percentage rate between 1973 and 1987.

Figure 5.2. Real wage rigidity and unemployment

ment during the 1980s may be explained as a continuing, entrenched, and perhaps intensified resistance of wages to respond to unemployment.

Such a situation could be expected to make employers reluctant to recruit additional labor, and would also adversely affect the ability of small businesses to become established. Hence wage rigidity helps to explain reduced outflows and increased durations of unemployment.

Although detailed research has demonstrated that wage rigidity is an important explanatory factor, it is difficult to say how important it is in comparison with other factors, including other kinds of rigidity. Research has tended to concentrate on wage rigidity, perhaps because wages are comparatively easy to measure and because the idea that wages in some way play a central role fits neatly with economic theory. Other explanatory factors that are less likely to interest economists may have been overlooked. Also, it may be that measures of wage rigidity are in part a proxy for other kinds of rigidity, such as lack of geographical mobility among the labor force. In fact, geographical immobility is likely to be an important factor for older workers, although it is less plausible as a factor in youth unemployment. However, the idea that differences in geographical mobility might explain national differences in unemployment rates has not been adequately tested.

A range of other types of inflexibility has been mentioned in the literature, such as low wage differentials, high nonwage labor costs, strong employment protection regulations, and labor legislation that hampers flexible contracting. These are static features, whereas wage rigidity is a description of the dynamics of the market. It is hard to see how static features such as employment protection regulations could explain why unemployment fell in some countries but not in others after the initial rise. However, these static features could in turn help to explain wage rigidity itself. There is no good evidence that any of these factors do have force in helping to explain cross-national differences in unemployment rates. Some of the low-unemployment countries certainly have low wage differentials, high nonwage labor costs, and strong employment protection legislation (*Sweden, Japan*). In the present state of knowledge, therefore, wage rigidity is the most important factor yet identified as explaining differences among countries in unemployment rates.

Explanations of youth unemployment

A particular reason for the relatively high rate of youth unemployment is the generational crowding associated with the increased size of the youth cohorts resulting from the postwar baby boom. A comparative study by the OECD (1986, pp. 106–133) shows that the bulge in the youth cohort occurred in different countries at different times. In *North America, Ireland, New Zealand*, and *Australia*, it appeared during the 1960s and persisted until 1980. In *Belgium, Finland, France, the Netherlands, Norway*, and *Sweden* it began as early as 1960 and was less marked and of short duration. In *Austria, Germany, Italy, Spain*, and the *United Kingdom*, the bulge was even more moderate, spread over a longer time period, and more noticeable after 1970. Finally, in *Australia* and *Japan* the baby boom was more recent, and its effects had not yet been felt by the mid-1980s.

From this summary, it is clear that in many of the high-unemployment countries, the increase in the relative size of the youth cohort occurred well before the big rise in unemployment in the second half of the 1970s. The OECD's comparative research shows that economic opportunities are reduced for members of large youth cohorts; this is reflected both in a decline in relative youth earnings and in an increase in unemployment, and there is, in addition, a trade-off between these two effects.

Thus, generational crowding has had an influence in increasing the level of youth unemployment at an earlier period, but it hardly helps to account for the rising levels of youth unemployment in high-unemployment countries from the late 1970s onward.

To some extent, the high rate of youth unemployment no doubt reflects the period of experimentation associated with the transition from school to work. However, it would be wrong to argue from this that it has little impact or imposes few costs on the young people concerned. There is, in fact, a high rate of job turnover among young people and, probably associated with this, a high rate of recurrent unemployment. The implication is that a considerable proportion of young people experience multiple spells of unemployment, in addition to the substantial proportion who experience at least one long spell (OECD, 1985b, pp. 99–119).

Strong evidence indicates that the pattern of youth employment is related to pay structures. A number of studies (e.g., Wells, 1983) have suggested that low youth pay relative to adult pay improves youth access to jobs and training. However, detailed cross-national research suggests that low youth pay may not in itself be effective unless it is grounded in an appropriate system of training and qualification.

In a study of six European countries, Marsden and Ryan (1986) used data about the youth share of employment in each of a number of industries, the adult pay, and the youth pay relative to adult pay in those same industries. They found a strong relationship in all six countries between the level of adult pay and the share of youth employment, such that youth employment tended to be highest in industries where adult pay was lowest.

In three of the countries studied—*West Germany*, the *United Kingdom*, and the *Netherlands*—they found in addition a relationship between youth pay relative to adults and the youth share of employment, such that the share of youth employment was highest in industries where the ratio between youth and adult pay was lowest. In the remaining three countries studied—*Belgium*, *France*, and *Italy*—there was no significant relationship of this kind. On the basis of a later analysis (Marsden & Ryan, 1990) the same authors modified the conclusion that there was a sharp distinction between countries where relative youth pay did and did not determine the employment share of young people. They concluded, instead, that relative youth pay had some importance in all countries studied, but had more importance in some than in others.

Marsden and Ryan explain these findings by assuming that in high-wage sectors, the wage structure is determined by rules that specify a rate for a particular job irrespective of the personal attributes of the person filling it. Firms in the high-wage sector are therefore unlikely to hire young workers, because there are experienced applicants (attracted by the high pay) and inexperienced applicants are unlikely to do the job as well. In the low-wage sectors, by contrast, either the rate for the job is low or the firm is free to pay whatever it finds appropriate. Adult workers will find such jobs less attractive, but young workers will be viewed more favorably by employers faced with a shortage of adult applicants. So far, this explains the general relationship between adult pay and the youth share of employment.

The second finding suggests that in some countries, but not in others, youth relative pay is also related to the youth share of employment—in these countries, the youth share could apparently be increased if youth pay were reduced. The interesting question is why this should apply in certain countries only. In seeking an explanation, it is useful to distinguish between occupational and internal labor markets. According to Marsden and Ryan (1990):

> Occupational markets encourage the mobility of qualified workers among employers and work best with a system of standardised vocational qualifications. . . . Internal markets are organised around particular work-places or employers; jobs above entry level are filled by internal promotion, skills are learned mostly as part of employment, and qualifications are of secondary importance. (p. 352)

Internal markets play a larger role in France and Italy than in Britain or West Germany. This can be seen, for example, in a contrast between training arrangements in the two pairs of countries.

Occupational markets rely on transferable vocational qualifications obtained at the workplace, such as apprenticeship (traditionally widespread in Britain and West Germany), and internal markets upon informal upgrade training (far more common in France and Italy). In countries oriented toward occupational labor markets, such as the United Kingdom and West Germany, youth pay is on average 57 to 58 percent of adult pay, whereas in countries such as France and Italy (oriented toward internal labor markets) youth pay is between 76 and 82 percent of adult pay. That is because in the occupational labor markets, youth pay has been negotiated downward on the understanding that the employer provides training leading to a transferable qualification.

The youth share of employment apparently is more sensitive to the level of youth pay in countries where the occupational labor market is more dominant. Although it is not entirely clear why this should be so, it points to the importance of the distinction between the two types of arrangements.

Barriers to entry of youth into employment tend to be highest in countries where internal labor markets are dominant, such as France and Italy, which have high ratios of youth to adult unemployment (see Table 5.3). Youth unemployment is lowest in West Germany and other German-speaking countries. These have an occupational labor market based on a unique type of apprenticeship system that covers both white- and blue-collar occupations in all branches of the economy, including banking and insurance, public administration, health, personal social service, and retailing as well as industry (Casey, 1986, from which the following account is also taken).

Apprenticeship in West Germany comprises training in a job skill and socialization into the world of work. Because the syllabus is determined and the examinations conducted externally to the enterprise, there is an emphasis on more general skills. Apprenticeship training is funded by the enterprise. The incentive to enterprises to take on apprentices is that they only have to pay them a fraction of the rate paid to a qualified adult worker. According to Casey, the rate of pay for a third-year apprentice in West Germany is about one-third that of a qualified adult worker. This is considerably lower than the figure quoted earlier from Marsden and Ryan (1986), which refers to the average rate of pay for all youth workers as a percentage of the average for adults. Although the proportion of apprentices who stay with the firm after qualifying is not particularly high, it has been shown that the policy of enterprises is rational if understood as based on investment in human capital. Problems in the transition from apprenticeship to employment are minimized by the possession of a generally recognized qualification.

There is little doubt that this apprenticeship system has been the main instrument in maintaining youth unemployment in Germany at a much lower level than in other countries. Of course, starting from a different institutional base, other countries would encounter substantial problems in moving toward the German system.

Economic explanations of wage rigidity

The existence of wage rigidity over long periods, and alongside persistent high levels of unemployment, poses a profound theoretical challenge to classical and neoclassical theories. How can such long-term wage rigidity be reconciled with the underlying assumptions of individual agents acting competitively in the labor market?

Considerable promise of an explanation is offered, at first sight, by the insider-outsider theory (Lindbeck & Snower, 1988) and the efficiency wage theory (Akerlof, 1982; Lindbeck & Snower, 1985). Both of these pay particular attention to employers' recruitment and turnover costs. In the insider-outsider theory, it is the capacity of existing workers (the insiders) to inflict increased turnover and recruitment costs on employers that permits them to extract a rent or premium and to prevent employers from replacing them with lower-cost outsiders. In the efficiency wage theory, it is the employer who takes the initiative in keeping wages high, to reduce labor turnover and, more generally, to retain effective and well-motivated workers. (The theory was partially anticipated in Adam Smith's *Wealth of Nations*, where he points out the advantages of paying high wages.)

Both the insider-outsider theory and the efficiency wage theory permit nonclearing labor markets, even though the actors in the labor market behave rationally and competitively. However, neither provides a convincing account of the historical course of unemployment in the United Kingdom, or of the reasons that U. K. unemployment should be particularly deep and prolonged. For example, under conditions where labor supply becomes more plentiful (including the availability of many experienced and skilled workers), labor turnover costs should fall and employer power should increase: This should bring down the insider rent or the efficiency wage, leading to relatively rapid adaptation. Yet, in the United Kingdom in the early 1980s, average real wages increased at an unprecedented rate despite the existence of mass unemployment. One would have to assume that, in the early 1980s, either insider militancy increased—which would be at variance with available indicators of industrial conflict—or (more plausibly) employers began placing a higher valuation on their existing employees. The underlying explanation of events, therefore, once more shifts outside the domain of formal economic theory. A recent analysis of cross-national data (Holmlund, 1991) also suggests that existing evidence provides very poor support for insider-outsider or wage efficiency theory.

An alternative path to economic explanation of wage rigidity and unemployment is through the effects of the system of unemployment benefits and income support. One line of argument (see Minford, Davies, Peel, & Sprague, 1983) is to suppose that state benefits set the "floor" for wages, effectively creating a minimum wage regime. So, as benefits increase, lower-paid jobs are "squeezed out" and available employment (especially for less-skilled workers) is reduced. Alternatively, wage rigidity can be attributed to unemployed people themselves, via some version of job search theory: Jobs are not sought if their wages are too close to state benefit levels.

Evidence from comparative analysis of social security systems and unemployment rates is not entirely clear-cut. The OECD has recently published the results of a comparative study of this kind covering 17 industrialized countries (OECD, 1991, pp. 199–236). The study is based on a complex measure of the "replacement rate"—the proportion of earnings replaced by social security payments—that takes account of the different payments made to people in different family circumstances and at different durations of the spell of unemployment. Findings show no correlation between a country's total unemployment rate and replacement rate (for 1987). Some countries with high unemployment, such as the *United Kingdom* and *Ireland*, have low replacement rates; other countries with average or low unemployment—*Denmark, Finland, Germany,* and *Sweden*—have high replacement rates.

A weakness of this analysis is the use of an average replacement rate when in practice the benefit system will have sharply contrasting effects on different people depending on their particular circumstances. More detailed analysis within the same study does show a weak relationship between some aspects of the social security system and the *structure* of unemployment. The share of long-term unemployment in total unemployment is weakly related to the ratio of the long-term to the average replacement rate indicator: This suggests that the structure of benefits paid over time may influence average durations of unemployment. Also, the share of women in long-term unemployment is related to whether benefits are payable to an unemployed married woman with a husband at work. These findings suggest that social security systems have certain highly specific effects, especially with regard to married women. More concrete evidence of such effects is quoted later.

A further analysis of the OECD database (Layard et al., 1991) finds that open-ended benefit systems are (along with wage rigidity) a major explanation of differences among countries in unemployment rates. In Sweden, for example, where benefit ends after a year, the unemployment rate is low.

For aggregate data, the average rate at which people leave unemployment tends to decrease with the duration of unemployment, but it seems that this is largely or entirely because these data lump together distinct groups of people whose chances of exiting from unemployment differ widely. When these subgroups are considered separately, it seems that the rate of exit remains constant or rises as the duration of unemployment increases. This fits with the findings of studies of the unemployed that show that motivation to find work and job search continue even after long periods of unemployment. However, a number of U.S. studies (summarized in OECD, 1991) have shown that the rate of exit rises as the end of the benefit period approaches. This fits with the finding of the cross-national study by Layard and colleagues (1991). It seems, therefore, that the length of entitlement may be an important factor. It is plausible that systems that provide generous benefits in the early period of unemployment (thus supporting active job search) but reduced benefits later are conducive toward lower levels of long-term unemployment, and so far this is supported by available research.

However, there is no evidence that the *level* of benefits can explain differences in unemployment among countries. This conclusion is strongly supported by historical and other data for the *United Kingdom*. It is true that benefits rose relative to wages in the late 1960s and 1970s, when earnings-related supplements to benefits were available, and this may have been a contributory cause of wage rigidity in the early phase of rising unemployment. But between 1978 and 1988—the period of persistent high unemployment—average benefits for unemployed people fell by about 5 percent in real terms (Atkinson & Micklewright, 1989), whereas average real wages increased by about 40 percent. Furthermore, unemployed people in the United Kingdom appear to have only the weakest adherence to reservation wages, and display considerable persistence in job search and flexibility in accepting low-paid jobs (Daniel, 1990; Narendranathan & Nickell, 1989; White & McRae, 1989). Indeed, according to the econometric analysis of Narendranathan and Nickell, leisure is negatively valued by unemployed men.

Institutional theories of wage rigidity

To give a more convincing account of wage rigidity, it is necessary to take an institutional view of wage fixing. Much of the relevant research is cross-national in perspective (Casey & Bruche, 1982; Bornschier, 1989; Garrett & Lange, 1986; Schmidt, 1987; Therborn, 1986), but the institutional background varies substantially from one country to another: Here the main focus is on the United Kingdom.

One way of summarizing much of the cross-national analysis is in terms of the conceptual continuum of "free-market versus corporatist" systems. (There are various classifications in the literature; we follow that of the OECD, 1989a.) At one extreme are the free-market economies such as Canada, Japan, Switzerland, or the United States, where unions are weak, wage fixing is highly decentralized and left to the marketplace with minimal intervention by the state, and welfare provision is low. At the other extreme are the corporatist economies of the Scandinavian countries and Austria, where wage fixing is highly centralized (for example, through tripartite arrangements involving the state, employers' organizations, and unions) and where welfare systems are well developed. Between these extreme and highly consistent systems (which tend to be underpinned by long-term political consensus) lie the mixed, and to some extent inconsistent, systems characteristic of most of the large countries of Western Europe, including the United Kingdom. An OECD chart (see Figure 5.3) shows that both the free-market and the corporatist economies succeeded in restraining the growth of unemployment during the period 1973–1987, whereas the intermediate and less consistent economies, including that of the United Kingdom, experienced large increases in unemployment.

Therborn's notion (1986) of institutional prioritization of full employment provides an alternative way of thinking about these issues. In that view, what the free-market and corporatist countries had in common was that they made achieving full employment their first priority. In pursuit of that priority, they were able to make the various institutions work together in a consistent way.

The notion of some inconsistency, or internal conflict, between free-market forces and collectivist, welfare-oriented aspirations is fruitful in explaining the British case. As they affect wage fixing, U.K. institutions are contradictory to the point of chaos. The overall tendency has been toward increasing decentralization and fragmentation. This, however, is far from creating a "free-market" structure like that in the United States or Japan, because of two structural factors. First, trade-union membership remains high (still above 40 percent nationally) and is particularly high in the public sector and the large-firm market sector; moreover, public appreciation or acceptance of trade unions, after dipping at the start of the Thatcher decade, has apparently recovered and is at a remarkably high level (see Edwards & Bain, 1988; Gallie, Penn, & Rose, in press). Second, employment in the market sector is highly concentrated in large companies, which accordingly enjoy great labour-market power. The fragmentation and decentralization of wage fixing are, therefore, combined with structural conditions that encourage both employers and trade unions to adopt strategies that make use of power rather than obey market forces. Recent government policies to reduce trade-union power have (perhaps unintentionally) strengthened the labor-market power base of large corpo-

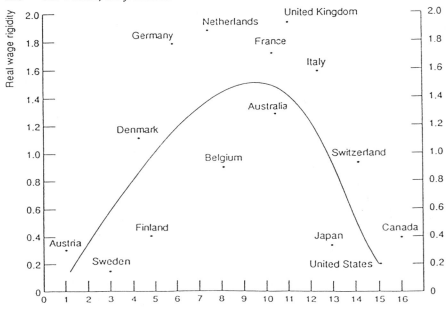

Figure 5.3.   Real wage rigidity and degree of corporatism

rations, which is a very different matter from creating free-market conditions.

Our own interpretation of wage rigidity in the United Kingdom
(White, 1991) rests particularly upon an historical interpretation of institutional power-based strategies. These can be seen as passing through three
phases, corresponding to the three phases of postwar labor market history
outlined in the first part of this chapter.

During the period of low unemployment, worker aspirations were
initially satisfied by the great increase in job security and continuity of
employment, coupled with slowly but steadily rising standards of living.
During this time, trade unions increased their membership and strengthened their local organization. During the 1960s, conflictual pressures
began to develop as unions and local workforces began to use their power
to attempt to extract larger shares, while firms were drawn toward capital-
deepening investment (see Freeman & Soete, 1987; Rothwell & Zegveld,
1979). Threats to worker security (emerging as a result of these changes)
led to further militancy. At the same time, manufacturing companies
moved towards the use of incentive payment systems on a large scale, and
then toward "productivity bargaining." In the face of union and worker

power, employers developed a habitual reliance on increasing pay to achieve the changes they desired and to minimize conflict.

By the beginning of the 1970s, the second phase of postwar labor-market history was fully established. The internal pressures generated by the first phase, coupled with the severe external shocks of 1971 and 1973, drove inflation rapidly upward, leading both Conservative and Labour governments to impose progressively more stringent wage controls. Significantly, employers gave little support to government wage policies. Instead, government became the common opponent of both employers and unions, which colluded to evade the restrictions. With rising unemployment, union power was ebbing, and the period of open industrial conflict was drawing to a close. Employers were able to consider the possibility of new strategies in which the (at least passive) cooperation of unions could be assumed.

With the advent of the Thatcher government and the second oil shock of 1979, followed by the deep economic recession of 1980, the third phase—that of persistent high unemployment—began. The key to the strategies of large companies in this situation was the need to raise productivity rapidly and to restore profitability. Technological change was one element in this but was less attractive than in other industrial nations, because there was an easier path in the United Kingdom.

The era of low unemployment and high union power, followed by the stagnation of the 1970s, had left behind a large surplus of underemployed workers and subefficient working practices. Rather simple methods of work intensification, coupled with selective site closures, redundancy programs, and reduction of recruitment, were able to achieve increases of productivity on a hitherto unparalleled scale (Haskel & Kay, 1990; Metcalf, 1989).

Unions almost everywhere cooperated with these programs of workforce reduction. In essence, the leading companies continued the tradition of incentive payments and productivity bargaining to raise earnings in compensation for reduced workforces, more intensive working, more efficient practices, and acceptance of new technology. Evidence of these changes can be found especially in the Workplace Industrial Relations Survey of 1984 (Daniel, 1987; Millward & Stevens, 1986), in analyses from the CBI Pay Databank (Confederation of British Industry, 1988; Ingram, 1991), and in various smaller-scale surveys and case-study researches (for sources, see White, 1991). Ingram shows that workforce reductions were associated with *higher* pay settlements, although Blanchflower, Oswald, and Millward (1991) show that they were also associated with a *higher* density of trade unionism.

Inherent in this conception of wage rigidity in the recent period is the notion of wage leadership. High-wage strategies adopted by leading, dominant employers are followed by far greater numbers of other firms, which do not necessarily reap the same benefits (see Millward & Stevens, 1986, Tables 9.17, 9.18, for detailed evidence of the importance of wage comparisons in U.K. bargaining). Far from weakening the leading employers, wage leadership creates adverse pressures on smaller competitors and imposes entry costs on potential competitors (Jacquemin, 1987).

This analysis has led us to firm conclusions about the origins of persistently high unemployment in the United Kingdom. We first of all accept the central importance of wage rigidity in the British case. Further, we agree with those (such as Brittan or Cornwall) who have attributed a particularly important role to trade-union power in the development of the wage inflation of the late 1960s and 1970s. However, too little attention has been paid in writings on wage rigidity to the evolution of employers' strategies during that period. In the 1980s, employers' wage strategies superseded those of unions as the most important single influence upon wage rigidity in the United Kingdom, even though the existence, character, and policies of unions remained important.

No doubt a detailed account of the origins of wage rigidity in other countries would vary substantially from the one we have developed for the United Kingdom. However, we would suggest that the explanation would still be found in institutional structures.

"Hysteresis" and state labor market policies

An earlier section showed that no evidence exists for a link between unemployment and the *level* of welfare benefits. It is now increasingly recognized that the level of benefits is only one of a wide range of labor-market parameters established by state policy. Even if benefit *levels* explain rather little about unemployment, the structure of benefit systems (such as the way they deal with family units), along with other aspects of labor-market policy, may be important.

A wider framework for considering the objectives of labor market policy is provided by the much-debated notion of "hysteresis." This springs from the assumption in classical economics that there is a "natural" rate of unemployment, which might, for example, be defined as the rate of unemployment at which inflation does not accelerate. Alternatively, it might be defined as the rate of unemployment at which real wages grow in line with productivity.

The idea of hysteresis is that if unemployment remains high, then the downward pressure that high rates of unemployment exert on wages tends to decline over time. In other words, the "natural" rate of unemployment no longer remains constant, but moves upward toward the prevailing rate. To the extent that this happens, it casts doubt on the original assumption that there is such a thing as a "natural" rate of unemployment.

The notion of hysteresis suggests that there is a historical asymmetry between the conditions of the labor market before and after the onset of high unemployment. The experience of long-term unemployment, for example, may lead to a deterioration in skills and work attitudes among some of those affected, and high unemployment provides employers with a simple screening device when deciding whom to employ. Hysteresis may be useful as a supplement to more fundamental explanations of unemployment, such as wage rigidity: It points toward the potential importance of second-round effects that may serve to perpetuate unemployment, unless there are countervailing influences. Such second-round effects may be either intensified or counteracted by state labor-market policies.

The design of the benefit system is a case in point. There are strong indications from cohort studies of the unemployed in the United Kingdom that the nature of the benefit system is an important factor leading women to give up their jobs. In the early 1980s, unemployment benefit was payable for up to 12 months, but when it expired an unemployed person became eligible for supplementary benefit. Unemployment benefit was payable to a married man regardless of his wife's earnings. By contrast, a wife's earnings were deducted from the value of supplementary benefit. The system of earnings deductions meant that unless she earned more than her husband's supplementary benefit, a wife received no financial gain from earning more than £4 a week.

When the unemployed were compared in terms of the type of benefit they were receiving, it was clear that wives were much more likely to leave employment when their husbands were on supplementary benefit than when they were on unemployment benefit (Moylan, Miller, & Davies, 1984, pp. 128–130). A faint echo of this type of effect was caught by the OECD's comparative analysis of social security in relation to unemployment referred to earlier (OECD, 1991). The U.K. results show that the design of the welfare system reinforced the tendency for unemployment to be concentrated in households and for the unemployed to become increasingly isolated from contact with the labor market as the duration of unemployment increases.

Layard and Nickell (1987) have drawn a distinction between labor market policies that are chiefly oriented toward income support for unemployed people and those that are oriented toward the active re-integration of unemployed people into employment. Policy in the *United Kingdom* is chiefly oriented toward welfare, whereas *Sweden* is taken as the leading example of more active labor-market policy. It is argued that the balance of policies developed in the United Kingdom tends to lead to large proportions of long-term unemployment.

The limitation of this type of explanation, once again, is that national labor-market policies may be constrained by more fundamental institutional characteristics. In Sweden, for example, a key role has been played by schemes for countercyclical temporary employment in the public sector (see Standing, 1988). Such employment creation is more easily introduced in a country with a low level of wage rigidity than in the United Kingdom: Indeed, the main scheme of this type introduced in the United Kingdom, the Community Programme, was constrained by problems of wages.

Nevertheless, despite the constraints of wage rigidity, there may be considerable scope for more effective labor-market policies by the state, to counteract hysteresis effects. For example, increasing evidence indicates that the intensive interviewing and counseling of unemployed people can be effective in reducing unemployment (and not just in driving people out of the labor market). An evaluation of labor-market policy in Sweden (Bjösklund, 1991) supports this conclusion.

A study by Disney et al. and colleagues (1992) using time series aggregate data shows that in Britain the Restart Programme (systematic interviewing and counseling of unemployed people at six-month intervals) had an effect in reducing unemployment; another study by White and Lakey (1992) using cross-sectional sample survey data also shows a similar effect. The OECD (1991, p. 215) quotes studies from a number of countries that suggest that higher levels of contact with unemployed people shorten unemployment durations. A number of U.S. studies, in particular, have shown (on the basis of random-assignment experiments) that "intensified counseling" has a measurable effect. Payne (1990) used survey data to suggest that an adult training program had positive effects upon the employment and wages of unemployed participants.

The Significance of the Distribution of Unemployment

In the first part, we drew attention to the uneven distribution of unemployment across social groups. Attempts to understand the significance of this distribution may be of two kinds. They may take the aggregate level of unemployment as given, and seek to explain why unemployment is distributed across groups in a particular way. Alternatively, they may start from the assumption that some of the causes of high unemployment are connected with the particular situation of specific groups in the labor market. To the extent that this second approach has value, analysis of aggregate statistics cannot provide a full explanation of persisting high unemployment. The explanations do not lie in the general structures or conditions of the labor market; instead, the situations of specific groups make a particular contribution to the growth of unemployment, and hence help to explain it.

An earlier section has already considered the special position of young people. This section goes on to consider some other groups, concentrating for the most part on evidence from the United Kingdom. Because most research has tended to use macroeconomic techniques to analyze aggregate unemployment, our understanding of the distribution of unemployment currently is based on comparatively weak evidence.

Employment shelters

Theories of labor-market segmentation provide one useful perspective on the differentiation of unemployment. The theory of "employment shelters" advanced by Ashton (1986) is an attempt to establish a link between precarious employment and the distribution of unemployment. Ashton states that "labour market shelters are analytically distinct from segments but are empirically-related features of the labour market" (p. 54). The distribution of unemployment is said to depend upon the degree of shelter from the effects of high unemployment provided by various segments of the labor market.

Among the institutions that create shelters are the state or public sector, market-sector employers with the power to control markets, and powerful trade unions or professional organizations. Social groups lacking access to any shelters tend to become marginalized in the secondary sector. Because shelters reduce the impact of unemployment in many parts of the labor market, a larger share of the burden of unemployment must be carried by those in unprotected positions, such as the secondary sector.

This explanation accounts for some significant variations in unemployment in the short to medium term. For instance, unemployment inflow rates have been disproportionately large from small firms: from construction, from the hotel and catering industry, from retailing, and from the whole of the market sector by comparison with the public sector (Daniel, 1990). Similar observations can be made about youth labor markets (White & McRae, 1989). However, high inflow rates should not be equated with high unemployment.

The hotel and catering industry has high turnover rates, but employment in this industry has been rapidly growing and reemployment prospects for experienced staff are good. Conversely, groups with low or average inflow rates to unemployment (e.g., those from the steel industry or textiles, or disabled workers who often literally come from "sheltered employment") have been found heavily concentrated in long-term unemployment (White, 1983).

This last point, further, illustrates the fact that a sheltered position, *which depends on the power of others* (e.g., employers), may in reality be a vulnerable one. Workers currently appearing to be sheltered by large employers may be made redundant in the next rationalization program. In addition, the importance of shelters in fact proves less impressive than the concept. Within the inflow to unemployment, two in three come from the large-firm sector or the public sector: Hence it is hard to claim that more than one in three comes from the secondary sector (Daniel, 1990). Similarly, the majority of workers in long-term unemployment have come from the large-firm sector or the public sector (White, 1983; White & McRae, 1989).

An unskilled underclass detached from the labor market

An alternative, influential view of unemployment connects it with skill or capacity. Unemployment is seen as allocated to those who fall below some cutoff point in the lower tail of the skill/capacity distribution. It also is argued that the cutoff point has been or will be moving upward, because of technical advancement, market sophistication, and other causes. Dore (1987) has claimed that unemployment will inevitably increase and become entrenched because of the difficulty of reconciling the falling marginal value of low-skilled labor in high-technology societies with the rising welfare minimum associated with societal affluence. Those falling below the skill level required for entry into employment will increasingly form an excluded underclass.

This kind of explanation of the growth of unemployment can be connected with wider debate, mainly in the United States, focused on the idea that there is a growing underclass of people concentrated in poor neighborhoods where public services and community networks have broken down and where rates of crime are high and rising (see Murray, 1984; Wilson, 1987).

It is suggested that these people are poor, that they lack education and marketable skills, that they are in work at best only intermittently, that they tend not to form stable family relationships (many are single mothers or fathers who have declined to take responsibility for their children), that they live in poor housing or are homeless, and that they often use illicit drugs. They are said to be an underclass because they are not integrated into the economic and social structure and have little stake in a society of which they are not full citizens.

However, this account of the idea of an underclass goes well beyond a definition to incorporate a whole set of interconnected explanations. At a minimum, the idea of an underclass is a counterpart to the modern idea of social class. The modern idea of social class, as distinct from older conceptions of rank, station, blood, and breeding, derives from Marx, who emphasized the relationship with the mode of production as the source of class distinctions. The array of social classes tends to approximate toward a hierarchy in wholly industrial or postindustrial societies, while at the same time different classes have different kinds of relationship with productive employment. The underclass are those who fall outside this class schema, because they belong to family units that have no stable relationship with legitimate gainful employment.

Whether there is a growing underclass in this sense in the United Kingdom and other high-unemployment countries is a question that has not yet been adequately researched. One question is whether there is among the unemployed (in the recent conditions of persistent high unemployment) a group of people who over long periods have become detached from the labor market. Members of such a group would tend to have had low skills initially, and over a period of increasing detachment from the labor market their skills would tend to erode and to become less appropriate to current job requirements. A separate question—well outside the scope of this chapter—is whether any such group is developing a specific culture, attitudes, and patterns of behavior that not only make them less employable but also bring them into conflict with legitimate institutions.

As already noted, research in the United Kingdom and elsewhere has so far failed to identify such a separate group among the unemployed. Job seeking and motivation to find work tend to be maintained even after long durations of unemployment, and the rate of exit from unemployment does not reduce with duration when the analysis is based on disaggregated data. However, there is a need for more research to be carried out well after the onset of persistent high unemployment.

There is, however, evidence for the United Kingdom that the unemployed tend to become isolated from contact with people in employment. The data are from the Social Change and Economic Life Initiative (SCELI), which included interviews in 1986–1987 with unemployed, employed, and inactive people in six British localities. (For a more detailed description, see Gallie, 1992, which is also the source of the following summary.) The results show that the unemployed were less likely than the employed to engage in leisure activities with people outside their own households. As the duration of unemployment increases, the pattern of sociability declines and then increases again, particularly among women. This suggests that there may be some process of adaptation to unemployment among the long-term unemployed. Women are more likely to make this adaptation than men, perhaps because of their distinctive patterns of sociability (which rely more heavily on neighborly visiting) and because of a lower stigma attached to women being without work.

As well as being less sociable, the unemployed also have social networks different from those of the employed. The social networks of those in employment consist primarily of others in employment, whereas among the unemployed, but particularly among unemployed men, contact with people in employment sharply declines to a low level as the duration of unemployment increases. Unemployed people, in Gallie's (1992) words:

> found themselves increasingly cut off from an effective support system that could help them meet financial difficulties, that could give psychological support and that could provide the information about jobs that was needed if people were to escape from the condition of unemployment. Changes in the pattern of sociability, then, increasingly helped to reinforce their exclusion from the labour market. (p.170)

There is some evidence to support the theory that changes in economic structure will encourage the development of an unskilled underclass: for example, the growing mass of evidence that new technology based upon computers and microelectronics requires more-skilled rather than less-skilled workers (Daniel, 1987; Gallie, 1988; Northcott & Walling, 1988). There has been a substantial decline in the number and proportion of low-skilled, routine jobs in the British economy as a whole, and this is expected to continue (Institute for Employment Research, 1989). These observations, however, are insufficient to account for more than a small proportion of the growth of unemployment. In the 1980s skilled manual workers and routine white-collar (mainly female) workers constituted a substantial proportion of the inflow to unemployment and of subsequent long-term unemployment. Also, work-history data showed that many supposedly unskilled workers in long-term unemployment had been downwardly mobile from former skilled employment (White, 1983). As to the specifically technological part of the explanation, the indications are that advanced new technology has so far had little displacement effect upon jobs in the United Kingdom (Daniel, 1987; Northcott & Walling, 1988).

To summarize the evidence on the idea of an underclass and its relevance to the growth of unemployment, it is possible, though not so far established, that a consequence of persistent high unemployment is the creation of an underclass increasingly detached from the labor market, but if so the existence of such an underclass cannot be an important cause of continuing high unemployment: This is because the underclass would be a small proportion of those so far affected by high unemployment and could not have had a dominant influence on the labor market.

Education and training

Whether education is considered as a factor deciding the distribution of unemployment among groups or a factor influencing the total amount of unemployment depends on which view is taken about the function of education in the economy. Very broadly, there are two types of theory. The first type of theory believes that education enhances the skills needed in production, and therefore directly influences economic activity and social welfare. This concept has been developed as "human capital theory" by Becker (1964) and others. The second type of theory puts forward the idea that education has an allocative function: It is used as a criterion to decide which individuals should do which jobs, but not necessarily because the education itself enhances their productivity. Econometric studies seem to support the view that educational attainment is a variable influencing economic performance, but the results of such studies are open to more than one interpretation (OECD, 1989b, pp. 47–93). There is no need to choose between the human capital theory and the allocative theory of education. A reasonable view is that educational attainment both increases the potential for economic growth and determines the distribution of well-being from growth.

The OECD has collected data on the relation between unemployment rate and level of educational attainment for 14 countries (OECD, 1989b, pp. 47–93). For most countries, there is a fairly strong tendency for higher levels of educational attainment to be associated with lower levels of unemployment. The largest differences in the unemployment rate are between the least educated and everyone else, and this applies to countries with widely different systems of education and training. Assuming that education has a more than allocative function, these findings imply that the greatest change in unemployment rates would be brought about by improving the attainment of the least educated.

When education is plotted against unemployment within age groups, the results show that the importance of educational attainment as a determinant of unemployment is greatest for the young. The probable reason is that educational qualifications are the only indicator available about a young person, whereas information about job experience and performance is available for older people.

The OECD was also able to analyze time-series data for six countries. The results suggest that through the period of rising unemployment, educational attainment became a more important factor in determining the rate of unemployment. This may be because employers became more selective as unemployment rose. It may also be due to the progressive disappearance of jobs requiring only minimal levels of attainment, and this of course relates to the earlier discussion about the possibility of a growing underclass.

For the *United Kingdom*, the growing disadvantage of nonqualification within the youth labour market in the late 1970s and early 1980s has been demonstrated by Payne and Payne (1985). At the same time as unemployment was rising, however, the proportion of nonqualification among school-leavers was falling. Comparing samples of long-term unemployed young people in 1980 and 1984, White and McRae (1989) found that the proportions who had no educational qualifications had decreased over the period. The same source also showed that, by 1984, the inflow to long-term unemployment among 18 to 24-year-olds differed little in terms of nonqualification from the same age group in employment, controlling for occupational level. Nonqualification, however, and level of qualification, had a substantial effect upon the outflow, with qualifications increasing the probability of moving back into employment. These findings could be taken to suggest that qualification has played a purely allocative role.

However, recent econometric studies support the idea that education has a role in reducing the overall level of unemployment. A recent analysis by Jackman, Layard, and Savouri (1990) has attempted to link differential rates of unemployment—which they term "mismatch"—to the formation of wage barriers. Although unemployment is seen as initially arising from more fundamental imbalances or shocks, they see mismatch as affecting the long-run level of unemployment through subsequent slowing of adaptation, and calculate that its contribution to U.K. unemployment may be around one-third. The main substantive idea used in this analysis is that of "entry costs." As employment in one section (industry, occupation, etc.) decreases and another increases, the labor market can only clear through mobility, but this may be obstructed if the entry costs (such as training or relocation) are high.

The postwar period, as a whole, has been one in which the higher occupations (managerial, administrative, technical, scientific, and professional) have expanded greatly in the United Kingdom, while manual occupations have contracted. In the earlier part of the postwar period, this structural change created substantial opportunities for upward social mobility (Goldthorpe, Llewellyn, & Payne, 1980). But entry into white-collar occupations has become increasingly controlled by criteria of qualifications. Indeed, even at the time of the 1972 Oxford Mobility Studies, the probability of a man entering white-collar employment, given educational qualifications, was more than three times greater than that of a man without educational qualifications, when both had fathers from white-collar occupations (Heath, 1981). Even during the period of rising and high unemployment, white-collar occupations and especially higher white-collar occupations have continued to expand. But lack of educational qualifications among manual workers has meant that entry cost barriers obstructing upward mobility (except perhaps through the narrow entrances of supervisory jobs or self-employment) have been high.

The conclusion of such an analysis, then, is that the disadvantage of manual workers with regard to unemployment does not lie in personal lack of skills and capacities (such as might be reflected in low productivity) but rather in a lack of the educational attainments that enhance mobility (especially upward mobility) through reducing training costs. Thus education ceases to be simply a personal characteristic and takes on the role of a structural variable with the power to enter into explanations of long-term developments.

Low average levels of qualification reduce the overall adaptability of the labor force in the face of economic change, contribute to wage rigidity through mismatch, and hence increase and sustain aggregate unemployment. A low average educational level also may have been an influence or constraint upon the choice of strategies adopted by employers, as previously discussed in relation to wage rigidity.

Toward a social class perspective

The foregoing analysis might also be usefully extended by introducing a social class perspective. Historically, forms of education in the *United Kingdom* have been divided sharply along class lines, with resources heavily concentrated into providing routes into and through higher education for the elites. Only in the 1960s were efforts begun to extend the scope of qualifications beyond the elite groups, and these have achieved only a slow rate of advance. Even currently, at least 20 percent of school- leavers can be regarded as effectively unqualified, and 50 percent lack the level of qualification that would facilitate entry into white-collar careers or into advanced vocational training (Hannan, Bovels, van den Berg, & White, 1991). In short, the educational system in the United Kingdom has tended to reflect the preexisting social class structure and hence to retard economic and social adaptation.

A social class interpretation also draws attention to other longer-term historical disadvantages of the working class with regard to unemployment. The main class divisions, as defined by Goldthorpe (1983) and colleagues (1980), are particularly constituted by differences in the nature of the employment relationship. Surveys of unemployment have shown the extent to which entrants have lost their previous employment at extremely short periods of notice (Daniel, 1990). Indeed, it seems that the protections offered under employment law are widely disregarded in the United Kingdom by employers, and unknown to workers in lower positions. Again, the provision of benefits to protect workers against the consequences of illness, or to permit early retirement under the advantageous conditions of occupational pensions, remain considerably more widely distributed among white-collar and especially higher occupations than among manual workers. Ill health has been a common precipitating condition for those in long-term unemployment (White, 1983).

Further, the progressive contraction of manufacturing industry, through technical advance, rising productivity, and the international division of labor, has chiefly affected the job opportunities of manual workers. This has been a natural consequence of the way in which manual work is organized along the lines of narrow tasks closely interdependent with machines.

The design of tasks and jobs in relationship with technology also defines class positions. The worker whose training is confined to a single type of special-purpose machine is likely to be deemed a semiskilled operative, whereas the worker trained to use generic knowledge to control a wide range of machines tends to be regarded as a technician. The scope for mobility in response to technical change, in the two cases, is different. This difference both reflects, and further accentuates, initial differences in the educational preparation of those working in the two positions.

Hence the employment relations and position in the production system of manual workers (and also of the more routine levels of white-collar work) are connected in a straightforward way with their high probability of entering unemployment. The British educational system has been designed to provide workers at this level with an average level of educational qualification, which creates barriers to upward mobility, slows down the process of adaptation (especially in a period when the expansion of employment is chiefly in higher occupations), and can be assumed to contribute toward wage rigidity and hence to aggregate unemployment.

Conclusion

This chapter has selectively reviewed some of the main explanations for high and persisting unemployment that have been advanced by economists, sociologists, and political scientists. It has tested them against the main facts about the historical development of unemployment in the postwar period, its analytical components (especially the relation between flows and durations), and its distribution among social groups.

Since the late 1960s the world economic order has been increasingly turbulent, with an international financial system in almost continuous difficulty, unprecedented variations in the price of energy, and rising expectations of workers in industrial nations leading to new bargaining behavior. The primary causes of unemployment can reasonably be assigned to these pressures and to the incapacity of governments, separately and collectively, to manage them in a way that maintains steady growth. Yet this is barely to be counted an explanation because it fails to show why there has been a remarkable divergence in the 1980s between industrialized nations that have contained unemployment at very low levels and others that have experienced persistent high unemployment. Low-unemployment countries include some free-market economies, where wage fixing is highly decentralized, and some corporatist economies, where wage fixing is highly centralized and social welfare systems are highly developed.

Strong evidence from international comparative research indicates that the central reason for divergence between the two groups of countries is wage rigidity: the failure of wages in the high-unemployment countries to adjust downward quickly to compensate for a sudden increase in aggregate unemployment. However, this account would be incomplete without an explanation of how and why wage rigidity develops in some economies. The United Kingdom has shown an exceptionally high level of wage rigidity coupled with an exceptionally large rise in unemployment. Our analysis of the origins of wage rigidity has therefore concentrated on the British case.

We have argued that explanations of wage rigidity in terms of economic theory (such as the insider-outsider theory or wage efficiency theory) are inadequate. Another line of economic argument, which concentrates on the effects of the social security system, was also shown to be incapable of providing a general explanation, even though social security systems do have relevant specific effects. Instead, we have sought to explain the development of wage rigidity in the United Kingdom in terms of the structure and interactions of labor market institutions and government.

The importance of trade-union and worker power in creating wage pressures has become a preoccupation of much economic analysis. We have argued that this was a historically one-sided account that had become particularly inadequate to handle the observed behavior of wages in the United Kingdom of the 1980s. We have drawn attention to the power of leading employers in the labor market, to their strategies of productivity enhancement through work intensification, and to their learned dependence upon wage incentives to achieve their goals. We have also pointed out that the United Kingdom industrial system, neither free market nor corporatist, was dangerously incoherent: too fragmented for central coordination or control, yet with too much power concentrated in large employers and trade unions for markets to develop according to a fully competitive model. Wage rigidity offers a largely convincing explanation of U.K. unemployment, but only if the roles of both employers and unions in bringing it about are recognized.

Britain has been taken as a case study to illustrate how wage rigidity may be explained by the structure of labor-market institutions. Case studies of other countries would show substantially different structures, but we suggest that the explanation of wage rigidity would still be found in the workings of labor-market institutions.

The concentration of unemployment among young people, manual workers, and people with low educational attainment requires further explanation. We have argued that relatively high youth unemployment arises from an unfavorable combination of wage structures and training arrangements. The apprenticeship system in German-speaking countries has been uniquely successful in overcoming these problems and delivering a low relative rate of youth unemployment. Within this system, young people receive clearly defined training and obtain widely recognized and transferable qualifications while in a job; the incentive to employers to take on apprentices within this framework is that their wages are very low.

We have argued that education and occupation do more than explain the distribution of unemployment among social groups. The reason is that educational and class barriers not only determine the distribution of unemployment, thereby working to the disadvantage of the uneducated and the manual worker, but also reduce the capacity of the economy to adapt, thereby limiting growth and total welfare. A class analysis of unemployment may be capable of integrating a number of explanations: It is particularly valuable in drawing attention to the role of the system of educational qualification in accentuating vertical divisions between occupations and in obstructing the mobility needed for adaptation to economic pressures and shocks.

The idea that there is a growing underclass of people increasingly detached from the labor market is supported by only limited evidence as yet. Any such group is a consequence, not a cause, of the period of persistent high unemployment and is much too small to explain the fundamental changes that have arisen in the functioning of the labor market during this period.

References

Akerlof, G. A. (1982). Labor contracts as partial gift exchange. *Quarterly Journal of Economics, 97*(4), 543–569.

Ashton, D. N. (1986). *Unemployment under capitalism: The sociology of British and American labour markets.* Brighton, UK: Wheatsheaf.

Atkinson, A., & Micklewright, J. (1989). Turning the screw: Benefits for the unemployed 1978–88. In A. Dilnot & I. Walker (Eds.), *The economics of social security.* Oxford: Oxford University Press.

Becker, G. S. (1964). *Human capital: A theoretical and empirical analysis with special reference to education.* New York: Columbia University Press.

Bjösklund, A. (1991). Evaluation of labour market policy in Sweden. In OECD, *Evaluating labour market and social programmes: The state of a complex art* (pp. 73–88). Paris: OECD.

Blanchflower, D., Oswald, M. & Millward, N. (1991). Unionism and employment behaviour. *Economic Journal, 101*(407), 815–834.

Bornschier, V. (1989). Legitimacy and comparative economic success at the core of the world system. *European Sociological Review, 5*(3), 215–230.

Brittan, S. (1975). *Second thoughts on full employment policy.* London: Centre for Policy Studies.

Casey, B. (1986). The dual apprentice system and the recruitment and retention of young persons in West Germany. *British Journal of Industrial Relations, 24*(1), 63–81.

Casey, B., & Bruche, G. (1982). *Work or retirement? Labour market and social policy for older workers in France, Great Britain, the Netherlands, Sweden and the USA.* Aldershot, Hants, England: Gower.

Confederation of British Industry (CBI). (1988). *The structure and processes of pay determination in the private sector.* London: Author.

Cornwall, J. (1983). *The conditions for economic recovery: A post-Keynesian analysis.* Oxford: Martin Robertson.

Daniel, W. W. (1987). *Workplace industrial relations and technical change.* London: Frances Pinter/Policy Studies Institute.

Daniel, W. W. (1990). *The unemployed flow.* London: Policy Studies Institute.

Disney, R., Bellmann, L., Carruth, A., Franz, W., Jackman, Layard, R., Lehmann, H., and Philpott, J. (1992). *Helping the unemployed.* London: Anglo-German Foundation.

Dore, R. (1987). Citizenship and employment in an age of high technology. *British Journal of Industrial Relations, 25*(2), 201–205.

Edwards, P. K., & Bain, G. S. (1988). Why are trade unions becoming more popular? Unions and public opinion in Britain. *British Journal of Industrial Relations, 26*(3), 311–326.

Freeman, C., & Soete, L. (Eds.). (1987). *Technical change and full employment.* Oxford: Basil Blackwell.

Gallie, D. (1988). *Technological change, gender and skill.* (ESRC Working Paper no. 4). Oxford: Nuffield College.

Gallie, D. (1992). Effets individuels et psychologiques du CLD en Grande-Bretagne. In O. Benoit-Guilbot & D. Gallie (Eds.), *Chômeurs de longue durée* (pp. 169–174, chap. 6). Poitiers, France: Actes Sud.

Gallie, D., Penn, R. & Rose, M. (Eds.), (in press). *Social change and trade unions in Britain.* Oxford: Oxford University Press.

Garrett, P., & Lange, P. (1986). Performance in a hostile world. *World Politics, 38,* 517–545.

General Household Survey 1990. (1992). London: HMSO.

Godley, W. (1991, January 11). An old limousine. *New Statesman and Society, 3*(133), 18–21.

Goldthorpe, J. H. (1983). Women and class analysis: In defence of the conventional view. *Sociology 17*(4), 465–488.

Goldthorpe, J. H., et al. in collaboration with C. Llewellyn & C. Payne (1980). *Social mobility and class structure in modern Britain.* Oxford: Clarendon.

Hannan, D., Bovels, B., van den Berg, S., & White, M. (1991). *Early leavers from education and training in Ireland, the Netherlands and the United Kingdom.* Conference paper, workshop on early leavers, June 1991. London: Policy Studies Institute.

Haskel, J. E., & Kay, J. A. (1990). *Productivity in British industry under Mrs. Thatcher* (Working Paper No. 7). London: London Business School, Centre for Business Strategy.

Heath, A. (1981). *Social mobility*. London: Fontana.

Holmlund, B. (1991). *Unemployment persistence and insider-outsider forces in wage determination* (Working Paper No. 92). Paris: OECD.

Hughes, P. (1982, December). Flows on and off the unemployment register. *Employment Gazette, 90*(12), 527–530.

Ingram, P. N. (1991). Changes in working practices in British manufacturing industry in the 1980s: A study of employee concessions made during wage negotiations. *British Journal of Industrial Relations, 29*(1), 1–13.

Institute for Employment Research. (1989). *Review of the economy and employment: Occupational assessment*. Warwick, UK: Author.

Jackman, R., Layard, R., & Savouri, S. (1990). *Labour market mismatch: A framework for thought* (Discussion Paper No.1). London: London School of Economics, Centre for Economic Performance.

Jacquemin, A. (1987). *The new industrial organisation*. Oxford: Clarendon.

Keynes, J. M. (1964). *The general theory of employment, interest and money*. London: Macmillan. (Original work published 1936)

Layard, R., & Nickell, S. (1987). The labour market. In R. Dornsbusch & R. Layard (Eds.), *The performance of the British economy*. Oxford: Oxford University Press.

Layard, R., Nickell, S., & Jackman, R. (1991). *Unemployment, macroeconomic performance and the labour market*. Oxford: Oxford University Press.

Lindbeck, A. and Snower, D. (1985). Explanations of unemployment. *Oxford Review of Economic Policy, 1*(2), 34–59.

Lindbeck, A., & Snower, D. (1988). *The insider-outsider theory of unemployment*. London: MIT Press.

Maddison, A. (1982). *Phases of capitalist development*. Oxford: Oxford University Press.

Marsden, D., & Ryan, P. (1986). Where do young workers work? Youth employment by industry in various European economies. *British Journal of Industrial Relations, 24*(1), 83–102.

Marsden, D., & Ryan, P. (1990). Institutional aspects of youth employment and training policy in Britain. *British Journal of Industrial Relations, 28*(3), 351–369.

Metcalf, D. (1989). Water notes dry up: The impact of the Donovan reform proposals and Thatcherism at work on labour productivity in British manufacturing industry. *British Journal of Industrial Relations, 27*(1), 1–31.

Millward, N., & Stevens, M. (1986). *British workplace industrial relations 1980–1984*. Aldershot, UK: Gower.

Minford, P., with Davies, D., Peel, M., & Sprague, A. (1983). *Unemployment: Cause and cure*. Oxford: Martin Robertson.

Moylan, S., Miller, J., & Davies, R. (1984). *For richer for poorer? DHSS cohort study of unemployed men*. London: Her Majesty's Stationery Office.

Murray, C. (1984). *Losing ground: American social policy 1950–1980*. New York: Basic Books.

Narendranathan, W., & Nickell, S. (1989). Modelling the process of job search. In S. Nickell, W. Narendranathan, J. Stern, & J. Garcia (Eds.), *The nature of unemployment in Britain*. Oxford: Oxford University Press.

Northcott, J., & Walling, A. (1988). *The impact of microelectronics*. London: Policy Studies Institute.

OECD. (1985a). The labour market implications of international migration in selected OECD countries. In OECD, *OECD employment outlook 1985* (pp. 47–63). Paris: Author.

OECD. (1985b). *OECD employment outlook 1985.* Paris: Author.

OECD. (1986). *OECD employment outlook 1986.* Paris: Author.

OECD. (1987). *OECD employment outlook 1987.* Paris: Author.

OECD. (1988). *OECD employment outlook 1988.* Paris: Author.

OECD. (1989a). *Economies in transition.* Paris: Author.

OECD. (1989b). *OECD employment outlook 1989.* Paris: Author.

OECD. (1990a). *OECD economic surveys 1989/90: United Kingdom.* Paris: Author.

OECD. (1990b). *OECD employment outlook 1990.* Paris: Author.

OECD. (1991). *OECD employment outlook 1991.* Paris: Author.

Payne, J. (1990). *Evaluation of adult off-the-job skills training.* Sheffield, UK: Training Agency.

Payne, J., & Payne, C. W. (1985). Youth unemployment 1974–81: The changing importance of age and qualifications. *Quarterly Journal of Social Affairs, 1*(3), 177–192.

Pigou, A. C. (1927). *Industrial fluctuations.* London: Macmillan.

Pigou, A. C. (1933). *The theory of unemployment.* London: Macmillan.

Roberts, K., & Parsell, G. (1988). *Opportunity structures and career trajectories from age 16–19.* (Occasional Paper No. 1). London: City University, ESRC 16–19 Initiative.

Rothwell, R., & Zegveld, W. (1979). *Technical change and employment.* London: Frances Pinter.

Schmidt, M. G. (1983). The welfare state and the economy in periods of economic crisis: A comparative analysis of twenty-three OECD nations. *European Journal of Political Research, 11*(1), 1–26.

Schmidt, M. G. (1987). The politics of labour market policy: Structural and political determinants of full employment and mass unemployment in mixed economies. Paper presented at the World Congress of the International Political Science Association, Paris.

Standing, G. (1988). Training, flexibility and Swedish full employment. *Oxford Review of Economic Policy, 4*(3), 94–107.

Therborn, G. (1986). *Why some peoples are more unemployed than others: The strange paradox of growth and unemployment.* London: Verso.

van der Wee, H. (1986). *Prosperity and upheaval: The world economy 1945–1980.* Harmondsworth, Middlesex, England; New York, NY: Viking.

Wells, W. (1983). *The relative pay and employment of young people* (Research Paper No. 42). London: Department of Employment.

White, M. (1983). *Long-term unemployment and labour markets.* London: Policy Studies Institute.

White, M. (1991). *Against unemployment.* London: Policy Studies Institute.

White, M., & Lakey, J. (1992). The restart effect: Does active labour market policy reduce unemployment? London: Policy Studies Institute.

White, M., & McRae, S. (1989). *Young adults and long-term unemployment.* London: Policy Studies Institute.

Wilson, W. J. (1987). *The truly disadvantaged: The inner city, the underclass, and public policy.* Chicago: University of Chicago Press.

III. Individual perspectives

6. Concepts of causation, tests of causal mechanisms, and implications for intervention

MICHAEL RUTTER
Medical Reserach Council,
Child Psychiatry Unit
London

There is a widespread assumption among both policy makers and members of the general public that more resources should be poured into the prevention of psychological disorders. This view is frequently accompanied by the parallel assumption that the knowledge required to set up effective preventive programs is already available. The problem, it is supposed, lies in inertia and vested interests to keep things as they are (Keniston & Carnegie Council on Children, 1977; Segal, 1975). After all, there is a wealth of evidence on the variables associated with all manner of psychological disorders. Surely, this gives us a good enough appreciation of the causal features; all that remains is the task of designing interventions to impact on those features and then test which form of intervention works "best." That scenario would involve a fair number of practical difficulties but, at least, the general way forward would be clear.

However, the picture is a seriously misleading one (Rutter, 1982). The issues involved in gaining an adequate understanding of causal mechanisms are much more complicated than generally appreciated. The question of what is the basic cause of any psychological disorder, or indeed any social circumstance, is far from straightforward.

This is not a matter of ivory tower academic niceties; rather it is central to the whole enterprise of prevention and intervention, whatever the target of concern. If we are to be able to devise effective measures, it is essential that we appreciate the complexities inherent in concepts of causation. However, in putting forward this view, it is *not* being argued that the matter is so difficult that nothing useful can be accomplished. To the contrary, it is suggested that an understanding of causal processes *is* attainable and that this understanding can and will provide a basis for effective intervention. The caveat is simply that well-meaning attempts to intervene before we understand these causal processes may, and often do, bring about more harm than good (Rutter, 1982).

As the U.S. biologist Lewis Thomas (1979) put it in his provocative essay entitled 'On Meddling':

> Intervening is a way of causing trouble.... Whatever you propose to do, based on common sense, will almost inevitably make matters worse rather than better. You cannot meddle with one part of a complex system from the outside without the almost certain risk of setting off disastrous events that you hadn't counted on in other, remote parts. If you want to fix something you are first obliged to understand, in detail, the whole system. (pp. 110–111)

Thomas was applying this caveat to both biological and social systems, and, similarly, in reviewing concepts of causation there will be a deliberate span of both domains. That is both because biology encompasses the social when dealing with social animals such as *homo sapiens* and because the causal concepts apply generally and not just to social phenomena. However, because the topic of this volume concerns employment, the general concepts will be related to this specific concern whenever possible.

Three key questions need to be tackled: (1) the definition of the target problem, (2) the various different meanings of cause, and (3) the methods by which hypotheses about causal mechanisms may be tested empirically. The issue of cause has been introduced in terms of the need to assess causation in order to plan preventive policies, but obviously, the issues relating to concepts of causation and their testing apply much more broadly.

Definition of the Target "Problem"

It is appropriate to begin with the question of how to define the target problem. Frequently, social scientists write as if this posed no difficulties, but clearly very considerable complexities and dilemmas are involved.

The point may be illustrated by taking a medical example. It might be thought that everyone would agree that preventing death is a good thing and that this, therefore, constitutes a sound medical target. The first objection, of course, is that this is an impossible goal: Everyone must die sometime. The objective therefore becomes translated into one of increasing life expectancy. At first sight, that seems unobjectionable, especially when you are dealing with developing countries where there is a very high death rate in childhood and early adult life. Indeed, in industrialized nations, too, the massive increase in life expectancy over the past century—in British women, from 42 years in 1851 to 75 in 1971 (Rutter, 1979/1980)—does reflect marked improvements in people's health. However, in recent times gerontologists have begun to question the goal (Fries, 1990). If prolonging life means that people die slowly of progressive dementia in their 80s rather than suddenly, through a heart attack in their 70s, that is not self-evidently a health gain. Accordingly, researchers and clinicians in the field of old age are coming to redefine the goal in terms of what has been called "compression of morbidity." In essence, this means the aim is to reduce the period of incapacity before death intervenes, rather than postpone death per se. Of course, many health measures will do both, but the priority is now being placed firmly on the former. That seems to make excellent sense when viewed either from the individual perspective of quality of life or the community perspective of cost benefits.

Let us take drug abuse as a rather different example. Once again, at first sight, that seems straightforward; who would defend drug abuse as desirable? But what is abuse? Which drugs should be included? And why is it a matter of concern?

There is a natural tendency to define *drugs* in terms of those that we do not take personally. Hence, many people would rule out caffeine, nicotine, and alcohol. However, that does not seem acceptable. After all, it is clear that smoking carries with it serious risks to the health of the individual and, through passive smoking, to the health of anyone in the vicinity (Royal College of Physicians, 1983). Similarly, alcohol leads not only to personal illness in the form of cirrhosis of the liver, heart damage, and so forth, but also to serious risks to others by means of mechanisms such as deaths caused by drunken driving or damage to the fetus through mothers' heavy consumption of alcohol during the pregnancy (Royal College of Psychiatrists, 1986). It may be argued that these risks do not apply to moderate drinking. As a consequence of these considerations, perhaps the problem should be redefined as an uncontrolled or excessive use of drugs. That may be reasonable with alcohol, but the argument cannot be applied to smoking, where any level of smoking constitutes a degree of health hazard. The target in this case may be shifted to efforts to make the drug safer. The attempt to replace the smoking of cigarettes by the chewing of nicotine gum is an example of this kind (Jarvis & Russell, 1989). These approaches focus on the direct ill effects of drug-taking, but many people would argue that the main damage comes from indirect effects.

Thus, the focus turned to the problems of the spread of AIDS through sharing contaminated needles used for injectable drugs, and of the criminal activities involved in the distribution of drugs or in the obtaining of money to buy illegal drugs. This form of reasoning lies behind the policies of prescribing drugs to addicts with the aim of avoiding both criminalization and infection (Strang, 1989). As it will be appreciated, there can be no one "right" answer on the choice of target, as each has a complicated mix of advantages and disadvantages.

How do these considerations apply to unemployment?

Probably everyone would accept that there are circumstances in which the lack of a paid job is desirable or, at the very least, not necessarily a bad thing. After all, it is generally assumed that, at some point in their lives, people should be able to retire from work. Also, traditionally, some women have chosen to make homemaking and parenting, rather than a paid job outside the home, a full-time career. In addition, many women, and some men, choose for a time to interrupt their work careers to look after their small children full-time. Or again, many young people, after leaving the university, decide to take a year off to travel, working from time to time in order to have enough to live on. Of course, none of these groups would see themselves as unemployed because the option of not working was selected voluntarily by them.

The solution would seem to be to redefine the variable in terms of involuntary unemployment. But then we have to ask ourselves why that might be undesirable or harmful. That it is indeed harmful is evident from longitudinal studies, which are agreed in showing that school-leavers who remain out of work maintain relatively high levels of anxiety and depression, whereas those who obtain paid employment show reducing levels of emotional distress (Banks & Ullah, 1988; Patton & Noller, 1984). Moreover, the unemployed who gain work show a fall in distress levels (Kessler, Turner, & House, 1987). The causal connection is well demonstrated. Similarly, in another longitudinal study, Farrington, Gallagher, Morley, St. Ledger, and West (1986) showed that London youths committed more delinquent acts during periods when they were unemployed than during periods when they were working. It is clear that both personal and community costs are attached to unemployment.

That finding, however, still leaves open the question of what it is about unemployment that creates the psychosocial risk. Several different facets need to be considered as possible candidates. First, and most obviously, job loss is likely to lead to a marked drop in income, with financial strains making a major contribution to the adverse psychological effects. It is relevant that Farrington and colleagues (1986) found that it was only crimes involving material gain that increased during unemployment. Banks and Ullah (1988) found that emotional disturbance in the unemployed was greater when the lack of a job led to severe financial strains. If that were the only psychologically relevant aspect of unemployment, the target should perhaps be shifted from unemployment as such, to financial strain. In that case, one solution would be to ensure that those who became unemployed would not also become financial losers.

That might indeed be helpful if financial strain constitutes the only relevant consideration. Jahoda (1981) argued, however, that paid work also contributed to psychological well-being in five main ways:

First, employment imposes a time structure on the working day; second, employment implies regular shared experiences and contacts with people outside the nuclear family; third, employment links people to goals and purposes that transcend their own; fourth, employment defines aspects of personal status and identity; and finally, employment enforces activity. (p. 188)

Accordingly, it might be thought that the loss of self-esteem associated with being made redundant (or being "given the sack") may be as influential as the loss of income. The loss of a person's position in society that went with having a job may make a similar psychological impact. The effects of the jobless environment are likely to be relevant, too; the satisfaction that a rewarding job provides is also lost. In addition, there may be strains stemming from a lack of work routine, together with the stresses on the family of having an extra person at home during the day when the family life has been organized on the basis of him or her being at work.

That these nonfinancial, social consequences of work are truly psychologically important is shown by empirical research findings. For example, Bolton and Oatley (1987) found that depression following job loss was most likely to develop when the person had few social contacts *outside* work and was least likely when the person had good continuing social support. It is evident that jobs are important as a source of social interactions that provide people with a sense of their own worth. Similarly, Banks and Ullah (1988) found that how young people managed their time when out of work made a difference to the likelihood that they would exhibit psychological distress. Those unemployed people who stayed at home most of the time, going through the same routine each day, with long periods of inactivity, were most likely to be depressed. Conversely, the maintenance of psychological well-being was associated with a definite time structure to the day, shared experiences and contacts with people outside the immediate family, the existence of definite goals and purposes, and a degree of activity. The availability of emotional support from other people also reduced the risks of emotional disturbance.

These considerations might make one take the emphasis off unemployment as the "bad" feature to be targeted and, instead, focus attention on people's social network of relationships and activities and on how they organize their time when out of work. The implication is that, if people's social needs were met in adequate fashion, it might not matter quite so much if they didn't happen to have a paid job. However, the implications of what people do about seeking a new job raises other issues.

Banks and Ullah (1988) found that, in the longer term, people's attitudes and activities in relation to finding work made a psychological difference. Depression was most likely to occur among those who continued to devote the greatest energies to finding work and who fell under the greatest pressure to get a job. To a degree, "scaling down" job-seeking efforts seemed to protect the unemployed from the depression that stemmed from failure in those attempts (it did not appear to alleviate anxiety, however). Although counterproductive in relation to reestablishing a work career, the psychological acceptance of unemployment may do something to reduce short-term stresses.

The long-term consequences of this style of coping may not be quite so positive for two different reasons. First, and most obviously, it is likely to reduce the chances of obtaining employment. Second, it means that persons have had to come to terms with an alternative that is socially less acceptable—namely, being indefinitely out of work. The California longitudinal studies analyzed by Elder, Liker, and Cross (1984) showed that, for vulnerable men, the loss of self-esteem and assertiveness associated with unemployment in the Great Depression of the 1930s left them less able to cope with the stresses and adaptations that accompanied old age many years later.

Distribution of unemployment

Up to this point, there has been a focus on the effects of unemployment as it impinges on the individual, without any consideration of whether it matters which individual is affected. Of course, that is an important issue. It is clear from the studies cited, together with others, that unemployment (like other stress situations) tends to have its worst effects on those individuals who are already coping least well psychologically and socially (Rutter & Rutter, in press). Accordingly, it could be suggested that the goal should be to change the pattern so these people are protected from unemployment, leaving the hardier members of society to cope with the stresses of being out of work. A case can be made for providing the sick and susceptible with extra protection, but that does not seem likely to constitute a practical general solution.

Let us broaden the topic of distribution of unemployment by asking whether the target problem should be thought of in individual terms at all. Posing the problem in relation to the individual presupposes that it is necessary to accept that unemployment will always be with us to some degree and that our aim must be to reduce the stresses for the individual that are entailed in being out of work. But is that a reasonable supposition?

Let us leave aside for the moment the question of whether the overall level of unemployment could ever be reduced to zero without radical changes in our society and, instead, consider distributional issues. For any given level of employment in society, there is a potential choice in how widely it is distributed among its citizens. At present, the majority of the population never experience more than very transient periods of unemployment, whereas a minority spend quite a lot of their supposedly "working" lives out of work. We need to ask whether that is the optimal distribution.

How might it be changed? Clearly, there are many alternatives. For example, the level of unemployment could be markedly reduced by cutting short the duration of work careers. This shortening could be done at either end of the career span: at the beginning by prolonging education (and therefore delaying work entry), and at the end by making retirement come at an earlier age. Alternatively, the distribution of work could be altered *during* work careers. For example, there could be a general reduction in working hours (thereby creating new jobs if work demands and productivity remained static), or an increase in part-time working, or an arrangement whereby people have to have a period of unemployment when they change jobs.

This is not, of course, an argument for any particular solution. Each has its own set of advantages and disadvantages with a range of desirable and less desirable knock-on (domino) effects. The point, and it is a fundamental one, is that it is not self-evident that the "problem" of unemployment should be seen in individual terms. The target also can be defined in distributional terms. For any given level of employment opportunities, these can be distributed narrowly or broadly, and it may be that the main problem lies in the degree of dispersal of the experience of unemployment.

Quite apart from the degree to which unemployment is distributed widely or narrowly, we need to pay attention to inequalities and biases. For example, in the United Kingdom (as elsewhere) there are marked geographical differences in unemployment levels. Ethnic minorities are at particular risk. White and McRae's (1989) survey of long-term unemployment among young adults in the United Kingdom showed that young Asian men and young Afro-Caribbean women had among the highest qualification levels but among the lowest chances of getting jobs. It is apparent that racial discrimination still plays a part in unemployment. It could well be the case, too, that its operation in the job market may serve to increase existing racial tensions. Accordingly, the target problem probably should include the element of inequitable distribution of unemployment.

This is, of course, very much a key issue in a wide variety of spheres of life. For example, in the United Kingdom, infantile mortality rates vary markedly by social class (Townsend & Davidson, 1982). At birth, and during the first month of life, the risk of death of infants in families of unskilled workers is double that of infants in professional families. During the remainder of the first year after birth, the gap widens. For the death of every one male infant of professional parents, there are almost two among infants of skilled manual workers and three among those reared by unskilled manual workers. The striking feature of these statistics is that the social disparities have remained remarkably great in spite of a marked overall reduction in infantile mortality rates.

Income levels provide an interesting contrast in terms of the huge *changes* in distribution over time. Over the decade or so of Thatcherite Tory rule in the United Kingdom, the affluent experienced a massive rise in income (Northcott, 1991). By sharp contrast, the incomes of the poor scarcely changed at all. The increase in social divisions in terms of income has been dramatic. It need not represent a causal connection, but it is notable that in countries (such as the United Kingdom and the United States) where the socioeconomic spread has broadened, there has been less improvement in infantile mortality than in countries such as Japan (Marmot & Smith, 1989), where the spread is less extreme. Thus, in 1960, the United Kingdom ranked fifth lowest in infantile mortality, but in 1988 only thirteenth in the world (United Nations Children's Fund, 1990). Socioeconomic gradients with respect to health status have become steeper in the past decade in parallel with economic gradients (Smith, Bartley, & Blane, 1990).

Scholastic attainment provides yet another contrasting example. Within many countries there has been much discussion of the merits and demerits of streaming or tracking, which involves dividing up school classes so those of higher ability make up one group and those of lower ability, another. The evidence is reasonably clear-cut in showing that this makes little or no difference to the overall level of attainment, but it does have an effect on spread (Rutter & Madge, 1976). Research findings show that there is a tendency for those in upper streams to increase their levels of attainment and for there to be a decrease among those in lower streams.

Distribution issues have been discussed at some length because they bring out several crucial considerations. First, the extent to which any psychological or social feature has adverse effects may be in part a consequence of its distribution in society. Therefore, distributional considerations need to play a part in defining the target problem to be addressed. Second, the study of factors influencing distribution has the potential of casting crucial light on causal processes. It is surprising, for example, that so few social scientists have put effort into determining the reasons that there are such marked social differentials in infantile mortality (but see Wilkinson, 1986, for a useful set of reviews of the issues involved in the links between social class and health). Third, as the scholastic attainment example showed, distributional variations may have consequences for individuals affected by them without necessarily affecting average levels in the population as a whole.

The last distributional point to bring out is of a rather different kind—namely, the question of whether people are influenced more by absolute or by relative differences in their circumstances. This is, of course, the distinction that was raised, and well discussed, by Runciman (1972) 20 years ago in relation to social deprivation. Put in simplistic terms, we may ask whether, for example, we are more likely to suffer psychologically through our absolute level of poverty or poor living conditions or through the fact that (regardless of level) we are worse off than other people. That is no trivial consideration, because it has huge implications for the policies we ought to pursue. Thus, since the turn of the century, absolute living standards in the United Kingdom (as in other industrialized nations) have risen dramatically, however you care to measure them (Rutter & Madge, 1976).

It is not apparent that this has brought any significant psychological benefits. If anything, psychological disturbances have probably somewhat increased in frequency (Rutter, 1979/1980). That does not necessarily mean relative deprivation is more important, but that could well be the case.

The question has recently received new life from an unexpected direction—behavioral genetics (Plomin & Daniels, 1987). The key finding is that for most (but not all) psychological characteristics, within-family differences have turned out to be more influential than between-family ones. That is, the differences in experiences between two children reared in the same family seem more influential than the differences between families. The evidence in support of this, at first sight, surprising inference stems from the *lack* of similarity between siblings—especially those who do not share their genes (e.g., adopted siblings)—reared in the same family. Dunn and Plomin (1990) have argued that the limited evidence available so far suggests that it may matter more to children that, for example, compared with their brother and sister, they are loved less by their parents than that the family as a whole is an unloving one lacking in warmth and affection. We all have a very basic tendency to compare ourselves with other people, and the argument is that we suffer when these consequences turn out to be mostly unfavorable to ourselves. In that connection, it is important to appreciate that the tendency is to compare ourselves with others in our network of social or working contacts and *not* with the hypothetical average for the population as a whole or with the few extremely privileged individuals in the country whom we never meet (Kelvin, 1969). With respect to unemployment, the implication is that adverse sequelae may stem as much from people's feelings of being ill-treated compared with others in their social network (because *they* are out of a job whereas others are in paid work), as from the absolute effects of unemployment as they impinge on individuals.

Plomin and his colleagues have put these arguments strictly in terms of the need to explain why within-family differences in experiences are so important. It is necessary to note that here the issue has been generalized more widely: If the comparison explanation is a valid one, it should also serve to account for the observation that between-family differences seem to matter more in some circumstances than in others.

The Variety of Causal Questions

It follows from the points made about the different ways of defining the target "problem" that there must be equally varied ways in which causal questions can be posed. Traditionally, cause has been considered in terms of the factors that account for individual differences. Thus, for example, the causes of delinquency are conceptualized with respect to the factors that explain why "X" is delinquent, whereas "Y" is not. Similarly, causes of unemployment often focus on the characteristics that differentiate between individuals in regular jobs and those who are out of work. That is a perfectly legitimate way of viewing causation, and indeed it is an essential part of the causal story, but as we have seen, it is by no means the only way of conceptualizing causation.

At least three other causal concepts must be taken on board. First, we need to ask the question in terms of *level*, rather than population *variance*. Of course, in some circumstances, the same factors may be responsible for both, but often they are quite different. For example, height is one of the most strongly genetic of personal characteristics; genetic factors account for most of the variation among individuals at any one point in time. There is no reason to suppose that that has changed over time. But it is also true that since the beginning of the twentieth century there has been a most dramatic increase in the average height of the population. The average height of London schoolboys, for example, increased by about 10 centimeters in 50 years (Tizard, 1975). Although we do not know for certain what has brought this about, it seems highly likely that the explanation lies in better nutrition.

Similarly, suicide rates in the United Kingdom dropped markedly with the detoxification of domestic gas used in cooking (Rutter, 1979/1980). Pricing and licensing controls of alcoholic drinks have been shown to effect the overall level of alcoholism in the population, too (Rutter, 1979/1980). In each case the effect on levels in the population as a whole has come from some key influence that is population-wide and that makes little impact on individual differences.

The parallel with unemployment is obvious. It is evident that the sort of causal explanations for why one person is unemployed and another is not are scarcely likely to be the same as those that account for, say, the massive rise in unemployment in the United Kingdom during the last 12 years of Tory rule. Personal factors such as low skill level, poor educational/vocational qualifications, inadequate personality functioning, and physical ill health are quite important with respect to individual differences (Rutter & Madge, 1976; White & McRae, 1989), but it is *not* changes in any of these that caused the number of people out of work to rise so dramatically. Although people may disagree on the precise nature of the causal processes, it is clear that the explanation is likely to lie in political, economic, and social policies rather than personal attributes.

The second causal concept applies to the degree of dispersal of the feature in the general population: whether a few people have a heavy and prolonged experience of unemployment or a large number of people have a light and brief experience of being out of work. Again, it is likely that the causal influence will need to be sought in broad sociopolitical factors rather than individual characteristics.

The third causal concept concerns bias or uneven distribution of the feature among subgroups of the general population. Perhaps the most investigated example of this kind concerns delinquent acts as they vary by geography and social circumstances (Clarke, 1985; Giller, 1983). It is clear that the likelihood that delinquent acts will be committed in any one place and time is much influenced by opportunity and situational factors. Effective surveillance and well-maintained properties reduce the rate of theft and vandalism.

The evidence on this topic emphasizes that an individual propensity to behave in a particular way is one thing but that the translation of that propensity into actual behavior is another. The factors influencing the two are rather different. So far as unemployment is concerned, the role of opportunities is obvious in terms of geographical differences in the availability of jobs. However, personal factors also may play a part in the overall effect of these varying opportunities. Thus, for example, the availability of personal transport may increase the geographical spread of jobs open to an individual (Banks & Ullah, 1988), and a willingness to move to another part of the country, or to be retrained for a different job, increases the scope of jobs even more. Personal attributes and social forces come together in the already mentioned role of racial discrimination in unemployment.

Casual Chain and Interconnections

We turn now to the rather separate issues involved in elucidating causal processes and mechanisms. Let us suppose that the prior questions of the target problem and the type of causal questions have been sorted out and that the challenge is simply to determine the causes of one of these. What do we need to bear in mind in that endeavor? There are four main considerations: (1) multifactorial determination, (2) person-environment correlations and interactions, (3) the need to consider protective as well as risk mechanisms, and (4) indirect causal chain effects.

Multifactorial determination

The basic fact that most personal behaviors or disorders and most social circumstances are multifactorially determined is generally accepted and needs no detailed justification by me. It is sometimes assumed that this does not apply to medical diseases where there is some identifiable necessary causal agent—such as a bacterium or virus in an infectious disease. However, that is not usually so. Thus, for example, it is well known that people's vulnerability to infection (such as tuberculosis) is greatly increased by malnutrition. That may not be a major consideration in modern Europe but it is in poor, developing countries, and it was so in Europe in earlier times.

The further point that needs to be made about multifactorial determination is that the balance in importance between different causal factors will vary with circumstances (the malnutrition and tuberculosis example illustrates that effect); also the meaning and/or impact of causal variables may be influenced by social context. For example, more than 30 years ago Christensen (1960) used aggregated data to suggest that the relationship between an unmarried woman discovering that she was pregnant and getting married varied greatly according to the sexual mores of the society. Somewhat similarly, it appears that variation exits among social groups and among societies in the extent to which dating—young people going out together as couples—is influenced by pubertal status (Rutter & Rutter, in press; Stattin & Magnusson, 1990). Thus, the effects of puberty on dating in the United States vary by both ethnicity and gender (Bancroft, 1991; Udry, 1990). Also, puberty has a greater effect on dating among female ballet dancers than among nondancers (Gargiulo, Attie, Brooks-Gunn, & Warren, 1987). It should be added, too, that, there is a two-way interaction between physiological and psychosocial variables. Thus, there is evidence from both human and animal studies that sex hormones influence behavior but, equally, there is evidence that psychological experiences and behavior lead to changes in hormone levels.

These considerations suggest that, in thinking about causes of unemployment, we need to be aware that it is likely that multiple factors will be involved and that their relative importance may well vary over time and across sociocultural groups. The variables, for example, that apply most strongly in males may be less important in females; those that are most influential in young people may not be quite the same as those with most effects in later life; and racial discrimination will be a relevant variable only in those subject to its operation.

Person-environment interplay

The second main consideration is that it is common for there to be an interplay between characteristics of the person and those of the environment (Rutter & Pickles, 1991). In other words, it is usual for the environment to impinge differently on different people. That is a general biological feature. Thus, we are aware that pollens bring on hayfever more readily in some people than others; that dietary factors affect cholesterol levels to a great extent in some individuals but make little difference in others; and that people's general physical well-being (and level of psychosocial stress) affects their resistance to infection.

It is clear that this issue also applies in the field of unemployment. Individual differences are influential both in terms of variations in the likelihood of becoming unemployed when economic and business conditions alter and in terms of variations in psychological vulnerability to the ill effects associated with the experience of unemployment.

An example of the first type (i.e., variations in the likelihood of being unemployed) is provided by the finding that during the late 1970s and early 1980s in the United Kingdom, long-term unemployment particularly affected young people. White and McRae (1989) suggested that this was because a relative contraction in manual occupations meant that those without qualifications were particularly at risk. This impinged on young people to a disproportionate extent because it affected job vacancies more than redundancies, because older workers were relatively protected by having behind them a prolonged period of job experience, because early retirement reduced the number of older people in jeopardy, because a sharp reduction in apprenticeships combined with high wages put young people especially at risk, and because the time period coincided with a relatively large proportion of the population in the young adult age group.

An example of the second type (i.e., variations in vulnerability to the ill effects of uemployment) is provided by the California longitudinal studies, which showed that men tended to be more affected than women by the stresses associated with unemployment during the Great Depression and that adolescents were often strengthened by the experience of their parents being unemployed whereas younger children usually suffered (Elder, 1979). It seemed that if people were able to cope successfully with the adaptations and challenges, in the long run the stressful experiences could prove "steeling," whereas if their circumstances were such that successful coping was not possible they responded adversely and were sensitized so that their vulnerability to later stresses increased.

A further point needs to be made about the interplay between person and environment characteristics: The interplay can arise in two somewhat different ways. First, it may be due to person-environment correlations that reflect a tendency for people to shape and select their environments. Second, it may be due to individual differences in people's susceptibility to the same environment. There is evidence that both occur but, until recently, the first mechanism has received relatively little attention. However, as Scarr (1988; Scarr & McCartney, 1983) has emphasized, people's determination of their own experiences may represent the more important effect. Certainly, it is one that focuses attention on a rather different set of causal processes; moreover, it is one with implications for intervention strategies.

Thus, it is relevant that antisocial boys have much increased unemployment rates in adult life compared with the general population. For example, in her classic long-term follow-up of child psychiatric clinic attenders, Robins (1966) found that 23 percent of antisocial boys were currently unemployed compared with 2 percent of control boys—a more than tenfold difference! Moreover, of those in both groups who had experienced unemployment during the last ten years, the antisocial boys were more likely to have experienced chronic unemployment. More detailed examination of the findings showed that this consequence was likely to be due to the fact that antisocial boys showed a much increased tendency to drop out of school, with the result that they lacked educational credentials and qualifications.

Protective and risk mechanisms

The third consideration is that we need to consider protective as well as risk mechanisms. On the face of it, it might be thought that those represent mirror images of each other, but that is a misleading oversimplification of the processes that apply (Rutter, 1990). The basic point is that protective mechanisms are those that *alter* the effect of risk processes by some kind of reverse-catalytic effect, in other words, an *interactive* effect rather than a directly beneficial one. The corollary of that point is that the processes involved in protective mechanisms may be rather different from those involved in risk. Once more, a medical example may serve to illustrate the point. Malaria is an infection spread by mosquitoes; the risk stems from the blood parasite conveyed by the bite of the mosquito. However, a *resistance* to malaria is afforded by the gene for sickle cell disease (Rotter & Diamond, 1987). This protective mechanism obviously involves a rather different process from that which gives rise to the disease.

Until recently, there has been relatively little research into protective mechanisms involved in psychosocial disorders or social circumstances. However, the limited available evidence (Rutter, 1990) suggests that protection may derive from (1) a reduction of the risk impact by virtue of effects on the riskiness itself or through alteration of exposure to or involvement in the risk, (2) a reduction of the likelihood of negative chain reaction stemming from the risk encounter, (3) a promotion of self-esteem and self-efficacy through the availability of secure and supportive personal relationships or successes in task accomplishment, and (4) an opening up of opportunities.

In relation to unemployment, it is not difficult to see how these mechanisms might apply. For example, education and training that provided people with the skills and attitude to enable them to learn new jobs as employment opportunities altered, and/or to move geographically to take up job opportunities further afield, would be likely to increase the chances of retaining employment in a falling or changing job market. Similarly, the resilience and self-efficacy deriving from having coped successfully with previous life crises may serve to protect people from the stresses that accompany being made redundant. In that connection, we need to be reminded that, biologically speaking, resilience and protection do not usually stem from the avoidance of risks; rather they derive from having coped successfully with similar risks in the past. Thus, the benefits from immunization come from *exposure* to, not avoidance of, the pathogenic bacterium. What makes the experience protective is that it takes place in a manner that greatly increases the chances of the body "coping" successfully and so acquiring relative immunity. The challenge in the psychosocial arena is to develop strategies and tactics that may serve to enable young people to cope successfully with minor stresses so they are better able to cope with larger ones later, if and when they arise.

Indirect causal chain effects

The last and most fundamental point to make about causal processes is that very frequently they involve indirect chain effects of one kind or another (Rutter, 1989). There is a tendency, perhaps especially among medical people but also among social scientists, to assume that there must be one basic primary cause, that this constitutes the first point in the causal process, and that, ideally, prevention should be focused on that basic primary cause. It is easy, however, to demonstrate that the first point in the causal chain and the basic mediating mechanism are by no means synonymous. For example, the causal association between smoking and lung cancer is dependent upon a basic mediating mechanism of chemical carcinogenesis. However, that is not the first point in the chain, because it is necessary to ask why some people smoke whereas others do not. The answer to that question lies in a mixture of social experiences and genetic factors as they apply to personality variations. These operate at an earlier point in the causal chain but in no sense can they be thought of as basic to the carcinogenic process. Even the choice to smoke cannot be considered as the ambiguous first point in the chain; the availability of cigarettes could be postulated as prior.

The real issue is not which cog constitutes the beginning of the chain; on the one hand the decision is necessarily somewhat arbitrary and, on the other, when causal processes are circular (as they often are), the very notion of a first point is meaningless. In the case of smoking and lung cancer, there is in a real sense a basic causal mechanism that is important to identify and understand. However, in many circumstances the causal chain does not involve any one link that can be seen as basic in the sense of the chemical carcinogenesis effect. For example, in our own research, one of the several chains that led to unemployment started with the qualities of the school attended at the secondary stage (Gray, Smith, & Rutter, 1980). Going to a less effective school had an adverse effect on school attendance, which in turn was associated with lower school performance, which then had an effect on the skill level of the job obtained after leaving school, which had a further effect on the likelihood of unemployment. It would be difficult, and not particularly meaningful, to select any one of these steps as the most basic.

Another consideration regarding causal chain effects is that the same variable may have different (and sometimes opposite) consequences at different points in the causal chain. For example, Robins, Davis, and Wish (1977), in their studies of drug abuse in Americans who served in the armed forces in the Vietnam War, showed that demographic variables had dramatically different and opposing effects at the beginning and end of the causal chain. Thus, older white men who lived *outside* central cities were the *least* likely to use narcotics in Vietnam (an adjusted 33% vs. 70% in young, inner-city blacks), but they were *ten* times as likely to be addicted if they continued the use of narcotics on their return to the United States (41% vs. 4%).

If all steps in the chain are put together into a multivariate analysis, demographic variables seem to have little effect and, insofar as they make any impact, the atypical users (older whites from outside the inner city) do not seem an at-risk group. However, they have an exceptionally high risk at a key point in the causal chain, and Robins and colleagues argued that they may, therefore, constitute the *most* appropriate and hopeful group to target in prevention.

Another example is provided by the findings on risk factors for heart attacks associated with coronary artery diseases. In adult life, the risk is substantially increased in those people who are markedly overweight. However, the risk is also greatly increased for adults who were very *under*weight in the first year of life (Barker, 1991). The reversal of the weight effect between infancy and middle age is at first sight surprising, but it may be a result of a sensitivity mechanism whereby relative sub-nutrition in infancy makes people more vulnerable to the damaging effects of a very rich diet later in life. As with the drug dependency example, the mechanisms are probably different at different points in the causal chain, with the consequence that what seems to be the same variable has opposite effects early and late in the chain processes.

Timing comes in also as a mechanism in the *effects* of a risk variable. Two examples serve to illustrate this point. Robins and McEvoy (1990), using Epidemiological Catchment Area (retrospective) data, showed that conduct disorder in childhood much increased the risk of drug abuse but that one of the important mechanisms by which it did so was by lowering the age of first exposure to psychoactive substances. This was relevant because, other things being equal, early exposure much increased the risks of later abuse. They suggested, only half tongue-in-check, that the Reagan campaign for youngsters to "just say no" to drugs should, if that fails, be supplemented by a "just say later" exhortation, as that might prove protective!

The second example comes from our follow-up of girls reared in group foster homes (Quinton & Rutter, 1988). The findings showed that, compared with controls, they were much less likely to exert planning in relation to earlier marriage and careers. As a result, there was a much increased rate of hasty teenage pregnancies and marriages to a behaviorally deviant spouse. This, in turn, was followed by a much increased rate of marital discord and marital breakdown. Detailed analyses showed that the lack of planning exerted its effects through two distinct routes: an effect on timing of marriage and an effect on choice of partner, meaning an increase in very early marriage and an increase in the likelihood of having a deviant spouse (Pickles & Rutter, 1991). The first route was important because it led to the second. Again, the findings suggested that it would be protective to delay marriage (because delay increased the pool of potential marriage partners and by so doing reduced the chances of having a deviant spouse).

One further consideration needs mentioning in relation to chain effects, and that is that different points in the chain may involve a shift from individual to family or from individual to population-wide mechanisms. An example of the first shift is provided by our comparative study of children living in the Isle of Wight (a community of small towns off the southern coast of England) and children of the same age living in inner London (Rutter, 1979/1980). We found that rates of psychiatric disorder were twice as high in inner London. This might seem to suggest that children suffered directly from the stresses of inner-city life, an effect that might apply most strongly to adolescents, who are most involved in outside-the-family activities. However, detailed analyses showed that the effect was greatest in the case of disorders beginning in early or middle childhood, not adolescence, and that the effect was largely explicable in terms of inner-city life leading to an increase in *family* problems (discord, break-up, overcrowding, etc.), as compared with the situation on the Isle of Wight (Rutter & Quinton, 1977). When children from like families in the two geographical areas were compared, there were no significant differences. The inference was that we needed to focus on city life effects on families rather than on children.

An example of the second type is provided by the findings on alcoholism (Rutter, 1979/1980). To become an alcoholic, a person must have the means of access to alcohol. The evidence from comparisons over time and across countries shows that access is influenced by both cost of alcoholic drinks and ease of buying as influenced by licensing laws. In this case, then, going back one step further in the causal chain meant a shift from an individual to a communitywide mechanism.

It is clear that all of these considerations are relevant in relation to unemployment. For example, the White and McRae (1989) finding that a lack of qualifications was a key risk factor for unemployment in young people has been mentioned already. Moving forward in the causal chain, it is important to note however, that the immediate mediating variable in the chain was not lack of qualifications per se but rather seeking or having an unskilled job. Moving backward in the chain at an individual level, our own findings (Gray et al., 1980) showed that a lack of qualification was related to individual variables (especially conduct disturbance), family variables (social disadvantage), and school variables (with some schools having much higher rates of leaving school without qualifications). Both studies showed that qualifications were not as protective in ethnic minorities as in white teenagers. Moving to a population, rather than an individual, perspective, White and McRae (1989) pointed out that increasing young peoples' qualification levels will not do much good unless young people also allocate themselves differently across occupations. In other words, there must be both qualification and occupation restructuring. The disproportionate burden of unemployment experienced by ethnic minorities, of course, also means that interventions need to include steps to reduce racial discrimination if maldistribution of unemployment is to be reduced.

These few selective remarks on the implication for unemployment of indirect causal chain mechanisms are not meant to provide a prescription for preventive policies. The point is simply that such policies will need to be based on a realization that the causal mechanisms, at both an individual and a population-wide level, usually will involve causal chains with a variety of different mechanisms operating at different points in the causal process.

Testing Causal Hypotheses

In discussing the variety of causal concepts, it has been assumed that it is possible to determine the nature of causal mechanisms, and it remains to be considered how this may be accomplished. Social scientists are often rightly criticized for being content with weaving ideologically acceptable stories on the basis of correlations and associations, while avoiding the challenge of putting causal hypotheses to empirical tests. We are taught in our undergraduate and postgraduate training that correlations do not prove causation and that causal hypotheses can be tested only through controlled, contrived experiments. Because very few psychosocial features can be subjected to experiments in the laboratory (obviously such experiments are not practicable in the case of unemployment), we sometimes slide into the assumption that causal hypotheses cannot be tested in the social sciences. That is *not* so. To the contrary, it is *mandatory* that we seek to test causal postulates in a rigorous manner. Indeed, unless we can use our data to bring about an understanding of causal mechanisms and processes, we have achieved very little. That means that, following Popper's dicta, we must set about trying to *disprove* our hypotheses. Only by surviving multiple tests of disproof does the causal hypothesis begin to achieve possible validity as an explanation.

How may this be accomplished? The situation lies in the search for, and use of, so-called "experiments of nature" (Rutter, 1981). The principle is quite straightforward (although the identification of the required quasi-experimental conditions often is very difficult). The experimental method has been expressed simply as the operation of "waggling" one variable in order to determine wether it causes some other variable to "move," and doing so in such a way as to find out whether this "movement" is brought about systematically and regularly in varying circumstances. The translation of this concept into the practical requirements for "experiments of nature" is most easily considered in relation to the causal hypotheses about individual differences, although the broad principles apply to any type of causal mechanism. Seven main needs have to be met.

First, it is necessary to have *longitudinal* data so actual change can be measured, rather than inferred from cross-sectional comparisons. Second, the data must be organized so change can be measured on an *intra-individual* basis, rather than at a group level. Third, unless the causal hypothesis specifies a permanent change, *reversal* effects must be examined. These first three requirements are met by longitudinal studies demonstrating that individuals show an increase in psychological distress when they lose their jobs and that unemployed individuals show a reduction in such distress when they succeed in obtaining work (Banks & Ullah, 1988; Kessler et al., 1987; e.g., Patton & Noller, 1984).

That finding provides strong support for a causal inference. However, the experimental paradigm requires that the effect be systematic, repeatable, and occur regularly under a variety of different conditions. Accordingly, two other requirements beyond the first three must be met.

The fourth is the basic requirement in science of multiple replications. The fundamental rule is that no finding, however striking, can be accepted until it is replicated in a different sample by an independent set of investigators. Statistical significance, however great, is no substitute; it is only the poor person's prop, serving as an index of the *likelihood* of replication. Of course, we are all poor men in that respect, but the rule has to be followed in social science, just as it does in the biological sciences. Replication is crucial.

The fifth requirement involves an extension of the fourth—namely, the specification that the same effect be found in samples that *differ* markedly in their other characteristics. This is necessary to check that the effect is not an artifact brought about by some correlated confounding variable. The effect of unemployment on psychological distress has begun to survive these two further requirements; it has been replicated in samples that range in a number of features.

The sixth requirement is that there should be a "dose-response" relationship within the affected group. Of course, that involves moving beyond the risk variable to specify a risk *mechanism*. Thus, in the case of the effects of unemployment in increasing psychological distress, it is necessary to postulate that the effect is brought about by the loss of income, the limitation of social contacts, or the loss of esteem in the community (or some other consequence or accompaniment of unemployment). Ordinarily, unless there is a threshold effect, it may be expected that the greater the change in the hypothesized risk feature, the greater the risk on the outcome variable; that is what is meant by a dose-response relationship. Because there is continuing uncertainty about the risk mechanism or mechanisms that underlie the effect of unemployment on psychological distress, this sixth requirement has not been met clearly as yet.

The last requirement is that the effect should be biologically plausible. That need is not so easily met with a feature such as unemployment. However, what it means is that there is reason to suppose that the risk mechanism *might* operate in the way suggested, a not unreasonable requirement.

These requirements have been put in terms that apply to causal influences on individual differences, but it is an easy matter to see how they may be extended to other types of causal concept. Thus, to understand the effects of economic policies on *levels* of unemployment, it is necessary to translate the first requirement of intra-individual change to one of intragroup change in level. The other specifications still apply. Thus, for example, it would be necessary to determine wether the economic policy effects applied similarly in different countries that varied in socioeconomic circumstances and in the same country over different eras or time periods (see, for example, White & Smith, this volume).

I have dwelt on the need to test causal mechanisms because the design of policies of prevention and intervention requires that we know the processes involved. The testing of causal hypotheses in social sciences may be more difficult than in sciences where the variables can be manipulated at will in the laboratory, but, with ingenuity and creative imagination, it is still possible to take the testing quite a long way.

Decisions on Intervention

It is necessary to end by noting that policy decisions—on which point in the chain to choose for interventions, on which segment of the population to target and how to intervene—need to be based on an understanding of the relevant causal concepts. The choice should not be based on misleading notions of what is *the* basic primary cause or on variables that have the supposedly greatest effect overall when all links in the causal chain are put together in one large multivariate "soup." Rather, careful decisions need to be taken on the basis of an understanding of the different mechanisms operating at different points in the causal process, or the strength of different mechanisms at each point, on the likelihood that an intervention could actually alter what was happening; and on the ease of obtaining adequate population coverage of the at-risk groups. That is no easy matter and, necessarily, a complex weighing of costs and benefits is needed. However, such decisions are likely to be made on a sounder basis if the complexities involved in causal processes are better understood. These are susceptible to quantified empirical analysis, and it is essential that these analyses be carried out if we are to be in a position to devise and implement really effective preventative policies.

References

Bancroft, J. (1991). Reproductive hormones. In M. Rutter & P. Casaer (Eds.), *Biological risk factors for psychosocial disorders* (pp. 260–310). Cambridge: Cambridge University Press.

Banks, M. H., & Ullah, P. (1988). *Youth unemployment in the 1980s: Its psychological effects*. London: Croom Helm.

Barker, D. J. P. (1991). The intrauterine environment and adult cardiovascular disease. In G. R. Bock & J. Whelan (Eds.), *The childhood environment and adult disease* (pp. 3–10). Ciba Foundation Symposium No. 156. Chichester, UK: John Wiley.

Bolton, W., & Oatley, K. (1987). A longitudinal study of social support and depression in unemployed men. *Psychological Medicine, 17*, 453–460.

Christensen, H. T. (1960). Cultural relativism and premarital sex norms. *American Sociological Review, 25*, 31–39.

Clarke, R. V. G. (1985). Delinquency, environment and intervention. *Journal of Child Psychology and Psychiatry, 26*, 505–523.

Dunn, J., & Plomin, R. (1990). *Separate lives: Why siblings are so different*. New York: Basic Books.

Elder, G. H., Jr. (1979). Historical change in life patterns and personality. In P. Baltes & O. G. Brim (Eds.), *Life-span development and behavior* (Vol. 2, p. 20). New York: Academic Press.

Elder, G. H. Jr., Liker, J., & Cross, C. (1984). Parent-child behavior in the Great Depression: Life course and intergenerational influences. In P. B. Baltes & O. G. Brim, Jr. (Eds.), *Life-span development and behavior* (Vol. 6, pp. 109–158). New York: Academic Press.

Farrington, D. P., Gallagher, B., Morley, L., St. Ledger, R. J., & West, D. J. (1986). Unemployment, school leaving and crime. *British Journal of Criminology, 26*, 335–356.

Fries, J. F. (1990). Medical perspectives upon successful aging. In P. B. Baltes & M. M. Baltes (Eds.), *Successful aging: Perspectives from the behavioral sciences* (pp. 35–49). Cambridge: Cambridge University Press.

Gargiulo, J., Attie, I., Brooks-Gunn, J., & Warren, M. P. (1987). Girls' dating behavior as a function of social context and maturation. *Developmental Psychology, 23*, 730–737.

Gray, G., Smith, A., & Rutter, M. (1980). School attendance and the first year of employment. In L. Hersov & I. Berg (Eds.), *Out of school: Modern perspectives in truancy and school refusal* (pp. 343–370). Chichester, UK: John Wiley.

Jahoda, M. (1981). Work, employment, and unemployment: Values, theories, and approaches in social research. *American Psychologist, 36*, 184–191.

Jarvis, M. J., & Russell, M. A. H. (1989). Treatment for the cigarette smoker. *International Review of Psychiatry, 1,* 139–147.

Kelvin, P. (1969). *The bases of social behaviour: An approach in terms of order and value.* London: Holt, Rinehart & Winston.

Keniston, K., & Carnegie Council on Children. (1977). *All our children.* New York: Harcourt Brace Jovanovich.

Kessler, R. C., Turner, J. B., & House, J. S. (1987). Intervening processes in the relationship between unemployment and health. *Psychological Medicine, 17,* 949–961.

Marmot, M. G., & Smith, G. D. (1989). Why are the Japanese living longer? *British Medical Journal, 299,* 1547–1551.

Northcott, J. (1991). *Britain in 2010.* London: Policy Studies Institute.

Patton, W., & Noller, P. (1984). Unemployment and youth: A longitudinal study. *Australian Journal of Psychology, 36,* 399–413.

Pickles, A., & Rutter, M. (1991). Statistical and conceptual models of "turning points" in developmental processes. In D. Magnusson, L. R. Bergman, G. Rudinger, & B. Törestad (Eds.), *Problems and methods in longitudinal research: Stability and change* (pp. 133–165). Cambridge: Cambridge University Press.

Plomin, R., & Daniels, D. (1987). Why are children in the same family so different from one another? *Behavioral and Brain Sciences, 10,* 1–15.

Quinton, D., & Rutter, M. (1988). *Parenting breakdown: The making and breaking of inter-generational links.* Aldershot, UK: Avebury.

Robins, L. (1966). *Deviant children grown up.* Baltimore, MD: Williams and Wilkins.

Robins, L., Davis, D. H., & Wish, E. (1977). Detecting predictors of rare events: Demographic, family and personal deviance as predictors of stages in the progression toward narcotic addiction. In J. S. Strauss, H. M. Babigian, & M. Roff (Eds.), *The origins and course of psychopathology: Methods of longitudinal research* (pp. 379–406). New York: Plenum.

Robins, L., & McEvoy, L. (1990). Conduct problems as predictors of substance abuse. In L. Robins & M. Rutter (Eds.), *Straight and devious pathways from childhood to adulthood* (pp. 182–204). New York: Cambridge University Press.

Rotter, J. I., & Diamond, J. M. (1987). What maintains the frequences of human genetic diseases? *Nature, 329,* 289–90.

Royal College of Physicians. (1983). *Health or smoking? Follow-up report of the Royal College of Physicians.* London: Pitman.

Royal College of Psychiatrists. (1986). *Alcohol: Our favourite drug.* London: Tavistock.

Runciman, W. G. (1972). *Relative deprivation and social justice.* Harmondsworth, Middlesex: Penguin.

Rutter, M. (1979). *Changing youth in a changing society: Patterns of adolescent development and disorder.* London: Nuffield Provincial Hospitals Trust. (1980, Cambridge, MA: Harvard University Press)

Rutter, M. (1981). Epidemiological/longitudinal strategies and causal research in child psychiatry. *Journal of the American Academy of Child Psychiatry, 20,* 513–544.

Rutter, M. (1982). Prevention of children's psychosocial disorders. *Pediatrics, 70,* 883–894.

Rutter, M. (1989). Pathways from childhood to adult life. *Journal of Child Psychology and Psychiatry, 30,* 23–51.

Rutter, M. (1990). Psychosocial resilience and protective mechanisms. In J. Rolf, A. Masten, D. Cicchetti, K. Nuechterlein, & S. Weintraub (Eds.), *Risk and protective factors in the development of psychopathology* (pp. 181–214). New York: Cambridge University Press.

Rutter, M., & Giller, H. (1983). *Juvenile delinquency: Trends and perspectives.* Harmondsworth, Middlesex: Penguin.

Rutter, M., & Madge, N. (1976). *Cycles of disadvantage: A review of research.* London: Heinemann.

Rutter, M., & Pickles, A. (1991). Person-environment interactions: Concepts, mechanisms and implications for data analysis. In T. Wachs & R. Plomin (Eds.), *Conceptualization and measurement of organism-environment interaction* (pp. 105–141). Washington, DC: American Psychological Association.

Rutter, M., & Quinton, D. (1977). Psychiatric disorder—Ecological factors and concepts of causation. In H. McGurk (Ed.), *Ecological factors in human development* (pp. 173–187). Amsterdam: North Holland.

Rutter, M., & Rutter, M. (in press). *Growing minds: Personal development across the life span.* Harmondsworth, Middlesex, and New York: Penguin and Basic Books.

Scarr, S. (1988). How genotypes and environments combine: Development and individual differences. In N. Bolger, A. Caspi, G. Downey & M. Moorehouse (Eds.), *Persons in context: Developmental processes* (pp. 217–244). Cambridge: Cambridge University Press.

Scarr, S., & McCartney, K. (1983). How people make their own environments: A theory of genotype—environment effects. *Child Development, 54,* 424–435.

Segal, J. (Ed.). (1975). *Research into the service of mental health: Report of the Research Task Force of the National Institute of Mental Health* (DHEW Publication no. [ADM] 75–236). Rockville, MD: National Institute of Mental Health.

Smith, G. D., Bartley, M., & Blane, D. (1990). The Black Report on socioeconomic inequalities in health ten years on. *British Medical Journal, 301,* 373–377.

Stattin, H., & Magnusson, D. (1990). *Pubertal maturation in female development.* Hillsdale, NJ: Lawrence Erlbaum.

Strang, J. (1989). "The British System": Past, present and future. *International Review of Psychiatry, 1,* 109–120.

Thomas, L. (1979). *The medusa and the snail: More notes of a biology watcher.* New York: Viking.

Tizard, J. (1975). Race and IQ: The limits of probability? *New Behaviour, 1,* 6–9.

Townsend, P., & Davidson, N. (1982). *Inequalities in health: The Black Report.* Harmondsworth, Middlesex: Penguin.

Udry, J. R. (1990). Hormonal and social determinants of adolescent sexual initiation. In J. Bancroft & J. M. Reinisch (Eds.), *Adolescence and puberty* (pp. 70–87). New York: Oxford University Press.

United Nations Children's Fund. (1990). *The state of the world's children.* Toronto: Oxford University Press.

White, M., & McRae, S. (1989). *Young adults and long-term unemployment.* London: Policy Studies Institute Publications.

Wilkinson, R. G. (Ed.). (1986). *Class and health: Research and longitudinal data.* London and New York: Tavistock.

7. Individual differences as precursors of youth unemployment

JEYLAN T. MORTIMER
Life Course Center
University of Minnesota

Unemployment can be usefully examined from a variety of disciplinary perspectives. Economists and sociologists generally focus on levels of unemployment, either in the society as a whole or in particular regions, industries, or population segments. Unemployment rates are viewed as the result of macrosocietal forces, such as technological changes, migratory patterns, monetary policies, economic cycles, or the operations of the world economy. According to this perspective, individual attributes, especially those that reflect human capital investment (e.g., education and experience), will influence the degree of success in obtaining employment, given their impact on a job seeker's placement in the employment queue. Moreover, stable "tastes for employment" will influence the propensity to seek work.

Psychologists tend to focus on other characteristics that people bring to the employment market, especially values, self-concepts, motivations, and psychological well-being, that could predispose them to become unemployed. These characteristics are usually viewed as quite stable and as sources of variability in both work-related behaviors and the ability to maintain employment over a period of time. Still, experiences of unemployment and work are acknowledged by many sociologists and psychologists as sources of personal change. Operating under the assumption that unemployment is largely dependent on external forces, but maintaining the psychological focus on the individual, social psychologists have studied its personal consequences, as unemployment is seen as a source of economic and social strain with manifold psychological and behavioral implications. Thus, at the individual level, the relationship between the work situation and the person is best conceptualized as truly reciprocal.

Taken to a more general level, it is evident that the educational resources and technical skills of a population can affect both economic growth over a period of time and the degree of adaptability of an economy to changing macroforces. Societal differences in aggregate psychological characteristics may also be more or less conducive to economic activity in general or to particular kinds of economic organization, such as entrepreneurship. At the same time, it is plausible to assume that the distinctive experiences of work and unemployment across societies or historical times are reflected in the psychological character of entire populations.

Recognizing the complementarity of these structural and psychological approaches is consistent with House and Mortimer's (1990) contention that analysts must attend to the reciprocal causal processes through which social structure and personality influence one other. This chapter addresses just one aspect of these dynamic interrelations: the extent to which individual differences are precursors of youth unemployment. It ignores, for the most part, the large literature on structural unemployment and on the psychosocial consequences of unemployment experience, given that other chapters in this book focus on these topics. But because a focus on any one element in the complex causal system linking the person and the work situation is incomplete, both sociological and psychological concepts and findings are drawn upon in an attempt to explain the linkages between individual attributes and employment outcomes.

Individual Differences as Correlates of Unemployment

The fact that the unemployed have distinctive individual characteristics is widely recognized. Clearly, unemployment is not randomly distributed. Among U.S. household heads aged 35–64 who were studied during a ten-year period (1968-1977) by the Panel Study of Income Dynamics, 5 percent of the sample accounted for almost half the aggregate unemployment time for the entire panel (Corcoran & Hill, 1980). Among those who were unemployed, the average duration of unemployment was 27 weeks during this ten-year period; but for the top 5 percent, who were the most frequently jobless, it was 96 weeks. Numerous studies in the United States (see, e.g., Kessler, Turner & House, 1989) and other countries report that the unemployed, in comparison to employed labor-force participants, are more likely to be young (DiPrete, 1981), female (Banks & Ullah, 1988; Dayton, 1981; Feather & O'Brien, 1986b), black (Banks & Ullah, 1988;

DiPrete, 1981; Lichter, 1988), less well educated (DiPrete, 1981; Miller, 1988, pp. 330–332), of lower academic ability (Dayton, 1981), and judged to have less "academic potential" (Feather & O'Brien, 1986b; O'Brien & Feather, 1990). Marital status is likewise implicated, as single persons have higher rates of unemployment than those who are married (U.S. Department of Labor, 1991). Low socioeconomic background has also been found to be associated with unemployment (Dayton, 1981; Millham, Bullock, & Hosie, 1978). The problem of unemployment in the United States appears to be exacerbated for individuals who have particular combinations of these characteristics, such as those who are black, young, and poorly educated (Lichter, 1988).

These patterns may be illustrated with seasonally adjusted U. S. unemployment data (U.S. Department of Labor, 1991). Whereas the total unemployment rate for the civilian, noninstitutionalized labor force was 7.0 percent in June 1991, it was three times higher—21.2 percent—among 16- to 19-year-olds who were not enrolled in school. Among 16- to 24-year-old (nonenrolled) black young people who had not completed high school, 39.9 percent were unemployed. Similarly, in Britain, young people with fewer educational qualifications, ethnic minorities, and women are found to be especially vulnerable to unemployment (Banks & Jackson, 1982; Millham et al., 1978).

Young people are at risk, given their relatively low levels of work experience; this risk increases when they also lack other forms of human capital investment such as education or job training. As workers obtain more occupational experience, they acquire skills that make them more valuable to employers (but this process may not operate at the lower levels of a segmented labor market, where competent performance is attainable after a brief period of training). Moreover, DiPrete (1981) speculates that as workers learn more about the job market, they have less need to "shop" for jobs and voluntary terminations decrease. As workers acquire job tenure and are rewarded for firm-specific skills by higher wages, they may also find it more difficult to find new jobs that would pay as well as those they already have. Moreover, the probability of involuntary terminations decreases with tenure because of seniority clauses in collective bargaining agreements (DiPrete, 1981).

The relationships between individual-level variables—such as age, education and skill level, occupational experience, and job tenure—and unemployment are not immutable, but vary across time and social context. For example, educational deficits have more negative implications today than a generation ago, especially for urban youth. Because of the change from a goods-producing to a service industrial base in U. S. inner cities, and the movement of jobs to the suburbs, the job skills of young urban blacks no longer match the needs of the labor market (Wilson, 1987). The decline in entry-level blue-collar jobs most severely affects young adults seeking their first jobs, who have too little education to obtain higher-level employment. Largely as a result of these trends, we now hear of the "hard-core unemployed" (Lichter, 1988) or "unemployable youth."

In addition to this kind of "structural unemployment," a host of negative psychological attributes (see Banks & Ullah, 1988; Jackson, Stafford, Banks, & Warr, 1983, p. 525; Kasl, 1979, p. 188) have been found to be associated with unemployment. Unemployed people have been found to exhibit high rates of depression and anxiety, low self-esteem, and an external control orientation. The special psychological features, problems, or deficits that are found to be particularly pronounced among the unemployed have two plausible sources. First, consistent with the psychological approach noted above, they could be causes of unemployment—personality features that either interfere with effective job search or lead to ineffective performance and involuntary job termination. But they also could be the consequence of unemployment that is the result of structural forces. A considerable body of research has demonstrated psychological change in individuals, indicating decrements in psychological well-being that occur in response to the unemployment experience (Banks & Jackson, 1982; Cohn, 1978; Hamilton, Hoffman, Broman, & Rauma, 1991; Hoffman, Hamilton, Braman, & Rauma, 1991; Jackson et al., 1983; Kessler et al., 1989; O'Brien, 1986; Patton & Noller, 1984; Winefield, Tiggemann, Winefield, & Goldney, 1991).

In some circumstances, for example, when entire plants close, unemployment cannot reasonably be attributed to individual characteristics (Hamilton et al., 1991; Hoffman et al., 1991; Rosenthal, 1991). But more often both hypotheses—that individual differences affect the likelihood of unemployment and that unemployment produces individual psychological deficits—are plausible. The covariation of employment status and individual psychological attributes, and even some biological features (such as ill health), cannot be construed as unequivocal evidence for either explanation. Most likely the truth lies with both, in complex reciprocal interrelationships between unemployment experience and individual psychological functioning.

Longitudinal Designs

Given the problems in interpreting cross-sectional data, a longitudinal design is essential to begin to unravel the causal dynamics underlying the relationships between employment status and individual differences. Moreover, only with longitudinal data can one monitor changes in the effects of individual variables over time (Rosenthal, 1991). Three alternative longitudinal strategies can be found in the literature. The first type of study begins with a sample of students, usually those who are about to leave (Dayton, 1981; Dowling & O'Brien, 1981; Feather & O'Brien, 1986a, 1986b; Kandel & Yamaguchi, 1987; Layton & Eysenck, 1985; O'Brien & Feather, 1990; Patton & Noller, 1984; Winefield & Tiggemann, 1985; Winefield et al., 1991) or have recently left (Banks & Jackson, 1982; Jackson et al., 1983) secondary school or college (Mortimer, Lorence, & Kumka, 1986), and follows these persons over time. Typically, the investigator attempts to predict, on the basis of data collected while the students were still in school, who becomes employed and who becomes unemployed some months, years, or even a decade later. In this kind of study trajectories of change in individual characteristics for both groups can be charted. This is a good design for identifying individual, psychosocial variables that may be precursors of youth or young adult unemployment.

A second design enables consideration of a broader age range of workers, in all phases of the career. A community sample or another representative sample of adults is selected, including those who are employed and those who are unemployed (Corcoran & Hill, 1980; DiPrete, 1981; Kessler et al., 1989). These persons are then followed over a period of time. In a variant of this approach, a representative sample of adults is selected who are (or were) employed in a particular industry, such as auto workers (Hamilton et al., 1991; Hoffman et al., 1991); or from a restricted number of firms (Layton & Eysenck, 1985). Using the sample of persons who are employed at the first data collection point, the researcher can then examine whether psychological variables measured initially predict who becomes unemployed later in the work career. Among the unemployed, the researcher examines whether prior psychological variables distinguish persons who, after a period of time, become reemployed from those who remain unemployed.

In a third type of study, the researcher commences with a sample of unemployed (Banks & Ullah, 1988; Rosenthal, 1991; Shamir, 1986) and monitors their work status over time. Alternatively, an unemployed sample may be chosen and its characteristics examined in relation to the duration of already experienced unemployment (Hui, 1991). Although the second and third designs do not allow one to address the causes of the initially observed unemployment, they may be useful in identifying psychosocial factors that predict successful or unsuccessful employment searches among those who are already unemployed. In this way, the precursors of persistent unemployment may be identified.

It is sometimes assumed, particularly by investigators who take the first approach, that the causal relationship between individual differences, measured initially, and subsequent employment outcomes is unidirectional; meaning that individual differences cause employment outcomes. Although this assumption is probably the most tenable with respect to the first type of study, even students still in secondary school may have sought part- or full-time jobs and may have had varying levels of success in the youth labor-market. Such prior labor-market experience is especially likely to have occurred in the United States, where it is common for students to be employed while they are still in high school (see Mortimer, 1991). In addition to providing adolescents with advantages in finding jobs after leaving school (Millham et al., 1978, p. 21), students' experiences of job search, employment, and unemployment could engender psychosocial differences related to subsequent employment outcomes. Any assumption regarding the exogeneity of individual characteristics in the second and third types of study, in which the investigator follows adults, is completely untenuous. Given the findings of prior research that demonstrate the pervasive influence of adult work experience on individual change (see Kohn & Schooler, 1983; Mortimer et al., 1986), there is strong reason to believe that adult attributes have been affected by the prior work history. Moreover, a prolonged spell of unemployment may reduce the motivation to seek work after subsequent unemployment spells (Layton & Eysenck, 1985). Thus, in all three of these study types, individual traits that predict subsequent unemployment experience could be causes and/or effects of prior labor-market experience.

Still, the first design leads to the least ambiguous interpretation of findings because it may reasonably be assumed that most secondary-school students have had minimal labor-market experience in comparison to that of adults. Because of this, and because this book is focused on the phenomenon of *youth* unemployment, I give most attention to findings drawn from the first type of study, that which follows a sample of students as they leave full-time schooling. However, I also consider the results of other relevant longitudinal studies.

It should be noted at the outset that panel studies focused on this topic sometimes lack adequate initial response rates (Shamir, 1986) or retention rates over a period of time (Banks & Jackson, 1982; Winefield & Tiggemann, 1985; Winefield et al., 1991); these problems raise the possibility of selection bias. Small sample size (Patton & Noller, 1984) or a small number of unemployed (Layton & Eysenck, 1985; Winefield et al., 1991) likewise diminishes the value of some research on this subject. Acknowledging these deficiencies, we focus here on the degree of convergence across empirical studies.

Psychosocial Factors as Precursors of Unemployment

Psychosocial factors believed to foster unemployment tend to be conceptualized somewhat differently in the various social science disciplines. Psychologists speak of work motivation, need for achievement, sense of efficacy, expectations, and perceptions of the opportunity structure (see, e. g., Feather, 1986). Sociological social psychologists have examined values (Mortimer et al., 1986), self-conceptions (Schwalbe & Gecas, 1988), and distress (Kessler et al., 1989) as factors likely to precede joblessness or an unstable work history. Economists attach considerable importance to the "reservation wage," which is, "the minimum offered wage necessary to induce an unemployed person to take up employment" (Hui, 1991, p. 1341). Economists also examine "tastes for employment" and the "propensity to work" or, conversely, the "propensity for unemployment," the "taste for leisure" (Corcoran & Hill, 1980), and "taste for vacation" (Coe, 1978). Corcoran and Hill (1980) note that unemployment can be stable over time because of personal preferences, motivations, or talents, which they refer to as worker "heterogeneity" (see also Baker & Elias, 1991). But if, as in their analysis, heterogeneity is defined by the past experience of unemployment itself, conceptualized as standing for a host of unmeasured individual factors, the question as to which particular individual attributes account for unemployment is, in effect, bypassed.

These diverse psychosocial features may be grouped in four broad categories: first, psychological orientations, such as attitudes, values, "propensities," and "tastes"; second, attributes of the self-concept, such as self-esteem or self-efficacy; third, variables reflecting distress or psychopathology; and fourth, differences in work-related behavior. Are they, in fact, predictive of unemployment? Whereas there appear to be far more studies of the ways in which unemployment fosters change in psychological orientations than on psychological differences as causes of unemployment, there is evidence that each of these categories of psychosocial attributes is implicated in employment success.

Psychological orientations

Several studies of school-leavers have found that psychological orientations predict subsequent employment status. For example, a measure of adherence to the "Protestant work ethic" distinguished students who found jobs one year (Feather & O'Brien, 1986b) and two years (O'Brien & Feather, 1990) after leaving Australian secondary schools. Greater perceived need for a job also characterized those who were subsequently more successful in finding work (Feather & O'Brien, 1986b). Dayton (1981) points to the importance of having clearly crystallized employment goals, and found that U.S. youth themselves perceive their absence as problematic in their job-search efforts. However, although the earlier need for achievement predicted employment status in another study of Australian school-leavers (Winefield & Tiggemann, 1985), this effect vanished when socioeconomic background and indicators of academic interest and potential were controlled (Tiggemann & Winefield, 1989).

In a factor analytic study, Feather (1986) found two dimensions of orientations toward future job prospects among Australian secondary-school students that he believes are relevant to future employment success. The first is a value factor—the importance of work, including indicators of interest in work, job need, and job want. The second is a factor reflecting expectations, which he calls "unemployment disappointment." The latter reflects the degree of helplessness or pessimism regarding job prospects, including the level of confidence about finding a job, the difficulty of doing so, the amount of time it will take, and the sense of helplessness or personal control regarding employment outcomes.

Possibly also relevant to future job prospects are young people's work values. Dowling and O'Brien (1981) found that Australian respondents who were unemployed one year after leaving school did not differ from their employed counterparts in their prior intrinsic occupational values. But in an older and better-educated group of U.S. school-leavers, extrinsic values measured in the senior year of college were found to predict men's employment stability in the decade after graduation (Mortimer et al., 1986). Those college seniors who valued the achievement of high income, advancement, and prestige more highly while they were still in college had less unemployment, involuntary part-time employment, and underemployment, as well as fewer changes in career direction, during the ten years following college graduation.

Finally, there is evidence that a high reservation wage fosters longer spells of unemployment (Baker & Elias, 1991; Hui, 1991). That is, those whose minimal acceptable wage offers are higher must typically wait longer to receive such offers.

Self-concept

Evidence regarding the self-concept as a precursor of unemployment is mixed. Research on a large panel of U.S. young people in Washington State found that women who had higher self-esteem in high school experienced less subsequent unemployment (measured in months) over a 13-year period following (with father's occupational status controlled); however, no such effect was observed for men (Spenner & Otto, 1985). Winefield and Tiggemann (1985) report that Australian students who manifested lower self-esteem when they were still in high school were more likely to be unemployed two years later. However, Tiggemann and Winefield (1989) find that self-esteem no longer had predictive power with respect to employment outcome when socioeconomic background and variables indicating academic aspiration and potential were controlled. Moreover, in another Australian study, self-esteem in the last year of secondary school did not differentiate students who became employed, unemployed, or returned to school five months later (Patton & Noller, 1984). Similarly, earlier self-esteem did not influence reemployment six months after the initial data collection among a sample of Israeli unemployed (Shamir, 1986).

Whereas self-esteem refers to a global sense of worth, another kind of self-conception, referencing the perceived ability to achieve one's objectives, is also relevant to job prospects. Such self-perceptions—including internal control, self-efficacy, and sense of competence—reflect the individual's expectations regarding the likelihood of successful goal attainment, such as finding a job (see Bandura's [1988] summary of a large body of research demonstrating the importance of self-efficacy for work-related behaviors). They are akin to Feather's (1986) notion of "unemployment disappointment," but conceptualized as a self-conception, an enduring attribute of the self. Self-rated confidence in finding a job distinguished subsequently employed and unemployed Australian school-leavers one year (Feather & O'Brien, 1986b) and two years (O'Brien & Feather, 1990) later. Similarly, those whose general sense of personal competence was weaker while still in school were more likely to be unemployed one year later. However, Spenner and Otto (1985) did not find that personal control orientation, measured during high school, predicted duration of unemployment over a 13-year period thereafter. Tiggemann and Winefield (1989) also find that locus of control does not predict employment status measured one, three, and five years after high school when academic potential and socioeconomic background are controlled. (Internal verses external locus of control in the last year of high school also failed to predict subsequent employment status in Patton and Noller's [1984] research.)

Distress

The third set of variables linked to unemployment experience refers to distress or psychopathology. Some evidence indicates that young people who are more distressed have greater difficulty in the job market. Several studies have shown that indicators of depressive affect and other psychological problems predict subsequent unemployment. Members of a sample of school-leavers in Adelaide, South Australia, who were found to be unemployed had lower life satisfaction, manifested greater stress, a less positive attitude, and more depressive affect when they were still in school two years earlier (Feather & O'Brien, 1986b; O'Brien & Feather, 1990). In another Australian study (Winefield & Tiggemann, 1985), young people who became unemployed expressed more boredom and depression, and males who became unemployed expressed more loneliness, before leaving school. However, depressive affect was not a significant predictor of future employment status in a later analysis using different statistical procedures and predictive intervals (Tiggemann & Winefield, 1989).

A similarly designed study showed that English school-age (mean age 16) subjects scoring high on the Psychoticism Scale on the Eysenck Personality Questionnaire were more likely to be unemployed one year later (six months after leaving school). The authors describe high scorers as "immature, irresponsible, troublesome, solitary, hostile, anti-authoritarian, independent, non-conformist, querulous and generally difficult to handle" (Layton & Eysenck, 1985, p. 388). They speculate that such persons may lack sufficient social skills to present themselves favorably to employers and that they also may be disinclined to seek work (Layton & Eysenck, 1985).

However, a study of school-leavers with relatively poor educational qualifications in the City of Leeds showed that prior differences on a measure of minor psychiatric disorders were not present in groups differentiated by subsequent employment status (Banks & Jackson, 1982; in a subsequent analysis, Jackson et al. [1983] found that differences between employed young people who were to remain employed and those who became unemployed were significant only in one of four subgroups). It could be that minor psychiatric problems are not very consequential for obtaining the kinds of lower-level employment that such young people sought. There also were no significant differences in depression for school-leavers in Australia who subsequently became employed, unemployed, or returned to school (Patton & Noller, 1984); but this study included a very small number of unemployed.

Hamilton and colleagues' (1991) quasi-experimental study in the United States of a wider age range of workers in four closing (and a control group of 12 nonclosing) General Motors plants from 1987 to 1989 found that depression, in fact, was a significant precursor of subsequent unemployment. Both unemployment and depression at wave 1 predicted unemployment at wave 2, one year after the plant closed; and unemployment and depression at wave 2 similarly predicted unemployment at wave 3 (2 years after the closing). Depression was found to be a more powerful predictor of unemployment than anxiety.

Still, depressive affect at time 1 did not influence reemployment (employment status six months after the initial data collection) in a sample of Israeli unemployed (Shamir, 1986). Furthermore, 17- to 62-year-old male skilled and semiskilled English workers facing dismissal from a job who scored higher on a scale of "psychoticism" were not less successful than other workers in obtaining future jobs (Layton & Eysenck, 1985).

Kessler, and colleagues (1989) report, on the basis of their study of a community sample in areas of Detroit that had high unemployment rates, that *greater* prior distress was associated with reemployment of the unemployed (controlling age, sex, education, race, and marital status) over a one-year period. There were also weak *positive* associations between reemployment and prior depression and anxiety ($p < .10$ for both). Somewhat paradoxically, the authors speculate that the more distressed unemployed may have engaged in more strenuous job-search efforts, encouraged by improving economic conditions in the Detroit area. On the basis of this evidence, we must conclude that the relationship between subclinical individual psychopathology and employment outcomes is equivocal.

Behavioral differences

Only a few studies have focused on behavioral predictors of future job status. Kandel and Yamaguchi (1987) report that U.S. students' (residing in New York State) level of drug use, while still in school, predicted subsequent unemployment and job separation. Similarly, young Australians who were unemployed one year after leaving school exhibited lower activity levels while still in high school (Feather & O'Brien, 1986b). One might expect that persons with poor work habits would be more likely to become jobless. Coe (1978) notes that absenteeism, while on the job, is associated with subsequent involuntary termination.

Causes of Pychosocial Differences Linked to Unemployment

Though the body of evidence reviewed in the previous section is not entirely consistent, several longitudinal studies have, as we have seen, demonstrated significant individual-level precursors of unemployment. In view of this evidence, it becomes important from both a scientific and a policy perspective to know what causes these psychological and behavioral differences. Some economists posit that there is a small group of individuals who have repeated unemployment because of the characteristics they bring to the labor market (Corcoran & Hill, 1980). A social-psychological perspective points to processes of socialization early in life—related to social class, gender, family characteristics, peer relationships, or school experiences—that lead to the development of personal attributes that are relevant to job search (Feather & O'Brien, 1986a). For example, Feather (1986) finds that eleventh-grade students who received job guidance while still in school, who had high levels of high school performance, and who had work experience prior to leaving high school had lower levels of helplessness and pessimism in relation to future job prospects. In this study, students of higher social class origin believed that unemployment was attributable to more internal causes, and this belief was negatively related to helplessness and pessimism.

   In considering the origins of psychosocial differences related to employment, attention must be directed to gender. Though a review of gender differences in psychological attributes that may be related to employment is far beyond the scope of this chapter, there is considerable evidence that adolescent girls are at a disadvantage with respect to many of the psychosocial dimensions that have been linked to employment outcomes. For example, they have been found to have lower self-esteem (Simmons & Blyth, 1987), higher levels of depressive affect (Rutter, 1986), and a weaker sense of self-efficacy (Gecas, 1989, p. 305; Maccoby & Jacklin, 1974; Simmons & Blyth, 1987). Our own findings from an ongoing study of a representative sample of high school students confirms this pattern for all three psychological dimensions (see Finch, Shanahan, Mortimer, & Ryu, 1991; Shanahan, Finch, Mortimer, & Ryu, 1991). Moreover, whereas adolescent boys are more strongly focused on achievement-related issues, for girls of this age interpersonal considerations are more prominent (Gilligan, 1982).

Furthermore, even though adult women in the United States and in European countries are increasingly likely to be employed, adolescent girls still encounter traditional values emphasizing the importance of appearance, popularity, marriage, and parenthood, which may interfere with achievement-related effort and occupational advancement. By observing the experiences of their mothers and other adult women, adolescent girls may become increasingly aware of the dilemmas and role conflicts posed by the attempt to combine family life and career, as well as the sex-typed job market and other obstacles to women's achievement.

Ambivalence about future work, when coupled with lower levels of self-esteem, efficacy, and well-being, relative to boys, could engender considerable psychological disadvantages for young women with respect to future employment outcomes. Moreover, reduced expectations about future job prospects, though realistic in view of the contemporary market situation, could erode achievement ambitions in favor of more traditionally female objectives. Hui (1991, p. 1347) finds that young Australian women's reservation wage is about 17 percent lower than that of males (and notes two other studies that similarly find reservation wage differentials in favor of men [Jones, 1989; Lynch, 1983]). Consistent with this pattern, our own ongoing study of St. Paul, Minnesota, youth shows that adolescent girls are significantly less likely than boys to believe that they will be able to obtain a job that pays well in the future. However, the importance that girls in our study attach to future work is not lower than that of boys (this pattern is consistent with Jackson and colleagues' [1983] finding that commitment to employment does not vary by gender).

Evidence that processes of vocational socialization in the family may underlie the development of psychological orientations that are relevant to employment derives from our longitudinal study of male students at a highly selective U.S. public university (Mortimer et al., 1986). We found that paternal support had a direct positive effect on career stability (including unemployment, involuntary part-time employment, and underemployment, as well as change in career direction). Paternal support also had indirect positive effects on sons' early career histories through the stronger extrinsic work values and higher levels of work involvement that characterized students who reported closer and more communicative relationships with their fathers.

As noted earlier, once an individual has entered the workforce, employment and joblessness, as well as the quality of work (Kohn & Schooler, 1983; Mortimer et al., 1986), can influence a range of psychological attributes that may be implicated in subsequent employment success.

Our longitudinal study of teenagers in the United States has found that job stressors influence depressive affect and control orientations among the youngest workers—those that pursue part-time jobs while they are still in high school (Finch et al., 1991; Shanahan et al., 1991). Adolescent part-time work has been found to be positively associated with employment and income in the years immediately following high school (Freeman & Wise, 1979; Meyer & Wise, 1982; Millham et al., 1978; Mortimer & Finch, 1986), but these benefits appear to accrue to white and Hispanic, but not black, youth (Steel, 1991). U.S. young people themselves apparently also recognize the utility of summer and after-school work for obtaining subsequent employment (Dayton, 1981). The benefits of early employment may derive from several sources: increased skill levels and productivity, enhanced sense of efficacy resulting from prior job success, greater familiarity with the job market and the process of job search, useful contacts obtained at work, or the fact that some youth retain their early jobs after leaving school. Corcoran & Hill (1980, p. 40) comment that the proposition that work conditions influence job-relevant worker behavior is consistent with dual labor-market theory: "men whose first jobs are unstable and fail to reward tenure, punctuality, and so forth may become alienated, develop poor work habits, and/or become less attached to the labor force."

It is also plausible that prior experiences of joblessness would foster the development of psychological characteristics that affect the likelihood of locating future employment. Studies have found evidence for causal links between unemployment and distress, self-blame, and other psychopathology (Hamilton et al., 1991; Kessler et al., 1989) that could jeopardize future success in the job market. (With long duration of unemployment, the reservation wage also declines; see Hui, 1991.) Moreover, frequent or persistent unemployment may lead U.S. black (and other) workers (DiPrete, 1981) to become discouraged, dropping out of the labor force because they believe work is unavailable. Thus, unemployment could alter tastes, skills, and motivations in such a way that unemployment is sustained (Baker & Elias, 1991). However, given the importance of work conditions for the development of individual attributes that may influence employment success, it is not sufficient to simply provide employment to avert negative outcomes. Corcoran and Hill (1980, p. 54) conclude, on the basis of their analysis of data from the Panel Study of Income Dynamics, that "unless job creation programs also . . . identify and alter those skills, attitudes, or habits which influence work stability, they will not lower future unemployment."

Although the effects of unemployment on individual attributes have been found to occur in diverse samples, they may be particularly potent among youth, given that their work orientations and behaviors are in an especially formative stage. A wide body of evidence indicates that individuals are particularly malleable, and responsive to social experiences, during the period of transition to adulthood (see Mortimer, 1991). Work autonomy has a stronger effect on job satisfaction and the commitment to work among young adults than among older workers (Lorence & Mortimer, 1985; Mortimer, Finch, & Maruyama, 1988). However, Miller, Slomeczynski, and Kohn (1985) find that the substantive complexity of work similarly influences intellectual flexibility in all age groups in the United States and Poland.

Other Individual Differences as Precursors of Unemployment

Individual psychosocial variables have been discussed at some length in the preceding section, and individual differences related to demographic features, human capital, and social location were alluded to briefly in the introduction (e.g., age, race, gender, educational attainment, socioeconomic status). There are other individual-level variables, likely to be implicated in the unemployment experience, that have been given relatively little attention, such as marital and parental status, career stage, health, and various biological factors.

It is commonly believed, for example, that married men are better job prospects than those who are unmarried; they are viewed as more "settled down," as having greater need for a job, and therefore as less likely to quit their jobs (Osterman, 1989). Responsibility for dependents certainly does increase the need for income, which might be expected to be negatively related to unemployment (DiPrete, 1981). However, it also typically increases absenteeism due to the need to care for other family members during working hours, which increases the likelihood of involuntary termination (Coe, 1978). At least partly because the latter responsibility primarily affects women, employers may not link women's marital and parental statuses to "stability" in the same way as they do with respect to men.

As noted earlier, the effect of age on employment status is largely due to the covariation of age with work experience or tenure in particular jobs, but DiPrete (1981) finds that age also moderates the effects of job tenure. Finding a higher association between instability in the recent employment history and unemployment risk for older workers, he explains that in youth, unemployment is part of the "sorting process" through which workers establish themselves in a career (see also Baker and Elias's [1991] discussion of the search model). But workers with chronic problems (presumably including personality and other individual deficits) will continue to suffer frequent and prolonged spells of unemployment even after the age when most workers will have "settled down."

As for biological factors, levels of intelligence and other cognitive capacities influence problem solving, as well as skill and knowledge acquisition (Gottfredson, 1986), and these may be at least partially genetically determined. Moreover, there are undoubtedly threshold levels of such capacities below which it is not possible to adequately perform particular kinds of work or, possibly, at the extreme end of the distribution, any job. Similarly, persons of all ages who have chronic health problems would also appear to be at risk of unemployment. Indicators of mental and physical health are significant predictors of employment for both women and men (Mullahy & Sindelar, 1990). Worker illness is a major cause of absenteeism, which is linked to employment instability (Coe, 1978); because women suffer more health problems than men, and blacks more health difficulties than whites, gender and race also are implicated in the health-unemployment nexus. However, other than at the extremes of the distribution, it is reasonable to suppose that biological factors such as these are more strongly related to the types of jobs that persons hold than to employment per se.

Directions for Future Research

Several questions need to be addressed in future studies to further scientific understanding of individual differences and unemployment. Of greatest importance, we need to know more about the intervening mechanisms through which individual differences might influence employment outcomes. Whereas prior studies predict subsequent unemployment on the basis of individual traits, we know little about the processes that generate these relationships. For example, it is important to understand how the various psychological precursors influence the individual's definition of the situation either upon entering the workforce for the first time or upon loss of a job. As Hamilton and colleagues (1991) point out, those who become unemployed may construct several alternative interpretations. Most obviously, they may see themselves as unemployed and looking for a new job. But such individuals also may define themselves as temporarily out of the workforce (which they found was a more typical definition among workers in closing GM plants who had more seniority, those who were older, and those who were female [see also Warr, Jackson,

& Banks, 1982]). They may also see little prospect of finding a new job and become so-called discouraged workers, dropping out of the labor force entirely. Finally, they may consider themselves to be retired.

Given these alternative definitions, great care should be exercised in defining the particular groups that are compared in studies of individual-level precursors of employment outcomes. The U.S. Department of Labor's definition of unemployment applies only if a person is not employed and has actively sought work during the past four weeks. But researchers use a varied set of definitions; unfortunately, these are not always explicit. Hamilton and colleagues (1991) defined the unemployed as those who were not employed and not retired, irrespective of whether there had been active job-search attempts. Some studies consider part-time and full-time workers to be employed (Hamilton et al., 1991), whereas others remove part-time workers from the analysis. Persons who are out of the labor force may be dropped from consideration, thus ignoring the "discouraged worker" syndrome, but sometimes they are considered to be "unemployed."

Operational definitions of the "employed" and "unemployed" are particularly important with respect to youth. There are a number of alternative social statuses that young people may occupy, and their determinants and consequences may be distinct. For example, many young people postpone entry into the labor force when labor conditions are unfavorable by prolonging schooling. Some continue economic dependency on their parents, without actively seeking work. Though not having gainful employment, such persons are not "unemployed"; some may be "discouraged workers."

Furthermore, attention must be given to gender differences. Whereas it is often noted that women are disadvantaged in the labor force and experience difficulty in the employment market (Banks & Ullah, 1988; Dayton, 1981; Feather & O'Brien, 1986b; Hui, 1991), the U.S. Department of Labor (1991) reports that women, in fact, have *lower* unemployment rates than men.[1] Among white youth, ages 16–19, 14.9 percent of girls were unemployed and 19.9 percent of boys. Although for both genders unemployment was higher among blacks, for black males the rate was 37.4 percent (including those in school and those not enrolled) and for females it was 28.9 percent. This paradox may be explained as follows: If women who are not employed do not actively seek jobs, they are defined as "out of the labor force," and they are therefore not counted among the unemployed. But this group is certainly quite diverse, containing discouraged workers as well as those who are not employed by choice. Warr and colleagues (1982) report that longer unemployment is associated with *lower* psychological distress among young women, a pattern that they attribute to the fact that many of their "unemployed" women have withdrawn from the labor market, and such women may be quite satisfied with their situation given that many are pursuing family-related objectives (see also Baker & Elias, 1991, pp. 230–231; Banks & Ullah, 1988, pp. 119–120).

It is plausible to assume that both men and women with lower self-efficacy may more readily become "discouraged" or, once an age threshold has been reached, "retired." Banks and Ullah (1988, p. 118) find that British youth who had low expectations about finding a job, and those who viewed job seeking as unlikely to lead to success, were more likely to be among the "discouraged workers" one year later. Hoffman and colleagues (1991, Table 6) show that those who were not employed and *not* looking for work in the second wave of their study of U.S. auto workers had somewhat higher levels of depression and self-blame at wave 1—but significance levels are not reported—than those who were subsequently unemployed and looking. In fact, not looking for a job (i.e., dropping out of the workforce) may be one way to protect a fragile psyche, for they show that to seek a job and not to find one increases depression. Those who were "not looking" and did not find work were less distressed than the active, but unsuccessful, job seekers (Hamilton et al., 1991; see also Banks & Ullah, 1988). Paradoxically then, given the various common definitions of the jobless situation, it could be that those who become unemployed have higher self-efficacy than those who become discouraged or retired. This effect would be entirely obscured if persons are deleted from the analysis who, after losing their jobs, move out of the workforce or become discouraged or retired.

In interpreting the linkages between individual characteristics, especially psychological variables, and unemployment, researchers often allude to their probable effects on job search. But there is little evidence that prior individual attributes influence search behavior. For example, Feather (1986) speculates that individuals with high scores on a scale signifying the importance of employment and low scores on a scale indicating helplessness and pessimism about job prospects (or the efficacy of job search attempts) would engage in more active job search. Kessler and colleagues (1989) also hypothesize that more extreme distress in the face of unemployment fosters more intense job search, especially when improvements in the economy generate hope that search efforts will pay off.

One empirical study that did attempt to link self-esteem with search behavior reports mixed findings. In research on unemployed workers in Israel, Shamir (1986) examined the relationship between self-esteem and the frequency of use of seven job-search methods: going to an employment service, reading newspaper want ads, placing personal ads, approaching friends or relatives about jobs, applying directly to employers by letter or telephone, personal visits, and interviews. He found no such relationship. However, among those workers who became reemployed, those with lower prior levels of self-esteem were more likely to use impersonal methods, such as the labor exchange or employment service. Those with higher self-esteem made more use of individualistic and active methods such as personal contacts and direct application to the prospective employer. (But Hui [1991] reports no significant relationship between informal versus formal methods of job search and unemployment duration.)

Another possible mediator of the relationship between psychological variables and employment status is the willingness to accept different kinds of work. In the same study of unemployed workers, Shamir (1986) reports that those who had lower levels of self-esteem exhibited greater flexibility concerning pay level and the professional content of the job (in relation to their professional training and experiences). Thus, they were more willing to accept jobs that did not match their income and job-content desires. Whereas such flexibility may be useful with respect to immediate employment prospects, it may have more negative long-term career implications. However, Kessler and colleagues (1989) did not find that greater distress led unemployed workers to take poorer jobs (in terms of earnings and job security) upon reemployment.

Of course, the effects of individual differences on employment are only partially mediated by such variables as psychological interpretations of the situation, job search, and related worker attitudes and behaviors. Employer discrimination (DiPrete, 1981; Hui, 1991) may be the source of much unemployment among women, minority groups, the physically and mentally disabled, persons who are obese or disfigured, the young, and the old. Moreover, after a time, unemployment may feed on itself as employers track workers with prior job instability into less secure jobs and career lines (Baker & Elias, 1991; Corcoran & Hill, 1980). If this were to happen, prolonged unemployment in youth could be especially pernicious. Clearly, there is a need for more research on the mechanisms through which psychosocial and other individual attributes generate unemployment.

In addition to such intervening mechanisms, we need to know more about moderating factors: for example, whether psychosocial determinants of unemployment differ depending on the circumstances of unemployment. Probably because studies generally focus exclusively on one or another particular group, most often school-leavers or household heads, there is little attempt to address, either theoretically or empirically, the possibility that there may be differing individual precursors depending on the stage of the life span. However, it is plausible to assume that unemployment following initial entry to the workforce after leaving school would have different precursors than unemployment at mid-career. A teenager, upon leaving full-time schooling, might be motivated to find a job, at least in part, by a desire for independence from parents and dissatisfaction with continued economic and other forms of dependency (Borman, 1991). In contrast, the older worker's job-search attempts may be more closely linked to family economic needs; the position of work in the "hierarchy of identities" (Stryker, 1985); and prior investment in, and commitment to, work. Relatedly, different individual precursors may be relevant to reemployment, depending on the immediate circumstances surrounding unemployment, such as whether it has come about as a result of voluntary termination or quitting or as a consequence of involuntary termination, such as by being fired or by plant closings.

The broader social context, and especially the structure of the labor market, is another potential conditioning factor. Although studies have been conducted in different national contexts—for example, in Israel (Shamir, 1986), Great Britain (Banks & Jackson, 1982; Jackson et al., 1983; Millham et al., 1978; Warr, et al., 1982), Australia (Dowling & O'Brien, 1981; Feather & O'Brien, 1986a, 1986b; Hui, 1991; O'Brien & Feather, 1990; Patton & Noller, 1984; Winefield & Tiggemann, 1985; Winefield et al., 1991), and the United States (Dayton, 1981; Hoffman et al., 1991; Kessler, et al., 1989)— there has been little attention to cross-national differences in culture, social structure, labor-market functioning, or the institutional linkages between school and work that would lead certain psychosocial dimensions to be more important in one context than in another.

Particularly welcome would be studies that explicitly compared the relevance of given psychosocial factors to youthful employment outcomes in countries that have looser institutional connections between school and work, such as the United States, and those countries that have more highly structured linkages, such as Germany or Japan. (For a comparative analysis of the problems of the school-to-work transition for youth who do not receive postsecondary education in the United States and Germany, see Hamilton, 1990.) Although the youth unemployment rate generally is lower where the transition from school to work is more highly structured, it may also be the case that different psychosocial variables are implicated in early work success depending on such cross-national differences. Rosenbaum, Kariya, Settersten, and Maier (1990) describe the transition from school to work in Japan as highly structured, due to institutionalized linkages between particular schools and firms. The student's prior academic achievement and teacher recommendations are highly consequential in obtaining placement in high-quality jobs. It may be that in such circumstances psychosocial variables that influence school achievement would have much greater relevance for youth employment or unemployment than in circumstances, such as in the United States, where employers may care less about recent school-leavers' academic performance, and schools may have few resources to respond to requests for transcripts and other records, when employers do want them (Borman, 1991, p. 41).

As discussed earlier, it may be misleading to focus on the antecedents of one employment status—unemployment—because the same kinds of psychosocial factors that predict unemployment may have numerous other typical sequelae, not only discouragement (and subsequent dropout from the labor force), but also employment in low-quality, unstable, and both extrinsically and intrinsically unrewarding jobs. Focusing on one problem, unemployment, diverts scientific and public policy attention away from these other employment outcomes. Studying the precursors of a wider range of employment statuses, both functional and dysfunctional, would enable researchers to identify the extent to which psychosocial precursors are general or status-specific. (See Aneshensel, Reutter, & Lachenbruch, 1991, for a parallel argument with respect to the mental health consequences of stress.) From a public policy perspective, unemployment may appear to be the most problematic, particularly in countries such as the United States, where attention focuses on the unemployment rate but not on the number of discouraged or subemployed workers. However, from a personal perspective, or from the point of view of human capital investment and economic productivity, the latter problems may be equally deleterious.

From a political standpoint, Jahoda (1981, p. 185) describes individual versus structural explanations of unemployment and links concerns about personal precursors of unemployment to a conservative worldview:

This view puts the blame for problems connected with work by and large on individual morality or its absence . . . character reform rather than social reform is required. . . . In sharp contrast, the radical world view puts the blame entirely on the system that produces alienation from work and unemployment. Without exploitation, work could be meaningful for all and unemployment eliminated through shorter hours.

She believes that those who espouse the conservative view look to studies of achievement motivation or sociobiology; the radical, who espouses "structural" explanations, finds supportive evidence in role and alienation theories. There is, in fact, empirical evidence that persons with more liberal political views do tend to see unemployment as due to societal causes more than to personal or internal psychological factors (Singer, Stacey, & Ritchie, 1987).

Though there may be some tendency for interest in individual precursors of unemployment to be linked to conservative ideologies, I do not believe that the studies reviewed here support conservative views or political prescriptions. For we know that the precursors that have been linked, theoretically and/or empirically, to unemployment—depressive affect, external control orientations, or pessimistic expectations about the likelihood of finding a job—are all potentially responsive to structural forces, such as poverty, unemployment rates, educational efforts (such as job counseling programs in school), and early experiences in the labor force (Finch et al., 1991; Shanahan et al., 1991).

Such "conservative" versus "radical" dichotomies are all too simple, reminiscent of the persistent debate between the proponents of "cultural" and "structural" explanations of poverty. Wilson (1987) finds that the cultural "pathologies" of the urban ghetto have structural origins. Given the responsiveness of individual personality, attitudes, and values to the structurally determined environmental situation (House & Mortimer, 1990), it is not easy to pinpoint specific "causes," for the empirical identification of antecedents, correlates, or predictors will depend on the particular point at which one enters the reciprocal, dynamic sequence of interrelations of personality and social structure. For example, given the economic, technological, demographic, and other structural trends that have eroded employment opportunities, youth in depressed U.S. inner cities—such as Detroit, Philadelphia, or Chicago—may have few job prospects or occupational role models. However, they do have chances to obtain income through hustling, crime, drugs, or welfare dependency. Educational and occupational aspirations, the motivation to seek jobs, and the sense of control over this process (as well as over life in general) are undoubtedly affected (Sullivan, 1989). Unsuccessful attempts to find paid work, perhaps accompanied by acts of discrimination (perceived or real), may only intensify pessimism and further weaken what economists call "the propensity to work." (For similar commentary on the situation of blacks in England, see Banks & Ullah, 1988.) Ogbu (1989), in addressing the paradox of high black aspirations and low achievement in the United States, draws attention to the "folk culture of success," which has been constructed over a long history of discrimination and reinforced by daily experience (e.g., observation of job ceilings and other barriers). According to Ogbu, this "folk culture" channels black youth away from schoolwork and toward behaviors that diminish the chances of legitimate employment success.

Furnham (1985, p. 109) recognizes such reciprocities in his literature review on youth unemployment:

> many of the studies seem to indicate the presence of a destructive vicious circle which young people experience when failing to get a job: stress and disappointment, leading to lowered self-esteem, a change in expectations, and minor psychiatric illnesses which handicap the job search and application process so making unemployment all the more likely.

Given this sequence of events, is it the person, or is it the structure, that is at the root of the unemployment problem? Clearly, the way we go about answering this question will depend both on our conceptions of social structure and on our assumptions about "human nature," motivation, and the malleability of the human being. This formulation of the question, and the ensuing political debate, corresponds well to relatively simple, linear, and recursive explanatory models in which individual differences "predict" employment outcomes *or* structural circumstances "determine" individual attributes. However, it does not do justice to the more complex, dynamic, interactive, and reciprocal interrelations of structural, psychological, and behavioral phenomena in the real empirical world.

Acknowledgments

This chapter was initially prepared for presentation at the Conference on Youth Unemployment and Society, sponsored by the Johann Jacobs Foundation, November 7–9, 1991, Marbach Castle, Germany. The author is grateful for the comments of Anne Petersen and other conference participants, which were taken into account in subsequent revision. She also thanks Carol Krauze and Katherine Dennehy for bibliographic assistance, and Kathleen Call and Michael Shanahan for helpful comments on an earlier draft. The author's research on youth work experience is supported by the National Institute of Mental Health and the National Center for Research on Vocational Education.

Note

1. Women also have been found to have longer spells of unemployment when they become unemployed (Hui, 1991; Rosenthal, 1991) and less likelihood (than that observed among men) of employment as the duration of unemployment increases (Baker & Elias, 1991). Young people with longer previous job tenure and higher past incomes experience shorter unemployment duration (Hui, 1991).

References

Aneshensel, C. S., Reutter, C. M., & Lachenbruch, P. A. (1991). Social structure, stress, and mental health: Competing conceptual and analytic models. *American Sociological Review, 56,* 166–178.

Baker, M., & Elias, P. (1991). Youth unemployment and work histories. In S. Dex (Ed.), *Life and work history analyses: Qualitative and quantitative developments* (pp. 214–244). London: Routledge.

Bandura, A. (1988). Organizational applications of social cognitive theory. *Australian Journal of Management, 13,* 275–302.

Banks, M. H., & Jackson, P. R. (1982). Unemployment and risk of minor psychiatric disorder in young people: Cross-sectional and longitudinal evidence. *Psychological Medicine, 12,* 789–798.

Banks M. H., & Ullah, P. (1988). *Youth unemployment in the 1980's: Its psychological effects.* London: Croom Helm.

Borman, K. M. (1991). *The first real job: A study of young workers.* Albany: State University of New York Press.

Coe, R. (1978). Absenteeism from work. In G. J. Duncan & J. N. Morgan (Eds.), *Five thousand American families—Patterns of economic progress: Vol. 6. Accounting for race and sex differences in earnings and other analyses of the first nine years of the panel study of income dynamics* (Chapter 5). Ann Arbor: University of Michigan, Institute for Social Research, Survey Research Center.

Cohn, R. M. (1978). The effect of unemployment status change on self-attitudes. *Social Psychology Quarterly, 41,* 81–93.

Corcoran, M., & Hill, M. S. (1980). Persistence in unemployment among adult men. In G. J. Duncan & J. N. Morgan (Eds.), *Five thousand American families—Patterns of economic progress: Vol. 7. Analyses of the first eleven years of the panel study of income dynamics* (Chapter 2). Ann Arbor: University of Michigan, Institute for Social Research, Survey Research Center.

Dayton, C. W. (1981). The young person's job search: Insights from a study. *Journal of Counseling Psychology, 28,* 321–333.

DiPrete, T. (1981). Unemployment over the life cycle: Racial differences and the effect of changing economic conditions. *American Journal of Sociology, 87,* 286–307.

Dowling, P., & O'Brien, G. E. (1981). The effects of employment, unemployment and further education upon the work values of school-leavers. *Australian Journal of Psychology, 33,* 185–195.

Feather, N. T. (1986). Employment importance and helplessness about potential unemployment among students in secondary schools. *Australian Journal of Psychology, 38*, 33–44.

Feather, N. T., & O'Brien, G. E. (1986a). A longitudinal analysis of the effects of different patterns of employment and unemployment on school-leavers. *British Journal of Psychology, 77*, 459–479.

Feather, N. T., & O'Brien, G. E. (1986b). A longitudinal study of the effects of employment and unemployment on school-leavers. *Journal of Occupational Psychology, 59*, 121–144.

Finch, M. D., Shanahan, M., Mortimer, J. T., & Ryu, S. (1991). Work experience and control orientation in adolescence. *American Sociological Review, 56*, 597–611.

Freeman, R. B., & Wise, D. A. (1979). *Youth unemployment.* Cambridge, MA: National Bureau of Economic Research.

Furnham, A. (1985). Youth unemployment: A review of the literature. *Journal of Adolescence, 8*, 109–124.

Gecas, V. (1989). The social psychology of self-efficacy. *Annual Review of Sociology, 15*, 291–316.

Gilligan, C. (1982). *In a different voice: Psychological theory and women's development.* Cambridge: Cambridge University Press.

Gottfredson, L. S. (Ed.), (1986). The g factor in employment [Special issue]. *Journal of Vocational Behavior, 29*(3).

Hamilton, S. F. (1990). *Apprenticeship for adulthood: Preparing youth for the future.* New York: Free Press.

Hamilton, V. L., Hoffman, W. S., Broman, C. L., & Rauma, D. (1991). *Aftermath: A panel study of unemployment and mental health among autoworkers.* Unpublished manuscript.

Hoffman, W. S., Hamilton, V. L., Broman, C. L., & Rauma, D. (1991). *Unemployment, depression, and self-blame among autoworkers.* Paper presented at the American Sociological Association Annual Meeting, Cincinnati, OH; August, 1991.

House, J. S., & Mortimer, J. T. (1990). Social structure and the individual: Emerging themes and new directions. *Social Psychology Quarterly, 53*, 71–80.

Hui, W. (1991). Reservation wage analysis of unemployed youths in Australia. *Applied Economics, 23*, 1341–1350.

Jackson, P. R., Stafford, E. M., Banks, M. H., & Warr, P. B. (1983). Unemployment and psychological distress in young people: The moderating role of employment commitment. *Journal of Applied Psychology, 68*, 525–535.

Jahoda, M. (1981). Work, employment, and unemployment: Values, theories and approaches in social research. *American Psychologist, 36*, 184–191.

Jones, S. (1989). Reservation wages and the cost of unemployment. *Economica, 56*, 225–246.

Kandel, D. B., & Yamaguchi, K. (1987). Job mobility and drug use: An event history analysis. *American Journal of Sociology, 92*, 836–878.

Kasl, S. V. (1979). Changes in mental health status associated with job loss and retirement. In J. E. Barrett, Robert M. Roos, and Gerald L. Klerman (Eds.), *Stress and mental disorder* (pp. 179–200). New York: Raven Press.

Kessler, R. C., Turner, J. B., & House, J. S. (1989). Unemployment, reemployment, and emotional functioning in a community sample. *American Sociological Review, 54*, 648–657.

Kohn, M. L., & Schooler, C. (1983). *Work and personality: An inquiry into the impact of social stratification.* Norwood, NJ: Ablex.

Layton, C., & Eysenck, S. (1985). Psychoticism and unemployment. *Personality and Individual Differences, 6*, 387–390.

Lichter, D. T. (1988). Racial differences in underemployment in American cities. *American Journal of Sociology, 93*, 771–792.

Lorence, J., & Mortimer, J. T. (1985). Work involvement through the life course: A panel study of three age groups. *American Sociological Review, 50*, 618–638.

Lynch, L. M. (1983). Job search and youth unemployment. *Oxford Economic Papers, 35*, (Nov. Supplement), 271–282.

Maccoby, E. E., & Jacklin, C. N. (1974). *The psychology of sex differences.* Stanford, CA: Stanford University Press.

Meyer, R. M., & Wise, D. A. (1982). High school preparation and early labor force experience. In R. B. Freeman & D. A. Wise (Eds.), *The youth labor market problem: Its nature, causes, and consequences* (pp. 277–347). Chicago: University of Chicago Press.

Miller, J. (1988). Jobs and work. In N. J. Smelser (Ed.), *Handbook of sociology* (pp. 327–359). Newbury Park, CA: Sage.

Miller, J., Slomczynski, K. M., & Kohn, M. L. (1985). Continuity of learning-generalization: The effect of job on men's intellective process in the United States and Poland. *American Journal of Sociology, 91*, 593–615.

Millham, S., Bullock, R., & Hosie, K. (1978). Juvenile unemployment: A concept due for re-cycling? *Journal of Adolescence, 1*, 11–24.

Mortimer, J. T. (1991). Employment. In R. M. Lerner, A. C. Peterson, & J. Brooks-Gunn (Eds.), *Encyclopedia of adolescence* (pp. 311–318). New York: Garland.

Mortimer, J. T., & Finch, M. D. (1986). The effects of part-time work on self-concept and achievement. In K. Borman & J. Reisman (Eds.), *Becoming a worker* (pp. 66–89). Norwood, NJ: Ablex.

Mortimer, J. T., Finch, M. D., and Maruyama, G. (1988). Work experience and job satisfaction: Variation by age and gender. In J. T. Mortimer & K. Borman (Eds.), *Work experience and psychological development through the life span* (pp. 79–107). Boulder, CO: Westview.

Mortimer, J. T., Lorence, J., & Kumka, D. (1986). *Work, family, and personality: Transition to adulthood.* Norwood, NJ: Ablex.

Mullahy, J., & Sindelar, J. (1990). Gender differences in the effects of mental health on labor force participation. In I. Sirageldin, A. Sorkin, & R. Frank (Eds.), *Research in human capital and development* (Vol. 6, pp. 125–146). Greenwich, CT: JAI.

O'Brien, G. E. (1986). *Psychology of work and unemployment.* Chichester, UK: Wiley.

O'Brien, G. E., & Feather, N. T. (1990). The relative effects of unemployment and the quality of employment on the affect, work values and personal control of adolescents. *Journal of Occupational Psychology, 63*, 151–165.

Ogbu, J. U. (1989). Cultural boundaries and minority youth orientation toward work preparation. In D. Stern & D. Eichorn (Eds.), *Adolescence and work: Influences of social structure, labor markets, and culture* (pp. 101–140). Hillsdale, NJ: Lawrence Erlbaum.

Osterman, P. (1989). The job market for adolescents. In D. Stern & D. Eichorn (Eds.), *Adolescence and work: Influences of social structure, labor markets, and culture* (pp. 235–256). Hillsdale, NJ: Lawrence Erlbaum.

Patton, W., & Noller, P. (1984). Unemployment and youth: A longitudinal study. *Australian Journal of Psychology, 36*, 399–413.

Rosenbaum, J. E., Kariya, T., Settersten, R., & Maier, T. (1990). Market and network theories of the transition from high school to work: Their application to industrialized societies. *Annual Review of Sociology, 16*, 263–299.

Rosenthal, L. (1991). Unemployment incidence following redundancy: The value of longitudinal approaches. In S. Dex (Ed.), *Life and work history analysis: Qualitative and quantitative developments*. London: Routledge.

Rutter, M. (1986). The developmental psychopathology of depression: Issues and perspectives. In M. Rutter, C. E. Izard & P. B. Read (Eds.), *Depression in Young People: Developmental and clinical perspectives* (pp. 3–30). New York: Guilford.

Schwalbe, M. L., & Gecas, V. (1988). Social psychological dimensions of job-related disability. In J. T. Mortimer & K. M. Borman (Eds.), *Work experience and psychological development through the life span* (pp. 233–271). Boulder, CO: Westview.

Shamir, B. (1986). Self-esteem and the psychological impact of unemployment. *Social Psychology Quarterly, 49*, 61–72.

Shanahan, M. J., Finch, M. D., Mortimer, J. T., & Ryu, S. (1991). Adolescent work experience and depressive affect. *Social Psychology Quarterly, 54*, 299–317.

Simmons, R. G., & Blyth, D. A. (1987). *Moving into adolescence: The impact of pubertal change and school context*. New York: Aldine.

Singer, M. S., Stacey, B. G., & Ritchie, G. (1987). Causal attributions for unemployment, perceived consequences of unemployment, and perceptions of employment prospects for youth among university students in New Zealand. *Journal of Genetic Psychology, 148*, 507–517.

Spenner, K. I., & Otto, L. B. (1985). Work and self-concept: Selection and socialization in the early career. In A. C. Kerckhoff (Ed.), *Research in sociology of education and socialization* (Vol. 5, pp. 197–235). Greenwich, CT & London: JAI Press.

Steel, L. (1991). Early work experience among white and non-white youths: Implications for subsequent enrollment and employment. *Youth & Society, 22*, 419–447.

Stryker, S. (1985). Symbolic interaction and role theory. In G. Lindzey & E. Aronson (Eds.), *Handbook of social psychology* (Vol. 1, pp. 311–378). New York: Random House.

Sullivan, M. L. (1989). *Getting paid: Youth, crime and work in the inner city*. Ithaca, NY: Cornell University Press.

Tiggemann, M., & Winefield, A. H. (1989). Predictors of employment, unemployment and further study among school-leavers. *Journal of Occupational Psychology, 62*, 213–221.

U.S. Department of Labor, Bureau of Labor Statistics. (1991). *Employment and Earnings, 38*(7).

Warr, P., Jackson, P., & Banks, M. (1982). Duration of unemployment and psychological well-being in young men and women. *Current Psychological Research, 2*, 207–214.

Wilson, W. J. (1987). *The truly disadvantaged: The inner city, the underclass, and public policy*. Chicago: University of Chicago Press.

Winefield, A. H., & Tiggemann, M. (1985). Psychological correlates of employment and unemployment: Effects, predisposing factors, and sex differences. *Journal of Occupational Psychology, 58*, 229–242.

Winefield, A. H., Tiggemann, M., Winefield, H. R., & Goldney, R. D. (1991). A longitudinal study of the psychological effects of unemployment and unsatisfactory employment on young adults. *Journal of Applied Psychology, 76*, 424–431.

8. The psychosocial consequences of youth unemployment

ADRIAN FURNHAM
Department of Psychology
University College, London

Introduction

During the past 20 years, since the problem first became acute in the Western world, there have been a number of important studies of youth unemployment in various countries: Australia (Gurney, 1981), Britain (Warr, Banks, & Ullah, 1985), Sweden (Hammarstrom, Janlert, & Theorell, 1988), and the United States (Raelin, 1981). Furthermore, there is a burgeoning literature on the psychological experience and consequence of being unemployed (Fryer & Payne, 1986; Warr, 1987).

The title of this chapter raises three issues. The first is the direction of causality with respect to the causes and consequences of unemployment. The second is whether there are unique and/or special effects of unemployment on the young as distinguished from other groups. The third issue concerns the consequences of employment, as opposed to unemployment, for young people. A central theme of this chapter is that the meaning and significance of employment status for youth vary in different social contexts; the consequences of employment are probably not the same for all young people.

Cause, Correlate, and Consequence

Historically there have been three major periods of research on unemployment in the twentieth century: the late Victorian/early Edwardian period, the depression years of the 1930s, and the decade of the 1980s. Whereas some of the earlier studies focused on the indolence and work-shy nature of the unemployed—suggesting that in many instances the unemployed are architects of their own misfortune—most recent studies have focused on the serious negative psychosocial consequences of unemployment. Economic and political conditions may have shaped this trend.

Because of practical issues such as time and money, most social science research is cross-sectional. Yet most researchers want to infer cause, which may be possible in laboratory-based research but is difficult, if not impossible, in interview-based or questionnaire studies. Although some interesting and important longitudinal studies in this field address the question of causality, they are few and far between (Feather & O'Brien, 1986a, 1986b; Warr, Jackson, & Banks, 1982; Winefield, Winefield, Tiggmann, & Goldney, 1991).

At issue is whether unemployment is a cause or a consequence of psychosocial distress (Furnham, 1990, 1992). The relationship between any two variables can take many forms. First, it is possible that psychosocial factors (personality, skills, the work ethic) determine, in some sense, various features of unemployment. The crucial axiom of this position is that psychosocial factors "causally" determine unemployment, along with other related variables (e.g., physical and mental health). A second position assumes that psychosocial factors are a result of being unemployed. This "model" is consistent with psychological theories of learning generalization and the structuralist-determinist position that society shapes thinking and behavioral patterns, which become set. Precisely how this occurs, or which aspects of psychosocial functioning are shaped by which features of the unemployment process, is not clear, but at the core of this position is the idea that psychological styles are primarily a function of the experience of unemployment.

A more common, cybernetic view suggests that psychological functioning is a result of unemployment and vice versa, or that there is bidirectional causality between the two. This position allows for one direction of causality to be primary and the other secondary, as long as it is acknowledged that each has influence on the other. There may be differences as to which aspects of personal functioning and which features of unemployment are singled out for reciprocal determinism. Some researchers have argued that because both psychosocial functioning and unemployment are multifaceted, it is possible that various relationships occur simultaneously: Some personal variables reciprocally determine some unemployment variables; some personal variables unidirectionally determine some unemployment variables, and vice versa; and finally, some personal traits are not determined by, nor determine, unemployment, and vice versa. The mixed effects are usually post hoc empirical findings, rather than those predicted by an *a priori* hypothesis. Finally, recognizing the number and complexity of variables operating in this area, some researchers suggest that both are determined by another variable or group of variables. This approach can take many forms, varying in the complexity of pathways and number of variables under consideration.

As of now, there is certainly no agreement on the salient personal variables, unemployment reactions, or "third variables" that are deemed important, or on the expressly causal links among them. Thus, though it is agreed that the relationship is complex, multifaceted, and multicausal, there are few explicit models of the interrelations of unemployment and psychological functioning.

Lynn, Hampson, and Magee (1984) tried to determine which variables predicted unemployment in young people. Cross-sectional data were collected on 701 adolescents, 15 to 16 years of age, comprising nearly all fifth-year secondary-school pupils in an Ulster town. Data were also collected on parents' education, father's occupation, intelligence (as measured by the Abstract Reasoning Scale of the DAT), personality (using Eysenck's Junior EPQ), and self-report measures of status aspiration and the work ethic. The study aimed to investigate which of these background factors could predict unemployment one year later. It was found that home background, intelligence, personality, school type, and educational attainment all had significant effects on unemployment. Lynn and colleagues were interested in testing the cycle of disadvantage thesis, which posits a recurring cycle wherein disadvantageous social and psychological conditions associated with low social class, poverty, and chronic unemployment are transmitted from one generation to the next. Lynn's study, however, has its limitations, particularly in the way intelligence was measured. Furthermore, the sample of unemployed young people was small and unrepresentative of the population of Great Britain. Yet despite these limitations the findings were surprisingly similar to those in the United States and attest to the role of personality, intelligence, motivation, and education in determining unemployment and employment in young people.

Whereas most studies on youth unemployment have been cross-sectional, some have been longitudinal. Although longitudinal studies have the potential to illuminate causal patterns, they often are plagued by testing effects, poor retention rates, and other problems (O'Brien, 1980). To understand the effects of unemployment one needs a population that moves in *and* out of employment and, ideally, back again.

Starting with a large, heterogeneous, and representative group of school-leavers, one could do a comprehensive audit of their beliefs, skills, aptitudes, personality, expectations, and job search, as well as other social factors, such as class of parents. After a period of a year one could then attempt to ascertain who has and who has not found employment, and then attempt to determine statistical discriminates of those who are successful versus those who are not. It is also important to understand the types of jobs the young people have accepted. Jobs are far from equivalent in their psychological, social, and material costs and benefits (Warr, 1987); some are obviously more desirable than others and presumably harder to get. Furthermore, some young people get part-time jobs; indeed, they may even have part-time employment while in school. Psychosocial factors may predict these features as well.

After some time (and this depends heavily on economic conditions and the "phase in the economic cycle"), some of those who have jobs lose them while others out of work find employment. In examining this process, the investigator must address the reasons for unemployment. Did a fixed contract time run out? Did the whole business close? Was unemployment voluntary?

The issue of cause and consequence is theoretically, as well as politically, important. Some politicians suggest that unemployment is largely voluntary and that it is the result of poor motivation of young people who have forsaken the work ethic. Others argue that the lack of motivation of some young people is the consequence of high unemployment, not its cause. What is quite possible is that young people are caught in a reciprocal trap in which failure to find work leads to depression, low self-esteem, and ineffective job-search and presentation strategies that are self-fulfilling prophecies (Furnham, 1984).

Longitudinal studies often suffer from high dropout rates. Attrition can occur for many reasons: Some people are unavailable or uncontactable because of illness or relocation or simply because they refuse to cooperate. This becomes most problematic when there are different rates of attrition, or when the pretest scores on the dependent variables for dropouts are different, across conditions. Methodological differences in sample size and homogeneity, study duration, and dependent variables contribute to the lack of comparability across studies (see Winefield & Winefield, 1992, for a discussion of the problems of doing longitudinal research). Furthermore, the economic environment can change significantly during the period of study, influencing the independent and dependent variables and the relationships between them: When the market is "bullish" the relationship between psychosocial factors and unemployment may be quite different from when the market is "bearish."

Problems such as these may be responsible for the inconsistency in the findings of longitudual studies of the psychological impact of unemployment on school-leavers. Thus, Banks and Jackson (1982) found that British school leavers who were unemployed showed an increase in psychological symptoms, whereas those who became employed showed a decrease. Yet two Australian studies could only replicate the increase in symptomatology of unemployed school-leavers (Patton & Notter, 1984; Feather & O'Brien, 1986b), not the increase in well-being among the employed. To further complicate matters, Australian researchers found only a general improvement in the psychosocial functioning of those who found employment, but no corresponding decline in the unemployed (Gurney, 1980; Tiggemann & Winefield, 1984; Winefield & Tiggemann, 1985).

Essentially, the longitudual studies suggest three possible scenarios:

1. Those seeking—but unable to find—employment suffer a decline in their well-being and psychological adjustment, but those who obtain work remain much the same.
2. Those who have found work experience an increase in well-being, but those out of work remain the same.
3. Both those who obtain work improve and those who become unemployed decline in their well-being and psychological adjustment.

However, these scenarios beg a number of questions:

1. What sort of job is obtained? Warr (1983) had distinguished between good and bad jobs, only the former of which provide psychological benefits.
2. Unemployment occurs over what period of time? Chronic unemployment may have quite different consequences during short, intermittent, or long periods of time.
3. How is well-being measured? Psychosocial well-being is a multifaceted concept including self-esteem, internal locus of control, absence of minor psychiatric morbidity, positive moods, and so on. Warr (1987) listed ten different measures frequently used in this field: happiness, pleasure, life satisfaction, negative affect, negative self-esteem, general distress, anxiety, strain, depressed mood, and positive affect.
4. To what extent is employment status a result rather than a cause of well-being? Are there demonstrable psychological factors that predict both employment status and the reaction to it? (Do healthy individuals get jobs that increase their well-being?)

Table 8.1 *Stage-wise theories of reactions to unemployment*

Hopson and Adams (1976)	Harrison (1976)	Hill (1978)	Briar (1977)
1. Immobilization	1. Shock	1. Trauma/denial	1. Shock
2. Minimization	2. Optimism	2. Depression	2. Optimism
3. Depression	3. Pessimism	3. Adaptation	3. Self blame
4. Acceptance of reality	4. Fatalism		4. Depression
5. Testing			5. Inertia
6. Search for meaning			
7. Internalization			

Despite the problems surrounding the attribution of cause, various researchers have attempted to construct theoretical models. For example, the stage approach describes the typical stages that an unemployed person passes through (Harrison, 1976; Hopson & Adams, 1976). Because unemployment involves reaction to loss, the extensive literatures on grieving and bereavement (Parkes, 1975), divorce (Levinger & Moles, 1979) and migration (Furnham & Bochner, 1986) are deemed relevant. These literatures rely heavily on early neo-psychoanalytic formulations (Bowlby, 1969). However, stage models are descriptive rather than explanatory. They rarely specify what factors determine whether a person moves from one stage to another or remains fixed in one stage. Stage models are linear but reactions may be cyclical, with erratic progressions and regressions. Furthermore, crucial individual differences and moderating variables are ignored in these general descriptions. Finally, the more stages a theory has, the more vulnerable it is to disproof.

Hayes and Nutman (1981) have reviewed a number of stage approaches to the reactions to unemployment. They include Hopson and Adams's (1976) seven-stage approach, the four stages of Harrison (1976), the three of Hill (1978), and the five of Briar (1977). They are listed in Table 8.1.

Although there are similarities in these approaches, there are clear differences. They are based on qualitatively and quantitatively different research and are often post hoc categorizations of observed differences. To what extent they predict or explain human behavior remains questionable. Most important, they assume that all people (young and old) proceed through these stages, for which assumption there is precious little evidence.

To speak confidently of cause or consequence may be unwarranted even after so much work has been done in the past decade. There are quite clearly psychosocial correlates of unemployment among young people, but it is not at all certain to what extent these factors actually led to the unemployment in the first place.

What Is Special About the Young?

Since the early 1970s, when the problem became most acute, there have been several studies of youth unemployment (Baxter, 1975; Clark & Clissold, 1982; Roberts, Duggan, & Noble, 1982; Winefield et al., 1991). Many of these have examined the same factors (e.g., health, self-esteem) that have been investigated in the adult population. The underlying causes of the increase in youth unemployment are manifold. They include demographic factors (change in the birthrate and an extension of the school career), micro- and macroeconomic changes (in technology, productivity agreements), and educational and training factors (the relevance and appropriateness of education). Changes in youth unemployment are naturally associated with changes in adult employment, but move with a greater amplitude. It has been calculated that if the unemployment rate for males rises by 1 percent, the unemployment rate for young males under 20 (excluding school-leavers) rises by 1.7 percent (Makeham, 1980). Compared with other groups, young people are more likely to be entering the labor force or changing jobs; hence, as a recession deepens and recruitment is cut, the young are the most vulnerable. Similarly, there is evidence that crime rates are higher for youth during periods of high unemployment (Farrington, Gallagher, Morley, St. Ledger, & West, 1986).

Are young workers different from older workers or the long-term unemployed? Warr (1987) believes that compared to middle-aged people, young people are *less* likely to suffer in four specific areas: availability of money, physical security, opportunities for interpersonal contact, and valued social position:

> For example, the income differential between having a job and being unemployed may be relatively small, especially for those teenagers with few qualifications. Money and material assistance are often provided by parents, and financial requirements are generally less than for older groups. Associated with that, physical security is often unchanged by the transition from school into unemployment, as many teenagers continue to live within the family accommodation. (p. 227)

Whereas older people become more isolated, friendless, and lonely after unemployment, young people, particularly school-leavers, carry forward a network of friends and leisure activities (Warr, 1984). This social contact may be extremely important for mental health, given the potential social support that young people receive (and give). The stigma attached to unemployment is no doubt less severe for the young, particularly in times of high unemployment (Furnham, 1985). With some pursuing higher education, others taking a "year off," and still others worrying about what to do with their lives, it is less conspicuous and unusual to be unemployed even in times of great economic prosperity.

Warr, Jackson, and Banks (1988) reviewed several factors that mediate the harmful impact of unemployment: employment commitment, social relationships, gender, ethnic group, social class, local unemployment rate, and personal vulnerability. They find fairly consistent evidence for a curvilinear association between age and mental health with younger (16- to 19-year-olds) and older (60- to 64-year-olds) persons having better mental health. Indeed, curvilinear relationships with age have been reported for financial stress, number of dependents, employment commitment, and job seeking. Unemployed men approaching retirement are less likely to have financial commitments and to suffer the stigma attached to being unemployed.

Warr (1987) believes that young people pay a high price when unemployed in the development of autonomy and competence. He believes that in adolescence gaining a job has special meaning in marking the end of childhood dependence and representing entry to the adult world. Earning money facilitates both independence and autonomy. Work signifies the acquisition of new skills and concomitant feelings of competence. Because jobs provide novel and challenging experiences, they are highly desirable to the adolescent; some experience fear of unemployment as a result. As Kelvin and Jarrett (1984) argued, in a society whose socioeconomic structure is determined by the division of labor, the unemployed are defined by what they are not—not integrated within that structure. It may well be that it is the self-concept, vocational identity, and self-esteem—related but not synonymous concepts—that render young people particularly vulnerable to the experience of unemployment. Many writers have noted change in the self-concept and identity of the unemployed. In their review of the psychological effects of unemployment in the 1930s, Eisenberg and Lazarsfeld (1938) note the development of apathy, depression, fatalistic beliefs, lowered self-esteem, resignation, and self-doubt.

Tiffany, Tiffany, Cowan, & Tiffany (1970) administered the Tennessee Self-Concept Scale to two comparable groups, one in work and one not, and found that the unemployed had lower self-esteem. The unemployed also had significantly less faith in themselves, saw themselves as less desirable, doubted their worth more, and felt more anxious, depressed, and unhappy than the employed. Briar (1977) has also noted secrecy and distancing in the unemployed, which appear to be ways of protecting themselves from being labeled failures and "welfare dependent."

It has been argued that the self-concept is a scheme that locates the individual within the social environment and shapes his or her interaction with it. Hence, becoming unemployed causes psychological dislocation and disorientation and a modification of the self-concept. Hodgson and Brenner (1968) found lower self-esteem in the previously unemployed compared to the previously employed. If employment shapes identity, self-concept, and self-esteem, and some young people never have the benefit of employment, their development may be seriously impaired. If it is assumed that there is a critical period in development when young people acquire a sense of competence and self-worth through the autonomy that work brings, youth may be particularly vulnerable to the deleterious effects of unemployment after leaving school.

The Consequences of Employment for Young People

It is the norm that after leaving full-time education (be it at school or college or university) young people obtain full-time employment. Even in times or places of high unemployment, this remains the norm. If there are psychosocial consequences of unemployment, in that young people change as a function of leaving education and becoming unemployed, it is equally likely that there are notable, theoretically predictable, and important consequences of going to work. Curiously, there are far fewer studies on this topic. Perhaps a thorough knowledge of the benefits and hazards of employment itself can be informative with respect to the implications of unemployment. The absence of work may preclude certain avenues for personal development and socialization. Jahoda (1979, 1981) has argued that, apart from money, work provides the opportunity for specific needs to be fulfilled. Some of these seem particularly relevant to young people.

Work structures time

Work structures the day, the week, and even longer periods. The loss of a time structure can be very disorienting. Feather and Bond (1983) found that unemployed university graduates were less well organized and less purposeful in their use of time, and reported more depressive symptoms, than those who were employed. The loss of time structure can have a very noticeable effect on young people's job-search strategies (Furnham, 1984).

Work provides regularly shared experiences

Regular interaction with nonnuclear family members provides an important source of social contact. Social support from family and friends buffers the major causes of stress and increases coping ability, thus reducing illness. Social isolation, in contrast, is related to disturbed mental states. If one's primary source of friends and contacts is work colleagues, then the benefits of social support are denied. One of the most frequently cited sources of job satisfaction is contact with other people (Argyle, 1983). However, this factor may be less important to young people, who often have fairly large social support networks.

Work provides experiences of autonomy,
and mastery and a sense of purpose

Both work organizations and the product of work imply the interdependence of human beings. Take away this daily experience and the unemployed are left with a feeling of uselessness. Work, even when not particularly satisfying, gives a sense of mastery or achievement. Creative activities stimulate people and provide satisfaction.

> A person's contribution to producing goods or providing services forges a link between the individual and the society of which he or she is part. Work roles are not the only roles which offer the individual the opportunity of being useful and contributing to the community but, without doubt, for the majority they are the most central roles and consequently people deprived of the opportunity to work often feel useless and report that they lack a sense of purpose. (Jahoda, 1979, p. 313)

Work may be very important for young people who are struggling with financial, emotional, and social issues relating to autonomy. By being a useful, contributing member of a nonnuclear family team, a young person can quickly establish such autonomy.

Work is a source of personal status and identity

A job determines relative status in society, both for the employed person and for his or her family. Employment links two important social systems—family and work—and confers identity in each. Many young people struggle with a sense of identity. Vocational identity helps considerably in establishing a sense of worth and knowledge about who one is. Not unnaturally, there can be a marked drop in self-esteem following unemployment.

Work is a source of activity

All work involves expenditure of physical or mental effort. Whereas too much activity may induce fatigue and stress, two little results in boredom and restlessness, particularly among extroverts. People seek to maximize the amount of activity that suits them by choosing particular jobs or tasks. The unemployed, however, must seek out other sources of stimulation to keep themselves active.

Furnham and Lewis (1986) have noted:

A number of points should be made about the list of the functions of work. First, it is not exhaustive and the functions are not mutually exclusive. Secondly, it is possible that other, even more obvious, functions could be mentioned, such as providing an income. Thirdly, these latent or manifest functions of work can be provided by other social institutions such as societies, clubs, etc., which provide a source of unpaid work. Finally, nothing actually prevents the unemployed from seeking out some of the benefits of work, such as creating a stable time structure to their day, though this may be difficult particularly for those most likely to be unemployed (school-leavers, unskilled laborers). (p. 124)

But not all work is beneficial. In accord with classic Marxist theory, work can be deeply alienating. Jobs that lead to a high degree of dissatisfaction may be more unhealthy for the individual than unemployment under good conditions. Warr (1983) has differentiated between "good" and "bad" jobs and "good" and "bad" unemployment in terms of nine variables that have proved discriminating in previous research (see Table 8.2). Thus, it may be the case that a person leaving a bad job will adapt well to a good unemployment experience. Just as not all jobs are satisfying, so not all unemployment is dissatisfying.

Assuming the advantages of a good job, social administrators and politicians have argued for both discretionary employment of secondary school–age children and, on occasion, mandatory work requirements for welfare recipients. Although these suggestions are justifiable if the nature of employment is "good," it seems particularly unwise to expose schoolchildren and the already unemployed to "bad" jobs that lead to disaffection, disenchantment, alienation, and ill health. Furthermore, some young people may experience depressive affect as a consequence of work (Shanahan, Finch, Mortimer & Ryu 1991). This seems particularly likely when they have bad jobs characterized by low status, long hours, dirty or heavy work, time-pressured work, insufficient resources, role conflict or ambiguity, and a lack of control. In addition, many jobs are

Table 8.2 *Characteristics of "good" and "bad" jobs and "good" and bad" unemployment (from Warr, 1983, pp. 309–310).*

	"Good" jobs and "Good" unemployment	"Bad jobs" and "Bad" unemployment
1. Money	more	less
2. Variety	more	less
3. Goals, traction	more	less
4. Decision latitude	more	less
5. Skill use/development	more	less
6. Psychological threat	less	more
7. Security	more	less
8. Interpersonal contact	more	less
9. Valued social position	more	less

characterized by low pay, no opportunity for advancement, the acute underutilization of abilities, lack of participation in decision making, and low job complexity.

It should be noted that the quality and quantity of a young person's nonwork or leisure activities may condition the outcomes of unemployment. That is, leisure activities may compensate for a poor working environment. Furnham (1990) has delineated various types of compensation: passive, supplemental, and reactive. If an unemployed young person can find structured, task-oriented, and social leisure activities, it may well be that they can substitute for the benefits of work. Just as retired people may very happily find "meaning in life" through their leisure, so young people (as long as they have adequate income) may not have to suffer negative consequences of unemployment.

These considerations support the almost tautological observation that only good jobs provide young people with psychological benefits. Although it is no doubt true that all work enables young people to become more emotionally independent of their parents and that the benefits of a good job may be manifold, the psychological consequences of a bad job may be worse than unemployment itself.

A Typology of Reactions to Unemployment

Although rarely addressed directly, the meaning and significance of employment status for young people differ as a function of social context, which means the consequences of unemployment may not be the same for all youth. A range of individual differences may be relevant, such as ability or aptitude, personality traits, and belief systems, as well as structural variables, such as the national or local unemployment rate, social security provisions, and so on.

		Motivation/Commitment	
		High	Low
Unemployment Rate	High	A	B
	Low	C	D

Two variables, representing individual and structural factors, have been found to be significant moderators of the effects of unemployment: the motivation or commitment to work and the unemployment rate. Warr, Jackson, and Banks's (1988) review suggests significant increase in psychological ill health for high-commitment people who become unemployed and a significant decrease in ill health for high-commitment people who become employed. Similarly, Furnham (1990) examined the moderating effect of Protestant work ethic (PWE) beliefs on the experience of unemployment. He developed the following hypotheses. First, unemployed people with strong PWE beliefs become more depressed, anxious, and apathetic than unemployed people who do not believe in the work ethic. Second, unemployed people with strong PWE beliefs participate more frequently in nonwork (but work-like or work-substitute) activities than people who do not believe in the PWE. Third, unemployed people with strong PWE beliefs persevere with more effort and over a longer period to get a job. Finally, Furnham (1990) hypothesized that belief in the PWE gradually decreases the longer a person remains unemployed.

It seems, then, that commitment, work motivation, and the work ethic are important determinants of a young person's reaction to employment and unemployment. Those motivated and committed seem much more sensitive to their work status, showing greater well-being when employed and greater distress when unemployed.

With reference to the local unemployment rate, Warr, Jackson, and Banks (1988) have noted:

> Two plausible hypotheses have been advanced about the relationship. On one hand, high local unemployment might be associated with poor psychological health, in line with mortality rates and other indicators of poor physical health, which are known to be higher in areas of high unemployment. Alternatively, high unemployment might be associated with relatively better psychological

health, because communities develop greater resilience in the face of a common threat, and unemployed people and their families find it easier to make external attributions of responsibility for lack of a job when many others are out of work. (p. 61)

Small-scale studies provide evidence for the latter hypothesis. Jackson and Warr (1984) found unemployed men in areas of chronically high unemployment to have significantly better psychological health than those in areas of moderate or lower unemployment. Similarly, Platt and Kreitman (1985) found parasuicide among unemployed men to be lower than that among employed men in parts of the city characterized by high levels of joblessness.

It is possible that these two factors, presumably independent of one another, lead to four quite different reactions to unemployment among young people. In the first case, young people, for whatever reason—parental pressure, the need for a positive identity—have a strong commitment to work, and hence motivation to seek it out, but live in an area or period of high unemployment. This scenario is probably most destructive for young people, because their repeated efforts are likely to meet with failure. Repeated unsuccessful efforts to obtain work can lower self-esteem, threaten identity, and increase anxiety, which, in turn, engender less effective job-search strategies. Alternatively, such young people may be driven to take a full- or part-time job that is psychologically and materially unfulfilling. A way out of this dilemma for some is to abandon the high commitment to work and closely identify with those out of work. However, the costs of lowering motivation may be very high (Furnham, 1990).

In the second scenario, the less committed young person is in an area of high unemployment. This is no doubt a situation that is fairly easy to cope with. If all of his or her peers are also unemployed and there are generous state support schemes, it may be quite easy for a young person to remain unemployed. The cost of this existence, however, in the long term may be great because if the job market improves, those young people may be poorly socialized to meet the demands of the world of work.

Third, when young people are highly motivated in an area or period of low unemployment it is probable that they get work before, or instead of, those less well committed. The fourth and final scenario in this taxonomy is the poorly work-motivated young person in an environment with low unemployment, whose indolence might be seen as rebellion. It is paradoxical that in times of economic growth and prosperity young people often reject what they see to be the "rat race" of materialism, preferring an alternative lifestyle. Though this may be an acceptable moratorium in the eyes of society, if it extends beyond a set period the young person may be stigmatized and rejected.

There are, of course, other possible typologies: young people in good/healthy jobs versus those in less healthy jobs, those with good or less adaptive coping skills, minority versus majority young people, and so on. Suffice it to say that the consequences of being unemployed do not affect every young person in the same way. Indeed, for some young people, remaining unemployed may even be a preferred way of life. There are probably several moderating factors that determine adjustment to "life on the dole." Warr, Jackson, and Banks (1988) noted eight quite distinct moderator variables affecting young people's reaction to unemployment.

Cognitive Consequences and Attributions About Unemployment

During the past 20 years, psychology has become much more cognitive, attempting to comprehend how people perceive and understand their social worlds. This orientation is reflected in research on youth unemployment as well, which focuses on aspirations, attributions, expectations, and explanations.

Empson-Warner and Krahn (1992) showed how the experience of unemployment following high school graduation leads to a reduction in occupational aspirations. Similarly, expectations about getting a job decline, and with them the motivation to work at all (Furnham, 1984). In a laboratory study, Fleming, Baum, Reddy, and Gatchel (1984) measured persistence and motivation to solve a laboratory task, comparing unemployed and employed people. The latter solved significantly more problems and tended (though nonsignificantly) to persevere longer than the unemployed. On arriving at the laboratory, the unemployed also exhibited significantly higher levels of both adrenaline and noradrenaline, suggesting strain.

Locus of control (the belief that internal or external forces control the various aspects of life) has attracted a great deal of attention in the psychological literature in general and in this area in particular (Furnham, 1992). A cross-sectional difference in locus of control scores has been reported by O'Brien and Kabanoff (1979), with greater externality among the unemployed. This difference remained significant when age, education, health, work values, leisure quality, and other variables were statistically controlled (O'Brien, 1984). A longitudinal study of Australian school-leavers revealed a significant increase in external locus of control for teenagers moving into unemployment and a decrease for those gaining a job (Patton

& Noller, 1984). Yet in another Australian investigation with the same design, Tiggemann and Winefield (1984) observed a decrease in externality of about the same amount for school-leavers, whether they became employed or unemployed. Feather and O'Brien (1986 a and b) found that unemployment had no effect on locus-of-control scores one year after school leaving; however, externality became significantly greater one year later among those who remained without a job. O'Brien (1986) points out that the unemployed's external orientation could signify a realistic recognition of their social impotence.

What do young people know about unemployment? Despierre and Sorel (1979) interviewed 51 French children in two age groups (11–12 years and 15–16 years) and two social classes. Their interpretations of five photographs were collected through semistructured interviews. Most 11-year-olds had an image of the concept of unemployment, attributing it to the moral or physical characteristics of the worker, whereas the older group defined unemployment in more global terms. The adolescents could distinguish among holidays, retirement, and unemployment, whereas many of the younger children confused these concepts. Ideas about unemployment differed by age, but not social class. The 11-year-olds said things like: "They made a blunder at work"; "They don't want to work because it tires them." When economic reasons were given, they were very succinct: "There is no work"; "Factories aren't working." But the older children were less certain. Laziness, a frequent theme, appears less a cause and more an effect to this age group.

A similar study by Webley and Wrigley (1983) confirmed these results. Forty British children from the same two age groups were asked to define unemployment, to indicate whether and how unemployed people differ from those with a job, and whether they would like to be unemployed. The results showed that understanding of unemployment became more abstract and global with age. Compared with younger children, adolescents offered more societal and fatalistic explanations for unemployment and saw the unemployed as fundamentally similar to the employed. They regarded the principal undesirable effects of unemployment as social-psychological rather than economic, identifying the lack of time structure as its worst feature.

A number of researchers have suggested that people out of work for long periods of time offer fatalistic explanations for the causes of their own and others' unemployment (Hayes & Nutman, 1981; Jahoda, 1979; O'Brien & Kabanoff, 1979). Common beliefs about unemployment may be seen as a special case of lay epistemology. Furnham (1982) examined differences in explanations for unemployment in Britain as a function of whether people were employed or unemployed, as well as age, sex, education, and voting pattern.

It was hypothesized that unemployed people would offer external social, economic, and political factors and fatalistic (luck, chance, fate) explanations for unemployment. Employed people, in contrast, would find individualistic explanations (internal, dispositional, and personality factors) more compelling. The results of this study showed a predictable pattern of differences between the employed and unemployed (see Table 8.3). Five of the individualistic explanations showed significant differences between the groups, but only two of these were in the predicted direction. Four of the differences in societal explanations were significant, with the unemployed attaching greater importance to social forces than the employed in three of them. In three of four instances, the unemployed reflected a more fatalistic attitude. This supports the work of Jahoda (1979) and O'Brien and Kabanoff (1979). Yet the employed sample tended to find worldwide recession and inflation more important as an explanation than the unemployed. More important, both the unemployed and the employed found most individualistic and fatalistic explanations for unemployment relatively unimportant. The most important explanations for both groups referred to present and past governments' actions and the worldwide recession.

Gaskell and Smith (1985) report evidence for the hypothesis that unemployed young people make more external attributions of unemployment (see Tiffany et al., 1970), but none showing them to make fewer internal attributions. Furthermore, according to Hayes and Nutman (1981), this tendency should increase the longer a person remains out of work. As national unemployment grows, even employed people may offer societal and fatalistic (external) explanations for unemployment, partly as a defense should they become unemployed themselves. Furnham and Hesketh (1989) were able to partially test this hypothesis by comparing British and New Zealanders' explanations for unemployment. The British, whose unemployment rate was nearly three times that of New Zealanders, rated societal factors as more important; the reverse was true for individualistic factors. A study by Payne and Furnham (1990) in the Caribbean also found employment status differences in explanations for unemployment, thus replicating this pattern even in a third-world country.

Table 8.3 *Means and F levels of the explanations for unemployment offered by employed and unemployed subjects (these numbers represent the mean on the following scale: Important 1 2 3 4 5 6 7 Unimportant).*

Explanations	Em-ployed	Unem-ployed	F Level
A. Individualistic			
Unemployed people can earn more money on social security	5.21	5.31	0.17
Lack of effort and laziness among unemployed people	5.13	4.81	1.72
Unemployed people don't try hard enough to get jobs	3.15	4.21	13.22*
Unemployed people are fussy and proud to accept some jobs	4.89	4.57	1.67
Poor education and qualifications among unemployed people	4.40	3.55	12.94*
Unwillingness of unemployed to move to places of work	4.32	5.51	10.60*
Inability of unemployed people to adapt to new conditions	4.77	4.38	3.44+
Lack of intelligence or ability among the unemployed	5.46	4.76	9.70**
B. Societal			
The policies and strategies of the present government	2.05	2.33	1.48
The policies and strategies of previous British governments	2.82	2.85	0.06
Inefficient and less competitive industries that go bankrupt	3.38	3.45	0.10
An influx of immigrants have taken up all available jobs	5.32	3.92	29.09*
Trade unions have priced their members out of a job	4.37	3.85	4.83+
Overmanning in industry which has occurred for too long	3.53	3.93	2.93
Incompetent industrial management with poor planning	2.94	3.46	5.98**
Weak trade unions that do not fight to keep jobs	4.80	3.58	26.05*
C. Fatalistic			
Sickness and physical handicap among unemployed people	5.14	3.74	29.32*
Just bad luck	5.73	5.27	4.63+
World-wide recession and inflation	2.19	2.57	3.69+
The introduction of widespread automation	3.70	3.09	6.14**

* $p<0.001$; ** $p<0.01$; + $p<0.05$.

La France and Cicchetti (1979) investigated social-class and employment-status determinants of perceived responsibility and blame for economic success and failure. Four groups of subjects—middle-class employed, middle-class unemployed, working-class employed, and working-class unemployed—were asked questions about a stimulus figure. The middle-class subjects, more than the working-class subjects, believed personality to be influential in success and failure. Overall, employed subjects assigned more responsibility to the stimulus person and saw luck as being less influential in the successful outcome than did the unemployed.

Nearly all of these studies used a limited and unrepresentative sample and a structured questionnaire. More recent studies are based on a free-response interview format with large, representative samples. In a free-response study, Lewis and Furnham (1986) asked 450 people how they believed unemployment could be reduced. Many answers were given, such as lowering the retirement age, increasing job creation schemes, or increasing public spending. Most people suggested stimulation of the economy or a redistribution of jobs, yet about 15 percent could provide no answer at all. In response to fixed-format questions, more than 90 percent of the sample indicated that the level of unemployment in Britain was unacceptably high, and 66 percent argued that the government should spend more money to reduce unemployment. There were some interesting and predictable sex, age, and employment-history differences: Women were against sacrificing their jobs if their husbands were unemployed, but did favor job sharing and reduced working hours, whereas younger people seemed more liberal than older people in their resistance to curbing immigration or women giving up their jobs. Heaven (1990) has replicated this work in Australia and shown how personal values are related to suggestions for reducing unemployment.

Lewis, Snell, and Furnham (1987) asked 900 British people to explain the causes of unemployment. Content analysis using 13 economic codes revealed that 28 percent of the explanations concerned falling demand for goods; 23 percent, inflation; 18 percent, government policy; and 17 percent, high wage demands. Curiously, there were very few demographic differences, although many were investigated (sex, social class, age, housing, trade-union membership). The explanations (many of which defied coding) were reclassified into three categories (Furnham, 1982): approximately three quarters were societal, a fourth fatalistic, and the remainder were individualistic. What was particularly striking about the explanations offered for unemployment was the fact that so few were purely economic—that is, lay explanations of economic phenomena are often normative, moralistic, or sociopolitical as well as economic. The fact that young people's beliefs were not dissimilar from those of older people does suggest a certain amount of consensus.

Furnham (1983, 1984) and Feather (1982) have argued that a potentially important factor in helping to explain an unemployed person's response to unemployment may be how that person, or a significant other, views the causes of not working. Although causal attributions have been studied in relation to psychological well-being, their relevance as moderators of the impact of unemployment has received less attention.

The theory of "learned helplessness" argues that attributions affect depression and other responses to uncontrollable negative events. For instance, internal (self-blame) attributions tend to lower self-esteem, whereas external (societal) attributions do not. Furthermore, stable (unchanging) attributions lower expectations of future success and increase the chronicity of helplessness in relation to a particular situation, whereas unstable (changing) attributions do not. Considerable clinical evidence demonstrates a strong relationship between internal, stable, and global attributions of negative outcomes and depression, indicating that people are likely to become particularly depressed if they believe themselves to be the cause of their plight. The most severe, enduring, and generalized forms of depression and concomitant mental illnesses develop when aversive stimuli (in this case, unemployment) persist despite the person's best efforts to avert them (by constantly seeking appropriate employment, for example) and when the person feels hopeless and helpless to change the situation. Thus, one would predict a positive relationship between depressive affect and internal attributions (i.e., a person holding him- or herself responsible) of the causes of unemployment. In contrast, external attributions may lead to anger.

Expectancy-value theory, which relates actions to the perceived attractiveness or aversiveness of expected outcomes, predicts that frustration in the desire to find work is associated with negative affects such as depression and sadness, but that these affects will be most intense among people who perceive work as attractive, have a high expectation of getting a job, and are very strongly motivated to find work.

Thus, much research has examined how young people explain their own, others', and the nation's unemployment. The type of attributions offered could have significant effects on their emotional well-being and their subsequent employment status. Consequently, many have argued that helping young people deal with unemployment is frequently best done at the cognitive level.

Final Comment

Research on unemployed young people during the past 15 years has yielded interesting and important findings. But do economic conditions shape how researchers view young people? It has been acknowledged elsewhere that periods of high unemployment stimulate research on its general psychosocial consequences, while in periods of low unemployment only the hard-core unemployed are deemed worthy of research (Furnham & Lewis, 1986). But are researchers' hypotheses, and indeed methods, influenced by the prevailing economic conditions? Enright, Levy, Harris, and Lasley (1987) believe they are. In a content analysis of psychology journals over a 60-year period, they were able to demonstrate that in times of economic depression and recession young people are portrayed as immature, psychologically unstable, and in need of prolonged participation in the educational system, whereas during wartime the psychological competence of young people is emphasized and the recommended duration of education reduced. Theories are seen as prescriptive (and proscriptive), reflecting the current social trend. They note:

> The field of adolescent psychology is not free from the societal influence that impinges upon legislators, educators and parents in shaping American adolescents. In fact, there is a strong correspondence between the ideas of adolescent psychology and the legislation passed by the US Congress. . . . The scientists' ideologies match those of the non-scientific policy makers. This is not to say that one is the cause of the other. The point is that all are influenced by the same economic conditions. (pp. 554–555)

Certainly, researchers would do well to examine how economic conditions have shaped their questions, methods, and theories. In periods of high unemployment, when many young people are unable to find work, researchers may tend to concentrate on the negative side-effects of worklessness and how to help young people overcome its deleterious effects. On the other hand, in times of prosperity and low unemployment, researchers may concentrate on issues of job motivation, commitment, and satisfaction. Thus, as now, when youth unemployment is high worldwide, researchers seem particularly concerned with negative psychosocial consequences.

That there is a complex causal relationship between youth unemployment and many psychosocial factors is beyond doubt. However, the research has demonstrated not only the complexity of this relationship, but also the large number of economic, psychological, and social variables moderating it. The fact that there are many such moderating variables means that unemployment is not experienced similarly by all young people. In the future, researchers may be able to describe and hence taxonomize the characteristic behavioral patterns of young unemployed people. Some attempt was made in this chapter to do just that, but the proposed taxonomy was based on only two variables. Research on the meaning and significance of youth unemployment in different contexts is only beginning. Because the topic is at the interface of a number of different disciplines, it is important that each discipline contribute its theories, explanations, and concepts. The socialization of young people into the adult worlds of work or nonwork can have important consequences for individual youth and the society at large. Hence this topic merits good applied research.

References

Argyle, M. (1983). *The social psychology of work*. Harmondsworth, UK: Penguin.

Banks, M., & Jackson, P. (1982). Unemployment and risk of minor psychiatric disorder in young people: Cross-sectional and longitudinal evidence. *Psychological Medicine, 12*, 789–798.

Baxter, J. (1975). The chronic job changer: A study of youth unemployment. *Social and Economic Administration, 9*, 154–200.

Bowlby, J. (1969). *Attachment and loss*. London: Hogarth.

Briar, R. (1977). The effect of long-term unemployment on workers and their families. *Dissertation Abstracts International, 37*, 6062.

Clark, A., & Clissold, M. (1982). Correlates of adaptation among unemployed and employed young men. *Psychological Reports, 50*, 887–893.

Despierre, J., & Sorel, N. (1979). Approache de la representation du chomage chez les jeunes. *L'Orientation Scholaire et Professionnelle, 8*, 347–364.

Eisenberg, P., & Lazarsfeld, P. (1938). The psychological effects of unemployment. *Psychological Bulletin, 35*, 79–96.

Empson-Warner, S., & Krahn, H. (1992). Unemployment and occupational aspiration. *Canadian Review of Sociology and Anthropology, 29*, 38–54.

Enright, R., Levy, V., Harris, D., & Lapsley, D. (1987). Do economic conditions influence how theorists view adolescents? *Journal of Youth and Adolescence, 16*, 541–559.

Farrington, D., Gallagher, B., Morley, L., St. Ledger, R., & West, D. (1986). Unemployment, school leaving and crime. *British Journal of Criminology, 26*, 335–356.

Feather, N. (1982). Unemployment and its psychological correlates: A study of depressive symptoms, self-esteem, Protestant ethic values, attributional style and apathy. *Australian Journal of Psychology, 34*, 309–323.

Feather, N., & Bond, M. (1983). Time structure and purposeful activity among employed and unemployed university graduates. *Journal of Occupational Psychology, 56*, 241–254.

Feather, N., & O'Brien, G. (1986a). A longitudinal analysis of the effects of different patterns of employment and unemployment on school-leavers. *British Journal of Psychology, 77*, 459–479.

Feather, N., & O'Brien, G. (1986b). A longitudinal study of the effects of employment and unemployment on school-leavers. *Journal of Occupational Psychology, 59*, 121–144.

Fleming, R., Baum, A., Reddy, D., & Gatchel, R. (1984). Behavioral and biochemical effects of job loss and unemployment stress. *Journal of Human Stress, 10*, 12–17.

Fryer, D., & Payne, R. (1986). Being unemployed: A review of the literature of the psychological experience of unemployment. In C. Cooper & J. Robertson (Eds.), *International Review of Industrial and Organizational Psychology* (pp. 235–278). Chichester, UK: Wiley.

Furnham, A. (1982). Explanation for unemployment in Britain. *European Journal of Social Psychology, 12*, 335–352.

Furnham, A. (1983). Mental health and unemployment status: A preliminary study. *British Journal of Counselling and Guidance, 11*, 197–201.

Furnham, A. (1984). Getting a job: School-leavers' perception of employment prospects. *British Journal of Educational Psychology, 54*, 293–305.

Furnham, A. (1985). The determinants of attitudes towards social security recipients. *British Journal of Social Psychology, 24*, 19–27.

Furnham, A. (1990). *The Protestant work ethic*. London: Routledge.

Furnham, A. (1992). *Personality at work*. London: Routledge.

Furnham, A., & Bochner, S. (1986). *Culture shock*. London: Methuen.

Furnham, A., & Hesketh, B. (1989). Explanations for unemployment in Great Britain and New Zealand. *Journal of Social Psychology, 129*, 169–181.

Furnham, A., & Lewis, A. (1986). *The economic mind*. Brighton, UK: Harvester.

Gaskell, G., & Smith, P. (1985). An investigation of youth's attribution for unemployment and their political attitudes. *Journal of Economic Psychology, 6*, 65–80.

Gurney, R. (1980). The effects of unemployment on the psychological development of school-leavers. *Journal of Occupational Behavior, 53*, 205–211.

Gurney, R. (1981). Leaving school, facing unemployment and making attributions about the causes of unemployment. *Journal of Vocational Behavior, 18*, 79–91.

Hammarstrom, A., Janlert, U., & Theorell, T. (1988). Youth employment and ill health: Results from a 2-year follow-up study. *Social Science and Medicine, 26*, 1025–1033.

Harrison, R. (1976). The demoralizing experience of prolonged unemployment. *Department of Employment Gazette, 4*, 339–348.

Hayes, J. & Nutman, P. (1981). *Understanding the unemployed*. London: Tavistock.

Heaven, P. (1990). Human values and suggestions for reducing unemployment. *British Journal of Social Psychology, 20*, 257–264.

Hill, J. (1978). The psychological impact of unemployment. *New Society, 12*.

Hodgson, J., & Brenner, M. (1968). Successful experience: Training hard-core unemployed. *Harvard Business Review, 46*, 148–156.

Hopson, B., & Adams, J. (1976). Towards an understanding of transition. In J. Adams, J. Hayes, & B. Hopson (Eds.), *Transition*. London: Martin-Robertson.

Jackson, P., & Warr, P. (1984). Unemployment and psychological ill-health: The moderating role of duration and age. *Psychological Medicine, 14*, 605–614.

Jahoda, M. (1979). The impact of unemployment in the 1930s and 1970s. *Bulletin of the British Psychological Society, 32*, 309–314.

Jahoda, M. (1981). Work, employment and unemployment: Values, theories and approaches in social research. *American Psychologist, 36*, 184–191.

Kelvin, P., & Jarrett, J. (1984). *Social psychological consequences of unemployment.* Cambridge: Cambridge University Press.

La France, M., & Cicchetti, C. (1979). Perceived responsibility and blame for economic success and failure. *Journal of Applied Psychology, 9*, 466–475.

Levingner, G., & Moles, O. (1979). *Divorce and separation.* New York: Basic Books.

Lewis, A., & Furnham, A. (1986). Reducing unemployment: Lay belief about how to reduce current employment. *Journal of Economic Psychology, 7*, 75–85.

Lewis, A., Snell, M., & Furnham, A. (1987). Lay explanations for the causes of unemployment. *Political Psychology, 8*, 427–439.

Lynn, R., Hampson, S., & Magee, M. (1984). Home background, intelligence, personality and education are predictors of unemployment in young people. *Personality and Individual Differences, 5*, 549–537.

Makeham, V. (1980). Youth unemployment: An examination of evidence on youth unemployment using national statistics (Research Paper No. 10). London: Department of Employment.

O'Brien, G. (1984). Reciprocal effects between locus of control and job attributes. *Australian Journal of Psychology, 36*, 57–75.

O'Brien, G. (1986). *Psychology of work and unemployment.* Chichester, UK: Wiley.

O'Brien, G., & Kabanoff, B. (1979). Comparison of unemployed and employed workers on values, locus of control and health variables. *Australian Psychologist, 14*, 143–154.

Parkes, C. (1975). *Bereavement: Studies of grief in adult life.* Harmondsworth, UK: Penguin.

Patton, W., & Noller, P. (1984). Unemployment and youth: A longitudinal study. *Australian Journal of Psychology, 36*, 399–413.

Payne, M., & Furnham, A. (1990). Causal attributions for unemployment in Barbados. *Journal of Social Psychology, 130*, 169–181.

Platt, S., & Kreitman, N. (1985). Parasuicide and unemployment among men in Edinburgh, 1968–1982. *Psychological Medicine, 15*, 113–123.

Raelin, J. (1981). A comparative study of later work experience among full-time, part-time and unemployed male youth. *Journal of Vocational Behavior, 19*, 315–327.

Roberts, K., Duggan, J., & Noble, M. (1982). Out-of-school youth in high unemployment areas. *British Journal of Guidance and Counselling, 10*, 1–11.

Shanahan, M., Finch, M., Mortimer, J., & Ryu, S. (1991). Adolescent work experience and depressive affect. *Social Psychology Quarterly, 54*, 299–317.

Tiffany, D., Cowan, J., & Tiffany, P. (1970). *The unemployed.* Englewood Cliffs, NJ: Prentice Hall.

Tiggemann, M., & Winefield, A. (1984). The effects of unemployment on the mood, self-esteem, locus of control and depressive affect of school leavers. *Journal of Occupational Psychology, 57*, 33–42.

Warr, P. (1983). Work, jobs and unemployment. *Bulletin of the British Psychological Society, 36*, 305–311.

Warr, P. (1984). Reported behavior changes after job loss. *British Journal of Social Psychology, 23*, 271–275.

Warr, P. (1987). *Work, unemployment and mental health.* Oxford: Oxford University Press.

Warr, P., Banks, M., & Ullah, P. (1985). The experience of unemployment among black and white urban teenagers. *British Journal of Psychology, 76,* 75–87.

Warr, P., Jackson, P., & Banks, M. (1982). Duration of unemployment and psychological well-being in young men and women. *Current Psychological Research, 2,* 207–214.

Warr, P., Jackson, P. & Banks, M. (1988). Unemployment and mental health: Some British studies. *Journal of Social Issues, 44,* 47–68.

Webley, P., & Wrigley, V. (1983). The development of conception of unemployment among adolescents. *Journal of Adolescence, 6,* 317–328.

Winefield, A., & Tiggemann, M. (1985). Psychological correlates of employment and unemployment: Effects, predisposing factors, and sex differences. *Journal of Occupational Psychology, 58,* 229–242.

Winefield, A., Winefield, H., Tiggemann, M., & Goldney, R. (1991). A longitudinal study of the psychological effects of unemployment and unsatisfactory employment in young adults. *Journal of Applied Psychology, 76,* 424–431.

Winefield, H., & Winefield, A. (1992). Psychological development in adolescence and youth. In P. Heaven (Ed.), *Life span development.* Marrionville: Harcourt Brace Jovanovich.

IV. Social consequences and interventions

9. Societal consequences of youth unemployment

HANNIE TE GROTENHUIS
B&A Group Policy Research and Consultancy,
Rotterdam, The Netherlands

FRANS MEIJERS
University of Leiden, The Netherlands

Introduction

In this chapter we examine three hypothetical consequences of chronic youth (ages 15 to 25) unemployment: a declining work ethic, a rising crime rate, and the emergence of a social underclass. As our considerations are mainly based on the employment situation in the Netherlands, we present some relevant information from that country in the first section. Next, we discuss empirical findings regarding the relationship among the work ethic, delinquency, and youth unemployment. We argue that a specific category of the young adult unemployed are at risk of becoming part of an underclass of socially, culturally, and economically marginalized people. Last, we explore the extent to which structural (youth) unemployment reveals the limitations of the welfare state.

Background

In the Netherlands attending school is obligatory until the age of 18. For 16- and 17-year-olds a so-called dual trajectory is allowed. After leaving junior secondary vocational education at the age of 16, one can enter the apprenticeship system. Apprentices are required to attend school for no more than two days a week (for 17-year-olds) or for one day a week (for 18-year-olds). But less than 10 percent of young people follow this trajectory, as Table 9.1 shows (under part-time education). Most stay in full-time education until the age of 20 and then enter the labor market.

Table 9.1 *Main pursuit of 16- to 26-year-olds in 1990 (in percent).*

	Full-Time Education	Part-Time Education	Em- ployed	Unem- ployed	Rest	Total
16- to 20-year-olds	61.3	9.6	19.0	7.3	2.8	100
21- to 26-year-olds	13.0	6.5	59.9	8.1	12.5	100

Source: Ministry of Social Affairs and Employment (1991a), p. 11.

In the past few years, the Dutch job market has strongly improved, especially for young people. In 1990, the demand for school-leavers even outnumbered the supply. As a result, youth unemployment dramatically decreased and is now below the 1980 level (Arbeidsvoorziening, 1991). Nevertheless, 7.3 percent of the 16- to 20-year-olds and 8.1 percent of the 21- to 26-year-olds are presently unemployed (see Table 9.1).

The overall unemployment rate in the Netherlands is 7.5 percent. Compared to other West European countries, this figure is quite high. One-fifth of all Dutch unemployed are below the age of 25. Compared to other OECD countries, however, a 20 percent share of youth in the total unemployed population is not a bad score (OECD, 1991). But this low figure should be put in proper perspective. First, it only pertains to unemployed youth who are registered at the labor exchange. Many 16- and 17-year-old school-leavers do not register because they are not eligible for unemployment benefits. Many young women (especially from ethnic minorities) do not register because they work in the family household. According to recent figures of the Ministry of Social Affairs and Employment, 12 percent of all 15- to 25-year-olds are looking for a paid job but cannot find one (Ministry of Social Affairs and Employment, 1991).

Second, about 40 percent of jobless youth have been unemployed for more than a year. Despite an improving economy, the percentage of long-term unemployed has hardly changed over the past five years (Boot, 1990). Long-term unemployment often means marginalization; the unemployed youngsters of the 1980's are the so-called lost generation (Grotenhuis, 1991).

Third, labor-market prospects did not improve for unqualified school-leavers. Their chances of remaining unemployed for more than one year have increased to more than 20 percent (Ministry of Social Affairs and Employment, 1991b).

Fourth, youth unemployment is concentrated more and more in minority groups. Whereas the unemployment rate among indigenous youngsters dropped by 50 percent between 1983 and 1989, it increased during that same period for Turkish (+13%), Moroccan (+59%), Surinam (+4%), and Antillian (+75%) youngsters (Bock & Hovels, 1991, p. 39). In 1991, the unemployment rate among 16- to 25-year-old immigrants was 3.5 times higher than among indigenous youth of the same age (Ministry of Internal Affairs, 1991; Veenman, 1991).

Finally, approximately 1 percent of Dutch adolescents are absorbed by the occupational disability system—not because of severe physical or mental handicaps, but because of social or psychological problems (Gemeenschappelijke Medische Dienst, 1989). These are not included among the officially counted unemployed.

Youth unemployed: An increasingly disadvantaged group

Youth unemployment is decreasing in prevalence. But it has become concentrated in an increasingly disadvantaged category of youngsters who are being crowded out of the market because they do not have the credentials that are now required. A disproportionately large number of unemployed youngsters are those from ethnic minorities, poorly educated youngsters, and youngsters from families where long-term unemployment is but one of many problems (Meesters, 1992; Werdmolder, 1990).

Due to an improved economy, the young unemployed are increasingly school dropouts. This especially holds true for those who, in principle, have the best chances on the labor market: white boys. Dropouts not only lack adequate schooling, but they also tend to have other problems that make an easy transition from school to work difficult: broken families, unemployed parents, negligence in the home, and alcohol and drug abuse (Grotenhuis, 1991; Junger, 1990; Ploeg & Scholte, 1990). These youngsters often have difficulties as early as elementary school. Behavioral problems, learning problems, or problems with teachers and classmates are not uncommon. Their educational careers often ended in failure even before they were old enough to legally leave school (Arbeidsvoorziening, 1991). Employers are not eager to employ these youngsters: They would rather employ those without any problems of this kind.

At present, the unemployed youngster is confronted with an increasingly difficult employment situation. Diplomas, a willingness and ability to learn, a high degree of flexibility, independence, and social skills are all demanded by employers. Junior vocational training no longer leads directly to work as a saleswoman or house painter. Additional training and capabilities have now become necessary, especially for poorly educated girls, young people from ethnic minorities, and long-term unemployed young adults. Without the "extras," they have very little chance of obtaining a place in the labor market (Kloosterman & Elfring, 1991).

Fighting youth unemployment

Since 1988, youth unemployment has not had high priority on either the political or the academic agenda. However, recently one of the most prestigious youth unemployment programs in Dutch history has been created, the Youth Employment Guarantee Plan (YEGP). It is not an exaggeration to say that at the moment, the entire Dutch youth unemployment policy has been compressed into YEGP. The new jobs created by YEGP are not supposed to compete with existing jobs, which is one reason only the public sector is involved in the program.

YEGP not only aims to deal with the present youth unemployment problem, but it also aims to prevent future mass unemployment for youngsters. After at least six months of unemployment, YEGP offers 16- to 22-year-olds a temporary job in the public sector or training.[1] An unemployed youngster can refuse the first offer, but the second has to be accepted to continue his unemployment benefits. A participant can stay at the same job for one year. If no regular job is obtained in the meantime, other temporary jobs will be offered. A participant who has failed to get a job before the 27th birthday, must leave the project.

The program had its official start in January 1992 and has not yet been evaluated. Nevertheless, there are doubts as to how successful it will be in dealing with youth unemployment. Youngsters who have been unemployed for at least six months belong to an increasingly disadvantaged group. Guaranteeing them a job is not feasible if only the public sector is involved, because not enough jobs are available in this sector. To make the program a success, the cooperation of the private sector is necessary. This is a large stumbling block: Employers have already stated they will refuse to cooperate with any policy that forces them to employ "marginal and underqualified" youngsters (Meijers, 1990).

During the past decade, the Dutch government has developed two additional strategies to treat and to prevent youth unemployment (Meijers, 1990). A decision to keep youngsters in the regular school system for as long as possible has been successful. Since 1985, attendance has risen more than could be expected on the basis of demographic changes. The education system serves a "warehouse" function (Ministry of Education, 1992). To reduce the gap between supply and demand, the dual system has been extended; a reinvestment in the apprentice system has been made.

Societal Consequences

Reactions to unemployment

From the 1930s onward research has been conducted on the relationships between work orientation and unemployment. The findings of earlier studies, however, differ in some important respects from those of studies conducted during the 1980s.

In their Marienthal study that began early in the 1930s, Jahoda, Lazarsfeld, and Zeisel (1933/1980) identify three types of prevalent coping behavior in families. The predominant type was called "resigned." The unemployed and their families resigned themselves to their situation. They arranged their lives as well as possible, no longer sought work, and were generally satisfied with their lot. The second and third types were called "unbroken" and "broken." When they still saw a future for themselves and were planning how to get employed again, the family was called "unbroken." These people still were strongly motivated to work and they were unsatisfied with their present situation. The reaction to unemployment was called "broken" when the unemployed person and his family were overwhelmed by despair and apathy. Jahoda, and colleagues (1933/1980) detected these features in a small proportion of cases; according to other authors, such as Zawadski and Lazarsfeld (1935), they were common.

In most of the studies conducted in the 1930s, unemployment was seen as a phenomenon that afflicts not only the unemployed person, but also his family and even his community. The unemployed individual (as well as his social environment) is typically seen as passing through stages of optimism and pessimism and arriving at a position of fatalism (see Eisenberg & Lazarsfeld, 1938).

Bakke (1934) perceives unemployment as a phenomenon that affects family life in five phases. In the first phase, called "momentum stability," the situation of unemployment closely resembles that of pre-unemployment. In the second phase, "unstable equilibrium," the negative aspects of unemployment worsen. In the third phase, "disorganization," the unemployed individual and his family give up any hope of returning to the stability experienced before unemployment. In the fourth phase, "experimental readjustment," the family members begin to accept the fact that life has irrevocably changed. In the fifth phase, termed "permanent readjustment," the most successful coping mechanisms are selected and consolidated.

Being unemployed is still a highly unwanted status. Having a paid job is a dominant value for most individuals in Western societies (Feather & Bond, 1983; Tiggemann & Winefield, 1980; Warr, 1982). But despair, apathy, and crisis are now much less prominently present in the lives of the unemployed and their families. Instead, almost all researchers report the emergence of indifferent or even positive attitudes toward unemployment among the unemployed.

In a secondary analysis of data from a national survey carried out in 1982, Becker (1989) established that the unemployed reacted to their situation in four different ways. First, there is a reaction that he labels "general disorientation" (60% of participants), prevalent among persons with traditional work attitudes. It incorporates feelings of aimlessness, uselessness, and social isolation. The generally disoriented unemployed want to work but are not given the opportunity to do so. They are bored and experience other forms of socio-psychological stress. The second reaction (15% of respondents), appearing primarily among the unemployed without partners and/or with few or no friends, takes the form of health disorders. Here, unemployment intensifies a feeling of social isolation. Becker's label for the third reaction is "alternative" (10%). The unemployed finds that "the essential elements [of unemployment] are greater freedom, greater ability to pursue one's hobbies and the ability to draw an income without having to work for it" (Becker, 1989, p. 167). This is especially likely for unemployed persons with nontraditional attitudes toward work who are unencumbered by a family and who generally work in the lower occupational categories. The fourth reaction (15%), emphasizing financial concerns, is found primarily among male breadwinners who do blue-collar work. It is characterized as "traditional working class." Attitudes toward work can be described as lukewarm: Work is not rejected but neither is it placed on a pedestal.

An "alternative" way of coping with unemployment is found particularly among the young unemployed. Huurne (1988) and Jehoel-Gijsbers (1990) found that almost 20 percent of unemployed youngsters hold "alternative values" with regard to work. This means they are unwilling to endorse the statement that work is a duty, they distinguish not only negative but also positive aspects of unemployment, and—last but not least—they are not eager to participate in training projects (such as the YEGP in the Netherlands or the Youth Training Scheme in Britain). Yankelovitch and colleagues (1984) report almost the same figures for the United States and for several Western European countries.

Several researchers argue that the existence of the welfare state provoked this alternative reaction to unemployment. In the 1930s, the financial consequences of unemployment were much more severe than in the 1980s. For Jahoda and colleagues (1933/1980), as well as for Bakke (1934), coping behavior was mainly determined by differences in the amount of money to spend. But nowadays, the social security system prevents unemployment from reducing whole communities to beggary. People know that they can survive when they become unemployed. Knowing that one's most important necessities of life are guaranteed gives an individual space to develop a so-called post-materialistic attitude to life (Inglehart, 1979). People can choose, many scientists and politicians argue, to be "voluntarily" unemployed (Furnham, 1982; Rose, 1985). Becker does not hesitate to call the alternative reaction to unemployment "an utterance of a post-materialist mentality" (Becker, 1989, p. 87). Is this a correct interpretation?

A declining work ethic?

At first sight, the emergence of post-materialism seems to be self-evident. Many studies show a change in the traditional work ethic during the past three or four decades (see Yankelovitch et al., 1984, for an overview). The Dutch Social and Cultural Planning Office (SCP) drew attention to the fact that more and more people value their leisure time more highly than their time at work. Only a small minority valued work more highly than leisure time (Social and Cultural Planning Office, 1984). Allerbeck and Hoag (1985) observed the same trend in the Federal Republic of Germany. Fewer think that paid work is an essential and indispensable part of a happy life. Very few people still state that only paid work can make them happy.

Noelle-Neuman (1981) reports that in a poll carried out in West Germany in 1980, about half the respondents declared that the time they really enjoyed was the time they spent away from work. In 1962, less than a third gave the same answer. She cites another study of German work values in which the respondents who thought that Germans worked too hard (42%) almost equalled those who took an opposite view (see also Otto-Brock, 1991).

On the other hand, even more studies, especially of young people, suggest that the vast majority of adolescents and adults—employed and unemployed—are committed to obtaining paid employment (Allatt & Yeandle, 1992; Baetghe, Hantsche, Pellul, & Voskamp, 1989; Banks & Ullah, 1988; Bogt & Praag 1992). And more important, as Rose (1985) stated in his review of research: "the primary motivation to secure employment does not appear to be financial. Most young people in these studies said that they would continue to work if it was no longer financially necessary to do so" (p. 116). Recently, Meijers (1992) reported that more than 90 percent of the immigrant and indigenous youngsters he interviewed held the same opinion. Apparently, having a paid job after finishing school is for almost all youngsters a valuable goal.

It is necessary to distinguish between those people who really do not value employment and those who do but are discouraged from looking for it. When we restrict ourselves to unemployed adolescents and young adults, we can detect these two groups very easily. The first group consists of highly educated, unemployed youngsters from the upper classes (and the highest stratum of the middle class) who feel comfortable in their unemployment. The second group consists of poorly educated, unemployed adolescents from the working class and the lower stratum of the middle class who cope successfully with their unemployment but would love to have a job.

In their longitudinal project, Huurne (1988) and Jehoel-Gijsbers (1990) found that young unemployed who hold alternative values with regard to work and, at the same time, are able to cope well with their unemployment (i.e., less than average stress, an internal locus of control, and no health problems) more often originate from a higher social class and have successfully completed a form of pre-university or general secondary education (see also Becker, 1989; Raaymakers, 1987). Further, their analysis shows that for this group (the so-called autonomous youngsters) no significant relationship exists between their alternative value orientations and their work careers. Two years after the first interview, autonomous youngsters were not less successful than the other respondents with regard to having a paid job. Jehoel-Gijsbers (1990, p. 102) even reports— contrary to her expectations—that autonomous unemployed youngsters more often than other respondents found a paid job two years after the first interview. Finally, Huurne and Jehoel-Gijsbers report that autonomous youngsters are more involved in voluntary work than other unemployed youngsters.

Whereas unemployed youth from advantaged backgrounds are more likely to hold alternative values, working-class youth may also develop them over time. Because the latter have fewer formal qualifications, their chances of becoming long-term unemployed are much greater (Diederen, 1991; Meesters, 1992; Ministry of Social Affairs and Employment, 1991). Banks and Ullah (1988) show that those people unemployed for long periods of time, when compared with those experiencing less unemployment, were putting significantly less effort into looking for work. However, this does not appear to be because they no longer wanted to have a job, since their level of employment commitment was high, and was similar to that of those who had been unemployed for a much shorter length of time. (p. 90)

Their lower levels of job seeking appear to reflect pessimism about the chances of obtaining a job. Hendry, Raymond, and Stewart (1984) reported that as the period of unemployment increased, there were increasingly negative attitudes toward looking for a job and lower expectations about the possibility of obtaining one. From here to "alternative values" is only a small step, especially because for these youngsters jobs are likely to be characterized by low wages, insecurity, and unpleasant working conditions. In contrast, unemployment at this age may not entail serious financial worries or be socially isolating. The important thing is that alternative values do not originate from an alternative "attitude to life" but from a growing sense of discouragement.

Unemployed adolescents from the middle and upper classes can afford to withdraw from the "world of labor" because their "social," "cultural," and "economic capital" (Bourdieu, 1979) guarantees them a paid job in the long run. Their unemployment is almost certain to be temporary and it gives them an opportunity to enjoy a period of "post-adolescence" (Keniston, 1968). "Personal growth" outside the labor market is a highly rewarded activity for the middle and upper classes (Ehrenreich, 1989; Meijers, 1992). Working as a volunteer in community development programs, adult education, or youth work fits in perfectly with this culture and, moreover, keeps the already acquired qualifications unimpaired. As soon as they have a paid job, however, their attitudes rapidly change (Boltken & Jagodzinski, 1984).

Unemployed youngsters (mainly from the working class) can best be described as "discouraged workers" (Flaim, 1973). They want to have a job, but change their values in the long run because they believe their search for a job will be in vain. As a result, their chances on the labor market are worsening. This process can be described through the concept of the "transactional relationship" (Lazarus & Launier, 1978): The unemployed individual changes his or her relationship with the environment on the basis of preceding attempts to cope with unemployment.

To conclude, in the lives of most unemployed young people a strong work ethic is still present. The values a person has acquired in primary socialization seem to be very stable and do not change easily, even if important circumstances do. Beliefs about paid work do not suddenly emerge at the end of full-time education, but are embedded in the family discourse of everyday life. The so-called institutionalization of the youth phase (Baetghe et al., 1989) gives unemployed youngsters with good prospects the chance to stay young for a time. There is, however, no reason for assuming that their work ethic is changing fundamentally or permanently.

For unemployed youngsters with bad prospects, however, discouragement can produce "alternative values" with regard to work. Expulsion from the labor market can eventually result in a life attitude in which the "Protestant ethic" (Weber) has completely vanished. If this attitude is transferred to children, their behavior is also affected by alternative values.

Crime as a consequence of youth unemployment

Scholars have often considered the relationship between unemployment and crime, with considerable difference of opinion (Freeman, 1983). Wilson and Herrnstein (1985) blame severe methodological problems and theoretical naiveté for this. Keeping their criticism in mind, we review some research findings on the relationship between youth unemployment and crime. First, however, we consider the main theoretical arguments underlying the hypothesis that unemployment causes crime.

According to Merton's (1967) "strain theory" of deviant behavior, people are socialized to pursue certain goals such as a well-paid job or a well-to-do lifestyle. But not everybody has access to the means of attaining these goals. This shortage of resources causes strain. Delinquency, then, is a way out of the conflict between the aspiration to achieve certain conventional goals and restricted opportunities. Unemployment is an unrelenting restriction of opportunities and resources; it frustrates most ambitions. If a person cannot or will not accept this, and if he or she feels fate is unfair, crime may be a solution (Ploeg, 1991).

A second line of reasoning comes from Hirschi's "social control theory" (1969). Hirschi wondered why everybody does not commit crime. According to Hirschi, people are kept from crime because of (1) bonds to conventional others, such as parents, teachers, and friends; (2) commitment to achievements, such as employment and education; and (3) beliefs concerning the dominant social and moral order. These three crime-inhibiting factors reflect bonds to society. The stronger the bonds are, the higher the cost of deviant behavior. The weaker the bonds, the greater the likelihood of delinquent behavior.

On the basis of these theoretical arguments, a strong relationship between unemployment and crime is not a realistic expectation. For most youngsters the bonds to society will be strong enough to make them accept their (temporary) situation. Most of them will be positively connected to parents and friends, with sufficient prospects to keep on trying and continue to have a law-abiding attitude. But a small proportion of the young unemployed may lack these inhibiting factors and try to achieve by crime what they cannot achieve in a conventional manner. Consequently, their crime will be crime for material gain.

Albrecht (1984) investigated the relationship between youth unemployment and crime in Germany. He analyzed labor-force data and police statistics to discover whether a rise in the number of young unemployed was followed by an increase in the number of unemployed juvenile offenders during the years 1977 to 1982. His findings are remarkable: Although the number of unemployed youngsters doubled between 1977 and 1982, the number of unemployed juvenile offenders remained fairly constant. Because, at the same time, the number of juvenile delinquents increased, Albrecht concluded that the total offender rate within the unemployed youth population dropped dramatically. Looking at this in more detail, Albrecht observed a shift within the group of unemployed juvenile offenders. Only among short-term unemployed youngsters did crime rates decrease; the propensity of long-term unemployed youngsters to engage in juvenile delinquency was unchanged.

Farrington, Gallagher, Morley, St. Ledger, and West (1986) analyzed data from the Cambridge Study of Delinquent Development, a longitudinal survey of crime and delinquency among 411 males. The authors relied on interview data from the early 1970s, when the boys were between 16 and 18 years old. Proportionally more crimes were committed by the boys during periods of unemployment than during periods of employment. Unemployment was related to crime especially at the younger ages (15–16). Criminal behavior was most frequently observed in the case of unemployed youngsters whose attitudes were more favorable to offending. Basically law-abiding boys did not alter their behavior in times of unemployment. Moreover, unemployment had a stronger relationship with crime when it occurred in the context of a lower-status job history. Finally, unemployment was associated with a higher rate of committing crimes for material gain, but not with a higher rate of committing other kinds of crime.

Thornberry and Christenson (1984) have criticized the fact that contemporary theories of criminal behavior are unidirectional. Based on the premise that various social factors (among them unemployment) cause criminal behavior, these theories ignore the possibility of reciprocal causation—that is, that crime also causally influences these same social factors. The authors investigated the reciprocal relationship between crime and unemployment by analyzing the juvenile and adult arrest histories of 567 persons born in the United States in 1945. The data were collected from the files of the Philadelphia police and the Federal Bureau of Investigation. The 567 subjects were interviewed at the ages of 25 to 30. Thornberry and Christenson found that unemployment has significant instantaneous effects on crime and that crime has significant—primarily lagged—effects on unemployment. Most interesting was their additional finding that the relationship between unemployment and crime was stronger for the less-advantaged groups: blacks and blue-collar workers.

The studies of Thornberry and Christenson and of Farrington and colleagues are limited, due to the small numbers of unemployed delinquents (Farrington et al.) and the long time that elapsed between the data collection and the report of the results. The research findings are nevertheless consistent with the results of two recent Dutch studies, considered below.

Kroes and Weerman (1990) analyzed police records between 1975 and 1988 in a medium-size Dutch city to gain more insight into the relationship between crime and unemployment. They observed a strong increase in crimes against property; other types of criminal offenses remained constant. Moreover, there was a growing percentage of unemployed delinquents; the percentage of working delinquents diminished. In 1985, 80 percent of the delinquents were unemployed men and women; in 1975 the figure was 65 percent. Unemployed people were found to commit more crimes than employed people. Kroes and Weerman estimated that 6 percent of the unemployed had a police record due to crimes against property, and 2 percent because of violence against persons. Only 0.6 percent of employed people had been recorded as committing these types of offenses. Table 9.2 shows the unemployed youngsters' crimes were more often for material gain. Thus, not only quantitatively, but also qualitatively, crime and unemployment are related.

Ploeg (1991) studied the relationship between socioeconomic position and delinquent behavior. About 300 long-term unemployed, low-income workers and high-income workers were interviewed about their actual delinquency and their tolerance toward breaking the law. Although Ploeg's study was restricted to 20- to 50-year-old men, Ploeg shows that unemployment does not push law-abiding men to delinquency, but it

Table 9.2 *Criminal offenses of working (w) and unemployed (u) persons who were booked by the police (per age group) (in percentages).*

		16–19	20–24	25–29	30–39	40–64
Theft	w	32.6	24.3	29.7	24.4	25.0
	u	39.9	39.9	42.4	37.9	42.9
Robbery	w	—	2.8	2.0	—	—
	u	2.7	4.9	3.0	4.6	1.4
Burglary	w	21.7	16.8	9.9	7.3	3.6
	u	33.8	29.4	22.2	17.9	5.7
Other offenses	w	2.2	7.5	6.9	11.4	19.6
	u	0.7	3.9	8.6	8.7	15.7
Violence against	w	30.4	29.9	25.7	30.9	33.9
persons	u	11.5	11.0	13.6	11.3	21.4
Vandalism	w	8.7	14.0	12.9	13.0	10.7
	u	8.1	6.4	7.6	10.3	10.0
Other violence	w	2.2	3.8	5.0	7.3	3.6
	u	2.1	3.6	2.0	4.6	1.4
Sexual offenses	w	2.2	0.9	7.9	5.7	3.6
	u	1.4	1.1	0.5	4.6	1.4
Total	w	100	100	100	100	100
	u	100	100	100	100	100
N		194	390	299	318	126

Source: Kroes and Weerman (1990), p. 194.

does encourage former delinquents to steal again. According to Ploeg, unemployment leads to feelings of deprivation, strain, and injustice; these attitudes, in turn, promote delinquency.

What can we learn from these studies? First, unemployment and crime are related, but in a more complex way than is often assumed. Ploeg and Farrington and colleagues show that unemployment results in recidivism far more than in first offenses. Thornberry and Christenson point to the mutual influences of unemployment and crime. Unemployment and crime are linked most strongly among "the less advantaged."

Underclass

Youth unemployment is not an isolated "fait social," but part of a social syndrome, related to other unfavorable social facts and experiences. In the foregoing sections, we considered the relationship between unemployment and social problems, such as the declining work ethic and crime. In this section we go one step further and examine whether structural youth unemployment results in a specific underclass of jobless, poorly educated, and socially marginal people. The term *underclass* implies a situation in which unemployment generates itself; attachment to mainstream society by way of education and work becomes the exception, and detachment the rule.

Belonging to an underclass means being socially isolated from mainstream society, facing strong structural constraints, and having very limited opportunities in the immediate environment. According to Wilson (1991), "What distinguishes members of the underclass from those of other economically disadvantaged groups is that their marginal economic position or weak attachment to the labor force is uniquely reinforced by the neighborhood or social milieu" (p. 474). An underclass, then, not only is detached from labor and other mainstream institutions, but it also is isolated from employed and attached people. Besides these structural circumstances, the underclass can also be distinguished by their cultural traits. Wilson refers to low self-efficacy as a central feature. Fatalism, low aspirations, and self-doubt could also characterize the underclass.

Do youth who are unemployed exhibit features of an underclass? To answer this question, we rely on two Dutch studies by Engbersen (1990)[2] and Grotenhuis (1991). Engbersen's (1990) research on long-term unemployment in the Netherlands was based on interviews with 271 men and women who were unemployed for at least two years; 70 of the respondents were 23 to 30 years old. Focusing on the coping strategies of the long-term unemployed, Engbersen distinguished four "cultures of unemployment": conformist, individualistic, autonomous, and fatalistic.

Conformists hold a traditional view of work. They feel it is their duty to work; therefore being unemployed causes a great deal of strain. When they are out of work, feelings of aimlessness and being left out dominate their lives. Compared with the other three groups, conformists go to great efforts to find a job and to maintain independence. Because they are socially integrated, a large part of their time is spent with relatives, friends, and neighbors. Their job-seeking behavior is strongly influenced by social pressure exerted by their relatives and neighbors. Conformists cannot easily accept welfare dependence. They perceive their benefit as a right, but at the same time they feel humiliated to be on welfare and not to be earning money by working.

The individualistic "culture" consists of "enterprising" and "calculating" respondents. Their large network of friends extends beyond the borders of the neighborhood. As a consequence, their life is not dominated by strong social controls. They have their own rules and values, which serve to help them get around the external rules of the authorities. Their work ethic is utilitarian: Work is important because it guarantees money to reach a certain consumption level and to gain access to a specific lifestyle. But if these things can be realized by alternative means—such as claiming welfare while having an income or committing crimes—individualists do not need a formal job. According to Engbersen, most of the calculating and enterprising respondents prefer the advantages of their situation to those of employment. They particularly appreciate the freedom and the leisure time they have while living on national assistance.

Autonomous unemployed—in general, the better educated—operate in a social context that is in some ways similar to that of the individualists. Their social environment is characterized by weak group ties and insignificant social control. The autonomous like to do things their own way and be as independent as possible. They are not very active in "network building" because they do not maintain social contacts with a view to acquiring extra income. Their social contacts fulfill intrinsic needs. The autonomous do not look for a job and reject illegal or dishonest income strategies. Some of them find satisfying alternatives to employment. The autonomous can be called "post-materialists" (Inglehart, 1979).

The fatalistic "culture of unemployment" is characterized by weak group ties and strong external regulations. Members of this category are socially isolated and extremely dependent on national assistance. The external regulations and control of the authorities dominate every aspect of their lives. The only "resistance" on the part of the fatalists is "withdrawal": They no longer seek or apply for jobs. This attitude is attributable to the absence of prospects and expectations. Boredom is widespread.

Of Engbersen's 70 young unemployed respondents, 45 percent, are conformist; 35 percent, individualistic; 11 percent, autonomous; and 9 percent, fatalistic. Compared to the older age groups, the youngsters more often adhere to the conformist or individualistic cultures. Older unemployed people are more often fatalistic. In essence, the fatalists belong to an underclass. Their economic and social positions are strongly marginalized and their level of self-efficacy is very low. But youngsters from the conformist culture of unemployment also run a risk. According to Engbersen, if unemployment continues and job-seeking behavior is unsuccessful, resignation and fatalism can be a consequence, engendering a fatalistic stance. Moreover, it can be expected that persons who cope successfully with their unemployment at any given time may fail to do so subsequently.

te Grotenhuis (1991) interviewed 23 indigenous youngsters in the Netherlands, whose ages ranged from 16 to 25. Thirteen were unemployed, and the other ten were employed or doing well in school. They lived in a working-class neighborhood; their parents did not finish any type of secondary education and worked in blue-collar jobs. Despite this common background, the unemployed youngsters differed from those who were employed and attending school.

Eleven of the 13 unemployed youngsters had unemployed parents. None of the unemployed youngsters had finished secondary education and 3 confessed they could not write or read properly. Five of the 13 had a police record and 2 had a father in jail. Their low self-efficacy, fatalism, and self-doubt were overwhelming. Three had too many troubles to worry about jobs and 3 were trying hard to find a suitable place where they could work and learn at the same time. Most of the unemployed youngsters lacked connections with mainstream institutions such as school and employment agencies, as well as with "conventional" others. Both parents and youngsters had little self-efficacy and lacked the skills and relationships needed to get a job or even to get the right information about job opportunities. Ten of the youngsters had been unemployed for more than one year. Seven of the unemployed boys and girls did not know how to look for a job and did not believe that applying for one could have a positive effect. te Grotenhuis found that not only the youngsters' but also their parents' social and economic positions were strongly marginalized. These findings are consistent with Wilson's view that low self-efficacy grows out of a weak attachment to school and the labor force and is reinforced by others in the neighborhood who are similarly situated and have similar beliefs.

An underclass implies the intergenerational continuation of a socially marginalized position. Payne (1987) reports that a child with unemployed parents or unemployed siblings has a considerably higher chance of becoming unemployed than does a child with employed parents and employed siblings. Unemployment runs in families as a result of the transmission of deprivation and inadequate coping strategies (Grotenhuis, 1991). Moreover, youngsters who have been unemployed once run a greater risk of becoming unemployed again in the near future (Meesters, 1992; Meesters & van de Pol, 1989).

In the Netherlands, as well as elsewhere, a growing and persistent class of unemployed and welfare-dependent men and women has emerged. A growing early school dropout rate perpetuates a hard core of long-term, unemployed youth. These youngsters are not reached by employment programs. The prestigious YEGP focuses on the recently graduated and short-term unemployed. As with employment programs for adults, YEGP creams off the most highly qualified. In the past, perhaps, the others could have been connected to society by way of unskilled or marginal jobs. Now they are needed less and less.

Mass youth unemployment during the 1980s seems to have resulted in a lost generation: the 25 to 34 age group is overrepresented in present unemployment figures. Some of today's unemployed youngsters may stay unemployed forever, or at best get work only intermittently. We can only guess what the consequences will be for the children of these unemployed.

Long-term unemployed people may be considered an underclass of society as soon as withdrawal, resignation, and social isolation from mainstream society become dominant. Engbersen claims that about 9 percent of the Dutch young unemployed in the 23 to 30 age group already belong to the underclass. Poorly educated youngsters, severely handicapped by a low level of self-efficacy and confronted with a myriad of problems, increasingly threaten to join this underclass.

Youth Unemployment and the Welfare State

Does youth unemployment undermine or threaten the welfare state (i.e., the social security system)? In one sense, the answer is yes. Nearly half of long-term unemployed youngsters—the individualistic and the autonomous ones—in the Engbersen study "successfully" coped with their unemployment, although most of them did not choose to be unemployed. Their work attitude, however, allowed them to be on welfare, to make little or no effort to find official employment, to develop alternative ways of life, and to withdraw from the formal labor market. Their attitude challenges the ideological basis of the welfare state. The modern welfare state is, according to Offe (1984), based upon the solidarity of the employed with the unemployed. This solidarity rests on the self-evident willingness of all who can work to do so. The refusal to work, therefore, destroys the ideological basis of the social security system.

But in another way, the answer to the above question is no. More than 50 percent of the unemployed youngsters—the conformist and fatalistic—in the Engbersen study wanted a job and hated being on welfare. They wanted to be independent, but not by means of illegal acts. The conformists are willing to accept all kinds of job offers. The fatalists do not look for work anymore; they have become resigned.

Offe (1987), among many others (e.g., Collins, 1979; Giddens, 1984), has argued convincingly that the mere existence of an underclass undermines the legitimacy of the welfare state in the long run. Until recently, continuous economic growth has made it possible to "buy off" groups that became marginalized by the sociocultural and socioeconomic developments that accompanied the development of the welfare state (Habermas, 1973). This strategy is no longer workable. The economic crisis of the 1970s and the "ecological crisis" of the 1980s have revealed the limits of economic growth, and the large number of persons needing support has generated a "fiscal crisis" for the central government (Wright, 1979).

By the end of the 1970s, many Western European countries felt that the central government had to develop a new policy in order to prevent an underclass from coming into existence. In the context of this new policy, politicians at first defined youth unemployment as an educational problem and, therefore, sought to increase the educational level of the unemployed. But soon the limits to this policy became clear, not only because of displacement and credentialism, but also because of the low level of "educability" of many youngsters, at least in formal educational institutions. The focus then shifted from the unemployed to the employers who excluded certain youngsters; to the trade unions who did not adequately react to these "strategies of exclusion"; and to the government, which failed to get disadvantaged youth into a competitive position in the "labor queue" (Kloosterman & Elfring, 1991). In many Western European countries, the central government has attempted to hold the organizations of employers and the trade unions co-responsible for a policy to decrease youth unemployment (Sellin, 1988). Most attention in this so-called social dialogue is paid to the question as to who is responsible for the qualification of the labor force.

Although in the Netherlands much progress has been made with respect to the reallocation of educational responsibilities, employers and trade unions find it very difficult to take on responsibilities that go beyond their "traditional" roles. This difficulty makes it impossible to accurately predict the future of the welfare state and the development of youth unemployment. The future depends on whether the central government and its social partners will be able to develop new ways of integrating disadvantaged marginal groups into the social and economic system.

Notes

1.   If YEGP is successful it will be applied in the future to all the young unemployed in the 16 to 27 age group (1988).
2.   An English translation of the Engbersen study is forthcoming (Boulder, Colorado: Westview Press).

References

Albrecht, H. J. (1984). Jugendarbeitslosigkeit und jugendkriminalitat. *Kriminologisch Journal, 101*, 218–229.

Allatt, P., & Yeandle, S. (1992). *Youth unemployment and the family: Voices of disordered times.* London: Routledge.

Allerbeck, K., & Hoag, W. (1985). *Jugend ohne zukunft: Einstellungen, umwelt, lebensperspektiven.* Munich/Zurich: List Verlag.

Arbeidsvoorziening. (1991). *Schoolverlatersbrief 1991.* Rijswijk, Netherlands: Minestre Van Sociale Zakenen Werkgelegenleid, Direct Draat-General Vdor de Arbeids Voorziening

Baetghe, M., Hantsche, B., Pellul, W., & Voskamp, U. (1989). *Jugend: Arbeit und identitat. Lebensperpectiven und idteressenorientierungen von Jugenlichen.* Opladen, Germany: Leske & Budrich.

Bakke, E. W. (1934). *The unemployed man: A social study.* New York: Dutton.

Banks, M. H., & Ullah, P. (1988). *Youth unemployment in the 1980s: Its psychological effects.* London: Routledge.

Becker, J. W. (1989). *Reacties op werkloosheid.* Rijswijk, Netherlands: SCP & Alphen a/d Rijn: Samsom.

Bock, B., & Hovels, B. (1991). *Zonder beroepskwalificatie uit het onderwijs: Deel 1. Een kwantitatief beeld van de groep voortijdig schoolverlaters.* Nijmegen, Netherlands: Instituut voor Toegepaste Sociale Wetenschappen.

Bogt, T. F. M. ter, & Praag, C. S. van. (1992). *Jongeren op de drempel van de jaren negentig.* The Hague and Rijswijke Social and Cultural Planning Office, Netherlands: VUGA.

Boltken, F., & Jagodzinski, W. (1984). Viel larm um nichts? In A. Stiksrud (Ed.), *Jugend und werte.* Weinheim/Basel, West Germany: Beltz.

Boot, P. A. (1990). De arbeidsmarkt in 1990. In *Economisch Statistische Berichten, 75* (3775), pp. 860–863.

Bourdieu, P. (1979). *La distinction; Critique social du jugement.* Paris: Editions de Minuit.

Collins, R. (1979). *The credential society.* Orlando, FL: Academic Press.

Diederen, J. (1991). *Loopbaan tussen 25 en 35 jaar. Van jaar tot jaar 4e fase: Over de effeckten van geslacht, milieu van herkomst, schoolprestatie, belangstelling en gevolgd onderwijs op beroepsloopbaan en levensloop.* Nijmegen, Netherlands: Instituut voor Toegepaste Sociale Wetenschappen.

Ehrenreich, B. (1989). *Fear of falling: The inner life of the middle class.* New York: Pantheon.

Eisenberg, P., & Lazarsfeld, P. F. (1938). The psychological effects of unemployment. *Psychological Bulletin, 35*, 358–390.

Engbersen, G. (1990). *Publieke bijstandsgeheimen.* Leiden, Netherlands: Stenfert Kroese.

Farrington, D. P., Gallagher, B., Morley, L., St. Ledger, R. J., & West, D. J. (1986). Unemployment, school leaving and crime. *British Journal of Criminology, 26*(4), 335–356.

Feather, N.T., & Bond, M.J. (1983). Time structure and purposeful activity among employed and unemployed university graduates. *Journal of Occupational Psychology, 56*, 241–254.

Flaim, P. O. (1973). Discouraged workers and changes in unemployment. *Monthly Labour Review, 96*(3), 8–16.

Freeman, R.B. (1983). Crime and unemployment. In J. Q. Wilson (Ed.), *Crime and public policy.* San Francisco: ICS.

Furnham, A. (1982). The Protestant work ethic and attitudes towards unemployment. *Journal of Occupational Psychology, 55*, 277–285.

Gemeenschappelijke Medische Dienst. (1989). *Statistische berichten 1989*. Amsterdam: Author.

Giddens, A. (1984). *The constitution of society*. Cambridge, UK: Polity Press.

Grotenhuis, H. te (1991). *The bottomside of prosperity: Children of long-term unemployed parents in the Dutch welfare state*. Manuscript in progress.

Habermas, J. (1973). *Legitimationsprobleme im spatkapitalismus*. Frankfurt: Suhrkamp.

Have, K. ten, & Jehoel-Gijsbers, G. (1985). *Werkloze jongeren: Een verloren generatie?* The Hague: Staatsuitgeverij.

Hendry, L. B., Raymond, M., & Stewart, C. (1984). Unemployment, school and leisure: An adolescent study. *Leisure Studies, 3*, 175–187.

Hirschi, T. (1969). *Causes of delinquency*. Berkeley: University of California Press.

Huurne, A. ter. (1988). *Werkloze jongeren, twee jaar later*. The Hague, Netherlands: Staatsdrukkesrij.

Inglehart, R. (1979). *The silent revolution*. Princeton, NJ: Princeton University Press.

Jahoda, M., Lazarsfeld, P. F., & Zeisel, H. (1980). *Die arbeitslosen von Marienthal: Ein soziographischer versuch*. Frankfurt Suhrkamp. (original work published 1933)

Jehoel-Gijsbers, G. (1990). Opleiding, waardenorientaties en arbeidsloopbaan. In M. DuBois-Reymond & L. Eldering (Eds.), *Nieuwe orientaties op school en beroep: De rol van sexe en etniciteit* (pp. 99–109). Amsterdam and Lisse, Holland: Swets & Zeitlinger.

Junger, M. (1990). *Delinquency and ethnicity: An investigation of social factors relating to delinquency among Moroccan, Turkish, Surinamese and Dutch boys*. Deventer, Netherlands and Boston: Kluwer.

Keniston, K. (1968). *Young radicals: Notes on committed youth*. New York: Harcourt, Brace and World.

Kloosterman, R. C., & Elfring, T. (1991). *Werken in Nederland*. Schoonhöfen, Germany: Academic Service.

Kroes, L., & Weerman, F. (1990). *Arbeidspositie en criminaliteit*. Groningen, Netherlands: Onderzoekscentrum voor criminologie en jeugdcriminologie.

Lazarus, R. S., & Launier, R. (1978). Stress-related transaction between person and environment. In L. Pervin & M. Lewis (Eds.), *Perspectives in interactional psychology*. New York: Reidel.

Meesters, M. (1992). *Loopbanen in het onderwijs en op de arbeidsmarkt*. Nijmegen: Instituut voor Toegepaste Sociale Wetenschappen.

Meesters, M. J., & van de Pol, F. (1989). Once unemployed, always unemployed? In B. F. M. Bakker, J. Dronkers, & G. W. Meijnen (Eds.), *Educational opportunities in the welfare state*. Nijmegen: Instituut voor Toegepaste Sociale Wetenschappen.

Meijers, F. (1990). Can job/training projects be successful? Some research results from the Netherlands. *British Educational Journal, 16*(4), 407–424.

Meijers, F. (1992). Being young in the life perceptions of Dutch, Moroccan, Turkish and Surinam youngsters. In W. Meeus, M. de Goede, W. Kox, & K. Hurrelmann (Eds.), *Adolescence, careers and cultures* (pp. 353–373). Berlin and New York: de Gruyter.

Merton, R. K. (1967). *Social theory and social structure*. New York: Collier-Macmillan.

Ministry of Education. (1992). *Voortgezet onderwijs in cijfers*. Zoetermeer, Netherlands: Author.

Ministry of Internal Affairs. (1991). *Actieprogramma minderhedenbeleid 1991*. The Hague: Author.

Ministry of Social Affairs and Employment. (1991). *Heroverwegingsonderzoek: Deelrapport 4*. The Hague: Author.

Noelle-Neuman, E. (1981). Working less and enjoying it less in Germany. *Public Opinion, 4*(4), 46–50.

OECD. (1991). *Employment outlook*. Paris: Author.

Offe, C. (1984). *Arbeitsgesellschaft: Strukturproblemen und zukunftperspectiven*. Frankfurt and New York: Campus.

Offe, C. (1987). *Disorganized capitalism*. Cambridge, MA: Polity Press.

Otto-Brock, E. (1991). Jugend und arbeit: Ein forschungsuberblick. *Zeitschrift fur Berufs- und Wirtschaftspadagogik, 87*(3), 208–224.

Payne, J. (1987). Does unemployment run in families? *Sociology, 21*, 199–214.

Ploeg, G. J. (1991). *Maatschappelijke positie en criminaliteit*. Groningen: Wolters-Noordhoff.

Ploeg, J. van der, & Scholte, E. M. (1990). *Lastposten: Of slachtoffers van de samenleving*. Rotterdam, Netherlands: Lemniscaat.

Raaymakers, Q. (1987). The work ethic of Dutch adolescents. In J. Hazekamp, W. Meeus, & Y. te Poel (Eds.), *European contributions to youth research*. (pp. 117–130). Amsterdam: Free University Press.

Rose, M. (1985). *Re-working the work ethic: Economic values and socio-cultural politics*. London: Batsford.

Sellin, B. (1988). *The social dialogue in the member states of the European community in the field of vocational training and continuing training—Synthesis report*. Berlin: Cedefop.

Social and Cultural Planning Office. (1984). *Sociaal en cultureel rapport*. The Hague: Staatsolrukkerij en Uitgeverij.

Thornberry, T. P., & Christenson, R. L. (1984). Unemployment and criminal involvement: An investigation of reciprocal causal structures. *American Sociological Review, 49*, 398–411.

Tiggemann, M., & Winefield, A. H. (1980). Some psychological effects of unemployment in school leavers. *Australian Journal of Social Issues, 15*(4), 269–276.

Veenman, J. (1991). *Allochtonen op de arbeidsmarkt: Van onderzoek naar beleid*. The Hague: Organisatie voor Strategisch Arbeidsmarktonderzoek.

Warr, P. B. (1982). National study of non-financial employment commitment. *Journal of Occupational Psychology, 55*, 297–312.

Werdmolder, H. (1990). *Een generatie op drift: De geschiedenis van een marokkaanse randgroep*. Arnhem, Netherlands: Gouda Quint.

Wilson, J. Q., & R. J. Herrnstein (1985). *Crime and human nature*. New York: Simon & Schuster.

Wilson, W. J. (1991). Public policy research and the truly disadvantaged. In C. Jencks & P. E. Peterson (Eds.), *The Urban Underclass* (pp. 460–481). Washington, D.C.: Brookings Institute.

Wright, E. O. (1979). *Class, crisis and the state*. London: Routledge and Kegan Paul.

Yankelovitch, D. et al., Aspen Inst. for Humanistic Studies, and Public Agenda Foundation. (1984). *Work and human values: An international report on jobs in the 1980s and 1990s*. New York: Octagon Books.

Zawadski, B., & Lazarsfeld, P. F. (1935). The psychological consequences of unemployment. *Journal of Social Psychology, 6*, 83–108.

10. Social roles for youth: Interventions in unemployment

STEPHEN F. HAMILTON
Cornell University
Ithaca, New York

Interventions designed to alleviate youth unemployment can only be assessed against criteria based upon beliefs about its causes and consequences. In the following pages, five criteria are set out and then applied to three interventions from three different nations. Schooling and voluntary service are considered as alternatives to interventions focused on preparing youth for work.

Criteria for Assessing Interventions

Interventions cannot be limited to the improvement of human capital; that is, to increasing the supply of qualified workers. Policy makers in the United States are especially apt to assume that youth unemployment can be reduced by improving the education and training of young people. However, unless the demand for skilled workers increases simultaneously, education and training serve only as waiting rooms, not launching pads. Both the demand for skilled labor and the supply of skilled labor must be part of the intervention equation.

Rutter's treatment of causality (in this volume) makes this point by associating the human capital strategy with the presumption that individual differences cause unemployment. He usefully points out that although different levels of education and training can explain differences in the individual propensity to be unemployed, they cannot explain overall levels of unemployment. Using his terms, differences in the average levels of human capital among subgroups can explain at least some of the distribution of unemployment. One reason young people suffer higher levels of unemployment than adults is because, as a group, they have less human capital—in the form of educational credentials, job skills, and personal qualities—than adults. In addition, they have poorer information about and connections to the labor market than adults (Rosenbaum, Kariya, Settersten, & Maier, 1990).

Thurow (1975) argues that interventions aimed at increasing unemployed people's job qualifications simply reorder the queue of job applicants. Beneficiaries of such interventions may move ahead of people who were previously in front of them, but the total number of jobless people remains the same. Interventions that merely change the order of the queue of job seekers risk reducing youth unemployment at the expense of other disadvantaged groups, such as women or minorities. They may change the dispersion or distribution of unemployment but not its level. Whenever there are more job seekers than jobs, some people will be unemployed.

To be fair, in a labor market characterized by low levels of human capital, interventions that improve human capital can reduce unemployment. Firms are more likely to expand if they think they can find productive workers. One can also argue that education and training contribute to a benign circle: More-qualified applicants displace less-qualified applicants in the labor market, who in turn seek to improve their own qualifications, thereby providing employers with the stock of human capital they need in order to expand. Such an argument is most persuasive in dynamic economies, such as that of the United States.

The point of this first criterion is not that education and training have no contribution to reducing youth unemployment. Rather, it is that if these are the only interventions, they are unlikely to affect the overall level of youth unemployment.

A second criterion, also requiring attention because of attitudes and approaches prevailing in the United States, is that in addition to thinking about *programs* to reduce youth unemployment, we must begin thinking of *systems*. Countries that rely heavily on free markets—such as the United States and more recently the United Kingdom—are inclined to attack youth unemployment by means of ad hoc and post hoc arrangements rather than with coherent systems that prevent its occurrence. (Such systems are more common in countries such as Germany and Sweden, which have corporatist economies.) Lessons can be learned across this divide without overhauling entire economic systems.

Programs serve a limited and defined group of people. Programs are often funded one or a few years at a time. They are viewed as having a special, often short-term purpose. When funds are limited, they must often cut back services, treat fewer clients, or close. The United States has Headstart programs, for example, that serve only a fraction of the preschoolers who could benefit. *Systems*, in contrast, are open to all who qualify. When more people want to use their services, the system must be enlarged, as is the case with the public school system. All children must attend school; if space is limited, schools must be built or enlarged.

A system has a place for everyone. It is as permanent as a social institution can be. Its structure enables entrants to see what will happen to them as they move through it. Other systems and institutions are linked to it in ways that provide recognizable paths from one to the other. Programs are more ad hoc. They are not necessarily part of a coherent set of opportunities.

Third, *prevention* of youth unemployment is preferable to treatment. The term *intervention* comes from medicine. It is appropriate, therefore, to carry the borrowing further and distinguish prevention, treatment, and rehabilitation. The last term is not so important here because, compared to adults, young people are, by definition, vulnerable only to relatively short-term unemployment.

Treatment of those already afflicted by unemployment is a necessary type of intervention. It has two advantages over prevention. One is that it can more readily be targeted to those most in need. Second, its results are relatively clear-cut because they can be reported in terms of numbers and proportions of afflicted people whose condition has been improved. However, by its nature treatment leaves the sources of the problem untouched. A treatment program with a 100 percent success rate would not eliminate unemployment because it would deal only with the results of unemployment, not with its causes. In medical terms, treatment does not reduce the incidence of a medical condition (which is the number of new cases); it alleviates the consequences of affliction (Albee, 1987). Ideally prevention is always preferable to treatment, but in the real world, treatment's advantages often win out. Ordinarily we try to do both at the same time.

Fourth, interventions must reduce the *marginalization* of youth and the demoralizing constraints on their future prospects, which are the most serious consequences of youth unemployment. For adults, the most serious consequences of youth unemployment are loss of income and status, but for youth, marginalization or social isolation (Hess & Petersen, 1991) and reduced prospects for future employment are more serious. This distinction is important because it means interventions that reduce unemployment without improving future prospects and without giving young people valid societal roles are inadequate, whereas interventions that improve future prospects by contributing to young people's education and socialization should be considered even if they do not reduce youth unemployment directly.

Even among youth, there are important differences in the consequences of unemployment. A brief period of unemployment between jobs for a white, male, high school student from a stable family is likely to be unimportant in the long term, and far easier to cope with than sustained chronic unemployment experienced by a poor, black, female without a high school diploma. This chapter primarily addresses chronic unemployment among young people who are no longer enrolled in full-time compulsory schooling.

Particularly if they are able to live with their parents, the most serious consequence of unemployment for youth in this category is not loss of income by itself but rather the inability to assume and maintain the role of worker, along with the related dampening of expectations for the future. Obviously, the seriousness of this situation grows over time. It causes greater distress for a 24-year-old than a 17-year-old.

Jahoda's (1981) "latent functions" of employment help to explain why the most serious consequences of youth unemployment are not strictly economic. Lacking the time structure, social contacts, transcendent goals, sense of personal identity, and enforced activity provided by employment, young people become ever more marginal and risk permanent alienation. An intervention that provides work without these functions is unlikely to be effective; one that performs these functions without providing employment may be quite effective.

Fifth, interventions must enable young people to function effectively in the *new work environments* that are emerging and will continue to evolve for the next half century. Equipping young people with the skills that served the twentieth century economy will not do. Because this point is not addressed in the other chapters, I consider working life in the future at some length.

Working Life in the Future

Prophecy is a risky business. False prophets are mocked and scorned; true prophets are often martyred for their truthfulness. It is especially difficult to prophecy with confidence during a period when the world order that has prevailed since the end of World War II has changed more rapidly and more dramatically than anyone could have predicted or even imagined. But the risks are unavoidable; our plans for improving the future can be no better than our predictions about what the future holds.

The majority of the workforce in the United States and Western Europe is increasingly engaged in work with people, data, and ideas rather than with things. Just as industrial production replaced agriculture as the major form of work in the nineteenth century, so services of various kinds are displacing manufacturing in the second half of the twentieth century. Notice that these successive shifts are changes in the *proportion* of people engaged in particular kinds of work. Workers in auto factories buy food produced by farmers and accountants buy automobiles. Manufacturing is not dying or even becoming marginal to developed economies; it simply requires a smaller proportion of the labor force than it did in previous decades and contributes a smaller share to the economy.

Historical shifts in the predominance of agriculture, manufacturing, and service have been driven by new technologies in both the established and the ascendent economic sectors. Today's driving technologies are based on microprocessors, which are transforming communication and data processing in both the manufacturing and the service sectors.

Just how these new technologies will affect the way people do their work, however, is not yet clear. The perennial debate regarding the impact of computers is whether they will require more workers or fewer, smarter workers who can program computers and interpret data, or less intelligent machine tenders who merely follow computers' instructions. Bailey (1988, 1989) has provided detailed accounts of how computerization changed the textile industry—with a boost from Asian competition—generally confirming the claim that computerization heightens knowledge and skill requirements for workers. Zuboff (1989), examining the introduction of computers into the textile and paper industries, has wisely pointed out that new technology can be put to different uses depending upon choices made by managers. In her terms, it can be used to "automate" processes—reducing human judgment and control—or to "informate," which means to provide a large volume of data to enable human workers to exercise and improve their controlling judgments.

The most compelling prediction is Kern and Schumann's (1986) "all of the above." They argue on the basis of German studies that the introduction of computer-driven machinery into manufacturing reduces the total demand for workers and greatly reduces the demand for minimally skilled workers. Although machine tenders and floor sweepers are still needed, the total demand for them is lower. Simultaneously, computerization creates a demand for highly skilled, flexible workers who can perform a range of tasks in conjunction with the new machines. Piore and

Sabel (1984) call these kinds of workers "flexible specialists" and see them as crucial to an emerging post-mass-production industry.

In the developed nations of Europe and North America a shift is well underway from the mass production of uniform commodities to customized production of specialized goods.[1] Changes in steel production provide a good example. The huge blast furnaces that formerly lit up the night around Pittsburgh and other steel-making centers in the United States are gone. Brazil and Korea can mass produce steel for less. U.S. steel making survives only in "mini-mills," small facilities that make specialty steels. Low volume is compensated by high prices. Frequent product changes and short production runs require a flexible plant and equally flexible workers. Instead of armies of semiskilled workers, mini-mills employ modest numbers of highly skilled workers who are required to learn new procedures and techniques to keep up with changing production demands. The difference in cost between raw materials and final product is much higher for specialized steel than for ordinary steel. Because workers add more value to the product, they earn higher wages.

A recent report on education and the economy in the United States urged the adoption of policies to foster industries that can pay high wages. The authors of *America's Choice: High Skills or Low Wages* (National Center on Education and the Economy, 1990) argue that productivity growth cannot be achieved by the means employed through most of the twentieth century: increasing output by investing in capital to speed up production and reduce labor costs. In an interdependent world economy in which developing nations contain some of the most modern factories, the only solution, they claim, is to foster the production of goods and services that take advantage of the country's store of human resources, goods and services that can only be produced with a well educated and highly skilled workforce. Study teams visited six countries (Germany, Japan, Sweden, Denmark, Ireland, and Singapore) for comparative purposes and found that all of them had made an explicit choice to follow this strategy.

Although this and other reports have given most of their attention to manufacturing, similar points can be made about services. The key phrase "high-performance work organizations" applies to all workplaces, including those in the public sector. Insurance companies provide a good example of the press to create high-performance work organizations in the service sector. Aetna Life and Casualty, for example, is beginning to reorganize so individual employees can handle all aspects of a customer's insurance needs. Rather than sending queries through an endless series of telephone contacts, each person knowing only part of the picture, they aim for "once and done" service. Computers and telecommunications make it possible for one person to have access to records that previously might have been stored in several company offices.

The people who perform this kind of service are equivalent to Piore and Sabel's "flexible specialists" in manufacturing. They must have a solid understanding of their company's policies and procedures and excellent communication skills in order to hear and respond to customers' concerns. They must master computerized data retrieval systems and be adept at collating and interpreting data from different sources. As such systems are established in the insurance industry, the need for clerks who process routine forms will decline rapidly.

A large gap exists, according to another report (Secretary's Commission on Achieving Necessary Skills, 1991), between such new demands for workers "who can put knowledge to work" and what U.S. schools are actually teaching. The report describes a "foundation" of basic skills, thinking skills and personal qualities, and needed competencies in five areas: use of resources, interpersonal interactions, use of information, understanding of systems, and working with technology. The report's most important contribution is to specify how changes in workplaces should affect education and training and to begin working out some of the details of setting and assessing standards of achievement. Although the report was based on conditions in the United States, the foundation and competencies identified are equally valid and important in other developed countries.

A refreshingly democratic message being conveyed by these reports is that traditional distinctions between manual and professional workers and in the levels of education they receive are diminishing. Workers at all levels increasingly need a combination of academic, job-specific, and personal skills formerly associated with university-educated professionals. Although differences will remain, educational and skill attainment must be raised across the layers of social class and organizational hierarchy.

Raising the qualifications of the workforce will not eliminate hierarchy. Neither will the need for unskilled workers disappear. Furthermore, labor markets are likely to grow increasingly rigid in the sense of requiring specific educational credentials, which constrain upward mobility. The day has already passed when corporate leaders began their careers in the mail room and worked their way up the ladder. Higher and more specialized educational qualifications separate the ladders within various careers, making it harder for people to climb very high without achieving educational credentials and leading employers to hire outside rather than promoting from within.

Only interventions that help young people prepare themselves for this kind of working life will succeed in reducing unemployment and marginality. Programs that consider themselves successful because they place young people in low-skill jobs without learning and advancement possibilities may contribute to lower unemployment statistics but they are unlikely to stave off marginality for long.

An Exemplary Program for Unemployed Youth

If youth unemployment is attributed to inadequate education and training, programs that attempt to improve the knowledge, skills, and behavior of unemployed youth are a logical intervention. Such programs are numerous and widespread; simply describing them would be an encyclopedic undertaking. Rather than taking on this task, I describe one, noting its distinctive features and assessing it in terms of the criteria stated above.

Transition to Working Life, or TWL, is the name of a program developed in the United Kingdom beginning in 1978. It is aimed at young people between the ages of 16 and 19 who have left school or soon will. TWL relies heavily on human interaction to achieve its goal of helping young people find jobs. The key person is a nonprofessional known as a "working coach." Working coaches are employed adults who are willing and able to spend two to four hours weekly with small groups of unemployed youth. Such groups usually number between eight and ten participants. Meetings are held in a workplace or other setting outside of school over a period of six months. They provide a time to talk about working, schooling, plans, and lifestyles. Finding a job and dealing with people in authority are common themes. Participants sometimes plan field trips to explore employment opportunities (see Grubb Institute of Behavioural Studies, 1982).

One of TWL's most remarkable early accomplishments was enlisting private employers in a youth program in the midst of a stagnant economy. Employers agreed to release working coaches from their normal duties for one day each week, not only as a public service but also because they lacked resources to train their own workers in supervision and saw the experience and support working coaches would receive through the program as a form of inservice training. Many working coaches were subsequently promoted to supervisory positions, confirming the value of their experience to them and their employers.

Working coaches were selected on the basis of a careful search process. Once welcomed into a firm by top managers, TWL staff sought nominations for working coaches from managers and union leaders, asking about which workers were sought after by their co-workers for advice on personal and career matters, and which were able to master new equipment and techniques quickest and then to teach others. People with previous experience as adult leaders in youth organizations and sports were avoided on the grounds that they would have too many preconceived notions of how to work with young people. Experience taught TWL staff that line workers made better working coaches than did managers, apparently because they were more like the young people in attitudes and background.

TWL staff use a memorable phrase, "releasing resources," to describe what they do with working coaches and with youth. Their presumption is that working coaches are capable of giving young people much of what they need and that the young people, too, have much to offer employers. What is needed is to make manifest capabilities that were formerly hidden even to their holders. Following this line of thinking, TWL does little formal training of working coaches. Instead, it relies on a system of advisers—professionals who meet weekly with working coaches to help them make decisions and solve problems. Rather than creating a new bureaucracy, TWL weaves networks among people who together can help unemployed youth.

Underlying TWL's program design is the belief that youth unemployment results less from limited academic achievement and technical competence than from unsuitable attitudes, behavior, and aspirations. The program grew in part from the fear that persistent unemployment among the British working class engendered a culture in which employment was exceptional. Under these circumstances, the primary concern was changing attitudes, teaching young people that it is both normal and possible to work. In this the goals of TWL are like programs in the United States, where the lack of "coping skills" (Walther, 1976) or a work ethic has been cited as the greatest barrier to employment among poor and minority youth. TWL staff acknowledge that it would ideally be used in conjunction with a training program imparting technical skills.

TWL is an appealing program to those who approach youth unemployment from the perspective of youth development rather than economic analysis. Its originators are remarkably articulate, thoughtful, and creative. Considering the state of the British economy when TWL was launched, the proportion of its completers who found employment is quite commendable. Yet some U.S. program operators who learned about TWL at a conference were unimpressed, pointing out that the reported rate of "positive terminations"—which is the percentage of program completers who were removed from the unemployment rolls by finding jobs, enrolling in school, enlisting in the military, or other constructive actions—was too low to sustain continued federal funding in the United States (Academy for Educational Leadership, 1977).

It seems unreasonable to try to compare one country's programs with another's on the basis of such statistics, given their dependence upon the labor market, not to mention such variables as certification requirements for workers, the duration of jobs found, and the definitions and procedures used for counting the unemployed. But pointing to the national economic context for TWL also raises another set of issues about the environment in which a program exists. The United Kingdom has endured slow and uneven economic growth and its educational system reinforces a highly stratified society. By helping some unemployed youth find jobs, TWL alters none of those factors. Young people lucky enough to get the boost that TWL provides simply move ahead of less fortunate young people in the imaginary queue of job seekers. Their success comes at the expense of others, without enlarging the demand for workers.

Neither does TWL constitute a preventive system. It is an excellent example of a treatment program. As such, it is unlikely to reduce the level of unemployment. However, TWL appears to stand up well under the fourth criterion of reducing marginality, largely because of its reliance on personal contacts, both between youth and adults and among a group of unemployed youth. Strong social support seems to be the key to TWL's effectiveness.

An Exemplary Treatment System

Sweden's youth centers were established for young people between ages 16 and 18 who are neither in school nor at work. Their effectiveness and creativity are enhanced by Sweden's unique set of social institutions, economic conditions, and values. Swedes view work as a right, not an obligation or a privilege. One of the state's duties is to assure that everyone has access to satisfying employment.

Until 1970, Sweden had a highly stratified school system, much like Germany's. College-preparatory high schools were elite institutions. The majority of secondary school-age young people attended vocational high schools or entered apprenticeships that were unconnected with school. The Swedes made a decision that took effect in 1970 that is typical of the country both in its aims and its sweeping impact. To reduce the social distinctions that accompanied enrollment in different types of secondary schools, and to assure that all young people had a chance at higher education, they abolished the divided secondary school system, consolidating formerly academic and vocational schools. At the same time, they located most vocational education in schools, greatly reducing the size of apprenticeship.

Patterned after U.S. comprehensive high schools, Swedish secondary schools now offer a range of course sequences, or "lines," that can last from two to four years.[2] Vocational and college-preparatory students attend school in the same buildings, even though they do not necessarily attend the same classes. After compulsory schooling is completed at the end of grade nine, about 95 percent of young people choose to continue in secondary school rather than attempting to enter the labor market without a diploma.

When young people exercise their right to leave school, the municipal school authority's responsibility for them does not end. That responsibility continues up to the age of 18, regardless of whether young people are enrolled in school. (A current proposal would extend that responsibility to age 20.) This responsibility means that someone must check regularly with those who are not enrolled in school to find out whether they are employed or have reenrolled and, if not, whether they would like to work or go back to school. Youth centers were created as a means of carrying out this responsibility.

The youth center I visited (which appears to host Americans frequently) is located in the small industrial city of Södertälje, north of Stockholm. Housed in a former factory building, it aggressively reaches out to young people by engaging in "door-knocking activities." That nice phrase means that staff do not merely sit in their offices and wait for young people to come to them. Instead, they call or visit homes. Staff have no control over what young people do. Their role is to ask questions and offer opportunities. The most attractive opportunity they have to offer is the chance to take a subsidized job in order to explore a career area for up to six months. But they can also give personal and career counseling, remedial instruction, and sometimes other supports. In Södertälje, for example, some young people are apprenticed to the bakery chef who works on the premises.

Several features of Swedish youth centers deserve attention and replication. The first is their active but empowering role. There is a movement to locate all youth centers in school buildings, but staff at Södertälje are convinced that this would be a mistake because of school-leavers' negative feelings about schools and because of the more controlling style of many school staff. Second, youth centers are organized to treat each young person as an individual. The heart of a center's work is the creation and implementation of a plan for each young person in its area. That plan may call for any combination of work experience, academic instruction, and counseling that is appropriate and may be oriented toward a goal of getting a full-time job or continuing in school.

Youth center staff have a rich blend of talents and backgrounds. Staff at Södertälje are organized in teams, each including a personal counselor, a career counselor, a teacher, and a nurse. The academic preparation for career counselors includes an equal number of courses in psychology, sociology, and economics.

On average, before their two-year responsibility terminates, youth centers have helped half of their charges return to full-time schooling. This is a remarkable proportion considering that the population in question is most disaffected from school. It is, on the other hand, a tiny proportion of the total youth population.

What is most impressive, and least reproducible, is Swedish youth centers' embeddedness in a society committed to assuring that every citizen has an opportunity for satisfying employment. Sweden not only spends a larger proportion of its budget than any other country on labor issues; it also spends a larger proportion of its labor budget on active labor-market policies (Larsson, 1988; *Policies for Structural Change in Sweden*, 1991). Those policies reflect the belief that it is preferable in both economic and human terms to help people find work than to pay them for not working.

Youth centers try to give unemployed young people the academic skills, information, and self-confidence they need to find and keep jobs, but they also alter the labor market by creating subsidized jobs. In addition, they actively seek out education and employment opportunities and try to match youth individually with them.

By treating unemployed youth as whole persons and addressing all their needs, youth centers give them a sense of their own possibilities. Persistent but noncoercive "door-knocking activities" are an ideal method of conveying the message that someone cares, but that the young person must decide.

Sweden's youth centers are not oriented specifically toward a new work world. The kinds of jobs unemployed youth can get through youth centers are not particularly up-to-date. Many of them are in retail sales.

The way in which youth centers can be said to prepare young people for working life in the future is through their direct connection to education. A placement in a department store is unlikely to be a good start toward a rewarding career unless it impels a young person to return to school for the learning and the credentials that will make career advancement possible.

Although the youth centers by themselves do not constitute a system, they are part of a coherent system of education, training, and social welfare that keeps most youth from becoming marginal. Combined with the openness of Swedish institutions, generous social benefits enable young people to make a leisurely transition to adulthood, one that is frequently highlighted by extensive travel abroad.

The greatest threat to the Swedish system comes from changing economic conditions. A new government was recently installed to preside over a severe reduction in the Swedish welfare state in order to reduce the tax burden. Swedish corporations and government agencies are also reducing their administrative staffs. Many corporations have expanded overseas to secure higher profits. However, the nation's strong commitment to equal opportunity and to the right of all people to dignity in work will persist.

An Exemplary System for Preventing Youth Unemployment

German apprenticeship is the most frequently cited exemplar of an active policy to prevent youth unemployment. (Similar systems exist in Switzerland, Austria, Denmark, and several Eastern European countries. For more information on [West] German apprenticeship, see Hamilton, 1990.) It was cited more frequently ten years ago than today, because in the 1970s West Germany seemed immune to the trend toward higher youth unemployment in OECD countries and apprenticeship was thought to be the reason. Slow economic growth combined with an oversupply of young people (as baby-boom cohorts entered the labor market) shook this notion. German youth unemployment rates edged upward in the mid-1980s, nearly matching those in the United States. Better economic performance and a reversal of the demographic picture reduced youth unemployment toward the end of the decade, when the incorporation of the former East Germany and of people of German ancestry from Eastern European countries became the principal labor-market policy issues.

Nonetheless, over time, German youth unemployment has remained low in comparison to rates in most other countries, and notably low as a proportion of total unemployment (see White & Smith, Bertram, and other chapters in this volume). In her authoritative overview, in *Youth at Work*, of six countries, Reubens (1983) noted that youth labor markets in Germany and Japan, unlike other countries, constituted a "nurturing, protective situation in which competition with other age groups is severely limited" (p. 320).

Apprenticeship is the institution that protects youth in the German labor market. It is a highly developed system for linking school with work experience in which workplaces serve as the principal learning environments for a majority of youth between the ages of 16 and 18. The standard distribution of time is four days per week at work and one day in school. Employers pay apprentices and undertake to train them over a period of two-and-a-half to four years for specific occupations. Special schools provide both general education (social studies and German) and instruction in occupation-specific knowledge and skills.

Both the power and the limitations of apprenticeship in preventing youth unemployment were demonstrated in the early 1980s. More young people applied for apprenticeships than employers could accommodate, creating tremendous pressure on the system. The Social Democratic Party (comparable to the Labour Party in the United Kingdom) tried to require employers to create sufficient places by threatening to invoke a law taxing firms that did not train apprentices in order to raise revenue for school-based alternatives. However, the law was invalidated. Exhortations from the more conservative Christian Democratic government succeeded in substantially enlarging the number of places, though the vast majority of new places came from small shops in the craft sector, which are unable to hire all trained apprentices. Faced with poor prospects of finding a good apprenticeship, many young people prolonged their school enrollment, primarily in vocational programs, some of which were created expressly to deal with the shortage of apprenticeships.

Adding apprenticeship places in the craft sector contributed to a new phenomenon, captured by the image of two "waves" of youth unemployment, the first wave following compulsory schooling when unsuccessful applicants for apprenticeships were classified as unemployed and the second wave following the completion of apprenticeship training, as older youth with new skills entered an unwelcoming labor market. This second wave clearly demonstrates the inadequacy of training alone to prevent unemployment. During this period, when too many applicants sought too few jobs, enlarging the training system simply postponed unemployment until after training was complete.

Expanding the range of school-based alternatives to apprenticeship had a comparable effect at the time of the first wave. Although it succeeded in preventing unemployment in the literal sense—young people without contracts as apprentices were counted among those enrolled in school rather than among those looking for work—the best hope among most enrollees was to find an apprenticeship. When they were successful in this search, they began at the same point where they would have started fresh out of compulsory school, with no credit for their additional schooling.

Young people's and employers' enduring preference for apprenticeship over full-time vocational schooling has been demonstrated convincingly by participation trends following the peak of the baby-boom population. In 1982, 52.2 percent of West German youth between 16 and 19 were apprentices. As the size of that group fell, the proportion who were apprentices rose, reaching 73.6 percent by 1989 (Der Bundesminister für Bildung und Wissenschaft, 1990, p. 102).

What is most remarkable about this participation level is that it has grown in tandem with rising enrollment in full-time schools. The proportion of youth neither in school nor in apprenticeships has been low for decades, between 5 and 10 percent. Increases in both forms of education have been possible because a growing number seek "double qualification," which is qualification based on *both* full-time vocational schooling and apprenticeship (Meister, 1985). In addition, a small but growing proportion of graduates from the college-preparatory *Gymnasium* has entered apprenticeship. Combining extended full-time schooling with apprenticeship has raised the mean age for apprentices. It also has qualified more apprentices to pursue further education.

Accepting the fact that training alone does not create jobs, German-style apprenticeship can be said to prevent youth unemployment in two ways. Most immediately, it can, even in times of high overall unemployment, provide sheltered niches in which young people gain skills and enact valued social roles while also earning a modest amount of money. There are limits, however, to how many young people can be absorbed by training firms and how many of them can find related employment after their training is completed. In a longer view, apprenticeship assures the German-speaking nations of a steady supply of skilled workers, human capital that fosters economic activity for the benefit of all. Germans take it as self-evident that their prosperity depends upon highly skilled workers who are able to make high-quality products for domestic and international markets.

Despite some distortions, apprenticeship remains connected to the labor market over time. Unlike schools or government-funded employment training programs, apprenticeship is paid for by employers, who will not pay unless it meets their needs. Ideally what employers need is skilled adult workers, and they train apprentices with the intention of hiring them. But some employers need cheap helpers and exploit apprentices for this purpose. Monitoring by both employers' organizations (chambers) and organized labor discourages this practice, which is most often found in small shops that are unlikely to hire their apprentices when training is completed.

Employers who expect to hire their apprentices will only maintain their training effort if trained workers are needed. For example, in 1983, no apprentices were admitted to the printing trades because the printing industry in Germany was being computerized, and all printers agreed not to increase the size of the workforce until this change had been accomplished and to invest their training funds instead in retraining experienced workers.

Apprenticeship not only gives young people work and moves most of them into careers, but it also assures constructive social contacts and a respectable social identity. Young people whose names appear in the newspaper are conventionally identified either by the school in which they are enrolled or by the occupation in which they are apprenticed. Unlike full-time students, apprentices spend most of their time in the company of adults. They must be punctual, reliable, and diligent, and if they are not, then their co-workers and customers suffer, not just their school grades.

Apprenticeship's effectiveness at preparing young people for the kinds of workplaces they will find in the future varies drastically. The best apprenticeships are extremely good on precisely this dimension because they are located in leading firms where the future has already arrived. For example, a leading manufacturing firm in Switzerland, after deliberating about the impacts of computer-integrated manufacturing, reorganized their apprenticeship training to combine seven formerly separate occupations. Now apprentices begin their four-year training with a systematic rotation among machining, electronics technology, and drafting. During the second year, they begin to focus on one area, but do not make a choice until the third year, after which they continue to learn at least one of the other specialties. This new approach postpones career choice until young people know what they are getting into and makes it easier for them to change their minds later on; instead of starting all over again, they need only go back to the point of specialization. From the firm's point of view, the greatest advantage is that machinists understand electronics and electronics technicians can do technical drawing and communicate effectively with designers.

A Danish manufacturing firm committed to maintaining a cooperative and creative workforce starts its apprentices in self-guided teams working on open-ended assignments such as designing and building a robot hand. This experience not only introduces apprentices to the firm and its resources, and to some of the technical knowledge and skills they will need to acquire (e.g., machining and computer programming), but also acquaints them with teamwork, problem solving, and taking initiative for their own learning.

Not all apprentices are so lucky. Girls are overrepresented in low-status occupations such as hairdresser and retail sales clerk where neither the technical demands nor their social environment are highly stimulating. The political power of small-business people (especially in Austria) has made it difficult to reduce the number of apprentices in such occupations.

Apprenticeship's contribution to the prevention of youth unemployment is not limited to its enhancement of individuals' human capital. It helps German youth avoid the "floundering period" (characterized by frequent job switches interspersed with periods of unemployment) typical among youth in the United States (Osterman, 1980). With some notable exceptions, it attracts young people into productive segments of the labor market and gives them the credentials they need to find long-term employment there. It fosters good work habits and the acquisition of basic academic skills that enable workers to continue their learning for a lifetime.

Schools and the Prevention of Youth Unemployment

The most widespread system for preventing youth unemployment in developed nations is the school system. It is easily overlooked because of its universality, but its role is too important to be taken for granted. School systems are central to human capital formation. Except in countries whose educational systems are badly out of balance with their labor markets, advanced schooling is associated with higher levels of employment, higher status, and higher earnings. Schools serve a second purpose, too. By occupying large numbers of youth, they reduce the number of youth who are in the labor force (i.e., either working or looking for work). In addition, the role of student is valued in most societies. To be a student is to have a place in society.

Compulsory schooling has been extended in many European countries during the past three decades, and a range of post-compulsory schools has been created. Historically there has been an inverse relationship between school enrollment and youth participation in the labor force. The prevalence of part-time employment among U.S. high school students has created an exceptional situation in which youth participation in the labor force has grown along with school enrollment. German apprenticeship makes another exception possible. Because apprentices attend school while also being counted as part of the labor force, the same combination is possible in the German-speaking countries and Denmark.

High rates of secondary-school enrollment in the United States reveal some of the limitations of extended schooling as an intervention to prevent youth unemployment. Older youth become, in the apt German (and Swedish) designation, "school weary." They are simply tired of school. Being a student is a passive role. Most schools throughout the Western world continue to practice lecture and recitation forms of instruction that treat students as sponges, whose task is to absorb knowledge and then regurgitate it upon demand. Students who are not adept in school become especially dissatisfied with their relative lack of success, but even good students become frustrated by the passive role they are expected to perform (Stinchcombe, 1964; Willis, 1977). This is one reason that paid employment is so attractive to U.S. youth, even when it is not very challenging or well paid (Greenberger & Steinberg, 1986).

Apprenticeship represents the closest possible integration of schooling with work, but other arrangements are also possible. Vocational schooling is the most prevalent; that is, schooling explicitly oriented toward preparation for specific kinds of employment, often including practical, hands-on instruction. For many young people, vocational education is more real and more accessible than academic instruction.

In the United States and in Sweden many vocational programs include work experience, which, though less extensive than apprenticeship, offers some of the same benefits. One reason for Sweden's move to extend by one year its vocational lines is to add more time for work experience. In the United States efforts are underway to improve vocational education by strengthening its academic content. One approach is establishing "career academies," relatively self-contained programs within larger comprehensive schools that organize the entire curriculum around an occupational area. Early indications are that these are promising innovations (Stern, Raby, & Dayton, 1992).

Service: An Alternative to Employment and Training

If marginalization and constrained future prospects are the chief consequences of youth unemployment, then it makes sense to seek means of ameliorating those consequences in addition to providing job preparation and actual employment. Aside from further schooling, opportunities to engage in service are the most promising. In the United States, the classic example of this approach is the Civilian Conservation Corps (CCC) of the 1930s (Sherraden, 1980). The CCC was created during the Great Depression to engage unemployed young men in conservation work on public lands. They received a small stipend plus meals and lodging, often living under quite primitive conditions. A place in the CCC was not an ideal job. It paid too little and the average length of service was only 10 months. But it was an honorable alternative to unemployment, giving young men a sense of their own worth while reducing pressure on the labor market. It also left an enduring legacy of improvements to public lands such as recreational facilities and newly planted forests.

So powerful is the aura of the CCC that when job training programs were developed in the 1960s, they were frequently patterned after it, most notably the Job Corps, which survives as the most effective program for severely disadvantaged youth. More recently, the CCC was invoked in congressional debates regarding the appropriation of federal funds to promote youth service, debates that ultimately led to the passage of the National Community Service Act of 1990, which authorized the expenditure of up to $287 million over three fiscal years, primarily to enlarge existing service programs.

Out of these debates has emerged a point that is critical in a time of governmental decentralization—namely, that offering a wide range of opportunities for service does not require creating a single national organization to control service activities (Eberly, 1991). Advocates and practitioners of service in the United States speak of multiple "streams" of service, including full- and part-time, paid and fully voluntary, and a diverse array of sponsors. Germany, in contrast, has a centralized youth service organization, partly as a means of providing alternatives to required military service—the status of a conscientious objecter is easily acquired. To provide a sufficient number of alternative service slots for the growing number of conscientious objecters, the *Zivildienst* has become a large organization (Kuhlmann, 1990).

Since William James (1910) recommended service as "The Moral Equivalent of War," military conscription has been juxtaposed with nonmilitary service. As the threat of war between superpowers recedes, advocates of nonmilitary service for youth may have opportunities to establish a wider range of options for a larger proportion of the youth population, but it is also possible that interest will fade as the need to find alternatives to military service becomes less pressing.

Although the probable reduction in military forces among the great powers is cause for rejoicing, it also requires some reflection on the youth unemployment prevention function of military service. Enlistment in the military gives a young person a valuable social role and all the other latent functions of employment, along with earnings and training. Military service has traditionally removed large numbers of youth from the civilian labor market. Civilian service opportunities may need to be enlarged and systematized to make up for reduced military requirements.

Conclusion

Youth apprenticeship matches the five criteria set out at the opening of this chapter better than any other intervention to prevent or treat youth unemployment. In addition to illustrating the difference between a program and a system, apprenticeship exemplifies *active labor-market policy*, a term used by labor economists to describe direct government intervention in the labor market to reduce unemployment. Creating jobs for unemployed people, retraining them, and providing placement services are the standard forms of active labor-market policy. They stand in contrast to more passive policies, notably, providing transfer payments to unemployed people and adopting macroeconomic policies designed to stimulate the economy in the hope of generating new jobs (Janoski, 1990). Short of apprenticeship and other forms of active labor-market policy, the intervention into youth unemployment that best matches the criteria is enlarging opportunities for young people to serve.

Extended schooling; training programs emphasizing job skills or, like TWL, work-related attitudes; and job-search and placement assistance can all contribute to reducing unemployment. They increase individuals' human capital and remove some youth from the labor market. Taking youth out of the labor market can be particularly helpful in bridging short-term cycles of high unemployment. However, the programs favored in English-speaking countries are unlikely to prove as effective in the long run as more comprehensive approaches, exemplified by Swedish youth centers, and coherent systems, such as German apprenticeship, which help to create jobs as well as prepare youth for work.

Notes

1. Peter Katzenstein (1989) has proposed that to understand economic trends in Germany (and by extension elsewhere) one must understand simultaneously the different and sometimes contradictory phenomena that occur at three levels: industrial plants (especially production methods and technology); national politics and social movements; and the international political system. He points out that many debates are carried out with arguments from these three different levels pitted against each other.
2. A recent experiment has convinced education policy makers to abolish the two-year lines. Gradually over the decade they will be replaced region by region with three-year lines that include a substantial work-experience component.

References

Academy for Educational Leadership. (1987). *Urban youth and school-to-work transitions* (Conference report). New York: Author.

Albee, G. W. (1987). Powerlessness, politics, and prevention: The community mental health approach. In K. Hurrelmann, F.-X. Kaufmann, & F. Lösel (Eds.), *Social intervention: Potential and constraints* (pp. 37–52). Berlin: de Gruyter.

Bailey, T. (1988). *Education and the transformation of markets and technology in the textile industry* (Technical Paper No. 2, Conservation of Human Resources). New York: Columbia University, National Center on Education and Employment.

Bailey, T. (1989). *Changes in the nature and structure of work: Implications for skill requirements and skill formation* (Technical Paper No. 9, Conservation of Human Resources). New York: Columbia University, National Center on Education and Employment.

Der Bundesminister für Bildung und Wissenschaft. (1990). *Grund- und Strukturdaten, 1990/91*. Bad Honnef, Germany: Bock.

Eberly, D. J. (Ed.). (1991). *National youth service: A democratic institution for the 21st century*. Washington, DC: National Service Secretariat.

Greenberger, E., & Steinberg, L. (1986). *When teenagers work: The psychological and social costs of adolescent employment*. New York: Basic Books.

Grubb Institute of Behavioural Studies. (1982). *Supporting young people in Transition to Working life (TWL): TWL network in practice, 1978–1981* (Special Programmes Occasional Papers, No. 2). Moorfoot, Sheffield, UK: Manpower Services Commission.

Hamilton, S. F. (1990). *Apprenticeship for adulthood: Preparing youth for the future*. New York: Free Press.

Hess, L. E., & Petersen, A. C. (1991). Narrowing the margins: Adolescent unemployment and the lack of a social role. Unpublished paper. Pennsylvania State University.

Jahoda, M. (1981). Work, employment, and unemployment: Values, theories, and approaches in social research. *American Psychologist, 36*, 184–191.

James, W. (1910). *The moral equivalent of war* (International Conciliation, no. 27, p. 3–20). New York: Johnon Reprint Co.

Janoski, T. (1990). *The political economy of unemployment: Active labor market policy in West Germany and the United States*. Berkeley: University of California Press.

Katzenstein, P. J. (Ed.). (1989). *Industry and politics in West Germany: Toward the third republic*. Ithaca, NY: Cornell University Press.

Kern, H., & Schumann, M. (1986). Limits of the division of labour: New production and employment concepts in West German industry. *Economic and Industrial Democracy, 8,* 151–170.

Kuhlmann, J. (1990). West Germany: The right not to bear arms. In D. Eberly & M. Sherraden (Eds.), *The moral equivalent of war? A study of non-military service in nine nations.* New York: Greenwood.

Larsson, A. (1988). *Flexibility in production, security for individuals: Some aspects of Sweden's active labor market policy.* Solna, Sweden: National Labour Market Board.

Meister, J. J. (1985). Press. übergansqualifikationen im wandel. In M. Kaiser, R. Nuthmann, & H. Stegmann (Eds.), *Berufliche verbleibsforschung in der diskussion* (Vol. 1). Nüremberg, West Germany: Institut für Arbeitsmarkt- und Berufsforschung der Bundesanstalt für Arbeit.

National Center on Education and the Economy. (1990). *America's choice: High skills or low wages!* (The Report of the Commission on the Skills of the American Workforce). Rochester, NY: Author.

Osterman, P. (1980). *Getting started: The youth labor market.* Cambridge: MIT Press.

Piore, M. J., & Sabel, C. (1984). *The second industrial divide: Possibilities for prosperity.* New York: Basic Books.

Policies for structural change in Sweden. (1991). Ministry of Industry, Ministry of Labour, Swedish Institute. Stockholm, Sweden.

Reubens, B. G. (Ed.). (1983). *Youth at work: An international survey.* Totowa, NJ: Rowman & Allanheld.

Rosenbaum, J. E., Kariya, T., Settersten, R., & Maier, T. (1990). Market and network theories of the transition from school to work: Their application to industrialized societies. *Annual Review of Sociology, 16,* 263–299.

Secretary's Commission on Achieving Necessary Skills. (1991). *What work requires of schools: A SCANS report for America 2000.* Washington, DC: Department of Labor.

Sherraden, M. W. (1980). Youth employment and education: Federal programs from the New Deal through the 1970s. In R. C. Rist (Ed.), *Confronting youth unemployment in the 1980s: Rhetoric versus reality* (pp. 17–39). New York: Pergamon.

Stern, D., Raby, M., & Dayton, C. (1992). *Career academies: Partnerships for reconstructing American high schools.* San Francisco: Jossey-Bass.

Stinchcombe, A. L. (1964). *Rebellion in a high school.* Chicago: Quadrangle.

Thurow, L. (1975). *Generating inequality.* New York: Basic Books.

Walther, R. H. (1976). *Analysis and synthesis of DOL experience in youth transition to work programs.* Alexandria, VA: Manpower Research Projects. (NTIS No. PB 272-435)

Willis, P. E. (1977). *Learning to labour: How working class kids get working class jobs.* Lexington, MA: Lexington Books.

Zuboff, S. (1989). *In the age of the smart machine: The future of work and power.* New York: Basic Books.

V. Implications for research

11. Youth: Work and unemployment—A European perspective for research

HANS BERTRAM
Humboldt-Universität zu Berlin Fachbereich
Socialwissen-Schäften Institut für Soziologie, Berlin

Studies involving international comparison are among the most elaborate, protracted, and difficult of research projects. This is because of the great effort needed for the coordination of the participating groups of researchers and for achieving measurement comparability across varying national and cultural contexts. The subject—youth, work and youth unemployment—can only be understood at all appropriately if it is considered in relation to a nation's particular economic, social, and educational policies.

In this chapter, I initially explain why European youth unemployment is a fruitful subject for international comparison. I then develop some hypotheses about youth and youth unemployment that can be subject to empirical test. I question whether the educational policy of the past 20 or 30 years, particularly, that which has promoted the academization of the educational system, has contributed to reducing the problem of youth unemployment or whether it has helped to produce youth unemployment. Because demographic change is being increasingly affected by migratory processes in Europe—at least in the case of the Central European countries—migration also must be taken into consideration.

Three years ago it would have been fairly easy to write this chapter, first, because it was quite simple to define Europe as Western Europe and Southern Europe (including Portugal and Spain) and, second, because the European Community (EC) and the Organization for Economic Cooperation and Development (OECD), as well as the great number of research cooperation projects between various European institutions, made it easy to identify institutions and colleagues who could work together on such a subject. This is no longer possible today, not only because East Germany has become part of the EC via German reunification, but also because

Central European countries such as Czechoslovakia, Hungary, and Poland look back upon some of the same cultural traditions as other European states. Furthermore, certain sociopolitical problem situations that arise in eastern Germany arise in a very similar way in Czechoslovakia and other countries as well.

These countries provide a much more interesting field of research from an epistemological point of view (for reasons I will state below). Moreover, only improvement in the sociopolitical and economic situations in these countries will permit the rest of Europe to continue its own favorable economic development.

Unemployment in Europe

In June 1988, just 7.8 percent of adult men and 13.2 percent of women were unemployed on the average in the 12 EC countries (see Table 11.1). By contrast, in the same month more than twice as many young men under 25 (16.6%) were unemployed, and more than two-and-one-half times (22.5%) more young women were unemployed than the average for all adult women in Europe.

Although these European averages do not reflect the great variability among nations, they do reveal two trends that seem to hold true not only for Europe but also for Western industrial nations in general. First, young people under the age of 25 have higher unemployment rates than other age groups. Second, young women are particularly disadvantaged because of their youth and their gender. Whereas the disadvantage of young people, particularly young women, is apparent across Europe and other Western industrial nations, these two general trends are more or less pronounced in different national contexts.

There is a group of countries, including Denmark, Germany, Luxembourg, and the Netherlands, in which the difference between overall unemployment and youth unemployment is less than in other European nations (see Table 11.1). Also, there is less disparity in these countries than elsewhere in unemployment rates between men and women, including young men and young women.

For example, in June 1988, the unemployment rate was 5.1 percent for all men and 5.3 percent for young men in West Germany. For all women it was 8.1 percent, and for young women, 7.2 percent. These differences are by no means as pronounced as those in other nations. In France, for example, where the average unemployment rate for all men is 7.2 percent, for young men it is almost 15 percent. Among all French women approximately 13 percent are unemployed, but for young women

Table 11.1 *Unemployment rates for comparison among member states, June 1988 (not adjusted for seasonal effects)*

	Men	Women	Men under 25	Women under 25
Europe (12)	7.8	13.2	16.6	22.5
Belgium	5.9	16.3	10.5	20.7
Denmark	4.4	7.7	7.0	8.9
Germany	5.1	8.1	5.3	7.2
Spain	14.9	29.7	36.1	52.2
France	7.2	12.9	14.8	24.2
Ireland	16.9	22.2	26.9	23.8
Italy	7.8	20.0	28.3	41.4
Luxembourg	2.0	3.3	3.7	4.3
Netherlands	8.0	13.4	14.0	14.8
Portugal	4.1	9.2	9.9	18.8
United Kingdom	8.8	7.8	13.6	11.2

Source: Eurostat, Subject matter 3: Population and social conditions, Series B: Economic cycles, *Unemployment in the community* (June 1988).

the rate of unemployment reaches 24 percent. The situation is even more extreme in Italy, where unemployment, especially among young women, is exceptionally high. The average unemployment rate of 8 percent among men contrasts with a rate of more than 41 percent for young women; this is twice as high as the overall female unemployment rate in Italy (20%).

Regardless of how one evaluates these figures, there can be no doubt that there are employment disadvantages for adolescents and young adults, and particular difficulty for young women. These disparities occur not only in countries with traditionally high unemployment, such as Spain and Ireland, but also in countries such as Italy and France, which have had low unemployment among men for the past decade due to a more favorable economic climate. These countries have markedly youth-specific and sex-specific labor markets that have fostered extreme unemployment among the aforesaid groups.

Educational Policy and Youth Unemployment

The educational expansion of the 1950s, 1960s, and early 1970s in Western Europe was justified by the argument that the technical/industrial revolution required increasingly qualified workers who could be trained only if there were corresponding educational reform. It was believed that only workers with relatively high educational qualifications had a chance in the future labor market. In view of the relationship between unemployment and poor educational qualifications, there were hopes that an increase in the educational attainment of the total population would solve individual unemployment problems among adolescents and young adults.

Germany's educational reform focused mainly on expanding the university system and the general school system. This was because at that time the United States was considered an exemplar with respect to both economic and educational policy in adapting to modernization processes. Most of West Germany's educational plans were oriented toward Anglo-Saxon models (e.g., comprehensive schools), including attempts to found elite universities in Constance and Bielefeld.

The traditional dual system in Germany and some other West European states was considered a major obstacle for further technical/economic development, because in this system children's future educational careers are decided when they are only ten years old. It was thought that much potential talent, yet unrealized, would not be recognized (Hamilton, 1990). This deficiency was to be remedied by introducing comprehensive schools intended to give all children equal opportunity to attain a university education, considered superior at the time, solely in accord with their talents and regardless of their social origins. Furthermore, the system in place at that time was criticized because employers had undue influence over vocational training. According to the popular argument, economic interests were given priority over young people's needs for training.

Up until the 1960s the German school system offered the same general instruction to all pupils only at the elementary-school level (usually the first to fourth classes or from ages six to ten). At the secondary level there were three separate forms: the upper division of elementary school (*Hauptschule*, fifth to eighth or ninth classes), junior high school (*Realschule*; fifth to tenth classes), and high school proper (*Gymnasium*, fifth to thirteenth classes). These involved different (and separate) vocational training courses and ultimately different (blue-collar, white-collar, and academic) vocations. Children's educational careers were thus settled by the age of ten. Thereafter, it was almost impossible to change a child's course of progress between the upper division of elementary school, junior high school, and high school (except sometimes in the downward direction). This very early selection, with its strong implications for eventual placement in the socioeconomic stratification structure, was one target of school reform plans in the 1960s. The same instruction for all children up to the sixth class (in so-called orientation stages) or up to the tenth class or longer (at comprehensive schools) was intended to keep the decision about future educational careers open as long as possible and to allow for later revision. This reform encouraged more and more children and youth to attend school for a longer period of time and to obtain higher school certificates.

The "dual system," involving the coupling of training and apprenticeship, is a special form of vocational training. Youths learn a trade, usually in three years, by participating in designated training plans within a company, while they simultaneously attend a vocational school. They are instructed by a trainer in the company and are also given training pay. Their qualification, acquired by an intercompany test, is highly valued on the labor market. Such training also confers general social esteem upon the student. Furthermore, a specific vocational qualification is an important component of vocational identity. The dual system is an effective way of integrating youths into the working world. In addition to providing vocational qualification and more general work-related and political socialization, it has a positive effect on the youth labor market (by making a great number of training positions available).

Whatever diverse motives drove the educational reformers at the time, and whatever measures were specifically taken in the various components of the educational system, Germany's dual system was not replaced. Today, we can therefore examine the effects of different educational systems and reform efforts on the employment of adolescents and young adults in varying national contexts. We can also assess their implications for the economic and industrial development of particular countries in Western Europe.

The European countries of Germany, Switzerland, Austria, and Denmark have minimal problems in the area of youth unemployment compared to all other European countries and the United States (White & Smith, 1991, pp. 10f). In countries where apprenticeship is part of the official course of training (i.e., the dual system), it is much easier to integrate adolescents and young adults into the productive process than in countries that provide an overall, general education and impart technical qualifications solely within this structure.

The immense flexibility of the dual system was impressively confirmed in West Germany, for example, when, from the mid-seventies to the mid-eighties, it enabled the society to effectively cope with rapid demographic change. When the demand for training positions clearly exceeded the supply—due to the increase in the youth population and the increasing willingness of adolescents and young people to look for an appropriate training position—training opportunities kept up with the quickly rising demand. Thus, the number of trainees in companies increased from 1.3 million in 1975 to 1.7 million in 1980, although West Germany had considerable economic problems during that period. The dual system has proven to be similarly flexible in integrating adolescents and young people into working life in the five new German states.

Joint action among employers, trade unions, and the government has actually caused employers' offers of in-company or intercompany training for adolescents and young people to far exceed the demand for such training. However, the real question is whether the companies or intercompany training institutions can ensure that adolescents and young people in fact find jobs at the end of such training.

Lappe (1991), like the Institute of Sociological Research (ISF) in Munich before him, has pointed out that in countries with a dual system there is something like a company-oriented labor-market policy. Large and small companies alike feel obligated to provide apprenticeship positions to ensure that there will be qualified staff available for their own workforces. Von Friedeburg, a central advocate of German educational reform and educational policy in the 1960s and formerly one of the sharpest critics of the dual system, has pointed out that in a dual system, 15- and 16-year-old adolescents and young adults seeking an apprenticeship position are generally not regarded as competitors by other workers in the labor market. Instead, they are viewed as young people for whom provision must be made. Parents, teachers, and supervisors feel responsible for helping these young people to be properly integrated into the productive process and to learn something useful. This company labor-market policy and the willingness to assume such personal responsibility for individual young people make the absorptive capacity of the working world much greater than in countries where the state alone, or educational institutions alone, are responsible for education both in the general sphere and in the vocational sphere.

In 1964, Picht, another initiator of educational reform in the 1960s, demanded that more adolescents and young adults attend universities in West Germany. A considerable opening of the educational system has doubtless taken place here. Although only 4 percent of the population ages 19 to 25 were university students in 1960, as many as 23 percent were students in 1990. Social inequality plays a far smaller part today in determining who will complete high school than it did in the 1950s and 1960s. Thus, many more children whose fathers and mothers only reached the upper division of elementary school graduate from a higher school now than was the norm 10 or 20 years ago. The inequality between boys and girls has also largely disappeared, at least in the general school system; one can even observe a slight advantage in opportunities for girls today. However, the most important success of this educational reform is that today almost all adolescents and young adults (except for about 6% to 7%) complete an apprenticeship or another form of vocational training, or a university education. This is quite a dramatic change from the mid-1960s.

The educational system of the United States was especially praised in Germany in the 1960s because it was assumed at the time that the U.S. system gave a much greater percentage of young people higher educational opportunities. However, OECD (1991b, Chapter 5) has ascertained that 81 percent of German 18-year-olds are either now in the general school system or in an apprenticeship; in contrast, only 58 percent of 18-year-olds in the United States still attend school. It may be that the dual educational system, having not only general school education but also a great number of highly differentiated application-oriented education courses, is attractive for a far greater percentage of adolescents and young adults over a longer period of time than is the present educational system of the United States. This is indicated by the fact that adolescents and young adults can leave school in Germany after nine school years, at the age of 15 or 16 years. At that point they can immediately go to work and within a short time draw considerable incomes in the labor market. Despite the existing job opportunities—especially in large urban regions—the share of adolescents and young adults who choose this option has dropped to 6 or 7 percent from approximately 35 percent in the 1960s (Achter Jugendbericht, 1990). Today all three forms of secondary school in the general school system (namely, the upper division of elementary school, junior high school, and high school proper) produce graduates who, via school, apprenticeship, or additional further training, either go through an apprenticeship or strive for a university education.

The current educational system in Germany is considered highly attractive not only in comparison to the United States, but also in comparison to Great Britain (Kupka, 1990). A comparative study of Liverpool and Bremen showed that young Britons manage to pass into working life two or three years earlier than young Germans. This later transition of young Germans into the workplace is not due to a longer stay within the general school system but rather to extensive involvement in vocational qualification processes. Young Germans are substantially more willing to obtain qualification through the dual system than their counterparts in the British educational system. This may be related to the fact that the status of a skilled worker entails a high degree of social prestige and economic potential in Germany.

Unfortunately, there are far too few studies of the relationships among training, in-company labor organization, and efficiency, and I must therefore refer once again to the above-mentioned study by the Institute of Sociological Research (ISF). This study examined similar production companies in Germany and France with respect to personnel, hierarchy levels, and income disparities.

To present only one example, the technical area of a German machine-tool factory had 17 foremen, 3 head foremen, and 1 production manager for 450 workers. The comparative company in France had 23 assistant foremen, 5 foremen, 3 head foremen, 2 deputy departmental managers, 3 departmental managers, 1 chief of production, 1 deputy production director, and one production director for 400 workers.

In the area of administration and operational accounting of a steel company, 8 departmental managers and 1 division manager were required for 127 desk officers in Germany, whereas 39 office people, 4 deputy departmental managers, 3 departmental managers, 3 main departmental managers, and 1 division manager were required for 174 desk officers in France. The disparities in income between workers and executive employees were 1:3.4 in France, whereas the discrepancy was 1:2 in Germany. The expenditure for executive personnel was accordingly lower in Germany than in France.

This study showed in exemplary fashion the greater bureaucratic differentiation and hierarchy, and the much greater income disparity, in French industry than in German industry. Moreover, it demonstrated that the promotion prospects for skilled workers were much greater in German industry because executive personnel were recruited to a much greater extent from the skilled workers and not from outside the company (from the universities).

From the German companies' point of view, the internal recruiting of skilled workers was satisfactory because the qualification profile of skilled workers was relatively high and homogeneous (as the companies themselves had been able to influence these qualifications). In France, industry's influence on applicants' level of qualification and course of training was virtually nonexistent due to the complete state control of the system.

I discuss the company training system in Germany in such detail here because of its relevance to the hypothesis that educational reform in the 1960s and 1970s in most Western European countries—with its extreme orientation toward a state- or publicly organized education at the expense of a dual education system—is possibly one essential cause of youth unemployment in Western Europe today. I presume that such a hypothesis, expressed by a German, is provocative. However, the fact that the unemployment rate of adolescents and young adults is hardly, if at all, higher than the general unemployment rate in countries with dual systems (whereas it is considerably higher in all other countries) should perhaps cause us to think about whether our orientation toward general education and the relatively blind expansion of the university system might not have been a misinvestment.

After all, the great need for academically trained people to support economic development, as espoused by antidual system proponents in the 1960s and 1970s, has not been verified empirically. It is indeed unfortunate that the social consequences of this inappropriate educational policy must be borne not by those responsible for making this policy but instead by adolescents and young adults. One can see that these considerations are not sheer invention by the fact that there is currently an intense debate in France, as well as in Spain, about whether a very much greater attempt than before should not be made to introduce the dual system, a system that has developed historically and been maintained in Middle and Central Europe up to the present time.

All training and education systems, including the university system, were traditionally coupled very closely with particular vocations and job descriptions. This applies not only to vocational training but also to all other courses of training including university education, from teachers' training, through training for the senior civil service, to medical training. Strictly scholastic education and training has increased at the expense of traditionally more practice-oriented courses of training in Germany, promoted by a belief that this would reduce social inequality. The question arises as to the consequences of this change for youth unemployment.

In European countries where general vocational qualifications are imparted in the scholastic education system, the actual ability to hold one's own in a job is imparted in the company. But such training is not systematic; it is instead concretely oriented toward application in a particular job. One must at least ask whether such within-company training can really be equated with systematic skilled workers' training and whether such forms of qualification develop the trainees' potentials to the same extent as does training in the dual system. Moreover, some young people receive little or no training in their initial jobs after leaving school. Hamilton and Crouter (1980) have pointed out that in the United States job experience does not necessarily contribute to the development of the personality, especially if the work has no particular meaning, makes no special demands on young people, and is thus felt to be more pointless than meaningful.

One must ask whether overly scholastic training systems are associated with specific problems that are relatively foreign to the dual system. Education systems that regard university training *a priori* as their culmination and conclusion, and education systems that are further differentiated within themselves (e.g., a hierarchy of large schools as in France or a hierarchy of universities as in the United States), are optimal from the individual perspective for all those who meet the academic criteria.

For example, those who excel in performance tests in the French system, as in the United States, have the opportunity to advance to top positions in a great variety of areas. However, there are those who do not have these school qualifications, who for whatever reason find scholastic learning to be problematic. Are not these the same people who were disadvantaged in the 1950s and 1960s, before the educational reforms, because they were unable to cope with the prevailing school standards and forms of school learning? For some, there may be difficulties in adapting to the scholastic school system because of cultural and/or linguistic divergence (e.g., recent migrants from other countries). Such people are excluded from such a system without there being a viable, socially respected alternative to the school qualifications. All those who do not meet the criteria remain in the lower stages of the education system, a system that offers no satisfactory training prospects for adolescents and young adults. These adolescents and young adults must therefore rely on state remedial programs or measures of the EC to maintain employment.

Almost all European countries with high rates of youth unemployment have developed a great number of remedial programs to give young people training on the job or to create job opportunities even if they involve little or no productive work. I will not comment specifically on these measures because the OECD (1984, 1991a) has presented a great number of detailed analyses of them, and there are many publications on these programs within the individual member nations. Also, it is extremely difficult to compare these programs and measures Europe-wide because the structures of the agencies are so different (e.g., state, schools, charity organizations, and municipalities in Germany).

By contrast, education systems that allow different educational goals to exist side by side and do not classify application and practice-oriented studies *a priori* as inferior might not be optimal for those who can meet high academic performance standards, but such educational systems have the great advantage of opening up meaningful work and life opportunities for the great majority of adolescents and young adults.

The considerations expressed here must be formulated very generally because, as OECD (1991b) recently ascertained, international comparison of the interrelations of social and economic policy, training, and youth unemployment has hardly been a subject of research. The OECD states rather tersely in its report that although many studies examine national differences in labor-market structures, virtually no studies have analyzed the very complex relationship among education, training, vocational qualifications, and the employment system. It is even difficult to make international comparisons because the country-specific databases are so differently organized. There is hardly an aspect of the labor market that is as difficult to grasp empirically as the relationship between the training system and the labor market. Perhaps it is necessary to make this relationship a central focus of research to determine whether the educational reform of past decades has been preferential to the more privileged, while it has more or less left behind those who are especially vulnerable to youth unemployment and downgrading processes.

It must further be assumed that those educational systems that have not entirely lost sight of the relationship among education, training, and employment will be economically superior to other systems. In comparison to systems that make a sharper distinction between manual work and brainwork, such educational programs will more likely foster abilities and qualifications that enhance adaptation to changes in technology and industry.

Internationally, remedial programs for unemployed young people who have fallen through the meshes of the educational system will always be necessary. But one must ask whether the extremely high percentages of those needing such aid are not the manifestation of an abortive educational policy. This problem cannot be corrected merely by devising further programs. What is needed is an educational system that recognizes the validity not only of intellectual, university-oriented goals, but also of vocational goals. More emphasis needs to be placed on vocational qualifications and abilities. Help could then really be focused on those groups who, for whatever reason, cannot make full use of the plural structure of offers even in the most efficiently organized educational system.

My hypothesis is thus that the high youth unemployment in some nations of Europe and in the United States stems, at least in part, from the separation of the education and employment systems. An educational system that has become so disengaged from the employment system leaves adolescents and young adults without any support when it comes to finding work. For example, Singell and Lillydahl (1989) examined the unemployment rate of high school graduates in the United States who do not remain in the education system, arriving at 30 percent for young white males in this group and at more than 65 percent for young black males. Regardless of how one sees these figures, there can be no doubt that educational systems that become disengaged from the labor market and the employment system saddle the entire burden of integration into working life onto young people. I consider this to be the essential cause of the high unemployment rates for young people in some European countries.

Regional and Demographic Causes for Youth Unemployment

When stressing that Germany and other European countries or the United States have dissimilar educational and employment policies, one must of course not forget that such comparison among nations conceals the diversities existing within individual countries. For instance, census data for overall unemployment and youth unemployment in German regions shows that the average national values of 7 percent to 8 percent for 1987 (a time prior to reunification) conceal regional variations within Germany that are sometimes even greater than those among the various European nations described by the OECD. For the reference year 1986, unemployment among young people is extremely low for such prosperous cities as Munich, regardless of other labor-market developments. This also holds true in mitigated form for service centers such as Frankfurt or Dusseldorf. The unemployment figures fluctuate between 3 percent for Munich and 12 percent or more for the North German Protestant cities.

Rural areas, such as the North German Protestant and the Bavarian regions, clearly differ in their unemployment patterns. Youth unemployment rises to 25 percent and is even higher among young women up to the age of 25. Unemployment is also particularly pronounced in the North German Catholic rural regions and in the Southwest German rural regions, which have an above-average unemployment rate both among young people overall and among young females.

This differentiation among the regions of West Germany permits several conclusions to be drawn. Even though certain general trends can be shown Europe-wide (at least rudimentarily), such as a particular disadvantage of young women and higher unemployment among adolescents and young adults compared to adults, there are very considerable differentiations among regions within a relatively small nation. Thus it appears advisable not to conduct analyses or establish programs that deal with the question and problems of youth unemployment on the sole basis of national perspectives and national analyses. Instead it is important to concentrate much more on comparing typical regions of Europe with each other.

Thus, comparing the average figure for youth unemployment in Germany with the average figure in France or Portugal has limited utility. It is much more interesting and more fruitful scientifically to compare developments in extended areas, such as Munich or Barcelona, Hamburg, Amsterdam, or Brest. A regional comparison might more clearly illuminate the structure, causes, and possible solutions of the unemployment problem for adolescents and young adults than would analysis on a national level.

Because the regional variations in youth unemployment are almost perfectly covariant in Germany with variations in birthrates, it is reasonable to hypothesize that regional variations in youth unemployment are essentially a function of demographic development. Integration into working life is more difficult in regions with a high birthrate and a high proportion of adolescents and young adults than in regions with a low birthrate and a low proportion of adolescents and young adults.

This relationship, in the German case, can be detected in the OECD's demographic database. There was a relatively high net reproduction rate until 1965 or 1967 in the European countries (which began to drop with varying strength and intensity). This high net reproduction rate could also be observed in the second half of the 1960s in the United States. Countries with traditionally high birthrates (for example, Italy with 20 per 1,000) decreased by almost half by 1985 (e.g., just under 10 per 1,000 in Italy). Thus, even these countries reached a level that either falls below or equals that of countries with traditionally low birthrates, such as Germany or France.

Because the drops in birthrate in both Canada and the United States were less clear-cut, one can speak today of different birth behaviors in North America and Western Europe. Most European countries are now definitely below the approximately 16 births per 1,000 reported in the United States and Canada, having 9 or 10 per 1,000 and at most 12 or 13 per 1,000. It is therefore no surprise that the percentage of 15- to 24-year-olds in the United States (approximately 19% of the total population [Bloom, Freeman, & Korenman, 1987]) is far above the percentage of the same age group in Germany (15%) or in Switzerland (only 13%).

As Bloom and colleagues explain in their survey of literature, the effects of cohort size on the unemployment ratios of adolescents and young adults are not the same in the United States and other countries. Most cohort studies have been conducted in the United States, where it is possible to take into account demographic development, labor-market development, the participation of different groups (such as men and women) in the labor market, and industrial development. Bloom and his coauthors conclude that a relationship can indeed be established in most studies between unemployment rate and cohort size in the United States, whereas an international comparison instead leads to the conclusion that the reaction of the labor market to different cohort sizes is highly dependent on the particular economic institutions and the very specific circumstances within the individual countries. Thus, despite the great interest in demographic models and the effects of a large cohort on unemployment, one can ascertain at least for most European countries that such a demographic approach is hardly suitable for meaningful analyses and comparisons in Europe.

One can develop complex models for changes in the labor market and changes in the economic structure of the labor market. Models intended to establish a relation between cohort size and job opportunities must assume *a priori* that cohort size is stable and that the age structure of those who leave the labor market is also just as stable as the participation of the total population in the labor market. However, cohort size, an important component of such models, has always been rather unpredictable in Europe because of immense migratory processes. For example, who could have predicted that political developments in Eastern Europe would make Germany the leader among all European immigration countries? How can this be incorporated into a demographic model?

I am not referring so much to those seeking asylum in Europe from all over the world, but rather to the enormous migratory processes from Eastern and Southeast Europe into Germany. These movements reduce all demographic models to absurdity if only because the very great majority of these immigrants belong to younger age cohorts and thus cause a structural change in cohort composition.

Thus, from a sociopolitical perspective, the question of unemployed young migrants in Europe is of much greater importance than the demographic effects of the so-called baby-boom generation. From a scientific perspective as well, the question of integrating migrants from entirely different cultural traditions and from nations with different economic conditions is much more central than cohort analyses, no matter how carefully elaborated they are, that attempt to calculate the effect of large and small cohorts on youth unemployment and job opportunities.

The composition of some cohorts is determined more by the number of migrants than by birthrates, and job opportunities possibly depend mainly on whether one is a migrant or the child of a migrant or whether one belongs to the native population. Migratory processes within Europe, including those movements that have been brought about in some countries in order to meet the need for workers, presumably constitute the central problem for youth unemployment in the 1990s from a demographic perspective.

Not only are the labor-market problems of the children of migrants and young migrants much greater than the labor-market problems even of the native baby-boom generation, but also migratory processes in Europe—like youth unemployment—vary considerably within individual nations, so the problem situations and difficulties in European regions may have much in common. In Germany, for example, the percentage of foreigners in the total population is extremely low in those regions with below-average youth unemployment, particularly in rural regions, so the number of unemployed foreigners and young foreigners in these regions is again lower than in regions where foreigners cumulate. In regions such as the North German Protestant rural districts, where the share of foreigners is just 2.7 percent, the unemployment rate of foreigners does not even reach the regional rate. Young foreigners also tend to be underrepresented among unemployed young people in these regions. In the city of Frankfurt, in contrast, the share of the foreign resident population is approximately 21 percent and the share of unemployed foreigners of the total unemployed is more than 27 percent. Young foreigners have much higher unemployment rates than older foreigners.

Because foreign population cumulates within large urban centers (at least in Germany), not only do very special problems of multicultural societies arise here, but also labor-market problems for adolescents and young adults appear. This migration problem will become more acute in the future if the economic imbalances within Europe and the bordering countries persist. Braudel (1985) shows that migratory processes have occurred throughout the history of Europe whenever economic imbalances among European countries were too great. Because these migrations, as the corresponding statistics within Germany show, are not evenly distributed within Europe but, rather, are generally concentrated in the large urban centers with accordingly homogeneous settlements of migrants, a great number of the ensuing problems pertain to urban youth unemployment. Finding solutions to these problems is a most urgent challenge.

As the official migration policy in Europe (Limage, 1987) was to admit migrants only if workers were required, a central problem in the 1970s and 1980s was how to integrate labor migrants' children—the so-called second generation—into the new cultures. Despite differences in government policies (e.g., in France and Germany—Limage, 1987, footnote 5; OECD, 1986), relatives and sometimes friends of the labor migrants who came into European countries as families were officially reunited through many unofficial channels. The integration of the children's generation initially posed a large problem, but one that could be solved—at least in Germany—if this second generation could be integrated into the country's training and company system.

However, the general success of this policy must not obscure the fact that the increasing qualification of this second generation has generally failed to close the gap between them and a multigenerational native population, leading to the development of an underclass. Educational reform has taken this native population a considerable step ahead in the area of educational qualification. At the same time (and this causes special difficulties, particularly in large urban centers), adolescents and young adults from migratory families who have not been appropriately integrated into the education system are precisely the group that is particularly affected by youth unemployment in Germany (Achter Jugendbericht, 1990).

However, this problem of migration exists alongside another one, which will presumably dominate the discussion in the 1990s, at least in Germany. Due to the economic collapses in Eastern and Southeast Europe, the inflow of ethnic German immigrants into Germany will continue to a considerable extent. Because here, too, these immigrants are mainly young people hoping to find work in Germany, the integration of these young people will pose a very central problem. These migrants constitute a much larger group than those applying for political asylum.

The influx of refugees can possibly be reduced if strategies could be developed that would enable these adolescents and young adults to obtain jobs and qualifications in their own native countries, thus launching favorable economic developments in their homelands as well. This problem, which has initially arisen above all in Germany due to historical and geographical circumstances, will definitely also affect other European countries such as France and Italy. After all, it is hardly conceivable that young people in the fringe countries of Europe can be kept from migrating to Middle and Western Europe if economic developments continue to be so disparate. The example of the United States shows how little protection there is against such migratory processes. Europeans are therefore well advised to address the question of how to create attractive living and working conditions for young adults in Central Europe that make it superfluous for them to emigrate elsewhere. As Braudel has shown in many of his publications, Europe has always been a continent in which peoples have migrated in accordance with economic conditions. These migrations took place not only in remote times but also—as the example of Germany shows—at the beginning of the twentieth century, when young Poles migrated to the Ruhr District and the first wave of Italian immigrants came, and in the 1960s and 1970s due to the labor shortage in Germany and other parts of Europe.

The Future Development of Youth Unemployment in Germany

Although a scientist must be extremely careful about making prognoses for the future, one can at least assume that certain structural changes in sectors of the economy inside and outside Germany will lead to specific problem zones and youth unemployment. One must assume that large shifts toward the tertiary sector will take place, drawing workers from the industrial production sphere and from agriculture.

Of all OECD countries examined, Germany had, in 1984, the highest percentage of people employed in producing industry of all OECD countries examined, namely 41 percent, followed by Switzerland with 38 percent (the United States had only 29% employed in the industrial sector but as many as 68% in the tertiary sector). In the agricultural sphere, Italy was the leader with 12 percent, and Great Britain and the United States showed the lowest employment rates in this sphere (OECD 1991b, Table 1: Civilian Employment by Sector, p. 36).

With respect to Central European states such as Czechoslovakia, Hungary, and Poland, all these countries still have a considerable percentage of their workers in agriculture: Czechoslovakia, 11 percent; Hungary, 20 percent; and Poland, 26 percent. Given these figures, it must be stressed that the reduction of the agricultural sector will entail both migratory processes and a particularly high measure of youth unemployment in such states as Italy, Hungary, Poland, and Czechoslovakia. Czechoslovakia, Hungary, and Poland also have a relatively high percentage of employees in the industrial sector (approximately 49%, 37%, and 37%, respectively); the domination of the industrial sector is particularly striking in Czechoslovakia (OECD 1991a, Table A4, p. 19).

It is quite interesting in this connection to observe that youth unemployment is above average in the agricultural regions of Northwest Germany. This is because the birthrate is still rather high there, whereas corresponding transformation processes have led to workers living in regions where there is a diminishing demand for them. One can therefore assume with some certainty that in the next few years and decades a high measure of youth unemployment will also exist in those regions of Europe that are still devoted primarily to agricultural production. This is because (1) the net reproduction rate is generally higher there than the average of the respective total population and (2) the adaptive steps in agriculture, in particular the pressure to adapt, will be especially extreme. For this area and particularly for the adolescents and young adults there will presumably not be very many possibilities of integration into the working world.

One possibility will be to migrate to large urban centers, places where there are new jobs. Another will be to leave one's native country altogether and migrate to economically prosperous regions of Europe. Up to now, it has been almost impossible to create jobs in the places where these adolescents and young adults have grown up. Programs for further training or retraining are particularly ineffective here because the jobs for which retraining or further training is provided are generally unavailable in these regions. Such measures themselves tend to increase rather than lower the pressure to migrate.

Tendencies toward urbanization will thus increase in view of such transformation processes in Southern Europe and in Middle Europe. The migratory process described by Braudel, as it has been observed in Europe during former centuries and decades, will be very substantially due to this as well.

Although regions with pronounced agricultural production are relatively easy to identify as future regions of high youth unemployment for the above reasons, this is much more difficult to do with respect to large industrial centers. It may be assumed that industrial production will decrease, but it is extremely difficult to say in what form and in what direction it will develop.

The category of the tertiary sector, which has become established in the OECD's statistics, frequently combines very heterogeneous developments. If one divides this tertiary sector into different segments, such as commerce, services, information, and communications and also public service or nonprofit organizations, one can show for Germany that these areas of the tertiary sector are very differently distributed and also that the relation of workers in the industrial sector to these segments of the tertiary sector is by no means always the same. The development of these individual segments is of crucial importance because these segments offer jobs in very different ways, in particular for women. For example, one can show for Germany that the percentage of female jobs is extremely high in the segments where the services sector is highly represented, whereas this is not as true of the commerce segments.

If one wanted to consider the extent to which shifts from the secondary sector to the tertiary sector could raise problems of youth unemployment in Europe (or in selected regions of Europe), one would have to determine for the individual regions (more precisely than I can here) the existing job structures, the shares of the individual sectors—differentiated to a greater extent than the mere classification into primary, secondary, or tertiary sector—and additionally cyclical factors in order to be able to state where certain problem zones already exist or where they will come about. Such regional analyses could be done without excessive effort because economics, unlike sociology, has attained a much higher degree of standardization and comparability in its variables. These analyses would be of extraordinary interest not only from a scientific perspective but also from a sociopolitical one, because they would permit a much more exact determination of the problem zones and problem situations within the individual regions of Europe. Clearly, different problems must be solved and different educational programs offered for those undergoing the transition from mainly agricultural economic structures to highly postindustrial structures than for those undergoing transitions from industrial production structures to postindustrial structures.

It is important to consider such different transitional processes not only to know which qualifications to impart to adolescents and young adults, but also to be able to take into account the motivation to work and work orientation in the different regions where such transformation processes take place. The debate about the change in work orientation and motivation to work in Europe suffers because a national comparison is generally drawn without regard for social and economic structures. Even such a thoroughly differentiated piece of work as Inglehart's (1989) *Cultural Upheavals* compares nations with respect to their orientation patterns even though national comparison permits only an average for highly heterogeneous regions.

For example, work orientations as well as post-materialism values measured by Inglehart (1989) are just as thoroughly differentiated in Germany when examined regionally (Bertram, 1991) as when they are compared on a national level with other nations. This is understandable, as very similar values and orientation patterns can be observed in tradition-ally rural regions of Germany and in traditionally rural Catholic regions of France, Ireland, or Italy. Conversely, the values and orientation patterns are presumably more similar in large European urban centers than are the values and orientation patterns within a nation. This applies analogously to Middle and Eastern Europe.

Analyses that take the transformation process of societies from the primary to the secondary and tertiary sectors as their starting point for considering the development of strategies and programs for avoiding youth unemployment should therefore investigate regional economic and social structures. Only such regional differentiations can permit proper consideration of the different cultural traditions and patterns of values. This, of course, also holds true for every scientific analysis, as there is absolutely no reason from a scientific point of view to assume that a young person from Zurich, Munich, or Milan will develop different values and orientations toward work than a young person from Stuttgart or Barcelona, for example.

Only on the basis of such regional differentiations can transformation processes be properly understood in relation to the development of labor markets for adolescents and young adults, including the motivation to work and work orientation. Only such analyses will make it clear, for example, why there is or is not a willingness to migrate to other regions for very different motives, or why young Spaniards from rural regions with extremely high youth unemployment do not migrate to Germany, whereas young Poles and young Russians try to do so. Without knowl-edge of such different configurations of motives it is impossible to do anything about such migrations, assuming such migrations are negative, if only for the regions being abandoned.

Summarizing Perspectives for Research

When we finally raise the question of what can be done by science, or offered by way of scientific policy advice, in view of these migratory processes, the increasing disengagement of the education and employ-ment systems, social transformation processes in connection with chang-ing production structures and also in the sphere of values and attitudes, and the very specific disadvantage of young women and migrants, there are basically two strategies to pursue. In accordance with the concept of step-by-step examination and correction of political programs (Albert, 1978), it would definitely be desirable to investigate the mode of action and efficiency of national programs for eliminating youth unemployment in selected regions of Europe. If at the same time, in accordance with the strategies proposed here, one focused on specific groups such as migrants and young women, considered the relation between educational policy and the employment system, and selected homogeneous economic areas, one could investigate both the effect of measures and programs and the effect of different educational policies on youth unemployment almost in the sense of classical socio-psychological experiments. Such a scientific analysis on the basis of concrete programs already in operation would definitely provide more knowledge about the changes and developments in Western and Middle Europe than the research programs currently supported by the EC, which generally confine themselves to investigating the values and attitudes of adolescents and young adults toward European tourism or toward Europe or the change of values in Europe.

If one could supplement such analyses of programs by relating young people's problems in the particular regions not only to the programs, but also to their living situations, one would surely obtain a very precise picture of the changes and developments in European regions in a comparative perspective. A comparison among nations may be useful from the perspective of government representatives, but it makes little sense from a scientific perspective aimed at examining the efficiency of national programs. After all, our problem today is not that we know too little about the consequences of youth unemployment for the biographies, attitudes, and life orientations of young people, nor is our problem that we do not exactly know the expenditures of the individual nations for these areas on an international level. Our perplexity really begins at the point when we ask why young people are so much more disadvantaged than older age groups in some regions of Europe and not in others. Our uncertainty begins only when we ascertain that certain governments go to relatively great lengths to eliminate the problem of youth unemployment without making any great headway at all, whereas others attain much more with much less effort. However, such research will be possible only if science itself deals with the activities and programs of governments and the EC, and is prepared not only to demand, but also to conduct policy relevant research to a much greater degree than in the past.

References

Achter jugendbericht. (1990). Bericht über bestrebungen und leistungen der jugendhilfe. Bonn: Der bundesminister für jugend, familie, frauen und gesundheit (Eds.).

Albert, H. (1978). Traktat über Rationale Praxis. Tübingen: Nnohr-Siebeck.

Bertram, H. (Ed.). (1991). *Die familie in Westdeutschland: Stabilität und wandel familialer lebensformen in Westdeutschland.* Opladen, West Germany: Leske und Budrich.

Bloom, D. E., Freeman, R. B., & Korenman, S. D. (1987). The labour-market consequences of generational crowding. *European Journal of Population, 3,* 131–176.

Braudel, F. (1985). *Der alltag.* Munich: Kindler Verlag.

Hamilton, S. F. (1990). *Apprenticeship for adulthood: Preparing youth for the future.* New York: Free Press.

Hamilton, S. F., & Crouter, A. C. (1980). Work and growth: A review of the impact of work experiences on adolescent development. *Journal of Youth and Adolescence, 9,* 323–338.

Inglehart, R. (1989). *Kultureller umbruch: Wertewandel in westlichen welt.* Frankfurt: Campus-Verlag.

Kupka, P. (1990). *Berufsplane und zukunftserwartungen jugendlicher: Ein deutsch-englischer.* Vergleich.

Lappe, L. (1990). *Jugend und Arbeit im Europäischen Vergleich: Skizze eines Projektes.* Munich: Deutsches Jugendinstitute e.v.

Lappe, L. (1991). *Jugend und Arbeit im Europäischen Vergleich: Skizze eines Projektes.* Munich: Deutsches Jugendinstitute e.v.

Limage, L. J. (1987). Economic recession and migrant/minority youth in Western Europe and the United States. *International Migration, 25,* 399–413.

OECD. (1984). *The nature of youth unemployment.* Paris: Author

OECD. (1986). *The future of migration* (Program, Conference of National Experts). Paris: Author.

OECD. (1991a). *Employment outlook.* Paris: Author.

OECD. (1991b). *Pathways for learning: Education and training from 16–19.* Paris: Author.

Singell, L. D., & Lillydahl, J. H. (1989). Some alternative definitions of youth unemployment. *American Journal of Economics and Sociology, 48,* 456–470.

White, M., & Smith, D. J. (1991). *The determinants of unemployment.* London: Policy Studies Institute.

12. Conclusion: Social structure and psychosocial dimensions of youth unemployment

WALTER R. HEINZ
Statuspassagen und Risikolagen im Lebensverlauf
University of Bremen, Germany

Introduction

The contributions to this volume repeatedly demonstrate that there is a need for a unified perspective on the structural causes, psychosocial consequences, and political solutions of long-term joblessness during the transition from youth to adulthood. My commentary, therefore, begins with the economic and social structures producing youth unemployment, its distribution, and its ups and downs in various countries. A theoretical interlude follows concerning the convertibility of family social capital into employment prospects and career resources for young people by putting the debate between Coleman and Modell in a wider theoretical framework of cultural reproduction. Finally, concepts of individual and social mechanisms assumed to be related to youth unemployment are reviewed to develop realistic proposals for intervention and prevention.

Economy, Education, and the Labor Market as Structural Contexts

As Michael White and David Smith demonstrate in their comparative analysis of the high unemployment rates in industrial nations in the 1980s, a focus on individual factors will only identify those persons who are selected for unemployment. To better understand the persistence of joblessness among the young population we have to instead look at economic structures and labor-market policies. There are severe problems for comparative analysis, though, even if one relies on the OECD or ILO statistics, because the formal definitions of unemployment differ among nations and economic periods. For example, in the United States someone who is counted as "unemployed" is supposed to have no job *and* to have been actively looking for work for the past month; in Germany the status of unemployment is not restricted to an active period of job search but depends on being registered as looking for employment at the local labor exchange. Moreover, the age classification of young unemployed persons differs. It may cover those under 20, those between 20 and 25, or those between 16 and 18; some countries only count young people who have accomplished their obligatory school years (e.g., in Germany 18 and older).

For sociologists and people who seek solutions to the social problem of youth unemployment, the focus on "relative changes in aggregate level of unemployment" (White & Smith) is important because it illuminates the reasons for differences in countries. Understanding the distribution of unemployment within countries requires assessment of the social structural circumstances and psychosocial responses to unemployment among different categories of young people. As the chapter by Hannie te Grotenhuis and Frans Meijers documents, there are psychosocial differences between working-class kids who are unemployed right after having left school and youth from upper middle-class backgrounds who select "voluntary unemployment" after college graduation to find out what their occupational interests really are. For such within-country analyses, it is useful to develop new criteria for defining unemployment. Following the ILO guidelines that define the unemployed according to three criteria—being without work, being currently available for employment, and seeking work—does not tell us much about what kind of work young people do not have, for how long they have been available for what sort of employment (part-time, unskilled, full-time, or skilled jobs), and which disappointments they have had to cope with in the process of job search.

According to White and Smith, there is a loss of employment opportunity because of company closures and severe cuts of jobs in various industries, which impair the employment prospects of young people. The current worldwide recession leads to increased industrial dismantling or to transferring jobs to low-wage countries. As the chapters by White and Smith and by Hess, Petersen, and Mortimer both argue, the health of the economy is critical to youth unemployment because young people generally have higher rates of unemployment than other age groups. Most recent OECD figures show that youth unemployment is rising again. Youth are especially vulnerable at times of economic downturn in countries that neither have an organized period of transition from school to work nor provide programs or training schemes for school-leavers who are barred from entry jobs (cf., the contributions by Bertram and Hamilton).

To understand this problem-ridden transition period for young people, not only the supply but also the demand side for recruiting new employees has to be analyzed simultaneously. According to most developmental psychologists, the youth phase is characterized by exploratory behavior and attempts to build one's own social identity from a variety of experiences. Thus, short spells of unemployment followed by work experiences in different social and work environments may contribute to finding out about strengths and weaknesses of one's skills and future perspectives, whereas long spells of joblessness in the formative period of personality development will have discouraging consequences for both identity construction and work orientations (see Mortimer's contribution). Therefore, it is important to distinguish between groups of young people whose risk of becoming unemployed during the transition to adulthood and whose chances for escaping from long-term unemployment differ.

In this respect, education, gender, the state of the local economy, and the supply of training and work-creation programs are major dimensions for comparative analysis. We should not forget, however, that cross-sectional and cross-cultural research has to be framed by "a historical interpretation of institutional power-based strategies" (White & Smith) that defines the scope of action young people have taken in accomplishing the transition from school to work. The state and collective actors at the local level can cooperate in establishing vocational education, training programs, and early vocational counseling. Such a strategy is needed to build bridges between young people who look for satisfactory employment and employers who look for skilled recruits or young people to be trained on the job. However, educational and counseling programs will not succeed in creating jobs. The state (in cooperation with industries) has to take on its responsibility to improve the general conditions of the labor market. Moreover, the bargaining power of specific groups of young people— especially women and ethnic groups—has to be strengthened by a combination of education and work experience to prevent them from experiencing unemployment.

Such a strategy could also prevent the creation of an underclass of unskilled young men and women who will, after a series of failed attempts to enter the labor market, decide to retreat from active job search. Depending on the formal definition of unemployment, most of them will not be counted as unemployed. This urban underclass is growing, mainly in the big cities of North America and England because these societies lack organized arrangements to stabilize the school-to-work transition and thus prevent the development of an underclass of the "truly disadvantaged" (Wilson, 1987). Building human capital in a society that emphasizes contest mobility over sponsored mobility means that young persons will have to cope with the chronic "mismatch" between their skills and credentials and the fluctuation in demand for their qualifications in various industries. This problem is especially acute in economies where manual occupations have contracted and have been replaced by casual jobs in the service sector.

Hence it is necessary to analyze the structural and psychosocial dimensions of youth unemployment in the context of economic development and social as well as educational policies. Furthermore, as Bertram's contribution shows, the problem of youth unemployment does not end at national borders; rather, international migration has become a major concern in European countries. This migration results from the fact that unemployment among adolescents and young adults is much higher in societies in Eastern and Southern Europe as compared to Western Europe. In the 1980s, West Germany became the most successful European state in containing the rise of economically induced joblessness among the young generation. Both Bertram and Hamilton explain this relative success by pointing out the flexibility of the traditional "dual system" in West Germany. Such a system not only provides a qualified workforce generation by generation, but also keeps potentially unemployed youngsters within the vocational and educational training system.

In contrast to mainly market-driven transition processes (characteristic of North America and England), the West German transition from school to work consists of a combination of vocational preparation and general education. It is based on an agreement among state, employers, and unions that the companies and regional governments are responsible for training young people for skilled jobs by offering three- to four-year apprenticeships and day-release education whose curricula and examinations are regulated by official training directives. This "dual system" has managed to keep young people on various tracks between school and employment in an efficient way that is documented by the high proportion of young Germans who pass an apprenticeship. Today almost two-thirds of each school-leaving cohort enters apprenticeship training, about 25 percent enter the academic track (with an increasing tendency), and only about 5 to 10 percent drop out of the organized transition system.

A recent study by a British-German research team has shown (Bynner & Roberts, 1991; Evans & Heinz, 1993) that the transition from school to employment, underemployment, or joblessness is accelerated in the British system compared to Germany because of the former's combination of market-driven status passages to work and temporary training schemes (such as YTS). These patterns are consistent with socialization experiences that emphasize educational and training credentials for young Germans in contrast to an early stress on becoming a worker and earning money among young Britons. The British system of vocational, general and further education will provide more options for the better educated and lead to fewer opportunities for those young people who do not accomplish the highest possible educational certificate.

According to Rosenbaum, Kariya, Settersten, and Maier, (1990), there are different organizing principles for the transition from school to work. They depend on the degree to which there are bridges that inform young people about the requirements of employers and give signals to employers about the skill distribution among young people who look for work. Such bridges could reduce the mismatch between levels and specifications of qualifications and the demands of the employment system and thus curb one of the causes of high youth unemployment mentioned by Bertram.

In the European context, there is another dimension of mismatch between supply and demand of young people in the labor market. Bertram calls our attention to the fact that many of the recent immigrants from Eastern and Southern Europe belong to younger age groups and increase the size and composition of the cohorts entering the labor market in Central Europe, especially in Germany. This situation has led to unexpected social conflicts that are targeted against migrants who look for work in Germany. The social and cultural integration of migrants from countries with different economic and industrial circumstances will be a major task of educational, social, and labor-market policy in Germany and other Central European countries for years to come. The prospects of young immigrants from predominantly agricultural regions of Europe will be dim in the more prosperous industrial and service-providing regions in Europe. If one looks at the composition of available apprenticeships and jobs in urbanized regions in Western Europe, one finds a growth of service, commerce, and communication as well as public-service jobs and a loss in manufacturing and the crafts. Such a situation will improve employment opportunities for young women in office work and personal and social services—mainly in part-time jobs—and reduce the opportunities for young people who have less than college education to move into the ranks of skilled employees with career perspectives.

Bertram (p. 292, this volume) argues convincingly that "transformation processes," including the motivation to work and other work orientations, can "be properly understood in relation to the development of labor market for adolescents and young adults." This suggests a research and policy perspective that examines psychosocial dimensions of work-related behavior in the context of local opportunity structures and institutional as well as social networks. Studies such as those by Mortimer, Finch, Shanahan, and Ryu (1992; Shanahan, Finch, Mortimer, & Ryu, 1991) in St. Paul, Minnesota; Elder, Conger, and Foster (1992) in Iowa; Anderson (1990) in Philadelphia; and the German-British group are examples of research at the micro-social as well as the contextual level.

Family Social Capital, Education, and Youth Unemployment

According to James Coleman, we live in a historical period in which economic and political changes have made children a marginalized group because they neither contribute to the family's survival nor support their parents in old age. He asks; "Who invests in the future of young people and where is the social capital that would provide the resources for building human capital in the young generation?" In the growth period of the industrial society, the family invested in children because of their value in terms of future productive capacity. It was rational for parents to motivate and socialize their offspring for education in order to build the human capital necessary to enter the labor market. In the present phase of the "advanced industrial society," argues Coleman, the family has lost its productive role for good; "it is no longer an institution spanning generations, but forms anew with each generation" (chapter 2, this volume). Referring to the United States, he describes an erosion of the social fabric, where the relationships between the working world of adults and the school world of young people have become separated. The breakdown of the family's economic and socialization efficiency has led to social problems in childhood, adolescence, and young adulthood. Dropouts, drug addiction, and unemployment characterize the young population in urban centers.

Coleman describes various ways in which human capital for the young can be built from investments in financial capital and social capital and concludes that "financial and social capital are not substitutes for one another" (chapter 2, this volume). He argues that in today's affluent society it is not the lack of monetary resources but the decline of motivation that creates problems for the accumulation of cultural capital in the young generation. Thus, the schools have to supply this social capital by instilling motivation among students to take advantage of educational opportunities to build their own human capital.

In this respect, however, there are vast differences between market-driven educational systems and those in welfare states (cf. Rosenbaum et al., 1990). In contrast to Western European models combining market and welfare principles, Coleman sees the attraction of private investors as the only solution for increasing investments in the education of the young generation. But who is to invest in the young generation in advanced industrial societies? Should business invest in public schools or establish privately owned and efficiently administered secondary schools? Coleman's advice is one of "wild west" capitalism: He proposes a "bounty" on the head of each member of the young generation, "a bounty collectible by whatever actor that undertook to develop a child in a way that would reduce the collective costs and increase the benefits" (chapter 2, this volume).

I want to add two critical points to John Modell's commentary. One concerns the role of the state, and the other, the conceptual shortcomings of Coleman's rational investment model. As Rosenbaum and colleagues (1990) have shown in their comparison of the transition from school to work in selected industrial societies, there are important differences between market-driven transition systems and those in welfare states. For instance, the Japanese system provides a strong linkage between companies and schools that makes parents select those schools where prestigious firms are recruiting their labor force. In Germany there is a "dual system," a training and socialization milieu that leads to vocational credentials for entering the skilled labor market. In contrast to these collective solutions to the problems of transition and youth unemployment, Coleman proposes a private-sponsor model to substitute for the family that does not live up to its socialization responsibilities. Such an investment strategy is limited with respect to reducing the risk of youth unemployment, because it does not build transition bridges from school to work that would be stable pathways for young people in good and bad economic times.

There are also questions concerning "social capital" as an explanatory concept. Coleman employs this concept in isolation from "economic capital" and "cultural capital." However, there is a more dynamic theory, developed by Bourdieu (see, e.g., 1986) in his studies of the education system in France (Bourdieu & Passeron, 1990), in which cultural, economic, and social capital can be converted to a certain degree.

The relationship between family and education is mediated by the dominant culture. The schools favor those social classes that possess economic capital and represent those elites who control the cultural standards. This is expressed by Harker (1990, p. 91) in an essay on Bourdieu's conceptualization of education and reproduction: "Disadvantaged families tend to make choices . . . by opting for known 'security' which for many families is a synonym for 'success'." Contrary to Coleman's assumption, the family participates in the reproduction of a balance between social, cultural, and economic capital by "selecting" educational institutions according to their sense of place in society. Parents will prepare their children to maintain their place in the social structure by using the appropriate educational pathways into the employment system (cf. Allatt & Yeandle, 1992). In societies with a comprehensive school system such as the United States and Canada, this means achieving high school graduation. But the diploma will not suffice for entering promising careers, because everybody—except the dropouts—gets it. Hence, employers apply selection criteria that relate to college education, self-presentation, and work experience.

To be able to convert social capital into cultural capital, family socialization has to be combined with the school system and transformed into educational capital (skills, knowledge, social competence, *and* certificates). To convert educational capital into social capital (e.g., job, social networks) and economic capital (monetary resources and property), the young person must gain access to the habitus of the society's elites. This is demonstrated in Coleman's example of the cultural productivity of Asian-American families' investment of social capital. Youth from disadvantaged families only have a chance to build enough convertible educational capital by entering prestigious institutions of learning with a scholarship. This example leads to the conclusion that it is not *the* modern family that fails to invest in social capital for their children that is the problem, but instead it is the unequal distribution of access to education and formal credentials. Parents who train their children for personal competencies and inculcate the value of independence do not act without responsibility; they rather anticipate a major social skill required by the employment system, namely, self-reliance and flexibility (cf. Baethge, Martin, Hantsche, Pelull, & Voskamp, 1988; Beck, 1992).

The exchange between family and school socialization thus stabilizes cultural and social distinctions that operate in class societies regardless of the individual families' investment policy in their offspring. Hence, in times of rising youth unemployment the schools offer courses on how to write a résumé and to prepare for a job interview instead of informing their students about the economic and political processes responsible for a recession. Moreover, schools tend to introduce more vocationally oriented courses in times of rising youth unemployment instead of preparing their students to cope with joblessness by continuing their education.

Modell makes another important observation that runs against the social capital theory: the expansion of more child-oriented socialization based on the assumption that a supportive relationship between parents and children will foster self-reliance and a positive attitude toward school and work during the preparation for adulthood. This support not only refers to the school-based "teenage culture," but also to the early introduction of young people into the world of work. Parents accept that adolescents perform part-time jobs after school, on the weekend, and through the vacation period. Contrary to Coleman's thesis of declining investment of parents in the schooling of their children, they also expect that their children will complete high school and enter college. This is not primarily motivated by the expected exchange value (i.e., highly educated children will be able to support their elderly parents), but by a conviction that their offspring will be better able to cope with the demands of adult life, as workers, parents, and citizens, the more advanced their educational background is.

Modell's cross-cultural exercise on the relationship between parents' involvement with children's school learning is less instructive than he assumes. Within each country are important regional variations (e.g., between rural and industrial regions, between prosperous and declining regions). If there is validity in Bertram's observations about the importance of regional variations in the pattern of transitions from school to work in European societies, then it is likely that there is more variation within societies than among them. To develop better understanding and social policy about the interrelationship among parental support, school efficiency, and the accumulation of human capital in the young generation, cross-national comparison has to be combined with accounts of historical change concerning the normative assumptions and specific regional opportunity structures youth are confronted with when entering the labor market.

This is the message of Helmut Fend's contribution regarding the social-historical contexts of the life course of young people. His basic assumption is that changing social circumstances influence the specific "pattern of individual properties" that give rise to differential risks of young persons to become unemployed. Fend uses the main dimensions of life-course analysis—historical *period*, school-leaving *cohort*, and chronological *age*—dimensions that have to be regarded simultaneously in order to explain timing, duration, and problems of the transition from school to work.

This framework takes into account recent developments in life-course theory and research, that assume that the modern life course is a social construction that consists of normatively expected status passages regulated by social institutions (cf. Elder, 1985; Hagestad, 1991; Heinz, 1991; Kohli, 1989). The transition to adulthood has become increasingly institutionalized by various combinations of education, vocational, and academic training. Adolescence and young adulthood cover an age period between 14 and the late twenties—depending on the timing of entry into and exit from the educational system. Like Coleman, Fend argues that the transition to adulthood has become an individual accomplishment that is valued positively. "Children are not expected to work for the family, to support their parents or to contribute to the family income but rather to prepare themselves for an independent life, for earning an income is essential" (pp. 12–13).

Societies differ in the degree of institutionalization of the adolescent and young adult stage in the life course. In North America there is no specific transition policy to adulthood—market mechanisms and special programs for low-income populations are the only societal investments. In England, there is still a school-leaving age of 16, and only a small segment of young people continue toward higher education. The main societal investment in the young population during England's economic and labor-market crisis throughout the 1980s was the creation of a variety of youth training schemes—devised mainly to keep youth unemployment down rather than to introduce a new transition structure. In Germany, in contrast, there is a three-tier educational system, linked to stable institutions for training young people to become skilled blue- and white-collar workers within the "dual system."

The dynamics of labor-market segmentation in advanced industrial and service economies make it very likely that in societies without an organized system of vocational training and preparation, young people will have to start their working life in the casual segment of the labor market (e.g., in part-time jobs of the service sector). Only those young adults who have at least college training and work experience will have access to entry jobs that will put them on career tracks to higher levels of skilled and secure employment. Under such conditions, the transition to adulthood will occur in separate trajectories, depending on the pathways between education and employment. Some youth will have substantial continuity and job rewards. Others, however, will spend several years in a discontinuous trajectory alternating between casual work, unemployment, and training schemes: They will be in a state of underemployment.

Unemployment and the Young Personality

Historical and comparative analyses of economic and societal contexts that affect the transition to adulthood contribute to the explanation of relationships between unemployment and the personality of young people. Such an approach makes sense, if the dynamics of the economy and the youth labor market are investigated by considering the interactions among family, school, and industry. Thus, research would be possible with specified populations in a contextualized longitudinal design, as proposed by Furnham and Rutter and practiced by Mortimer and colleagues in their study in St. Paul, Minnesota (1992; Shanahan et al., 1991).

In Europe there is an estimated number of 5 million unemployed in the age group between 15 and 25; about one-third are long-term jobless (those who have been unemployed for more than one year). In view of the high risk for many young people of becoming unemployed for more than one or two short spells, there is deplorably little sound comparative research that combines analysis of historically based social and economic circumstances with the psychosocial effects of unemployment in a life-course perspective (cf. Kieselbach, 1991).

From a life-course perspective, it is important not only to know the economic and social-political conditions that influence the risk of unemployment, but also to understand the personality dimensions that make young people especially vulnerable to unemployment in the process of job entry. Although social psychology and developmental psychology have primarily looked at the consequences of prolonged unemployment on the young person, Jeylan Mortimer emphasizes that theory and research have to "attend to the reciprocal causal processes through which social structure and personality influence one another" (p. 173, this volume). This is the same research perspective that has guided sociologists and social psychologists such as Kohn and Schooler (1983) or Hoff, Lempert, and Lappe (1991) in their studies of the reciprocal connection between work experiences and personality functioning. This approach supplements the well-known research tradition that started with the study by Jahoda, Lazarsfeld, and Zeisel (1933; Jahoda, 1982) and emphasized that joblessness is a deeply alienating experience that disconnects the individual from actively participating in socially useful activities. Today, for young men and women, short periods of joblessness will not necessarily result in a personal catastrophe. Youth's reactions will depend on their economic resources and the level of social support they can rely on in their social networks. Depending on their educational background, self-efficacy, and occupational aspirations, some may even prefer temporary unemployment to boring jobs without prospects. This is shown in the chapter by te Grotenhuis and Meijers, whose Dutch respondents expressed more preference for meaningful work than for jobs with high income. Young people with such an orientation, however, come from at least middle-class households and tend to be less distressed by the experience of unemployment, compared to those from working-class families who feel locked in a transition to underemployment.

Mortimer's review of recent studies supports the assumption that personality traits may be precursors of youth unemployment. This, however, does not tell us much about the causes of such personality differences. Therefore, the search for social and personal determinants that may have been influential during prevocational socialization is important in order to prevent the fallacy of blaming the victim, attributing the causes of youth unemployment to the individuals themselves.

Gender is associated with basic differences in psychosocial dimensions that are important for competitive success in the youth labor market. Whereas adolescent boys are socialized for achievement and self-efficacy, adolescent girls are more concerned about interpersonal and communicative issues. These psychosocial differences very likely interact with gender-related expectations concerning success in the job market. This, in turn, seems to reflect the long shadow of the segmentation of the labor market according to gender.

On the other hand, boys and girls in the United States who attend high school tend to have substantial experiences as teenage part-time workers. This experience is positively related to employment and wages in the years after high school. This issue, however, is still a controversial one (cf. Greenberger & Steinberg, 1986; Mortimer et al., 1992); the actual work conditions and skill requirements for teenage jobs in North America must be considered. There is evidence that white, middle-class boys and girls draw benefits from employment with respect to their job-related orientations and behaviors, in contrast to black young people, who are less likely to be employed while in high school. Favorable employment conditions can foster personal efficacy and promote mental health (Finch,

Shanahan, Mortimer, & Ryu, 1991; Shanahan et al., 1991). The situation of U.S. youth, in naturally occurring part-time employment disconnected from the educational system, differs substantially from the social and cultural assumptions concerning the transition from school to work of young people in European countries, most obviously in Germany. Though German youth are not yet treated as grownups and do not experience autonomy and self-determination at work, they are integrated in a well-organized system that combines education and qualification for an occupation that is a basic requirement for being recognized as an adult in Germany (cf. contributions by Bertram and Hamilton).

Thus, the search for individual antecedents of unemployment should be supplemented by investigations of young people's lives and their definitions of the situation, which may very well deviate from official definitions of unemployment status. Depending on their school record, experiences with applications, and the material resources of their families and other social networks, some young unemployed will see themselves as still looking for a job, as being temporarily out of the workforce, or as having dropped out of the job-search competition. Others will see their situation as one of postponing labor-market entry and staying in school voluntarily or because of parental or peer pressure. Still others may not actively look for work because they are provided with resources by their parents. Finally, as Mortimer mentions, not looking for a job may be one way to protect a person from continual experiences of failure.

The social circumstances and psychosocial dimensions of youth unemployment are not easily explained, given the complexity of causal mechanisms that Michael Rutter describes in this book. We are all convinced that unemployment creates costs to the person and the community, but this does not answer the question as to why unemployment causes psychosocial stress. Since the work of Jahoda (1982) we know that for adults the psychological consequences of joblessness are not mainly linked to financial strain. The unemployed person loses self-esteem, a time structure, and a sense of connection to society. Therefore, coping with unemployment by developing personal distance from the world of paid employment may reduce the pressure of getting a job and thus the possibility of falling into a depressive mood.

It is doubtful, however, whether this temporary adjustment will be effective in cases where joblessness becomes a long-term experience. The risk of being among the long-term unemployed depends not only on the state of economy, but also on the government's social welfare policies. In the United States and in Great Britain, conservative governments have done little to reduce income inequalities, but rather have contributed to rising numbers of people living in poverty and at risk of unemployment. In these countries, youth unemployment is much higher than in European countries such as Sweden or West Germany, where the state attempts to conduct an active training and labor-market policy. Therefore, it is important to emphasize Rutter's clear statement (p. 157, this volume) that "personal factors such as low skill level, low educational/vocational qualifications, inadequate personality functioning, and physical ill health are quite important with respect to individual differences, but it is *not* changes in any of these that caused the number of people out of work to rise so dramatically." In societies such as the United Kingdom and the United States, where heavy losses in manufacturing industries have not been compensated by job growth in skilled service jobs, young people who leave school at the age of 16 or after high school without further training have to face tremendous risk of becoming unemployed.

In a causal model as it is envisaged by Rutter, the chain of events should be modeled according to a life-course framework. The model should specify the chains of events linked to the timing and duration of status passages, starting with the school system and proceeding in sequences specific to gender, ethnic, and regional background. Such sequences lead to differential success at labor-market entry. If one wants to specify risk mechanisms that lead to unemployment in the hope of preventing negative causal chains, it is not only important to develop a methodology for testing particular causal hypotheses. We also need more general theoretical approaches that link social structural factors, institutional procedures, and individual orientation and behavior (cf. Heinz, 1993; Rosenbaum et al., 1990). I doubt whether it is sound advice to manipulate and test variables in a causal chain, as proposed by Rutter, without being able to establish a theoretically meaningful conception of how social structure and human agency are related to each other in the case of youth unemployment (cf. Giddens, 1984).

As pointed out by Adrian Furnham, there are no theoretically convincing models to explicate the complex interrelationships between unemployment and personality. We need stage-and-process conceptions that take into account causes and effects of moving into and out of work. Models of this kind will have to accommodate many moderating variables (e.g., work orientation, job experience, job opportunities, and types of jobs available for young people). The impact of unemployment after school graduation may first reduce occupational expectations (Empson-Warner & Krahn, 1992) and, the longer it lasts, may lead to distress and self-blame in cases where social support and financial resources are not available for buffering psychological stress (Banks & Ullah, 1988).

Furnham's observation that young people in Britain tend to attribute unemployment to economic conditions and government policy and not to a lack of motivation or skills among the jobless suggests that the attribution of reasons for being unemployed (external vs. internal) could moderate the effect of unemployment on distress. British youth's external attributions could be protective. However, we should be careful not to generalize this finding to societies such as Germany or the United States where the tendency to attribute causes of unemployment to personality deficits is much more prevalent in public opinion and policy making. Research on the attribution of unemployment, on both the collective and the personal levels, is timely because it may contribute to a better understanding of the extent to which young unemployed blame themselves and develop psychosocial distress and fatalism.

Irrespective of the moderating variables that may cushion the impact of unemployment on the personality of young people, there seems to be no alternative to meaningful work as a means to challenge and support personality development. A sense of purpose, participation in cooperative and productive activities, and the development of a positive social identity are all linked to employment in our work-centered societies.

But how are we to organize the transition to work in such a way that education and training programs become "launching pads" instead of "waiting rooms" (Hamilton)? Does the improvement of young people's human capital facilitate labor-market entry in a society where jobs are scarce or allow them to compete for scarce jobs? Hamilton's contribution points to a basic distinction between, on the one side, ad hoc arrangements to fight youth unemployment that establish training programs and qualifications schemes and, on the other, vocational and educational training systems operating in good and bad times to supply well-trained cohorts of young people and reduce the individual risk of unemployment. Thus, the best method to combat unemployment of young people is to stabilize the transition from school to work by providing vocational education and training that promote skill and personality development. The creation of short-term training schemes, however, tends to define structural problems as problems of young people. Such interventions may even have negative consequences because they often socially isolate or marginalize young people and thus reduce their prospects for employment in the future. Moreover, intervention programs usually aim at symptoms, by providing basic skills to improve employability and job-search techniques. They are not directed toward building skills and knowledge that are required to succeed in the job market of highly technological and service-oriented societies. White- and blue-collar jobs of the future will require intellectual flexibility, social and verbal competence, and readiness for lifelong learning.

As a final consideration, various youth training programs such as the British Youth Training Scheme or the Swedish youth centers emphasize different philosophies of why young people face unemployment. YTS maintains that unemployed youths lack work experiences and associated cognitive, interpersonal, and practical skills. The example of the Swedish youth centers demonstrates that even a successful program that improved unemployed young people's self-confidence, learning skills, and job-search strategies may be severely restricted when economic conditions are changing. In contrast to program-centered transition policies, the West German apprenticeship system is not primarily fighting youth unemployment, but provides the main learning and training context for young people who do not continue to higher education.

Long-term unemployment for young people, following Hamilton and Bertram, is best prevented by building bridges for the transition from family and school to employment. This solution should not be left to private investors in human capital. Instead, it is the responsibility of the welfare and education state to invest in transition institutions in order to rectify the unjust distribution of life chances.

References

Allatt, P., & Yeandle, S. M. (1992). *Youth unemployment and the family: Voices of disordered times*. London: Routledge.

Anderson, E. (1990). Racial tension, cultural conflicts, and problems of employment training programs. In K. Erikson & S. P. Vallas (Eds.), *The nature of work*, (pp. 214–234). New Haven, CT and London: Yale University Press.

Baethae, M.; Hantsche, B.; Pelull, W.: Voskamp, U., (1988). *Jugend: Arbeit ud Identitat*. Opladen: Leske & Burdich

Banks, M. H., & Ullah, P. (1988). *Youth unemployment in the 1980s: Its psychological effects*. London: Croom Helm.

Beck, U. (1992). *The risk society*. Beverly Hills, CA: Sage.

Bourdieu, P. (1986). The forms of capital. In J. C. Richardson (Ed.), *Handbook of theory and research for the sociology of education* (pp. 241–258). New York: Greenwood.

Bourdieu, P., & Passeron, C. (1990). *Reproduction in education, society and culture*. (2nd ed.). London: Sage.

Bynner, J., & Roberts, K. (Eds.). (1991). *Youth and work: Transition to employment in England and Germany*. London: Anglo-German Foundation.

Elder, G. H., Jr. (Ed.). (1985). *Life course dynamics, trajectories and transitions*. Ithaca, NY: Cornell University Press.

Elder, G. H., Jr., Conger, R. D., Foster, E. M. (1992). Families under economic pressure. *Journal of Family Issues, 13*, 5–37.

Empson-Warner, S., & Krahn, H. (1992). Unemployment and occupational aspiration. *Canadian Review of Sociology and Anthropology, 29*, 38–54.

Evans, K., & Heinz, W. R. (1993). *Becoming adults in England and Germany*. London: Anglo-German Foundation.

Finch, M., Shanahan, M., Mortimer, J. T., & Ryu, S. (1991). Work experience and control orientation in adolescence. *American Sociological Review, 56*, 597–611.

Giddens, A. (1984). *The constitution of society*. Berkeley: University of California Press.

Greenberger, E., & Steinberg, L. (1986). *When teenagers work*. New York: Basic Books.

Hagestad, G. (1991). Dilemmas in life course research: An international perspective. In W. R. Heinz (Ed.), *Theoretical advances in life course research* (pp. 23–57). Weinheim, West Germany: Deutscher Studienverlag.

Harker, R. (1990). Bourdieu—Education and reproduction. In R. Harker, C. Mahar, & C. Wilkes (Eds.). *An introduction to the work of Pierre Bourdieu* (pp. 86–108). London: MacMillan.

Heinz, W. R. (Ed.). (1991). *Theoretical advances in life course research*. Weinheim, West Germany: Deutscher Studienverlag.

Heinz, W. R. (1993). *Social structure, institutions and biography in research on youth and work* (Working Paper). Minneapolis: University of Minnesota, Life Course Center.

Hoff, E. H., Lempert, W., & Lappe, L. (1991). *Persönlich keitsentwicklung in facharbeiterbiographien*. Bern and Toronto: Huber.

Jahoda, M. (1982). *Employment and unemployment: A social-psychological analysis*. Cambridge: Cambridge University Press.

Jahoda, M., Lazarsfeld, P. F., & Zeisel, H. (1933). *Die arbeitslosen von Marienthal*. Leipzig, GDR: Hirzel.

Kieselbach, T. (1991). Unemployment. In R. M. Lerner, A. C. Petersen, & J. Brooks-Gunn (Eds.), *Encyclopedia of adolescence* (pp. 1187–1201). New York and London: Garland.

Kohli, M. (1989). Institutionalisierung und individualisierung der erwerbsbiographie. In D. Brock, H. R. Leu, R. Preiss, H. R. Vetter. (Eds.), *Subjektivität im gesellschaftlichen wandel* (pp. 249–278). Munich: Deutsches Jugendinstitut.

Kohn, M. L., & Schooler, C. (1983). *Work and personality*. Norwood, NJ: Ablex.

Mortimer, J. T., Finch, M., Shanahan, M., & Ryu, S. (1992). Work experience, mental health, and behavioral adjustment in adolescence. *Journal of Research on Adolescence, 2*, 25–57.

Rosenbaum, J. E., Kariya, T., Settertten, R., Maier, T. (1990). Market and network theories of the transition from high school to work. *Annual Review of Sociology, 16*, 263–299.

Shanahan, M. J., Finch, M. D., Mortimer, J. T., & Ryu, S. (1991). Adolescent work attitudes and depressive affect. *Social Psychology Quarterly, 54*, 299–317.

Wilson, W. J. (1987). *The truly disadvantaged*. Chicago: University of Chicago Press.

Index